The Goths

The Peoples of Europe

General Editors
James Campbell and Barry Cunliffe

This series is about the European tribes and peoples from their origins in prehistory to the present day. Drawing upon a wide range of archaeological and historical evidence, each volume presents a fresh and absorbing account of a group's culture, society and usually turbulent history.

Already published

The Lombards
Neil Christie

The English
Geoffrey Elton

The Bretons
Patrick Galliou and Michael Jones

The Franks
Edward James

The Huns
E. A. Thompson

The Illyrians
John Wilkes

The Basques
Roger Collins

The Gypsies
Angus Fraser

The Goths
Peter Heather

The Mongols
David Morgan

The Early Germans
Malcolm Todd

In preparation

The Sicilians
David Abulafia

The Irish
Francis John Byrne and Michael Herity

The First English
Sonia Chadwick Hawkes

The Spanish
Roger Collins

The Celts
David Dumville

The Portuguese
Kenneth Maxwell

The Armenians
Elizabeth Redgate

The Etruscans
Graeme Barker and Thomas Rasmussen

The Byzantines
Averil Cameron

The Normans
Marjorie Chibnall

The Romans
Timothy Cornell

The Scots
Colin Kidd

The Russians
Robin Milner-Gulland

The Picts
Charles Thomas

The Goths

Peter Heather

First published 1996

2 4 6 8 10 9 7 5 3 1

Blackwell Publishers Ltd
108 Cowley Road
Oxford OX4 1JF
UK

Blackwell Publishers Inc
238 Main Street
Cambridge, Massachusetts 02142
USA

British Library Cataloguing in Publication Data

A CIP catalogue record for this book is available from the British Library.

Library of Congress Cataloging-in-Publication Data

Heather, P. J. (Peter J.)
The Goths/Peter Heather.
p. cm. (The Peoples of Europe)
Includes bibliographical references and index.
ISBN 0-631-16536-3 (alk. paper)
1. Goths–History. I. Title. II. Series.
D137.H425 1996
909'. 0439–dc20

96 – 6725
CIP

Typeset in 10 on 12pt Sabon by
Words & Graphics Ltd, Anstey, Leicester
Printed in Great Britain by Hartnolls Ltd., Bodmin, Cornwall

This book is printed on acid-free paper

TO

JOHN RICHARD ALLAN HEATHER

16.4.91–19.4.91

EVEN THE HAIRS OF YOUR HEAD
ARE ALL NUMBERED

Contents

Plates

Figures

Preface

The last survey of Gothic history in English to take the subject all the way from Poland to Spain, prefaced its account with the following judgement:

> For three hundred years – beginning with the days of Tacitus – their history consists of little else than a dreary record of barbarian slaughter and pillage. A century later, the Goths have become the mightiest nation in Europe. One of their two kings sits on the throne of the Caesars; the other reigns over Spain and the richest part of Gaul. We look forward two hundred and fifty years, and the Gothic kingdoms are no more; the nation itself has vanished from the stage of history, leaving scarcely a trace behind.[1]

Apart from its rather moralizing tone, now somewhat out of fashion, this remains a perfectly fair characterization of the general outlines of Gothic history. Indeed, the reader interested enough to check will find considerable overlap between Henry Bradley's narrative of 1888, and my own of 1996. Little, certainly no substantial, new literary evidence, our main source of narrative information, has been discovered in the meantime.

There are a number of good reasons, however, why it would (I hope!) none the less not have been right simply to reissue Bradley's book. Not least, the intervening hundred years have seen the uncovering of vast amounts of archaeological evidence relevant to Gothic history. This material simply did not exist when Bradley wrote his book. The same period has also seen the rise of archaeology as a professional scientific discipline, and, with it, great debate over how

[1] H. Bradley, *The Goths* (London, 1888), 3.

to interpret such remains. Argument continues, and I think it is fair to say that Gothic archaeology has everywhere reached only, as yet, provisional conclusions. None the less, particularly in north-central and eastern Europe, but also in France and Spain, our understanding of Gothic history has been hugely advanced by a century of archaeological investigation.

At the same time, interpretation of the literary evidence has certainly advanced. Apart from individual matters of fact, this is an area of fundamental importance for Gothic history because of the existence of one particular source: *The Origins and Deeds of the Goths* or *Getica* of Jordanes. Written in sixth-century Constantinople, it provides many of the big ideas which have long shaped modern accounts of Gothic history. The Goths' supposed origins in Scandinavia, their trek to the Black Sea, and the creation there of the Visigoths and Ostrogoths, each ruled by its royal dynasty (the Balths and Amals respectively): all of these mainstays of traditional Gothic history have their origin in the *Getica*. But, as will emerge, sustained comparison of the *Getica*'s narrative with more contemporary evidence raises doubts about much of its testimony. In particular, Jordanes has imported Gothic socio-political patterns of his own day, the sixth century – when Ostrogoths and Visigoths existed, together with their ruling dynasties – anachronistically into earlier eras. First and foremost, perhaps, Gothic history of the Hunnic period (the fourth and fifth centuries) has to be correspondingly rewritten. Older accounts of this period, which saw Ostrogoths and Visigoths (together with their respective dynasties) as entities with a continuous history from *c.*300 to *c.*500, must be replaced with a vision allowing for greater diversity and even fundamental discontinuity. It is precisely the recognition of this discontinuity, and the whole new range of issues it raises, which above all separate the historical vision of this book from that of its predecessor.

Bradley was writing in an era which simply assumed that the social groups mentioned in ancient sources were ethnic groups, analogous to 'modern' nations. They had distinctive cultures, material and non-material, and were solid entities with continuous histories. This kind of perspective also underlay the earlier eras of archaeological investigation into Gothic history (up to about the 1950s). Since then, however, there has been a sea change. Anthropologists have shown that ethnicity cannot be measured by simple lists of concrete characteristics, and that, in many contexts, ethnicity is not the powerful binding force that it is (arguably) in modern nationalisms. Archaeologists, following the lead of anthropologists, have ceased to equate areas of similarity in physical remains (traditionally called 'cultures') with the boundaries of particular socio-political entities, and historians of all eras, but particularly those of the medieval period, have re-evaluated the social groups they encounter in their sources. For the Goths, this has generated great debate on the nature of the forces holding together groups described as 'Gothic', and the nature of any Gothic identity.

Above all, this book aims to contribute to this debate. The thread binding together its many individual arguments and analyses is an attempt to explore the nature and significance of Gothic identity in the four main contexts where Goths are met in historical sources: northern Poland in the first and second centuries, the northern hinterland of the Black Sea in the third and fourth, central and eastern Europe in the Hunnic period, and western Europe after the collapse of the Roman Empire. In analytical terms, therefore, it picks up where my previous attempt to write about the Goths left off.[2] The old certainties about the nature of the Goths have been replaced, I think it is fair to say, by a new orthodoxy which would confine social and political enfranchisement to only a very restricted elite within the known Gothic groups. Correspondingly, ethnicity has been devalued as a major organizing principle among the Goths. Gothic groups are now seen as Gothic simply because their restricted elite saw themselves as such. In such a view, the origins and affiliations of the bulk of any group's population is beside the point, and most so-called 'Gothic' groups were in fact multi-ethnic. My first book on the Goths focused on other issues and a restricted time-span. The general vision it incidentally suggested of Gothic history in the fourth and fifth centuries, however, made me doubt that envisaging ethnicity as the preserve of a *very* restricted elite did full justice to the evidence. In this book I have put the case for an alternative vision of 'Gothicness': one that encompassed a rather larger proportion of the population of Gothic groups – although still, I would emphasize, a minority – than the new orthodoxy would allow. In my view, 'Gothicness' was, from the third to the sixth centuries at least, an attribute of a particular caste of Gothic freemen, comprising somewhere between one-fifth and one-half of the total population of any Gothic group: in Procopius' terminology, the 'notable', 'distinguished', or 'best' men among the Goths. It is, of course, for the reader to decide on the success or otherwise of this argument.

There now merely remains to me the very pleasurable duty of

[2] *Goths and Romans 332–489* (Oxford, 1991).

thanking all who have aided me in this work. I would particularly like to thank the Fellows and Trustees of Dumbarton Oaks. I wrote the bulk of the text which follows in the course of an extremely rewarding term there as a Senior Fellow in autumn 1994. More particularly, I would like to thank colleagues who have helped me with access to recent archaeological data, and discussed its interpretation with me to my great benefit: above all, Heinrich Härke, Michel Kazanski and Gisela Ripoll Lopez. The latter two belong to the same group as myself within the European Science Foundation's project *The Transformation of the Roman World*. Participation in this project has helped me in more ways than I can list, and I would like to thank all the members of my group, not least for their willingness to listen. Thanks are also due to Pablo de la Cruz Diaz Martinez for many valuable offprints. Many friends and colleagues have also read part or all of the text, and, again, I would like to thank them, especially James Campbell, Mary-Lyon Dolezal, Emily Umberger and Michael Whitby. Like its predecessor, this book is above all the product of the happiness created by the existence of family and friends, without which creative writing would be impossible for me. *The Goths* is firmly dedicated to all of these, especially Gail and William, the great joys of my life, but also Carley and the boys (particularly J.C. who would be grumpy if not singled out). The need to feed the latter keeps me going when all else fails.

Peter Heather
University College London

Abbreviations

AM	Ammianus Marcellinus
CE	*Codex Euricianus*
CM	*Chronica Minora*
Coll. Av.	*Collectio Avellana*
CSEL	Corpus Scriptorum Ecclesiasticorum Latinorum
C.Th.	*Codex Theodosianus*
DOP	*Dumbarton Oaks Papers*
FHG	*Fragmenta Historicorum Graecorum*, ed. C. Müller, vols 4–5 (Paris, 1868, 1870).
HF	*History of the Franks*
Hyd.	Hydatius, *Chronicle*
JRS	*Journal of Roman Studies*
ILS	*Inscriptiones Latinae Selectae*, ed. H. Dessau
LV	*Leges Visigothorum*
PBSR	*Proceedings of the British School at Rome*
PLRE	*Prosopography of the Later Roman Empire*, 3 vols (Cambridge, 1971–92).
RgA	*Reallexicon der germanisches Altertumskunde*
SHA	*Scriptores Historia Augusta*

Acknowledgements

The author and publishers offer grateful acknowledgements to the following for permission to reproduce copyright material:

Plates: Uppsala University Library (cover); J. Kniecinski, University of Lodz (plate 1); Scala (plates 2, 20); Zeitschrift für Numismatik 36–7 (plate 3); Ukrainian Academy of Science, Institute of Archaeology; (plate 4); Archaologisches Landesmuseum der Christian Albrechts-Universitat, Schleswig (plate 6); Sonia Halliday (plates 7, 24); British Library Newspaper Services (plate 8); Trinity College, Cambridge (plate 10); Musée des Augustine, Toulouse (plate 12); Ancient Art & Architecture Collection (plates 13, 15, 16, 22, 23, 25); Museu d'Arqueologica de Catalunya, Barcelona (plate 14); Museo Nazionale dell Terme, Rome (plate 7); Instituto Arqueologico Aleman, Madrid (plates 26, 27); ICRBC (plate 28); Biblioteca Nazionale di Napoli (plate 29); Biblioteca Medicea Laurenziana (plates 30, 31).

Figures: 2.1, from Cornelii Taciti, *De origine et situ germanorum*, ed. J. G. C. Anderson (Oxford: Oxford University Press, 1938); 2.2, 3.2, 3.3, from M. Todd, *The Northern Barbarians 100 BC–AD 300* (London: Hutchinson, 1975); 2.3, 2.5, 7.4, 8.2, from E. A. Arslan et al. (eds), *I Goti* (Milan, 1994); 2.8, from M. Todd, *The Early Germans* (Oxford: Blackwell, 1992); 3.1, 3.5, from M. Kazanski, *Les Goths* (Paris: Editions Errance, 1991); 3.7, from P. Heather and J. Matthews, *The Goths in the Fourth Century* (Translated Texts for Historians; Liverpool: Liverpool University Press, 1991); 5.1, from P. Heather, *Goths and Romans 332–489* (Oxford: Oxford University Press, 1991); 9.3, from G. Ripoll and I. Velazquez, *La Hispania Visigoda* (Madrid: Temas de Hoy, 1995).

The publishers apologize for any errors or omissions in the above list and would be grateful to be notified of any corrections that should be incorporated in the next edition or reprint of this book.

1

The Gothic Problem

In the summer of 376, a large force of Goths came to the river Danube, the north-eastern boundary of the Roman Empire, and asked for asylum. Two Gothic kings had just died, and another been deposed, as they tried – and failed – to hold in check the expansion of Hunnic tribes into their territories on the northern shores of the Black Sea. Within two years, the Goths had precipitated, in turn, a crisis for the Roman state. On 9 August 378, just outside the city of Hadrianople (modern Edirne in European Turkey), they defeated and killed the Emperor Valens, ruler of the eastern half of the Roman Empire, along with two-thirds of his army. The victory unleashed a chain of events which changed the course of European history. On or about 17 September 476, the last Roman Emperor in the West, Romulus Augustulus, was deposed: the final act in the drama of Roman imperial dismemberment. The Roman Empire in western Europe, which had run Britain, France, Spain, Italy, together with parts of Hungary, Switzerland, Belgium and Germany as a single state for 400 years, had foundered. In its place, there stood a series of independent kingdoms constructed around the military power of immigrant groups.

In all this, Goths had played a central role. They were the first autonomous group of immigrants to force their way across an imperial frontier en masse and survive. They were responsible for Hadrianople, the single most resounding defeat of Roman armies in the entire period, when, as one Roman put it, 'our armies . . . vanished like shadows'.[1] They were also the first immigrants to sack the

[1] Themistius *Or.* 16, p. 296. 17ff.

imperial capital. Rome fell to armies of the Gothic king Alaric on the morning of 24 August 410. Two of the new European states were even Gothic: the Visigothic kingdom in Spain and southern Gaul, and the Ostrogothic kingdom in Italy. On one level, then, Gothic history is inextricably bound up with Gibbon's problem: the Fall of the Roman Empire. It encompasses much else besides.

Goths are first mentioned occupying territory in what is now Poland in the first century AD. Visigothic Spain, the longer-lived of the western kingdoms, did not fall to Muslim, Arab conquerors until the second decade of the eighth century. The history of people labelled 'Goths' thus spans 700 years, and huge tracts of Europe from northern Poland to the Atlantic ocean. Striking monuments mark their passage. The mausoleum of the first king of Ostrogothic Italy, Theoderic the Great, can still be seen in Ravenna, its roof composed of a single, massive block of stone (plate 22; see p. 251). Gothic treasures abound, including gem-encrusted eagle brooches of gold, and gold crowns from Visigothic Spain. The Goths were also the first Germanic group to produce a literature. Not only are the remains of literary Gothic linguistically of the first importance, but they survive in a manuscript, which is itself the greatest Gothic treasure of all. Now in Uppsala, the sixth-century *Codex Argenteus* preserves 188 folios of Gothic Gospel text in silver and gold ink on purple-dyed parchment (see front cover). The parchment is of such fineness, that it may have been produced from the skin of unborn calves.

Not surprisingly, the Goths have, down through the centuries, fascinated Europeans of many persuasions. Gothic kings regularly appeared in medieval heroic poetry, not least Theoderic, as Dietrich of Berne, in the *Niebelungenlied*. The range and grandeur of Gothic history has also made it a symbol for empire builders. Its potency in this respect is still visible on the Swedish royal coat-of-arms, where the second of three crowns lays claim to the kingdom of the Goths. This claim was generated in protracted, if discontinuous, debate between the fifteenth and eighteenth centuries over whether Swedish or Austrian Hapsburg kings were the true heirs of the Goths. More recently, visions of the supposed extent of the old Gothic kingdoms in what is now Poland, and of the Empire of the fourth-century Gothic king Ermenaric in Russia and the Ukraine, helped glorify Nazi territorial demands. The Polish port Gdynia-Gdingen was rechristened *Gotenhafen* ('the harbour of the Goths') after the conquest of Poland. Subsequent military advances generated earnest discussions among Nazi bureaucrats on the suitability of *Theoderichshafen* ('the harbour of Theoderic') as a new name for Sevastopol in the Crimea.[2]

This book is not, however, a study of the *Nachleben* of the Goths, but an attempt to get to grips with the central questions raised by the history of groups called or calling themselves Gothic in the first seven centuries of our era. What was their historical importance? How did they come to play such a wide variety of roles? And what relationship did the very different groups called Gothic in the course of these 700 years bear to one another? What meaning, in other words, can be attached at any point to the term 'Gothic'? In many ways, the Goths provide a particular case study of a general problem, which has, in recent years, generated considerable debate. What is the nature of ethnic identity, and how can it be transmitted over time?

A. *Understanding Identity*

In the nineteenth century, anthropologists cheerfully asserted that race, language, and culture (ways of thinking and doing, moral values etc.) were essentially coterminous. Thus there seemed to be adequate criteria to define ethnic identity in a straightforward and concrete manner. Any ethnic group would be recognizable by its unique racial, linguistic, and cultural profile. By the middle of the twentieth century, field studies had shown that ethnic identity was not so easy to define, but it was still regarded as an objective category. It could be measured in concrete ways. Research at this point concentrated on assembling a checklist of concrete categories: biological self-perpetuation, fundamental social values, interaction and communication, self-identification and identification by others. The underlying assumption was that, examined under such headings, a particular social group would display a unique set of objective cultural features, the component parts of its ethnic identity, which would distinguish it absolutely from surrounding groups. Each surrounding group would likewise have its own distinctive profile. The approach also implied that, if you started with two distinct social groups – A and B – and, over time, they exchanged concrete cultural features to such an extent that A came to resemble B closely, then the two groups would be found to have amalgamated.[3]

When identity was understood in such a way, it was only natural to

[2] After Wolfram, 1988, 3ff.

[3] A helpful introduction (among many others) is Bacal, 1991, ch. 1.

write about groups of the past, such as the Goths, as though they too were entities of a very concrete and coherent kind. But since the Second World War, understandings of identity have been transformed by two separate lines of research. The first originated with Leach's study of North Burmese hill tribes in 1954. His conclusions explicitly challenged the assumption that social groups and observable cultural features coincide sufficiently for the latter to be a guide to the former. His study showed that, on occasion, people with little or nothing in common (when investigated under the traditional, objectively measurable categories) would claim to belong to the same social group. Similarly, those with much if not everything in common might claim to belong to different social groups. Exchanging cultural features, then, did not necessarily lead to the amalgamation of groups.

The classic document of this revisionary approach came in 1969, with the publication of *Ethnic Groups and Boundaries*, a collection of essays assembled by the Norwegian anthropologist Frederick Barth. Because perceptions of identity do not always coincide with measurable cultural traits, Barth's collection switched the emphasis of research to subjective assessment as the basis of identity. What identity did individuals claim, and what identity was recognized in them by others? For Barth, the different cultural traits which ethnic groups tend to (but do not always) display were the *result* and not the *cause* of erecting a social boundary. Groups do not erect boundaries against one another because they are already different, but become different because of the original decision to erect a boundary. Diverging cultural traits are thus symbols of identity, not its substance.

The underlying implication of Barth's approach was that larger group identities were a voluntary element in the individual's make-up. Ethnicity was not an inherited given, but something to be taken on and accepted. His own work on Pathans observed some of them switching group identity when the social and economic patterns of their lives changed, whereas, in other contexts, similar socio-economic changes produced no such alterations. Barth consequently promoted the utilitarian explanation that individuals change their identity in contexts where it is better for them to do so. His thinking generated a whole approach to ethnicity: the so-called instrumentalist position. According to this view, identities are not inborn and unchanging, but manipulable and chosen: the product of personal choice. In some contexts, they can also take the form of ideologies deliberately fostered by elites who want to create senses of solidarity in subject peoples bound to them. In such cases, of course, the nature of ethnic identity would not be constant across all social classes within the same group. In Barth's words, ethnic identity is 'an evanescent situational construct, not a solid enduring fact'.

The second line of research – the so-called 'primordialist' approach – stemmed from close observation of individuals and their reactions, rather than the study of groups. These studies have shown that, in some contexts, inherited senses of identity cannot be manipulated at will, but push individuals to act in common with others sharing the same sense of identity, against the more obvious dictates of material calculation. In an awful phrase, primordialists have asserted 'the authenticity of ethnicity'. Differences in blood, speech (whether language or dialect), social practice, social values, and history can – once they exist – act as real barriers to individuals wishing to change their identity in subsequent generations. To some extent, they take on a life of their own, and restrict the individual's range of choice. A further strand in this research has shown that many of a group's defining characteristics are picked up unconsciously in the earliest years of life. They can thus shape individual behaviour on a very profound level.

These two lines of research have on occasion been held to contradict one another. When discussing the kinds of inherited cultural items which might constrain an individual's free choice of ethnic affiliation (religion, language, social values, shared history etc.), primordialists can seem to be holding to a view of ethnicity similar to that prevailing before the Second World War. In the primordialist position, however, it is not these items in themselves which constrain freedom of action, but the individual's reaction to them. Both approaches thus emphasize perception, rather than objectively measurable criteria, as the basis of identity. Likewise, both understand group identity as the individual's response to an account – whether true, false, or something in between – of a group's historical past and a series of established social norms (in jargon: a 'myth/symbol complex').

More fundamentally, the two approaches between them define opposite ends of a spectrum of possibility. Depending upon the context, inherited identities can exercise a more or less powerful hold on individuals born into any group. Indeed, it is entirely characteristic to find every conceivable position in between, with individuals displaying simultaneously an emotional dependence on their ethnic identity, and the ability to manipulate it in certain contexts. There is thus no absolute difference between groups exercising stronger and weaker holds on their constituent individuals. In both cases, identity consists of a claim or series of claims generated in individuals by their life experiences (particularly in their early years), and the willingness of those around them to recognize such claims. Likewise, according to circumstance, individuals may be able to make just one, or more than one claim, and find groups more and less willing to recognize their claim or claims.

This constraint is sometimes forgotten. The individual can make any claim he or she wants to, but, to have any effect, a claim must be recognized. If I turned up at New York's Kennedy airport claiming US citizenship, my stay would be brief. For individuals born into all but the simplest of contexts, identity comes in layers. Immediate family, wider kin, town, county, country, and, these days, international affiliation (such as to the EU) all provide possible claims. And where an individual's parentage is itself mixed, then the number of possible claims increases accordingly. Overall, groups exist who are more and less exclusive, and who exercise more and less powerful holds upon their individual members' loyalty. Barth's famous aphorism posits a false dichotomy. All ethnic group identities are situational constructs, but some are more evanescent than others.[4]

For the historian approaching a subject like the Goths, this prompts two major conclusions. First, there is no such thing as an unchanging identity. The recognizable components of identity – any group's myth/symbol complex – are bound to change over time. The 'myth' component, for instance, does not have to be entirely historical, but will reflect the continuing experiences of the group, changing as new episodes are added to its history. Continuity in group identity cannot be measured by the persistence (or otherwise) of individual cultural traits, therefore, but by the transmission over time of a perception of difference: the claim to a particular identity on the part of a number of individuals and the recognition of that claim by others.

Secondly, cases corresponding to both ends of the spectrum (more or less solid group identities) are well documented in the present day. It has been suggested, however, that the kind of powerful ethnic identity found in some modern contexts could not have existed in the past. Indeed, there has been a marked tendency in recent years to view socio-political entities of the early middle ages as highly 'evanescent situational constructs'. This, again, represents a necessary reaction to older writing which saw entities like Goths as unchanging,

[4] Barth, 1969, esp. introduction. For a review of subsequent literature, see (amongst many others) Bentley, 1987; Kivisto, 1989; Roosens, 1989; Bacal, 1991.

unproblematic historical phenomena. It must be correct – and this, I take it, is the central point – that modern western nationalisms represent a very specific kind of phenomenon generated by a particular set of unprecedented circumstances. Many have pointed out, however, that some group identities of the past, even if somewhat differently constructed, could exercise a powerful hold. Indeed, as will become apparent, some of the groups we will encounter in these pages exercised a significantly greater hold on their members' loyalty than did others.

We need not adopt a position on the likely nature of ethnicity among the Goths *a priori*, therefore, or even whether it was necessarily a significant factor at every stage in their history. According to circumstance, looser identities have been known to evolve into tighter ones, and vice versa. As a rough guide to when senses of ethnicity might be operating as an important phenomenon, I will use the well-known checklist put forward by the anthropologist Dragadze. She argued that given ethnic identities can be considered to be exercising a substantial effect upon its constituent individuals, when the following conditions are broadly satisfied: '[a functioning ethnic unit is] a firm aggregate of people, historically established on a given territory, possessing in common relatively stable peculiarities of language and culture, and also recognizing their unity and difference from other similar formations (self-awareness) and expressing this in a self-appointed name (ethonym)'. Gothic history, and the role within it of any powerful sense of ethnic identity, must be investigated with an open mind.[5]

The central purposes of this study should by now, I hope, be clear. Over seven centuries, the Goths played a dramatic role in the history of Europe. They made a major contribution to one sea change in the history of the continent: the dismemberment of the Roman Empire. They also left behind them some striking memorials. This book will attempt to describe and explain the main features of their history, and, at the same time, explore the evolving significance of the term 'Goth' at different moments and in different contexts.

[5] Dragazde cited in Renfrew, 1991. My thinking has been strongly influenced by Smith, 1986 (who posits a similar checklist at pp. 22–31). See also Smith, 1981; Gellner, 1983 with refs.

Part I

In Search of the Goths

Modern approaches to the history of the Goths have been decisively shaped by the survival of one particular text: the *Origins and Acts of the Goths* or *Getica* of Jordanes. Written in Constantinople in about AD 550, it is a unique document. Although its author wrote in Latin, he was of Gothic descent, and drew upon Gothic oral traditions. He explicitly claims personal acquaintance with such material, and there is no reason to disbelieve him (e.g. *Getica* 28, 43, 72, 79, 214). He was also, again by his own account, closely following the now lost *Gothic History* of the Roman Senator Cassiodorus, which was written in the 520s at the court of the Ostrogothic king of Italy, Theoderic the Great. Jordanes certainly shaped and added to what he learned from Cassiodorus, but his dependence upon it was very significant. Like Jordanes, Cassiodorus was also acquainted with stories that some Goths told of their past, and included some of them in his work.

To add a further level of interest, the *Getica* refers at three points to a third Gothic historian: one Ablabius (28, 82, 117). Nothing is known of him for certain, although he too seems to have been interested in Gothic traditions, and it is a fair guess that he worked at the court of Visigothic kings. Jordanes probably knew of him only at second hand, deriving the passages that mention him from Cassiodorus. Gothic existed as a literary language from the mid-fourth century, but there is no sign that it was ever used for anything other than ecclesiastical purposes. No history in Gothic has come down to us, and there is no indication that one was ever written. The *Getica* is thus the closest we will ever come to Gothic history as told by Goths.

A second feature of Jordanes' work also helps to explain its historiographical significance. Uniquely, the *Getica* provides us with an overview of the entirety of Gothic history (down to the moment of its composition). Many Greek and other Latin written sources from the first six centuries AD transmit a wealth of additional information about Goths, many more individual facts, indeed, than are contained in the *Getica*. In particular, there was a Greek tradition of writing detailed contemporary history. Thus a virtually unbroken line of authors from *c.* AD 200 to 600 tell us much of the doings of Goths. But the information preserved in these authors' works tends to be episodic. Hence, naturally enough, the *Getica*'s consolidated account has exercised enormous influence on the overall 'shape' of modern reconstructions of Gothic history. In particular, it has provided three central ideas. First, the Goths originated in Scandinavia before moving across the Baltic and south through Poland to the Black Sea (see pp. 11–12). Secondly, from at least the third century, the Goths were divided into two groups: the Visigoths and Ostrogoths (esp. *Getica* 42, 82). Thirdly, these groups were led by two families with unique royal prestige: respectively the Balthi and the Amals (esp. *Getica* 42, 78–81, 98, 146, 174–5). None of these ideas has won simple acceptance from modern historians and archaeologists. At the very least, however, they have set an agenda around which argument has raged. Indeed, the basic method of historical argumentation cannot help but consist, for much of the time, in the comparison of Jordanes' overview with the detailed materials preserved in more contemporary Greek and Roman sources.

The one exception to this pattern of discourse concerns the subject with which we must begin: Gothic history of the first three centuries AD. For this period, we have few written sources other than Jordanes. It has been greatly illuminated in recent years, however, by the work of Polish, Russian, and other east European archaeologists. Thanks to them, it is now possible to exercise at least some kind of control over Jordanes' account of even this earliest period of Gothic history.[1]

[1] This summarizes the view of Jordanes, Cassiodorus and Ablabius I have argued out elsewhere: Heather, 1991, pt. 1, 1993. Other accounts are Momigliano, 1955; Goffart, 1988.

2

From the Baltic to the Black Sea

The origins and early history of the Goths have generated, in different centuries, enormous heat and a voluminous literature, of more and less scholarly kinds. Swedish kings, Hapsburg monarchs, Romantic German nationalists, and Nazi imperialists: all have used and distorted early Gothic history for their own ends. Since the Second World War, however, new excavations have not only greatly increased the amount of evidence available, but also generated methodological and analytical advances of the first importance. As a result, much more of the reality of early Gothic history can be distinguished beneath the patina of past political ambition.

A. Gothic Origins

(i) Jordanes, Kossina, and beyond

Modern discussions of the origins of the Goths have centred on the coherent literary account of the subject produced in antiquity by the Gothic author Jordanes. Its key passage, therefore, is well worth citing in full:

[Chapter 25] Now from this island of Scandza, as from a hive of races or a womb of nations, the Goths are said to have come forth long ago under their king, Berig by name. As soon as they disembarked from their ships and set foot on the land, they straightway gave their name to the place. And even today it is said to be called Gothiscandza. [26] Soon they moved from here to the abodes of the Ulmerugi, who then dwelt on the shores of the Ocean, where they pitched camp, joined battle with them and drove them from their homes. Then they subdued their neighbours, the Vandals, and thus added to their victories. But when the number of the people increased greatly and Filimer, son of Gadaric, reigned as king – about the fifth since Berig – he decided that the army of the Goths with their families should move from that region. [27] In search of suitable homes and pleasant places they came to the land of Scythia, called *Oium* in that tongue. Here they were delighted with the great richness of the country, and it is said that when half the army had been brought over, the bridge whereby they had crossed the river fell in utter ruin, nor could anyone thereafter pass to or fro. For the place is said to be surrounded by quaking bogs and an encircling abyss, so that by this double obstacle nature has made it inaccessible. And even today one may hear in that neighbourhood the lowing of cattle and may find traces of men, if we are to believe the stories of travellers, although we must grant that they hear these things from afar. [28] This part of the Goths, which is said to have crossed the river and entered with Filimer into the country of Oium, came into possession of the desired land, and there they soon came upon the race of the Spali, joined battle with them and won the victory. Thence the victors hastened to the farthest part of Scythia, which is near the sea of Pontus. (*Getica* 25–8)

The story is not without its puzzles. No one is sure, for instance, who the Spali are supposed to be. Nevertheless, its outlines are straightforward enough. The Goths started life in Scandinavia – Jordanes is reflecting the norms of ancient geography in calling it an island – and via two distinct moves ended up beside the Black Sea ('the land of Scythia'). The moves are both portrayed as mass, armed migrations led by kings, and caused, at least in the second case, by over-population. How much of this can we believe?

Down to the late nineteenth century, Jordanes' account was simply accepted at face value. The lack of alternative literary sources, or other means of verification, prevented further research. In any case, the story seemed entirely plausible. The Viking period and, more recently, the nineteenth century, had both seen mass emigration from Scandinavia in search of greater wealth and more fertile land. Tongue in cheek, one Swedish scholar recently cited, in his discussion of the question, a fellow-countryman's report home, in pre-cholesterol days, from his new-found North American land of plenty: 'We eat only pork and dripping, and now my little woman is so fat that she can't get through the door of the cattle-shed'.[1]

Controversy was confined to dating the moves. The *Getica* places

[1] Svennung, 1972, 45.

material from two millennia of classical Greek history and pseudo-history between its account of Filimer's migration and the point at which it returns to genuinely Gothic activities in the Black Sea region. It was a standard conceit of late antique ethnography that there were no new peoples, just the same old ones under new names. For Cassiodorus, this offered the opportunity – grasped with both hands – of giving the Goths a grandiose pre-history. Their earlier doings could be illuminated by equating them with, amongst others, Scythians, Amazons, Getes, and Dacians. The histories and mythologies of these peoples could then illuminate the earlier doings of Goths. According to this view of the past, the kingdom of the Goths was founded well before the city of Rome, and Goths had even fought in the Trojan war. An incidental effect was to date Berig's crossing from Scandinavia to 1490 BC, and to give Filimer's move to the Black Sea, said to have occurred five generations later, an extremely early date.

The rise of archaeology as a professional discipline in the late nineteenth century made it possible, for the first time, to search outside the text of the *Getica* for some confirmation of its story. A pioneering role was played by the German scholar Kossina and the group of archaeologists who gathered around him. As increasing quantities of archaeological material came to light, these scholars began to group together some of the finds on the basis of similarity of artefact and custom. In response to this emerging picture of archaeological groups (often called 'cultures'), Kossina evolved the central tenet of his school. As he put it in the 1926 version of his *The Origin of the Germani*, 'clearly defined, sharply distinctive, bounded archaeological provinces correspond unquestionably to the territories of particular peoples and tribes'. For Kossina, each people or tribe mentioned in the ancient sources had its own distinctive material culture. From this it followed that archaeological remains could be used to confirm or deny literary accounts of migrations. If peoples had specific material remains, the changing patterns of such remains reflect their movements.

In the case of the Goths, Jordanes' account of their Scandinavian origins was 'proved' by the new discoveries, techniques, and assumptions. Central to this demonstration was the fact that certain artefacts and practices, dating from the early centuries AD, had been found both in Scandinavia and in the area of the river Vistula south of the Baltic. These resemblances were interpreted, after Jordanes, as marking the passage southwards of the Goths from Scandinavia to the European mainland. By about 1950, the so-called 'Gotho–Gepidan' culture was held to be identifiable on the basis of seven elements: inhumation burial (rather than cremation), a lack of weapons in graves, the use of stone circles and stelae (standing stones) in cemeteries, pear-shaped metal pendants, serpent-headed bracelets, S-shaped clasps and a particular type of pottery decoration which combined roughening with polishing.

Unfortunately, this easy correspondence between literary sources and archaeological remains was illusory. Leaving aside for the moment any other question, the seven 'Gothic elements' could prove that the Goths originated in Scandinavia, only if the European examples were later in date than those found in Scandinavia. The artefacts and customs must themselves have originated in Scandinavia if the argument was to work. For the most part, this has proved not to be the case. The earliest examples of stone circles in cemeteries are found in Scandinavia, but the other six elements of the Gotho-Gepidan culture all originated south of the Baltic.[2]

More fundamentally, the central tenet of Kossina's school begged important questions. Running very much in parallel with anthropologists' re-evaluations of identity (chapter 1), there has been a revolution in the general understanding of the material 'cultures' which have been traditionally identified in the course of archaeological investigation. The idea that the boundaries of such cultures *necessarily* reflect the boundaries of particular peoples has proved untenable. Archaeological 'cultures' are statistical constructs, areas where the geographical distributions of a number of artefacts coincide. Cultural areas will not always have the same significance, therefore, since distribution patterns can be created in a number of ways. Depending upon precisely what it is that is common to the particular area, an archaeological 'culture' might represent, for instance, an area of socio-economic interaction, an area of common religious belief, or, indeed, a political unit.

Taking Germanic archaeological remains of the Roman Iron Age (of which the Gothic problem is one particular instance), the point can be demonstrated very simply. As a comparison of figures 2.1 and 2.2 makes clear, there are incomparably more groups ('tribes' for want of a better word) named in the likes of Tacitus, Pliny and Ptolemy than there are identifiable, chronologically coincident, archaeological 'cultures'. Each of the named groups could not have had its own distinctive material culture. These archaeological cultures, at least,

[2] See generally, Ščukin, 1989, pt. 2 ch. 4. Critical landmarks in the debate: Oxenstierna, 1948; Kmieciński, 1962, 1972; Hachmann, 1970.

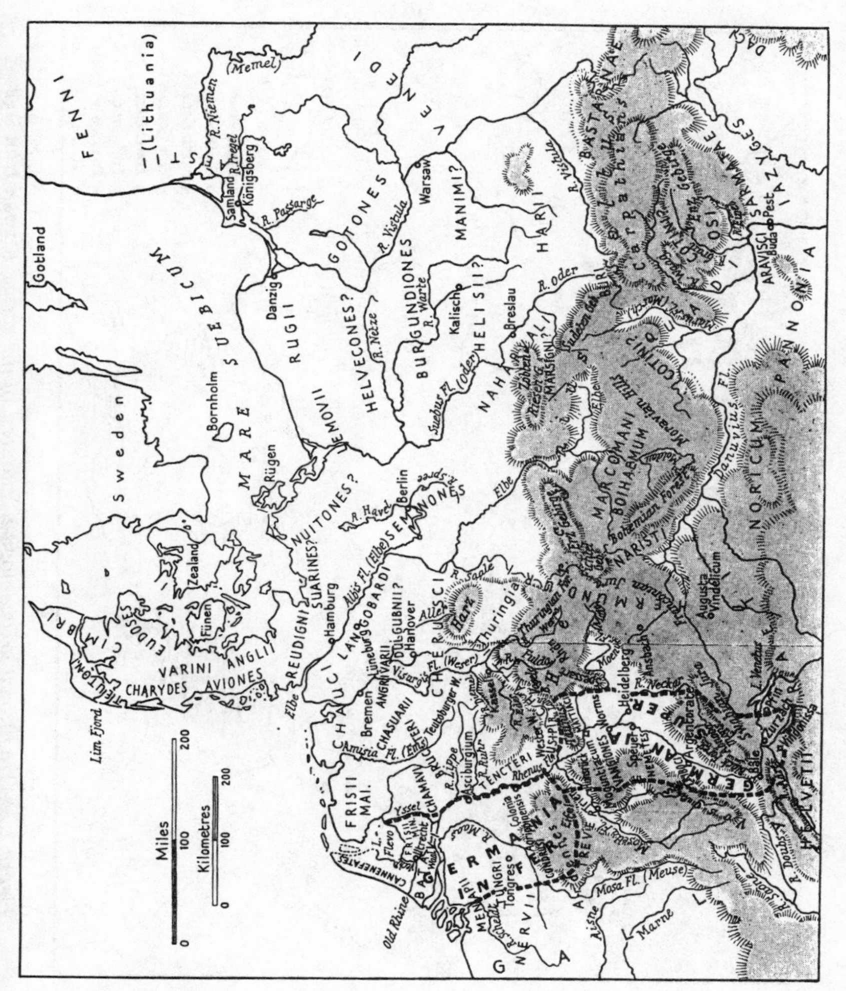

Figure 2.1 Groups named in Tacitus' Germania *and their approximate locations*

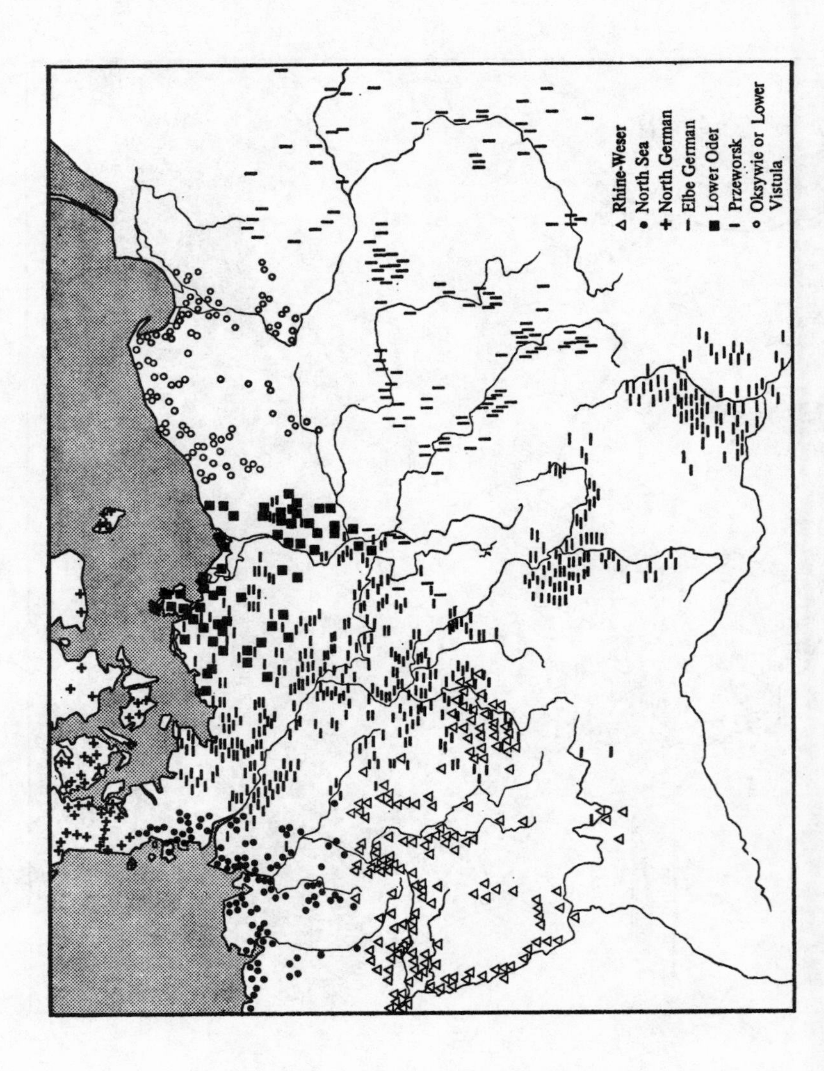

Figure 2.2 *Traditional archaeological 'cultures' of the earlier Roman Iron Age*

must reflect something other than the boundaries of primary political units.

All of this has profoundly changed archaeological understandings of observable cultural change. When the equation between cultures and individual groups was unchallenged, the tendency in prehistoric archaeology was always to explain change in terms of migration or diffusion. A basic rule of thumb operated. If a set of material remains underwent large-scale transformation, this was usually explained as the effects of migration. Smaller changes, by contrast, were signs of diffusion or influence, usually from a 'more advanced' group to a 'more primitive' one. Especially since the 1960s, there has been a strong reaction to these paradigms of causation, at least among anglophone archaeologists. Many have stressed that change, even drastic change, can come about by other means. So-called 'New' or 'Processual' archaeology switched the emphasis in causation away from movements of peoples or ideas, towards the adaptation of geographically stable populations to new conditions and stimuli. The appearance of a new custom or artefact does not always mean that immigration has occurred. The physical evidence for the mass adoption of the motor car in the twentieth century does not mean that the previously unknown 'motor people' have conquered large tracts of the earth (perhaps from outer space). Indigenous populations have simply learned to drive. As we shall see in the next chapter, many of the changes observable in Gothic (and other Germanic) societies in the first three centuries AD, probably should be explained along processual lines.[3]

But when this emphasis on indigenous adaptation extends (as it sometimes has) to a refusal to accept that migration might ever be an important factor in explaining observable change, processual archaeologists place themselves in a position as untenable as that of the old migrationists. As one commentator put it, a universal law of 'least inventions' (the migrationist/diffusionist approach) has been replaced by a new universal law of 'least moves'. The migration of human populations is, however, a well-documented phenomenon in the historical record. Likewise, one of the general features of homo sapiens as a species is the ability to occupy new ecological niches, a characteristic which does generate some tendency towards migration.

In recent years, much theoretical effort has gone into understanding

[3] The essays in Shennan, 1989 and Ucko, 1995 provide illuminating introductions; cf. more generally Renfrew, 1991, or, more particularly, Kobylinski, 1991.

migration as a specific phenomenon. For one thing, it has been pointed out that human populations, like those of seasonal plants and animals, have tended historically to maintain themselves by high birth and death rates. In such circumstances, conditions need become unusually favourable for only a relatively limited time to generate population explosions. This kind of phenomenon is recorded among population groups which did not have access to modern medicine, so that periodically accelerated rates of population increase are not a purely recent phenomenon. Likewise, the act of moving has been subject to more precise analysis, some of whose results are highly relevant. Migrations, not surprisingly, tend to follow established routes to known destinations, and the groups undertaking them are prompted by certain negative features of their current situation and positive expectations of where they aim to go (so-called push/pull factors).[4]

Archaeological cultures are not, therefore, in any straightforward way, the remains of specific peoples. Similarly, not much will be explained about any observed change simply by adducing migration. If there is good reason to think that migration is an important part of the story of any particular population group, however, there is no reason to rule it out *a priori*. With these points in mind, we can return to the history of the Goths in the first three centuries AD.

(ii) The Wielbark and Černjachov cultures[5]

A vast amount of new archaeological material has been unearthed in eastern Europe since 1945. The finds have shed light on many periods, not least on the general history of the first few centuries AD, and the history of the Goths. This has come about through the identification and analysis of two archaeological 'cultures' of the traditional kind: the so-called Wielbark culture of what is now northern Poland, and the Černjachov of the northern hinterland of the Black Sea. These cultures do not reflect the material remains of the Goths in the sense advocated by Kossina. A simple one-to-one equation of either set of remains with Goths is demonstrably mistaken. Both sets of remains

[4] E.g. Adams, 1978; Kershaw, 1978; Antony, 1990; Sallares, 1991, 66ff, Shennan, 1991.

[5] Since I am not an archaeologist, and have not worked directly on the remains, I have decided, for the most part, to abandon precise annotation when discussing the Wielbark and Černjachov cultures. I have instead provided bibliographical guidance to the reading which informs both what follows and the relevant sections of chapter 3.

clearly encompassed many other groups besides, and the population group designated by the term Goth was itself, as we shall see, subject to profound transformation over time. None the less, there is reason to associate both cultures with the spread of Gothic and other related Germanic groups in the first four centuries AD.

The mass of new material has, perhaps above all, enabled archaeologists to establish a broadly reliable dating system for objects from northern and central Europe. The basic problem has always been that the remains contain few precise chronological indicators. Imported Roman coins and closely dateable fine Roman *terra sigillata* pottery in closed finds (such as burials), provide the only precise indicators, but the time lag between production and deposition is always a matter of uncertainty. Thus another, related, approach has come to predominate. Typologies of individual objects have long been used to provide relative indications of date. The appearance of more-developed types of an object can be reasonably presumed to be subsequent to simpler, therefore earlier, forms. In recent years, the systematic analysis of an ever-increasing body of material has allowed the typologies of a whole series of objects to be defined with much greater security. But any individual type of brooch or buckle might have been adopted at different times in different areas, or, indeed, deliberately retained as antiques. Dating has come to rely, therefore, not on individual objects, but on groups of them. The greater the number of objects showing features of a dateable kind in any one find of material, the more secure its chronology. Hence chronological phases are now typically defined as consisting of an association of particular weapon-types with certain forms of brooch, buckle, pot and comb.

Three of the phases thus defined, concern us here: B (early Roman Iron Age), C (late Roman Iron Age) and D (Migration Period). Each of these phases has been further sub-divided (e.g. B1a, B1b, B2a etc.), and argument continues over details.[6] None the less, for early Gothic history, more than enough has been achieved to make it possible to use this system to work backwards in time and space from the Black Sea, identifying a Gothic involvement in both the Černjachov and Wielbark cultures. How precisely to associate the Goths with these remains is a separate question. The range of possible answers has been blown wide open by modern critiques of Kossina's assumptions, and we will return to this question in the next chapter.

In the fourth century AD, Gothic military power was dominant in

[6] Godłowski, 1970, esp. 101ff.

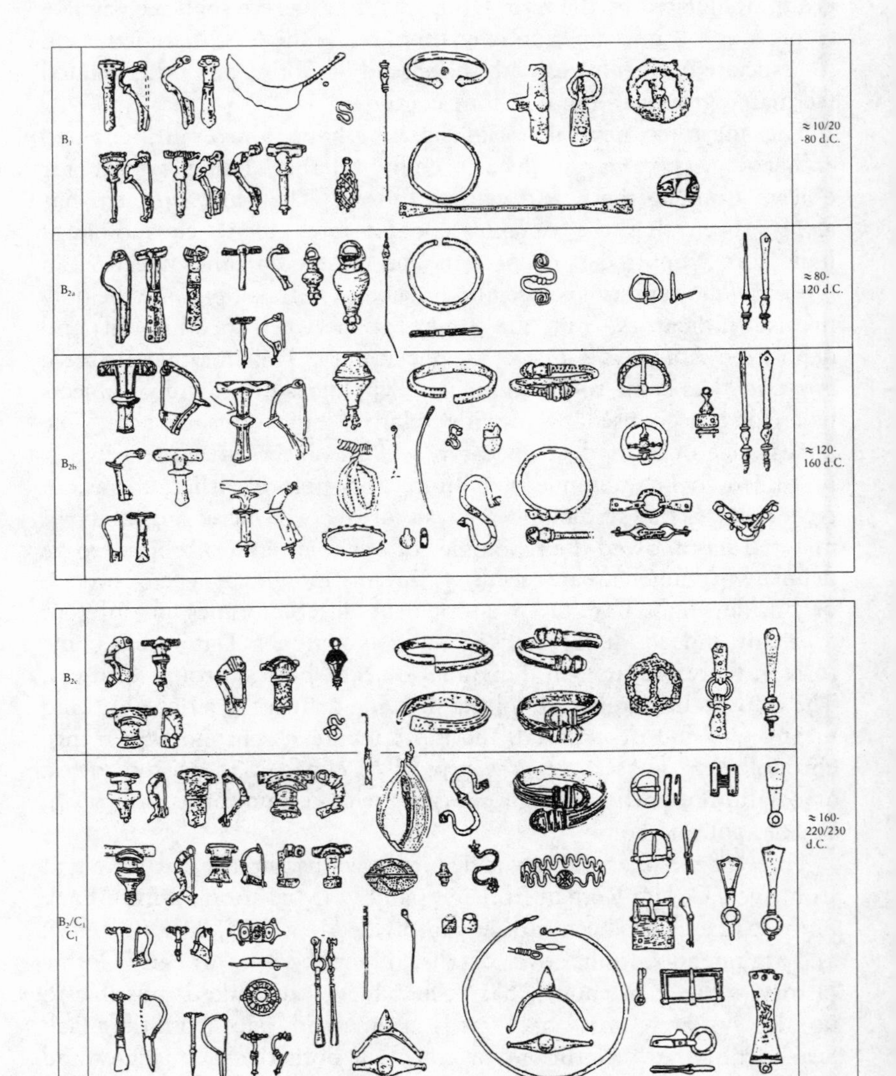

Figure 2.3 Dating the Wielbark culture

an area between the rivers Danube and Don. The Danube frontier of the Roman Empire marked its south-western boundary, and a reliable contemporary historian, Ammianus Marcellinus, tells us that the Alanic group on the Goths' eastern front were the Tanaites: 'the Don people' (31.3.1). Literary sources provide no information on the Goths' northern boundaries. It is now certain that a relatively rich and homogeneous archaeological culture found in the same area – the Černjachov culture – dates from precisely the same period. In archaeological terms, the Černjachov culture was generated in phases C1b–C2, and reached its fullest extent in phases C3–D. The equivalent absolute dates would imply the culture's formation in the later third century, and full flourishing in the fourth. Given the geographical and chronological coincidences between Gothic power and Černjachov remains, an association of some kind between the two is irresistible.

It was also noted long ago, almost as soon as the first Černjachov finds were published in the early 1900s, that some of them (particularly metalwork and personal ornaments) bore a striking resemblance to objects found in Poland, in cemeteries belonging to Kossina's 'Gotho–Gepidan' culture. In recent years, a wide programme of investigation has established the broad outlines of the development and spread of what has come to be known as the Wielbark culture. It is usually sub-divided into two broad horizons. The earlier – Wielbark–Lubowidz – took shape in the middle of the first century AD (phase B1b) in Pomerania and lands either side of the lower Vistula. Again, this is the broad area where our few literary sources place a group called Goths at this time.[7] The culture flourished in these areas for the best part of a century (particularly phase B2: earlier second century). In the second and third centuries, however, artefacts and customs typical of the culture in its second phase – Wielbark–Cecele – spread over a much wider area (figures 2.3, 2.4). Expansion first encompassed northern greater Poland and Mazovia east of the river Vistula in the phase B2–B2/C1 (= *c.* AD 160–210). Slightly later, the same kind of material remains spread south along the Vistula and the rivers San and Bug into Byelorussia, Volhynia and the northern Ukraine (phase B2/C1–C1a = *c.* AD 180–230).

The Wielbark culture thus spread into the precise geographical

[7] Tacitus *Germania* 43–4 places them not quite on the Baltic coast; Ptolemy *Geography* 3.5.8 locates them east of the Vistula; Strabo *Geography* 7.1.3 (if Butones should be emended to Gutones) broadly agrees with Tacitus.

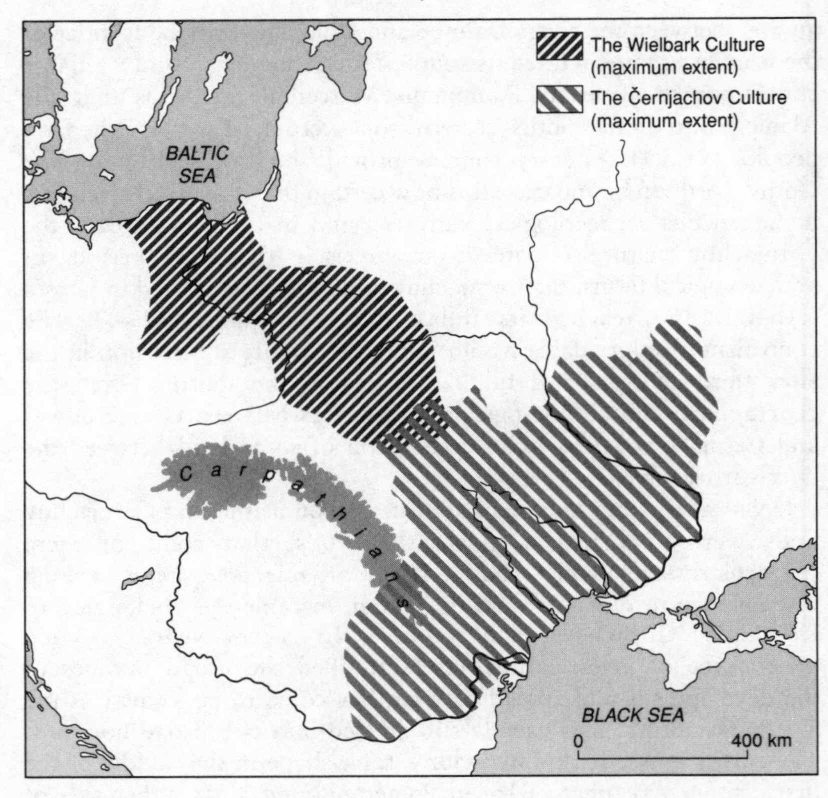

Figure 2.4 The Wielbark and Černjachov cultures

milieu where the Černjachov culture was to form, in the period immediately before the latter's generation. Literary sources, similarly, report the presence of Goths in the right areas at the appropriate times, suggesting an association of Goths with both sets of remains. More than that, certain distinctive elements of the Wielbark culture are also prominent in the remains of the Černjachov. Among artefacts, some of the handmade pottery, many of the fibula brooch types, and the style of female costume (see below) are identical. Likewise, some particular methods of house construction are common to both. More profoundly, two customs really distinguish Wielbark remains from those found in surrounding areas of northern central Europe. First, in Wielbark cemeteries, two types of ritual co-existed side by side: inhumation and cremation. Surrounding areas have produced only cremation burials, and, as we shall see, the partial adoption of inhumation is one of the main features distinguishing Wielbark-Lubowidz remains from earlier remains of the same area.

Secondly, the population of Wielbark areas did not bury weapons (or any other iron objects) with their male dead. Again, surrounding cultures continued to do so, and former populations in Wielbark areas had themselves previously done so too. Both of these habits – mixed cemeteries and weaponless graves – also feature in the material remains of the Černjachov culture, although there is a much greater variety of burial practice in the latter. This documented transfer of distinctive traits – to which we might add continuity in female costume – is extremely important. In these cases, we are dealing not with the spread of isolated objects from one area to another, but with the spread of customs expressing social norms (i.e. female costume) and even belief systems (burial rites).

Objects and customs from one area can be found subsequently in another without having been carried there by a substantial movement of population. As we have seen, such has been the reaction to the old migration-driven visions of European pre-history, that some scholars have virtually written migration out of their reconstructions of the past. In this particular case, likewise, some important features of the Černjachov culture have no precedent in Wielbark remains (see below). The former is not, therefore, simply a continuation of the latter. Nevertheless, human migration has sometimes been a major phenomenon in European history. And, in this particular instance, the recent archaeological finds suggest a series of good reasons for seeing a population movement south and east, from what is now Poland, as having played a major role in the creation of the Černjachov culture.

First, Wielbark sites increase in density in the first two centuries AD, and then become much sparser in their old Pomeranian heartlands in the third and fourth centuries (figure 2.4). Secondly, Wielbark elements found in the Černjachov culture are both numerous and distinctive, reflecting a transfer not just of certain objects but of basic beliefs and norms. Thirdly, as we will consider in more detail later, literary sources confirm that groups of people called or calling themselves Goths moved from Poland to the Black Sea, at exactly the same time as the Wielbark culture spread south and made its contribution to the Černjachov. The surviving narratives of the third century show Goths fighting around the northern and eastern borders of old Roman Dacia (i.e. Volhynia and the northern Ukraine: see below). And, as we have seen, Goths dominated at least some of the areas coincident with the

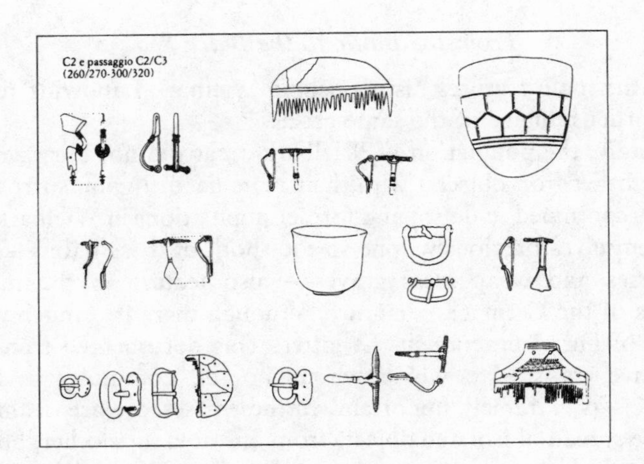

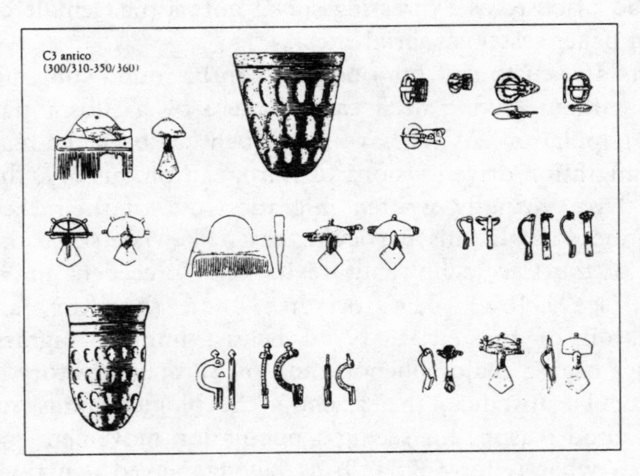

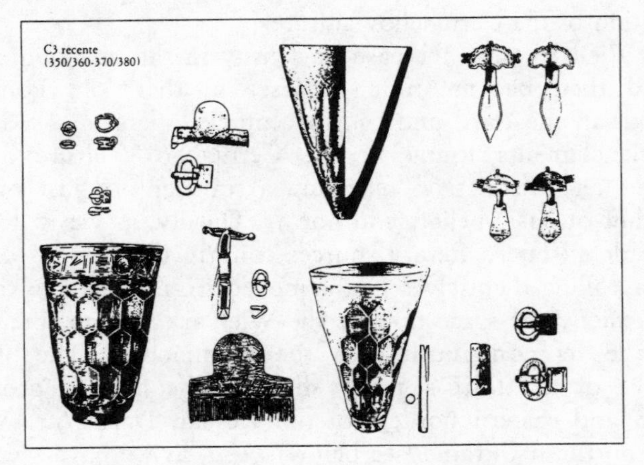

Figure 2.5 Dating the Černjachov culture

Černjachov culture in the fourth century[8].

Many questions remain. How are we to envisage the human history reflected in the expansion of Wielbark-type remains, and the creation of the Černjachov culture, and what was the role of Goths in these events? An attempt will be made to answer these questions later in the chapter, but, for the moment, we can leave the discussion with an intermediate conclusion. The archaeological evidence would seem at least partly to confirm Jordanes' account of Filimer's migration: the movement of Goths from the European mainland opposite Scandinavia to the hinterland of the Black Sea. Given that the events occurred some 300–400 years before the *Getica* was composed, at a time when the Goths were not themselves literate, Jordanes' account is more correct, it seems to me, than we have any right to expect. Can this judgement be extended to his story of Berig and the Goths' Scandinavian origins?

(iii) Poland and Scandinavia

The archaeological trail from the lower Vistula to Scandinavia is much weaker than that from the Black Sea to the Vistula. Only one feature of the earlier phase of the Wielbark culture, the appearance of stone circles in cemeteries (27 had been identified by 1983), was practised earlier in Scandinavia, than on the European mainland.[9] A number of other observations similarly minimize the extent of any possible Scandinavian contribution to the Wielbark culture.

First, the stone circles do not appear among the earliest Wielbark cemeteries. These can be dated B1b (early to mid-first century AD), while the stone circles are found only in cemeteries of the period B2 (*c.* AD 100 or later). If the stone circles do reflect a Scandinavian involvement in the Wielbark culture, it was not in its creation. Graeco–Roman literary sources, incidentally, already place Goths around the Vistula in the first century, *before* the use of such circles began.[10] Secondly, the same cemeteries were in continuous use in both the earliest phase of the Wielbark culture and the latest phase of the so-called Oksywie culture which preceded it. Much of the history of

[8] Recent investigations have also identified three local cultural horizons, where Wielbark and Černjachov elements are found mixed together, where the two overlap: the Volhynian, Ružičanki and Masłomęcz groups. All have been dated C1a/b, just prior to the full emergence of the Černjachov culture. On the Masłomęcz group, see 39.

[9] Cf. Kazanski, 1991, 15ff, with the map of stone circles at p. 17.

[10] Godłowski, 1986.

the creation of the Wielbark culture is the story of an indigenous population adopting new habits. In particular, they ceased to cremate all their dead and to bury men with weapons, both common practices of Oksywie people. Thirdly, enough is known of the general development of archaeological cultures around the Baltic in the centuries either side of the birth of Christ, to render it highly unlikely that a substantial emigration from Scandinavia occurred at any point in this period. From the archaeological evidence, therefore, the most that could be claimed is that a few 'Gothic' aristocratic clans migrated from Scandinavia to northern Poland. Even so, the indigenous population south of the Baltic had already adopted most of the new customs which made them archaeologically distinctive, and were already known as Goths. The core of any argument in favour of a link between the Goths and Scandinavia remains, therefore, the *Getica*'s account of Berig's migration, and we must consider it in more detail.

Plate 1 A Wielbark stone circle under excavation

Evidence for the Goths' Scandinavian origins has been found in two elements of the *Getica*'s text: the story of Berig (p. 11), of course, but also the names of some Scandinavian tribes which are mentioned just before it (*Getica* 19–24). The extensive knowledge of Scandinavian ethnography demonstrated in this second passage has been taken as proof that Gothic oral history retained clear memories of the tribe's first home. This section also names three Scandinavian groups which have 'Goth' as an element within them: Vagoth, Gauthigoth, and Ostrogoth. These have been seen as the names of Goths who never migrated, and who are responsible for some modern 'Gothic' place names: Ostergotland, Vastergotland and the island of Gotland.

In the sixth century, however, there existed close links between the Baltic world and Ostrogothic Italy, where Jordanes' main source – the *Gothic History* of Cassiodorus – was composed. Cassiodorus sent letters, in Theoderic's name, to the Aestii who lived on the southern shore of the Baltic, and an exiled Scandinavian king – Rodulf of the Rani – sought refuge at the Ostrogothic court. He is mentioned in the *Getica* just after its long list of Scandinavian tribal names (24), and it seems a fair guess that he, rather than Gothic memories of their first homeland, was the ultimate source for most of the *Getica*'s Scandinavian ethnography.[11]

There may even be an explanation for the idea of Scandinavian Goths. A Scandinavian tribe called the *Goutai* are already mentioned in Ptolemy's *Geography* of the second century AD (2.11.16). Both the 'Gothic' names in the *Getica* and also the supposed modern Gothic survivals (Gotland etc.) all correspond to the territory of this people. They are the Geats of *Beowulf*, and their subsequent history is known from medieval sources. It is not at all clear, however, that they were really Scandinavian Goths, directly connected to the groups which concern us here, rather than a quite separate population group with a not dissimilar name. The early Scandinavian stone circles, for instance, are not found in the areas of Sweden that the Goutai dominated. And even if we beg this question, and assume for a moment that these people were 'our' Goths, this still does not prove that Scandinavia was the original Gothic homeland. The Viking era makes us think instinctively of outflows of population from Scandinavia. Immigration, however, also occurred. The movement north of some Heruli in the sixth century, for instance, is well-documented (Procopius *Wars* 6.14–15), and all the Scandinavian peoples must have originally got there from somewhere.[12] Again, we

[11] The description used Graeco-Roman written sources too: Mommsen's notes to his edition of the *Getica*, pp. 58–60. Modern commentary: esp. Svennung, 1967 (stressing the accuracy of the *Getica*'s information).

[12] Hachmann, 1970, pt. 1. Svennung, 1967, ch. 9 takes an alternative view.

are led back to the story of Berig. Does its insistence upon Scandinavia reflect authentic Gothic tradition?

While there is no direct method of finding out, it is worth considering all that Jordanes has to say on the subject. Having recorded Filimer's victory over the Spali, the passage quoted above continues:

> [28] for so the story is generally told in their early songs, almost as a history. Ablabius also, a famous chronicler of the Gothic race, confirms this in his most trustworthy account.

A little later on, Jordanes returns to the question:

> [38] We do not find anywhere in their written records legends which tell of their subjection to slavery in Britain or in some other island, or of their redemption by a certain man at the cost of a horse. Of course if anyone in our city [Constantinople] says that the Goths had an origin different from that I have related, let him object. For myself, I prefer to believe what I have read, rather than put trust in old wives' tales [*fabulis anilibus*].

From these passages, we learn two things. First, the Scandinavian story was not the only one known to Jordanes. Secondly, he believed in its authenticity not primarily because it was told by the Goths themselves (although the first quotation would suggest that it was), but because he found written confirmation of it in Ablabius. As we have seen, Ablabius was probably known to Jordanes through Cassiodorus' *Gothic History*, and Ablabius himself seems to have collected Gothic oral traditions. It is certainly possible, therefore, that Scandinavia was explicitly mentioned in Gothic tales of the past.

What strikes me, however, is that the Berig story and the other variants more briefly referred to by Jordanes, all involved islands: Scandinavia, Britain or 'some other island'. The idea that a distinct people should have a distinct geographic origin seems to be a commonplace of oral traditions, and islands – conveniently surrounded by water to exclude intruders – fit the bill perfectly. In the sixth century, however, people do not seem to have been sure which island. Even a man of Gothic descent like Jordanes was not certain. He clearly favoured the Scandinavian hypothesis, but primarily on Ablabius' authority, and we simply do not know what Ablabius' source might have been. The story of Berig as told by Goths might have said Scandinavia. Given the variations reported by Jordanes, it is just as likely that it simply said *an* island, without giving a name. It would thus have been left to those investigating Gothic history (Ablabius, Cassiodorus and Jordanes) to work out which one. To one strand of Graeco-Roman ethnographic and geographic tradition, Britain and Scandinavia were mysterious northern islands (often associated with Thule) rather than well-documented localities, and either might have fitted the bill. Before describing Scandinavia, Jordanes includes a lengthy geographical description of Britain (10–15). The only possible relevance of this passage to what follows is that it was meant to prove that the Goths could not have originated there. Among other things, for instance, he reports that Britain's inhabitants are like Gauls or Spaniards, presumably drawing an implicit contrast between such peoples and the Goths.

I think it likely, therefore, that the story of Berig and his migration genuinely reflect Gothic story telling in some way, but I am less sure that the original Gothic stories mentioned Scandinavia. Indeed, the pattern of the evidence here is in some ways similar to the original stories which have survived for another Germanic people, the Lombards. Paul the Deacon's *History of the Lombards* and the *Origins of the Lombard People* both report that the Lombards' original home was Scandinavia. But there is reason to think that Paul was at least influenced by having read Jordanes. A third text, the so-called *Codex Gothanum*, although telling not dissimilar stories about some of the same people nevertheless situates the Lombards' first home on the extreme boundary of Gaul. This is exactly where they were located by Tacitus (*Germania* 40), and it is likely that Tacitus' account swayed our third author's choice. Similar intellectual processes were seemingly at work. Literate recorders of tribal traditions had to make sense of obscure, but possibly copious oral materials. Part of this process involved their comparison with Graeco–Roman geographical and ethnographical writings in order to locate the action. Such an approach is clearly marked in the *Getica*. Jordanes' discussion of Britain, for instance, borrows directly or indirectly from Tacitus's *Agricola* and Pomponius Mela.[13]

Exactly the same approach to chronological problems is visible in the *Getica*. Roman chronicles, for instance, have been used to identify the battle in which the dynasty of Theoderic the great, the Amals, first acquired the aura of semi-divine status. The choice fell upon a chronologically convenient battle in the first century, which had, in reality, involved Dacians, not Goths. In the *Getica*, however, a learned manipulator has turned the event into a great Gothic victory. Someone, probably Cassiodorus, clearly searched through the chronicles until he found a battle in the right time and place, with

[13] Cf. Mommsen's notes to his edition of the *Getica* at this point, pp. 56–7.

the right result (a Roman defeat).[14] The same concern, if differently expressed, is also apparent in the wealth of Graeco–Roman historical material, which, as we have seen, separates the tales of Berig and Filimer (*Getica* 39–78). The intellectual approach displayed in the *Getica*'s account of early Gothic history is thus consistent. The Goths and their stories have been carefully positioned against a classical and literary frame of reference.

This general characteristic makes the case for Scandinavia look still more doubtful. Jordanes' working methods in the case of the Berig story look suspiciously like those demonstrated elsewhere. Some obscure Gothic material has been given a secure Scandinavian location, not for any genuinely Gothic reason, but because classical geographical traditions seemed to suggest that this was the most likely locale. This choice was perfectly respectable given the information available in sixth-century Constantinople, but we need not regard it as authoritative. The trail of physical remains fizzles out in northern Poland, and Jordanes' evidence is too insecure a basis to take it further. The mutually confirmatory information of ancient sources and the archaeological record both suggest that Goths can first be identified beside the Vistula. It is here that this attempt to write their history will begin.

B. Rome and the Goths, c.AD 1–300

By the beginning of the first century AD, Roman imperial power had pushed out of Italy as far north and east, broadly speaking, as the rivers Rhine and Danube. About 100 years later, the Dacian kingdom, north of the Danube, was added to the Empire, but this was an isolated episode. Uncontrolled expansion in Europe seems to have been halted when an earlier plan to advance the frontier to the Elbe was abandoned, after the complete destruction of Varus' expeditionary force in the Teutoberger Wald in AD 9. A fairly straightforward cost-benefit analysis brought the legions to a halt. Not only were the lands beyond the Rhine and Danube difficult to subdue, but they were also lacking in the kinds of economic development which would have made them worthwhile conquests. Rome's European frontiers broadly coincided, in fact, with the spread of the so-called Oppida culture. This network of developed, wealthy societies, which

[14] *Getica* 76ff, the defeat of Cornelius Fuscus in AD 76. For another example concerning the career of Valamer, see Heather 1989; cf. below, p. 114.

flourished in western and south-central Europe in the last centuries BC, represented an attractive lure to Roman imperialism.[15] At the start of the first century, the Goths, established in northern Poland close to the Baltic, were nowhere near the main focus of Roman energies, and this, of course, is the main reason why so little is known of their early history.

In the first three centuries AD, the Goths themselves were essentially non-literate. Runes already existed, and there have been some exciting finds, such as an inscribed spearhead from Volhynia. Nothing suggests, however, that runes were ever at this time used to create documentary records of people, events, or goods. We are entirely dependent, therefore, for our knowledge of the Goths upon what authors from the Mediterranean world chose to record. These sources naturally concentrated upon groups and events of particular interest to the Roman Empire (usually those nearest the frontier), and our knowledge has been further curtailed by the chances of manuscript survival over the centuries. Notoriously, many third-century sources have failed to survive, and this, as we shall see, is precisely the moment that Goths began to make a bigger impact on the Roman world.

The first 150 years or so of the Christian era, after Rome abandoned further expansion, saw a reasonable degree of stability on Rome's Germanic frontiers. Defences were built, diplomatic alliances furthered, and client kings beyond the frontier sponsored.[16] From time to time, the rhythm of frontier life was broken by unrest. The first major upheaval – the so-called Marcomannic war – did not come until the second-half of the second century. As we shall see, extended military and diplomatic action enabled the Empire to restore order, but, this time, stability would not last so long. The central part of the third century was marked by severe disruption to both the European riverine frontiers. Historical fragments and archaelogical evidence combine to generate a clear picture of the intrusion, in the course of these two major periods of disruption, of Gothic power into the Graeco–Roman world.

(i) The Marcomannic war

For the whole of the first century AD, narrative sources specifically mention Goths in relation to only one incident. In AD 18, a young nobleman called Catualda, who, although not himself a Goth, had

15 A useful introduction is Whittaker, 1994, ch. 3.
16 On the latter, see esp. Klose, 1934.

sought refuge with them from the great Marcomannic king, Marboduus, returned 'with a strong force' to his homeland, right beside the Danube, to seize power (Tacitus *Annals* 2.62). The Goths' distance from the frontier, at this point, presumably made their lands a safe haven for Catualda, but it also meant that they were of little direct concern to the imperial authorities.

There is just a chance that Goths were also involved in a second political convulsion of the first century. Most individually named Germanic groups of the period seem to have belonged to larger associations or tribal leagues, quite possibly organized around religious cults. Tacitus, for instance, refers to the religious observances which united the confederation of the Suebi, and to the cult of the Earth Mother Nerthus which provided a focus for another large grouping.[17] The allegiance of the Goths is problematic. According to Pliny (*Nat. Hist.* 4.99), they formed part of the Vandalic confederation. This may or may not have been identical with the grouping known collectively as the Lugii, with whom they were associated by Strabo.[18] The question is relevant, because, in AD 50, king Vannius, again of the Danubian Marcomanni, was driven out of his kingdom by a large horde, consisting, amongst others, of Lugii. The invaders wanted to share out the vast wealth he had accumulated in the course of his 30-year reign (Tacitus *Annals* 12.25). If we follow Strabo, Goths may well have been involved in these events, which would cast them in much the same light as the Catualda episode. Too far away from the frontier to merit direct Roman attention, they were none the less participants in inter-Germanic politics. In particular, they displayed a healthily predatory interest in the wealth which clients of the Empire had a particular tendency to amass, the fruits of diplomatic gifts and licensed trade.

In the middle of the second century, frontier stability was shattered by the Marcomannic war. Hostilities opened with an attack by Chatti into Raetia and upper Germany between AD 162 and 165, but the main action unfolded south and east. In winter of 166/7, 6,000 Langobardi and Ubii raided Pannonia, in 168 Marcomanni and Victuali demanded admission into the Empire and, in the winter of 169/70, there followed the famous Marcomannic invasion of Italy, which was not fully repelled until the end of 171. At the same time, other Germanic and nomadic groups were causing trouble the length of the Danube. The Costoboci, from the north-east of Dacia, raided

17 *Germania* 38–40; cf. Hachmann, *The Germanic Peoples*, 81ff.
18 Strabo *Geography* 7.1.3; for further discussion, see Wolfram, 1988, 40.

Thrace, Macedonia and Greece. Nomadic Sarmatian Iazyges and Germanic Quadi caused further problems on the middle Danube west of the Carpathians, and two Vandal groups (the Astingi and the Lacringi) disturbed the northern frontiers of Dacia. Not surprisingly, much of the rest of the decade was taken up with Roman counter-measures. Far-reaching military campaigns (celebrated pictorially on the column of Marcus Aurelius in Rome: plate 2) were combined with a complicated web of diplomatic alliances. These involved both frontier groups, and others, such as the Buri and the Vandals, who lived at a greater distance. By these means, peace was eventually restored to the middle Danube and the fringes of Dacia.[19]

As this brief outline makes clear, the disruption affected many more groups than just the Marcomanni, and, in particular, involved geographical displacement on a substantial scale. The Langobardi and Ubii, whose attack on Pannonia opened proceedings, seem to have moved about 800 km south from their first-century homeland on the lower Elbe (Tacitus *Germania* 40). Geographical displacement is also apparent in the move south of certain Vandal groups into the territory of the Costoboci.[20] This may well have stimulated, in turn, the latter's invasion of Roman territory. Likewise, when defusing the crisis, the Romans admitted a group called the Naristi peacefully into the Empire. This, seemingly small, group had previously lived on the Danube frontier between the Marcomanni and Quadi. Marcomanni and Victuali also asked for the same treatment as the Naristi, but, in their case, permission was denied. All this suggests that frontier groups were feeling considerable pressure from the north. The king of the Marcomanni, Ballomarius, had earlier acted as spokesman before the Emperor for delegations from some 11 tribal groups. This confirms the extent of the problem.[21] The name generally given to the war is thus something of a misnomer. The attacks on the Empire by the Marcomanni stand in the middle of a sequence of disturbances affecting much of the Germanic world.

As far as we know, Goths were not involved in direct conflict with the Roman state in these years. Nevertheless, the southward movement of more northerly groups was central to the action, and geographical displacement of this kind was seen by one of our main sources, the *Scriptores Historia Augusta*, as the underlying cause of

[19] A good introduction is Birley, 1966, chs 6–8 with App. III; see also Böhme, 1975.

[20] Dio 72.11.6; 12.1–3 (ed. Loeb, vol. 9, pp. 14ff).

[21] Dio 72.3.1a, (ed. Loeb, vol. 9, p. 10).

Plate 2 The Marcomannic War (the column of Marcus Aurelius)

the war: '... not only were the Victuali and Marcomanni throwing everything into confusion, but other tribes, who had been driven on by the more distant barbarians and had retreated before them, were ready to attack Italy if not peaceably received' (*V. Marc.* 14.1).

At this point we face one of the many difficult problems which the *Historia Augusta* poses. The whole thing is in a basic sense a fabrication. It contains much historical information, but is a creation of *c.* AD 400 masquerading as one of *c.*300.[22] How reliable, therefore, is this particular statement? A writer of *c.*400 would have been only too well aware of a contemporary example of exactly this kind of sequence of events (the retreat of the Goths before the Huns after 375: chapter 4). Did he find his interpretation of the Marcomannic war in his source for the reign of Marcus Aurelius, or did he retrospectively apply a familiar model of causation? Fortunately, we do not have to rest the case for Gothic involvement in the Marcomannic war upon just this one remark.

The period from *c.* AD 150 onwards, the era of the Marcomannic war, was marked by substantial changes in the configuration of archaeological cultures on the territory of what is now Poland. It was in precisely this period (B2, B2/C1a), that the second phase of the Wielbark culture, Wielbark–Cecele, evolved and spread south from Pomerania into the northern part of Greater Poland (between the rivers Notec and Warta), and south-eastwards across the Vistula into Masovia (figure 2.6). These territories had previously been occupied by elements of the so-called Przeworsk culture. The chronological coincidence is too striking to be dismissed. Wielbark expansion, indicating a major upheaval in northern Poland, occurred at broadly the same time as the Marcomannic war, and was surely connected to it in some way. What the archaeological evidence cannot make certain, however, is whether this connection was cause or effect. Did the Wielbark take-over of northern and north-eastern Przeworsk territories force some of its component population southwards? The Przeworsk culture is traditionally associated, amongst others, with Vandals, who took part in the war. Alternatively, did Wielbark populations move into a vacuum created by a shift to the south of the interests of their Przeworsk neighbours?

If the spread of Wielbark finds over time is mapped, and the maps taken in chronological order, it becomes clear that settlement within the original Wielbark zone became more intense before the take-over of Przeworsk territory. A buffer zone had existed between the two cultures in the period B1, but was eroded by Wielbark expansion in the periods B2 and B2/C1a (figure 2.6). Similarly, as we shall see, while there is some evidence in Masovia for Przeworsk populations taking on Wielbark habits (below p. 89), there would also seem to

[22] E.g. Syme 1968, 1971a, 1971b.

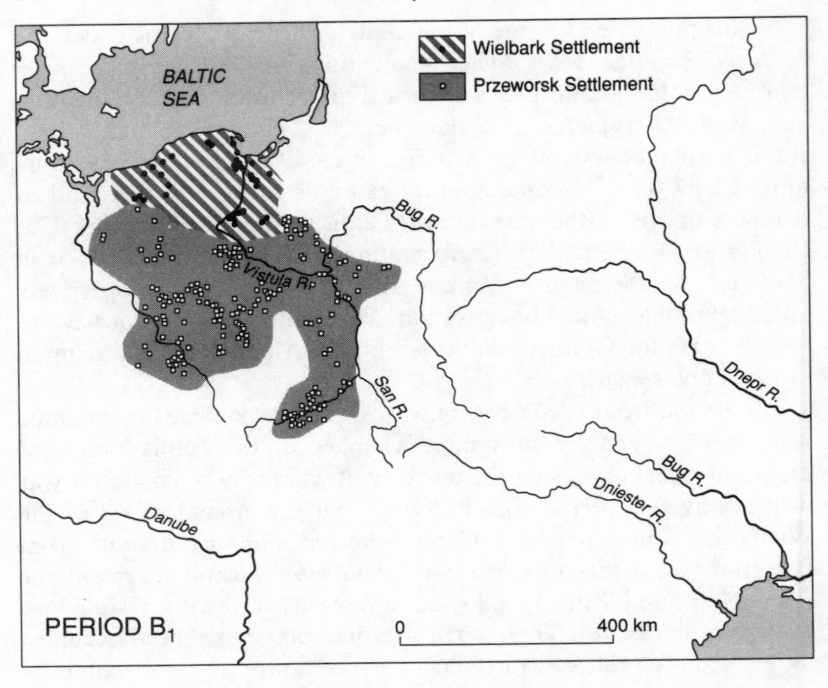
Wielbark Settlement
Przeworsk Settlement
BALTIC SEA
Bug R.
Vistula R.
San R.
Dnepr R.
Bug R.
Dniester R.
Danube
PERIOD B1
0
400 km

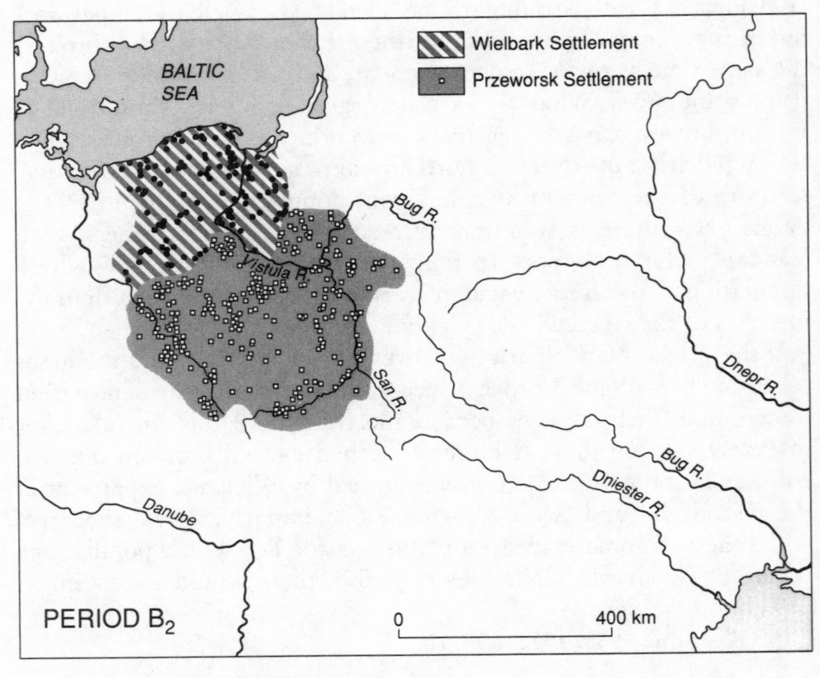
Wielbark Settlement
Przeworsk Settlement
BALTIC SEA
Bug R.
Vistula R.
San R.
Dnepr R.
Bug R.
Dniester R.
Danube
PERIOD B2
0
400 km

Figure 2.6(a)

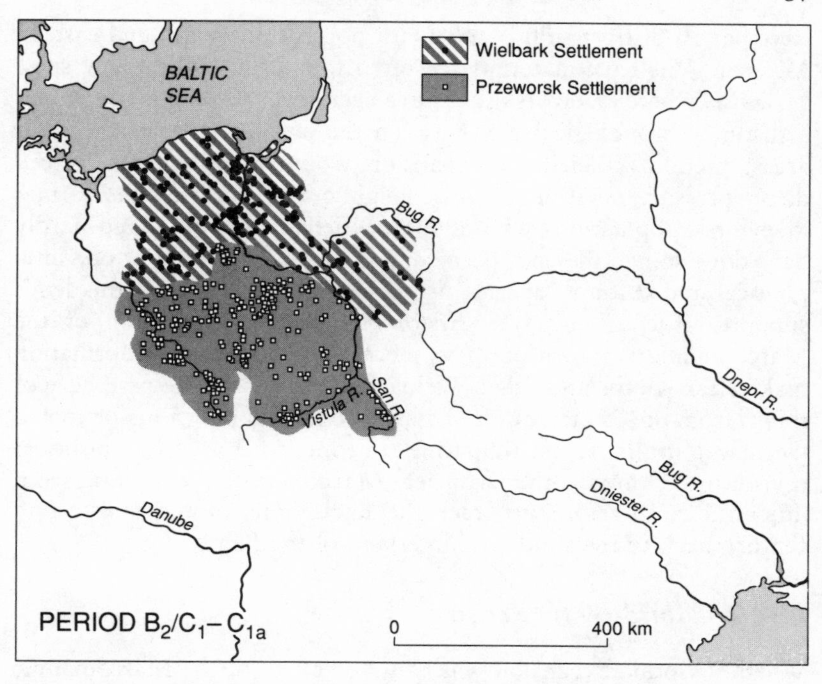

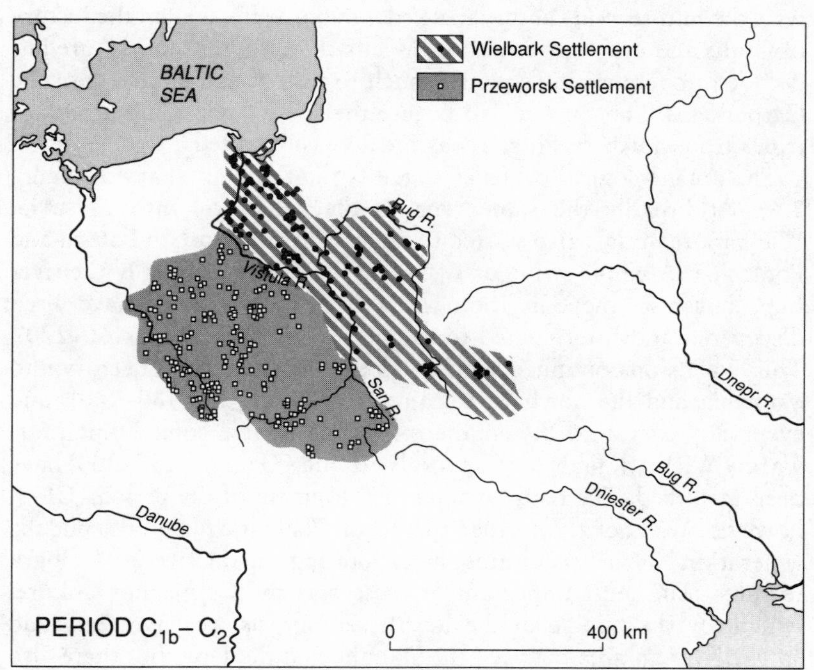

Figure 2.6(b) The chronological spread of the Wielbark and Przeworsk cultures

have been a distinct shift of Wielbark populations south and east. In Masovia, Wielbark materials are often found on entirely new sites. Likewise, where Przeworsk sites have been re-used, there is sometimes a distinct chronological gap between the layers. At least in certain areas, therefore, Wielbark expansion would seem to have placed direct pressure on its Przeworsk neighbours. And even the former Przeworsk populations who adopted Wielbark habits would hardly have done so had they not been coming under some kind of pressure: political and cultural, at least, if not demographic. All of this lends support, of course, to the *Historia Augusta*'s conception of the Marcomannic war. As our few pieces of first-century information make clear, Goths and other Wielbark tribes – if on the periphery of things from the Roman point of view – could still play a major role in Germanic politics, participating in one, if not two, political revolutions among the frontier Marcomanni. It is far from implausible, therefore, to trace the disruptions of the mid-second century back to the southern hinterland of the Baltic.

(ii) The third-century crisis

Whether Gothic expansion was cause or effect of the Marcomannic war, the mid-second century marked a major watershed in the history of Goths and other groups of the Wielbark culture. Marcus Aurelius' decade of counter-measures did much to restore stability west of the Carpathians, but, once it had begun, the south-eastern movement of tribes from northern Poland was not so easily halted.

The archaeological evidence suggests the following pattern (figure 2.6). At broadly the same time as the expansion into Masovia, Wielbark materials also started to appear further south in Polesia and Podlachia. A whole string of Wielbark sites along especially the river Bug, but also the San (both flow into the Vistula), have been discovered and firmly dated to the period B2/C1a (*c.* AD 160–220). This expansion continued slightly later along the same trajectory into Volhynia and the northern Ukraine (C1a/b = *c.* AD 180–220), and eventually even into the southern Ukraine, where some straightforwardly Wielbark finds of the periods C2 and C3 (*c.* AD 250–300) have been identified. The really striking development of the periods C1–3, however, was not the further spread of Wielbark materials, but the generation of new cultures incorporating distinctively Wielbark features. The most important of these was the Černjachov culture, which, by the middle of the fourth century, as we have seen, had spread over an area between the Danube and the Don, but there also the three so-called 'intermediate cultures' (above p. 25). The first of these, the Masłomęlcz group, was generated in the periods B2/C1a and C1a (= *c.* AD 180–220), even if most of its finds belong to C2. The other two in Volhynia and Ružyčanka were both generated in the period C1b (*c.* AD 220–260).

Questions of definition arise, however, because some scholars consider these to be not separate groups, but minor variations of either the Wielbark or Černjachov cultures. The Masłomęcz group continued to exist as a recognizably distinct entity, however, down to the Hunnic period. Such questions aside, the overall picture is clear. In *c.* AD 150 to *c.*220/230, there occurred a large-scale south-eastern expansion of the Wielbark culture. This was followed, shortly afterwards, by the generation of the Černjachov culture. The legacy of the Wielbark culture to the Černjachov, which proceeded to spread across much of the Ukraine and modern Romania, was profound and distinct.

What historical events created this pattern of remains? Although the available literary sources are fragmentary, it is quite clear that Goths were certainly involved. The first movements south along the Bug put Wielbark groups into virtually direct contact with Rome's northern Dacian frontier. At this point (*c.* AD 200), the imperial frontier was established right on the northern Carpathians. It can hardly be a coincidence, then, that evidence for close contact between Goths and Romans should begin at precisely this point. An inscription from Roman Arabia reads,

> Monument of Guththa son of Erminarius, commander (*praepositus*) of the tribal troops (*gentiles*) stationed among the Mothani. He died at the age of 14 years. In the year 102, Peritius the 21st [= 28 February, AD 208].

The personal names suggest that these might be Gothic auxiliary troops (*gentiles*) in the Roman army of the East. Their presence in such an out-of-the-way spot, betokens direct contact between Roman and Goth somewhere much further north, quite likely on the borders of Dacia. They were perhaps recruited by Septimius Severus after *c.* AD 196, when abortive movements of 'Scythians' (often used as a pseudonym for Goths in classicizing Greek sources) are mentioned in a fragment of Cassius Dio. They were about to make war, when lightning killed three of their chiefs. This they interpreted as an unfavourable omen. One can see their point.[23]

Gothic participation in the turbulence which affected the extra-

[23] Inscription: Speidel, 1977, 716–18. Dio 75.3 (ed. Loeb, vol. 9, p. 198).

Carpathian and Pontic regions later in the third century is also explicit.[24] We hear little of what was happening behind the Roman frontier, but Goths made numerous attacks across it. For the most part, the raids followed two well-defined routes. First, and most direct, Goths attacked across the Empire's continental frontiers. The Carpathian mountains provided the defenders of what would, at first sight, seem the most exposed Roman province in the region – Transylvanian Dacia – with a considerable advantage. Hence, attacks tended to unfold south of their protective encirclement, either directly across the lower Danube (the run of the river east of the so-called 'Iron Gates') or through the narrow corridor of territory – protected by belts of defences on and beyond the river Olt (the *limes transalutanus*) – connecting the 'Dacian salient' to the rest of the Roman Balkans (figure 2.7).[25] Penetrating the frontier by either of these routes allowed access to the relatively rich Roman provinces of Thrace, Macedonia and Greece.

The first known attack came in 238, when Goths sacked the city of Histria at the mouth of the river Danube (Dexippus fr. 14 = *SHA* Max. et Balb. 16.3). A series of much more substantial land incursions followed a decade later. In 249, Marcianople was ransacked by the Gothic followers of two chiefs called Argaith and Guntheric, but this was still only the prelude.[26] In the spring of 250, another Gothic chief, Cniva, broke through the *limes transalutanus* into the Dacian corridor, and, crossing the Danube at Oescus, turned south. Having captured Philippopolis south of the Haemus Mountains, he overwintered his forces. The following year he defeated a Roman army and killed its leader, the Emperor Decius, at Abrittus in 251.[27] Further attacks about which we know little – probably a sign that they were less successful – followed in 253 and 254 (Dexippus fr. 16).

After this, the raiders exploited a second route into the Empire, crossing the Black Sea by ship. They plundered first the south-western Caucausus, and then worked their way westwards along the coast. The first major sea-borne raids took place in three successive years, probably 255–7. A largely unsuccessful attack on

[24] Other general accounts: Demougeot, 1979, 394ff; Wolfram, 1988, 43ff.

[25] *Limes transalutanus*: Cataniciu, 1981, 31ff.

[26] *Getica* 91; *SHA* Gord. 31.1 recounting the deeds of one 'Argunt'; this probably represents a conflation of both Argaith and Guntheric.

[27] Main sources: Zosimus 1.23. *Getica* 101–3, Zonaras 12.20. Commentary in Paschoud's edition of Zosimus, pp. 146ff, n.50ff.

Pityus, was followed in the second year by another which sacked both Pityus and Trapezus, and ravaged large areas of the Pontus. Both of these initial raids were undertaken by the so-called 'Boranoi', who may have included Goths.[28] Their success, however, encouraged wider participation, and the third year saw the arrival of a much larger force, this time explicitly including Goths. This attack devastated large areas of Bithynia and the Propontis, including the cities of Chalcedon, Nicomedia, Nicaea, Apamea and Prusa.[29]

After a 10-year gap, there then unfolded, in 268, another enormous expedition, comprising both Goths and others besides. It also encompassed both the previous approaches. A large fleet left the northern shores of the Black Sea, moving south and west. Landings to assault Tomi and Marcianople were beaten off, as were further attacks on Cyzicus and Byzantium. At this point, the Dardanelles was forced, and the raiders spilled out into the Aegean for the first time, breaking up into three main groups. One, composed mostly of Heruli, landed in the northern Balkans around Thessalonica. The second – including both Goths and Heruli – devastated Attica, and the third rampaged through the coastal hinterland of Asia Minor, probably led by the Gothic chieftains Respa, Veduc and Thuruar. Rhodes and Cyprus were attacked, before the Goths turned their attention to Side and Ilium, and destroyed the temple of Diana at Ephesus. The other raids were less successful. The first group seems to have been defeated by the Emperor Gallienus in 268, the second by Claudius at Naissus in 270. In the meantime, the Aegean raiders had been driven back into the Black Sea in 269.[30]

The destruction wrought by this combined assault on land and sea was severe, and prompted a fierce Roman response. Not only were the individual groups defeated, but no major raid ever again broke through the Dardanelles. Measures were presumably taken, therefore, to close off this route of attack. Indeed, the raid into the Aegean was very much the high tide of third-century Gothic attacks. A further attack across the Danube occurred in 270, when Anchialus and Nicopolis were sacked. But the Emperor Aurelian counter-attacked across the river in 271, and defeated the Gothic king Cannabaudes

[28] The name may just mean 'northern peoples'; for further discussion, Heather and Matthews, 1991, 2–3, 8.

[29] Principal source: Zosimus 1.31–5. Additional sources and commentary, Paschoud's commentary on Zosimus, pp. 152ff, n.59ff.

[30] Zosimus 1.42–3, 46 with Paschoud's edition, pp. 159ff, n.70ff.

(*SHA* Aur. 22.2). This may imply that Cannabaudes had also led the initial raid. The years 276/7 also saw further sea-borne raids which ravaged the Pontus, and ranged further afield into Galatia and Cilicia. Overall, the impression transmitted by our rather fragmentary sources is that the third century saw two moments of intense Gothic destruction: the early 250s and the later 260s. Both were eventually controlled. Indeed, the fact that, in between, the attackers switched their assault from land to sea, suggests that a reasonably effective closing of one invasion route had demanded the subsequent adoption of another.

Figure 2.7 Gothic attacks of the third century

Gothic-inspired mayhem thus became an increasing and, for the first time, direct threat to the Roman Empire in the middle of the third century. The obvious match-up between the picture painted by the literary sources, and the archaeological evidence for the south-eastern expansion of the Wielbark culture hardly requires emphasis. Despite modern predilections for minimizing the importance of migration, the combined evidence of texts and remains would in this case appear convincing. The descendants of groups including Goths, whose power centre in *c.* AD 100 had been Pomerania in northern Poland, had by AD 250 become major players in the eastern and northern hinterlands of the Carpathians and Black Sea regions.

(iii) Patterns of expansion

This expansion was not, however, a simple process. A single group of Goths did not move to the Black Sea under an established leader in the manner implied by Jordanes' story of Filimer (*Getica* 26–8; above p. 12). First, the Wielbark culture did not consist solely of Goths. The relevant Graeco–Roman sources (especially Tacitus and Ptolemy) mention Goths as only one among a very long list of named Germanic groups (cf. above figure 2.1). It is extremely probable that more than one of these groups occupied land within the Wielbark culture's boundaries, even when they were at their smallest in the first century. The main elements which distinguish the Wielbark culture are bi-ritual cemeteries and a disinclination to bury weapons with dead males. These are both essentially matters of cultic belief and practice. It may well be, then, that the spread of the Wielbark culture really reflects that of a cult league of the kind known from other parts of contemporary Germania (above p. 32).

Correspondingly, there is every reason to suppose that the expansion mirrored in the spread of Wielbark remains did not just involve Goths. Heruli, for instance, figured strongly in the great sea raid of the late 260s. The name is not mentioned in first- and second-century literary sources, but they were certainly another group of Germanic intruders onto the northern Pontic littoral. They may well have been one of a constellation of groups, therefore, within the Wielbark culture. Gepids (from later events, a substantial Germanic group) and Taifali (clearly smaller, but probably Germanic) also first appear in the Carpathian region in the aftermath of the third century convulsions. Equally to the point is the case of the Rugi. Tacitus places them north of the Goths, right beside the Baltic Sea in the first century (*Germania* 44). This would situate them within the original Wielbark area (figure 2.6). No literary source mentions their involvement in the great upheavals of the third century, but, by the fifth century, at least some Rugi had established themselves on the Danube. Goths were neither the unique cause of Wielbark expansion, nor the sole source of

Wielbark contributions to the Černjachov culture.[31]

Moreover, even Gothic expansion into the Pontic region did not take the form of a single, royal-led, migration. Rather, it was accomplished by a series of separate, probably mutually antagonistic, groups. The raids of the third century show no sign of underlying unity. Gothic groups are found, as we have seen, operating in different ways over a wide geographical area: by land or sea, everywhere from the mouth of the Danube to the Crimea, and beyond. A whole series of individual leaders are also mentioned: Cniva, Argaith, Guntheric, Respa, Veduc, Thuruar and Cannabaudes. Some appear in alliance with one another, but no overall Gothic king is mentioned in any reliable source.[32] The end result of all this activity, likewise, was the creation not of one Gothic kingdom, but of several (chapter 3). Expansion was thus accompanied by a degree of socio-political fragmentation as a presumably originally unitary Gothic kingdom in northern Poland gave way to several successors.

Of such a process, we have some further evidence. The extensive Wielbark contribution to the Černjachov culture can probably only be explained by positing a substantial transfer of population from the former to the latter. But the Wielbark culture itself continued to exist, even after the creation of the Černjachov. The two continued side by side throughout the fourth century in Mazovia and Podlachia. Thus, not all the Wielbark groups involved in the general move south shared in the same outcome. Some followed one historical trajectory which led to their involvement in the Černjachov culture. Their northern cousins followed another, however, which generated no substantial change in the profile of their archaeological remains. Once again, this emphasizes that Wielbark expansion generated a fragmentation of experience, even if it is no guide to political affiliation.

Some memory of this would also appear to be reflected in a series of traditions preserved in the *Getica*. According to a sub-plot of the Berig story, the Gepids also crossed from Scandinavia to the European mainland with the Goths. They were sailing, however, in a third ship which lagged behind the first two containing the Goths proper (*Getica* 94–5 explicitly labelling Goths and Gepids as 'kin'). Likewise, Jordanes' account of Filimer's migration to the Black Sea

[31] On Gepids, Heruli and Rugi in the Danubian area in the fifth century, see Pohl, 1980.

[32] Jordanes *Getica* 90–6 records the third-century triumphs of the Amal Ostrogotha. The king is a mythical, name-giving invention, however, and his name has been added to known historical events: Heather, 1991, 22–3, 36–8.

(above p. 12) tells the story of the bridge which collapsed half way through a river crossing. As a result, some of the migrants failed to make it all the way to the Goths' new homeland beside the Black Sea. These stories could not more clearly preserve a sense of broken association, and there is every reason to situate this fragmentation in the context of second- and third-century expansion.

Such processes may well explain the appearance, after *c.*250, of Germanic groups with previously unattested names, such as Heruli, Taifali and Gepids. There has always been a tendency to treat the map of Germanic groupings, such as it can be reconstructed from Tacitus and Ptolemy, as a political order written in stone. But, while some of the names mentioned in the first century (such, indeed, as Goths) do have a long history, Tacitus' *Germania* is a momentary snap-shot of a situation liable to change. New groups could be born and old ones disappear. Tacitus' own narratives, for instance, describe the creation of the Batavi. A breakaway group from the Chatti, they subsequently pursued a quite separate course from their former associates (Tacitus *Hist.* 4.12, *Germania* 29). Tacitus also describes the total extermination of the Ampsivarii, Chatti and Bructeri (Tacitus *Ann.* 58, *Germania* 33). Gepids, Heruli and Taifali are just as likely to have been new creations of the third century, as old groups previously unattested.

The striking expansion of the Wielbark culture and the creation of the Černjachov in the later second and third centuries are phenomena probably best explained as follows. A whole series of armed groups left northern Poland to carve out new niches for themselves, east and south-east of the Carpathians. Many – although not all (see below) – came from Wielbark lands, but this does not mean that they formed a united front. Because of our sources' interests, we hear much more about the intrusions of these groups into Roman territory, than about the formation of new political units beyond the imperial frontier. This second strand of activity was probably just as important to the groups involved, however, as raiding the Roman Empire. It certainly underlay the creation of the fourth-century kingdoms which will concern us in the next chapter, and the same kind of disunited armed groups were presumably involved in both types of activity. How should we envisage them?

At least some of the action was carried forward by warbands: groups of young men on the make. The undeveloped agricultural economies of Germanic territories in the first centuries AD may well have regularly generated population surpluses which could not be accommodated at home (see further, chapter 3). Tacitus signals that the warband was a standard feature of first-century Germanic society,

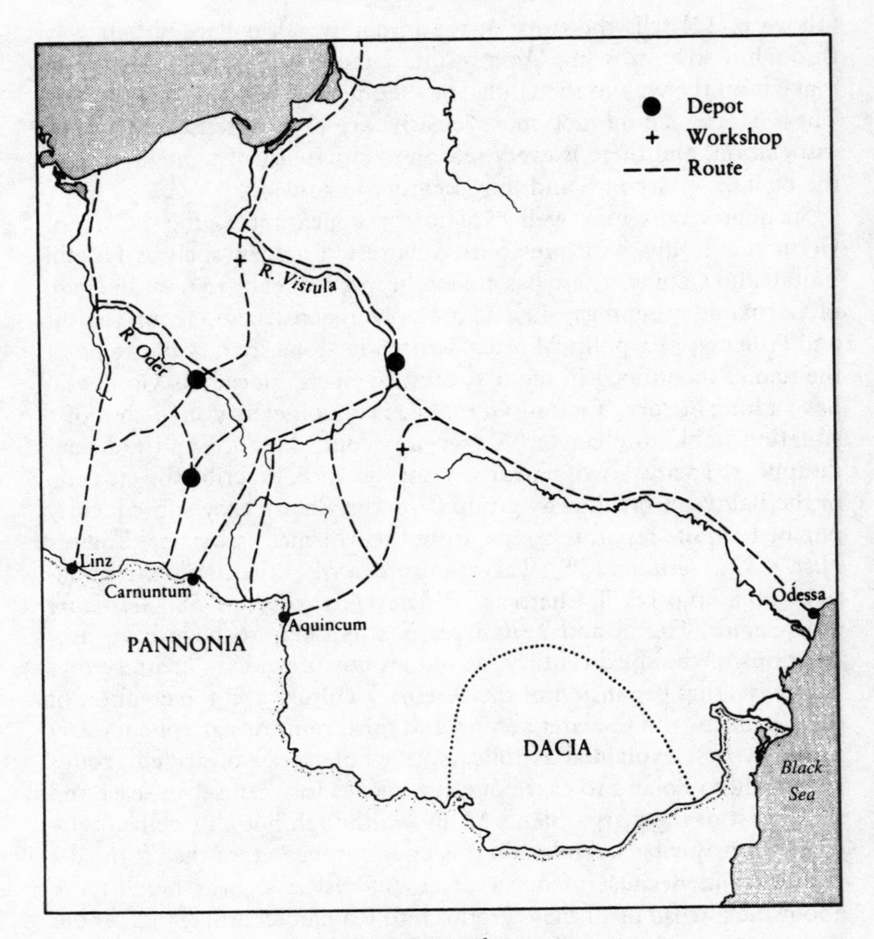

Figure 2.8 Amber routes

and it was still common in the fifth. As we shall see in the next chapter, weapon deposits in Danish bogs suggest that they were well organized, hierarchical military forces of a few hundred men. It is perhaps no coincidence either, that these weapon deposits seem to have become more frequent in the second and third centuries.[33] The disruptive, expansionary activity we have been observing at this time in eastern Europe, may have been characteristic of Scandinavia too.

Archaeological finds perhaps preserve just a little more specific evidence of the activities of such groups north of the Black Sea. From

[33] E.g. Ilkjaer, 1995.

the early phases of the Černjachov culture, a few cemeteries have been unearthed – Cozia-Iaşi, Todireni and Braniste – where, contrary to normal Černjachov practice, the dead were buried with weapons. All the other equipment found would suggest that the groups using these cemeteries were Germanic intruders from the north. The weapons suggest, however, that they originated somewhere outside the Wielbark culture, probably from within the area of the Przeworsk. The cemeteries are not large, and would be entirely in accord with a picture of small armed Przeworsk groups seeking their fortune.[34]

Third-century events cannot, however, be explained solely in terms of such small groups. Cniva could not have defeated the Emperor Decius had not his Gothic army numbered thousands rather than hundreds. Similarly, the Heruli defeated by Gallienus in 269 are said to have come in 500 boats and to have lost 3,000 men in the battle. It is also hard to believe that the great sea raid of 268–71 could have done so much damage had its component forces been much smaller than these kinds of losses would suggest.[35] More generally, the Germanic groups who moved into lands north of the Black Sea in the third century were not operating in a vacuum. They had also to compete with powers indigenous to the region. In 238, after the attack on Histria, an annual subsidy was granted by the Empire to the relevant Goths, on condition that they withdraw and return their prisoners. The arrangement provoked a howl of protest from the Carpi, who claimed to be 'more powerful' than the Goths (Petrus Patricius fr. 8). The latter were a group of 'free' Dacian tribes (i.e. they had not been brought fully under imperial rule) established in the hinterland of the Carpathians. As this episode suggests, Goths and Carpi were in direct competition with one another, and, over time, it was at the latter's expense that Gothic power grew in the region. In the end, the Carpi lost out completely. Their independence was totally dismantled, with large numbers of them being resettled inside the Roman Empire either side of the year 300.[36] Further east, the new Germanic powers in the land similarly subdued the Sarmatian

[34] Ioniţă, 1975.

[35] Heruli casualties: George Syncellus, ed. Bonn, I. 717. Other figures for the Aegean expedition: 3,000 boats and 320,000 men (*SHA* Claud. 8.2), or 2,000 boats (AM 31.5.15). Cannabaudes' defeat is said to have cost 5,000 Gothic dead (*SHA* Aur. 22.2). Much of this material derives from the contemporary account of Dexippus.

[36] Main sources: Aur. Vict. *Caes*. 39.43; Cons. Const. s.a. 295 (= *CM* 1, 230). See generally, Bichir, 1976, ch. 14. Six campaigns were fought against the Carpi during the reign of the Emperor Galerius (293–311).

kingdoms and old established Greek cities of the Pontus.[37]

The fragmented and chronologically extended nature of the action leaves plenty of room for envisaging small-scale initiatives. But more substantial groups, capable of fielding armies of a few thousands, also played their part. The extent to which these groups contained women and children, as well as men, still requires detailed study. One of the striking contributions of the Wielbark culture to the Černjachov, however, was precisely in the field of female costume (at least, burial costume). In both, women's clothes were held with two brooches (*fibulae*), one on each shoulder, and the same styles of necklaces, belts and brooches appear. It is hard to believe that such a striking continuity in female dress could have occurred without substantial numbers of women – and therefore, in all probability, children too – having trodden the road south.

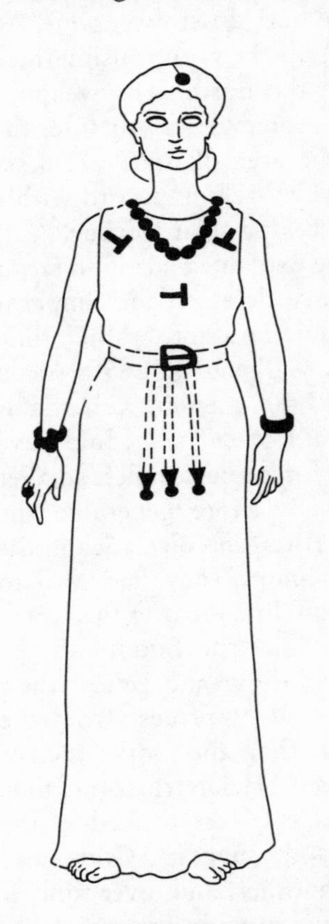

Figure 2.9 Female dress style of the Wielbark culture

Substantial population movement has for some time been out of vogue for explaining observable changes in patterns of archaeological remains. In this case, however, literary sources record the presence of Goths in northern Poland in the first century, and their disruptive intrusions into the Black Sea area in the third. Archaeologically, we have also seen that settlement density grew substantially in the original Wielbark areas in the first and second centuries (figure 2.6). This led to the colonization of new territories, and probably also to pressure on some of the surrounding Przeworsk groups to adapt to Wielbark ways. The evidence for the creation of the Černjachov culture is similar. The established order of the eastern Carpathian and northern Black Sea regions was overthrown. Groups such as the Carpi lost out in processes which, as we have just seen, resulted in population displacement. Likewise,

[37] On these, see Minns, 1913; Rostovzeff, 1922.

the striking Wielbark contribution to the Černjachov culture, and the seemingly substantial involvement of Wielbark females, all argue that migration in a more traditional sense played some part. Jordanes may have been mistaken in describing a single, mass migration led by one Gothic king. He was not so far from the truth in imagining large, mixed population groups – amongst others – as having moved south-east from the Baltic to the Black Sea.

Certain features of the evidence, moreover, are quite in accord with modern demographic studies of migration processes. Large-scale, mixed, population shifts, for instance, are often preceded by the activities of 'scouts': small groups largely of young men checking on the possibilities of new areas. The activities of Przeworsk and Wielbark warbands might be viewed in this light. Movements also tend to take the form of streams rather than of waves. A thin ribbon of sites will lead from old habitation centres to new ones, because migrants stick to known routes. The chain of Wielbark finds south along the line of the river Bug corresponds to such a pattern. Similarly, migration patterns are strongly dictated by flows of information, since people have to have good reason to abandon one habitat for another. The route north from the Black Sea up the rivers Dniester and Bug to the Vistula and the Baltic was an established trade artery in the early centuries AD. North along it flowed Mediterranean goods in exchange for the amber of the Baltic (figure 2.8). In this sphere too, therefore, Wielbark expansion fits established migration patterns.[38]

Questions, however, still remain. Why did the population in the original Wielbark areas increase in the first place? Patterns of human demography suggest that the possibility of rapid population expansion is always there, but conditions have to become favourable in some way (above pp. 17f). This is an area which requires much more work, but a substantial population increase is now considered to have been a general phenomenon of Germanic areas bordering the Roman Empire in the early centuries AD.[39] It obviously bore some relation to a simultaneous intensification in agricultural production which we will consider in the next chapter (pp. 75ff). Why a population increase in northern Poland should have generated migration seems rather less mysterious. The soils of northern Poland, original home of the Wielbark culture, are relatively poor. Further south, there is much better land. Areas such as the Hrubuieszów basin, where the

[38] For an introduction to migration as process, see Antony, 1990.
[39] E.g. Whittaker, 1992, 214ff; with further refs.

Masłocmęcz group established itself, would have been very attractive to northern migrants.

The same is true of the old Greek granary areas of the northern Pontus and the Greek cities of the Black Sea littoral. These had lost their independence in the early centuries AD, but political order in the region was maintained by Roman diplomatic subsidies, and considerable trade passed through the region. The profits of all this are visible in the substantial coinages produced by these cities down to the fourth century, and in the rich elite burials of the region from the first three centuries AD.[40] All of this would have acted as a magnet to predatory Goths, who, as we have seen, had substantial knowledge of the Black Sea region, because of the trade routes which connected it to the Baltic.

More generally, a considerable wealth differential was building up between areas closer to the Roman frontier and those further away. Roman merchants, diplomatic subsidies, the profits of trade all tended to make frontier groups, or certain elements within them, much wealthier than they had ever been before. Groups less advantageously placed were keen to share in the action. This was explicitly the motivation of the tribes from Poland who ransacked the capital of king Vannius of the Marcomanni in the first century (p. 32). The third-century raids towards, and, of course, beyond the Roman frontier should probably be seen as a more general expression, on a much larger scale, of the same phenomenon.

There remains much about the third century we do not know. The archaeological 'record' cannot supply details of the battles fought by the Goths and others to oust indigenous groups from their new homelands, nor, very easily, a detailed profile of the immigrant groups. There probably will be more information to come, and, in particular, the recently developed ability to extract DNA from ancient bones – now even, it seems, from cremated bone material – offers the tantalizing prospect of producing a more precise estimate of the extent to which northern populations migrated towards the Black Sea region. Much new light has already been shed, however, by archaeological investigation. As a result, substantial progress has been made towards understanding the nature, date and scope of the intrusion of Germanic groups into the Black Sea region. The kingdoms which emerged out of the chaos of these tumultuous events form the subject of the next chapter.

40 See e.g., Anokhin, 1980; Frolova, 1983; Raev, 1986.

3

The Fourth-Century Kingdoms

According to the Roman historian Ammianus, the fourth-century dominions of the Goths extended from the Danube to the Don, broadly coincident in time and space with the archaeological remains of the Černjachov culture. At its fullest extent, the latter spread over a broad belt of territory running east from the fringes of the Carpathian mountains to the rivers Dnieper in the south and Donetz in the north. In the west, it encompassed the fertile lands of Moldavia and Wallachia (figure 2.4, p. 22). Its eastern boundaries closely correspond to those of a particular ecological zone, the forested steppe, whose eastern extremity is marked by a line drawn roughly between modern Odessa and Kharkov. To the north and west of this line (the area within Černjachov boundaries), rainfall is reliable enough for agriculture to be possible without extensive irrigation.

The coincidence between Ammianus' account of the Goths and the Černjachov culture suggests very strongly that the latter can be taken in a broad sense to reflect the power of the Goths. The population of the Černjachov culture was not, however, composed solely of Goths. Suffice it to say for the moment, that literary sources suggest that groups other than Goths held positions north of the Black Sea in the fourth century, and that, within the Černjachov culture, a number of distinct sub-groups can be observed, even if their precise political or economic significance is uncertain (see below).

A. Kingdoms and Politics

(i) The kingdoms

It is traditional, on the testimony of the sixth-century *Getica* of Jordanes (esp. 42, 82), to conceive of the Goths as already divided, in the fourth century, into Visigoths and Ostrogoths. That is, the groups who later formed successor kingdoms to the Roman Empire in southern Gaul, Spain and Italy already existed north of the Black Sea in the fourth century. The boundary between them is usually placed on the river Dniester, because Ammianus reports that a king of the Tervingi (traditionally thought to be another name for the Visigoths) met some retreating Greuthungi (thought to be another name for the Ostrogoths) there in *c*.375 (31.3.5). Jordanes also reports that the fourth-century Ostrogothic king Ermenaric belonged to an ancient ruling dynasty – the Amals, to which also belonged Theoderic, the sixth-century king of Ostrogothic Italy – and controlled a vast multinational Empire between the Black Sea and the Baltic (116–20). But the Tervingi and Greuthungi known to Ammianus were not the same as the later Visigoths and Ostrogoths, nor can Jordanes' testimony about Ermenaric be accepted at face value.

If we use 'Visigoth' to mean the Gothic group which was settled in south-western Gaul in 418 and eventually created an independent kingdom there (chapter 6), it was not the direct descendant of the fourth-century Tervingi. As we shall see in more detail later, it was a new grouping largely composed of three previously separate units. By 418, it encompassed those Tervingi (not the entire unit) *and* Greuthungi who crossed the Danube in 376, and many of the followers of the Gothic king Radagaisus (not called either Tervingi or Greuthungi) who invaded Italy in 405/6. A similar story lies behind the Ostrogoths. Two Gothic groups, who had had separate histories for at least 50 years and initially competed with one another, eventually formed a united front against the eastern Roman Empire between *c*.474 and 489. Each of these major contributors to the Ostrogoths was itself built out of several previously separate units, and there were still other Goths in the fifth century who were not part of the process at all (chapter 5). Both Visigoths and Ostrogoths were thus created in particular fifth-century contexts, and their existence must not be backdated into the fourth century.[1]

[1] See in more detail, Part 2. Wolfram, 1988, 5–12, 24–7, 164ff, 168ff, 248ff (after Wenskus, 1961, 471ff). Taken further by Heather, 1991, ch. 1; cf. Liebeschuetz, 1990, 48–85 on Alaric and the Visigoths.

How should we envisage the political structure of the fourth-century Goths? No contemporary source provides us with a comprehensive account, so that the Gothic political order of the fourth century has to be deduced from the groups who came into contact with the Roman Empire after the arrival of the Huns in *c.*375. Twelve groups altogether are known, of whom five eventually contributed to the Visigoths and Ostrogoths:

Fifth-century Visigoths:	1	Part (most) of the Tervingi
	2	Greuthungi of Ermenaric
	3	Goths of Radagaisus
Fifth-century Ostrogoths:	4	Amal-led Goths
	5	Goths of Theoderic Strabo
Others:	6	Rest of Tervingi ? = Goths of Arimer
	7	Greuthungi of Farnobius
	8	Greuthungi of Odotheus
	9	Goths of Bigelis
	10	Gothic followers of Dengizich
	11	Goths of Crimea
	12	Goths of Sea of Azov

From Ammianus, we know that the Tervingi (Groups 1 and 6) had formed one political unit in the fourth century. Ermenaric's Greuthungi, to which the Greuthungi of Farnobius perhaps also belonged (Groups 2 and 7) were another. What of the rest? There are two basic possibilities. Either all the rest of the known groups (or their ancestors) – a total of eight including at least four very sizeable ones (numbers 3, 4, 5 and 8) – had earlier come under the domination of Ermenaric. Alternatively, there had been more than two Gothic kingdoms north of the Black Sea in the fourth century.

The first possibility is in line with Jordanes' description of the Empire of Ermenaric. On close inspection, however, the description turns out to be a deliberately expanded version of the account of Ermenaric that can still be read in Ammianus. Rather thin narratives of supposed victories, together with a list of Gothic equivalents for names common to classical ethnography and some Biblical references have been used to fill out Ammianus' account. The *Getica*'s Ermenaric has been intentionally recast as a Gothic precursor to Attila: the ruler of 'all the Scythian and German nations'. The reason emerges from the *Getica*'s Amal family tree (table 1, p. 54). For Ermenaric was used there to link together the ancestral line of Theoderic the Great with

Table 1 Amal Genealogy (after Getica *79ff)*

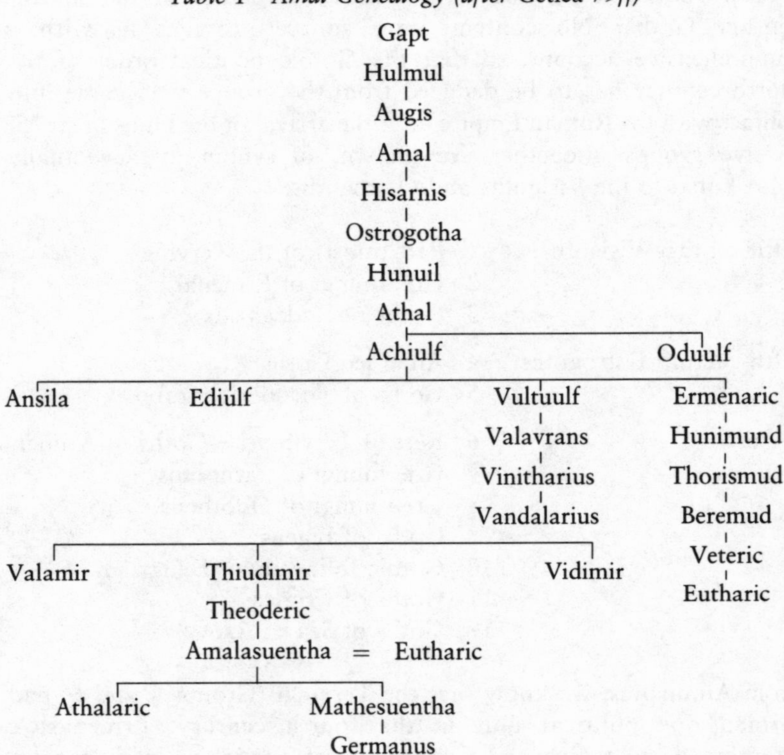

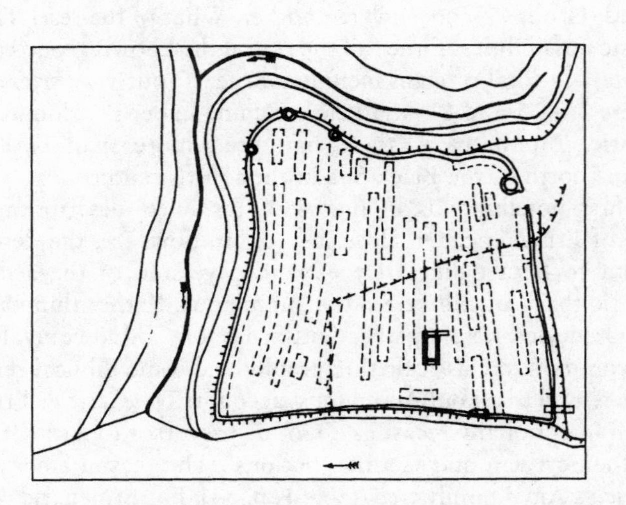

Figure 3.1 The Černjachov fortified site at Alexandrovka

that of Eutharic, his adopted heir and son-in-law, and hence fabricate a family link between the two. Since none of the details in the *Getica* suggest that its rewriting of Ermenaric was based on reliable sources, the real extent of Ermenaric's kingdom remains an open question.[2]

According to Ammianus, Ermenaric was a 'most warlike monarch' who ruled 'extensive and wide dominions' (31.3.1–2). He was obviously a substantial figure, but he probably did not rule every Goth who did not belong to the Tervingi. First, Ammianus' account reads as though all of Ermanaric's followers made their way across the Danube in 376 (31.3.3ff). It is certainly possible that Ammianus chose not to mention (or was ignorant of) political fragmentation among the Greuthungi subsequent to Ermenaric's death. But, for the *Getica*'s account to be correct, one large group must have fragmented into at least ten successors (all except groups 1 and 6 above), so that we would have to suppose him to have omitted a phenomenon of the first importance. He does chronicle such a process among the Tervingi (31.3.6–8).

Secondly, in 399, the Roman poet Claudian referred to 'Ostrogoths mixed with Greuthungi' inhabiting part of Phrygia (*Eutr*. 2.153). It is impossible to know precisely what Claudian meant by this, but, at face value, he would seem to be distinguishing Ostrogoth as another category of Goth apart from Tervingi and Greuthungi. Thirdly, while much work remains to be done, archaeologists have identified six Černjachov sites as political centres of some kind on the basis of size, fortification, and topography. Five have been found on the territory of the former Soviet Union – Basmachka, Alexandrovka, Novie Gorodok, Rumarov and Sovari – the sixth is a re-used Roman fort at Pietroasa in Romania (cf. figure 3.1). Alexandrovka, for instance, situated near the confluence of the Ingulec and Dnieper, was defended by a ditch, earth ramparts and stone walls with three towers. Inside its walls have been found the remains of 30 buildings, varying in size (15–150 long by 6–8 m wide).[3] The precise significance of these sites is uncertain. I have seen no comprehensive attempt to rank the different types of settlement found within Černjachov territories, and other areas had centres too. In the Hrubieszów basin, for instance, many smaller settlements clustered around the two larger ones of Masłomęcz and Gródek.[4] The latter, however, look more like larger

[2] Heather, 1989, 110–16 with refs., but see in particular Korkannen, 1975.
[3] Magomedov, 1995; Kazanski, 1991, 47–9; Gej, 1980.
[4] Kokowski, 1995, 45ff.

villages than an obvious centre of power such as Alexandrovka. It may well be, therefore, that these fortified sites represent the capitals from which independent Gothic political units of the fourth century were run.

Locally distributed characteristics have also led to the identification of a number of distinct sub-groups within Černjachov remains. A main group of sites and cemeteries has been identified on the middle Dnieper, in Podolia, Moldavia, Muntenia and Transylvania. In addition, there is a so-called Steppe group occupying the Black Sea coastal area between the rivers Dnieper and Danube. Further groups occupied territory around the upper Dniester, and in Volhynia and the Hrubieszów basin. There is no certainty that all, or indeed any, of these sub-groups represent politically independent entities. Their existence is another reminder, however, that groups living within the Černjachov area are likely to have been subdivided in a number of ways.

A more powerful objection to the existence of one large fourth-century kingdom arises out of reflections upon exactly how vast it would have been. It would have encompassed the vast majority of the Goths (ten out of the 12 known Gothic groups), and would certainly have been much more powerful than the contemporary Tervingi (the remaining two groups). It would even have commanded greater resources of Gothic manpower than the kingdom-founding Visigoths and Ostrogoths of the fifth century. This being so, the Greuthungi, occupying lands at no great distance from the Roman frontier, ought to have been the major focus of Roman foreign policy in the lower Danubian region. The Emperor Valens fought some of them in 369 (AM 27.5.6), but otherwise the Greuthungi barely intrude into the narrative of fourth-century Gotho–Roman relations (see below). It is difficult to believe that such a vast Gothic political unit could have left so little trace in what is a fairly substantial historical record.[5]

To my mind, therefore, we must envisage several independent fourth-century Gothic political units within the bounds of the Černjachov culture. The Tervingi and Ermenaric's Greuthungi (who crossed the Danube in 376) are two obvious units. Odotheus' Greuthungi, who tried to cross the river ten years later, might be a third. In addition, the obviously substantial Gothic groups who enter the action in the fifth century (especially numbers 3, 4 and 5) are probably all descended from independent groups of the fourth. This

[5] Cf. below pp. 84ff; I do believe that 'Gothicness' was stable enough to make this exercise worthwhile.

may well also be the case with at least some of the others. Half-a-dozen independent Gothic units, if not more, probably existed, therefore, north of the Black Sea before the arrival of the Huns.

(ii) *Gothic politics*

Each of these units had its own overall ruler. Whenever we meet Greuthungi, they are led by kings (AM 31.3.1–3). Leaders of the Tervingi, by contrast, are called 'Judge', a label which has generally led them to be viewed as somewhat lesser figures.[6] They have traditionally been characterized as temporary leaders, given special powers only in times of danger. But the office of Judge among the Tervingi descended through three generations of the same family, and one source refers specifically to the existence of a 'royal clan' (Zosimus 4.25.2; 34.3).[7] Likewise, whenever the Tervingi are mentioned in Graeco–Roman sources, they are always headed by one individual, and a whole array of contemporary sources found the office of Judge of the Tervingi eminently confusable with kingship. The Judge of the Tervingi looked to contemporary Roman eyes very much like a monarch, and there is every reason for us to follow their lead.[8]

One dimension of fourth-century Gothic politics follows from this conclusion. As we shall see in more detail below, processes of social differentiation had created, by the fourth century, a powerful political elite among the Goths, composed of a freeman class among whom there were already substantial differentials in wealth. These may have been both wide and rigid enough for us to think of greater freemen as an at least quasi nobility. Controlling these men was far from easy. The best sources portray fourth-century Gothic leaders 'urging' and 'persuading' their followers rather than just issuing orders, and leaders' counsels could be overruled (e.g. AM 31.15.7ff, 13). The boundaries of the political units, however many there were, may also have been far from rigid. Particularly successful leaders (like Athanaric of the Tervingi in the 360s, or Ermenaric) are likely to have expanded their kingdoms in the course of their lifetimes by

[6] AM 27.5.6, 9; Ambrose, *De Spiritu Sancto*, prol. 17; Auxentius 246. For comment, Wolfram, 1988, 67, 91–2; Thompson, 1966, 45.

[7] Wolfram, 1988, 62ff.

[8] Themistius *Orr.* 11 p. 221.9, 15 p. 276.5; *Anon. Val.* 6.31: a *rex* Ariaricus versus the *regalis* Alica of 5.27; Eunapius (and, following him, Zosimus) consistently refer to the 'King' of the Goths. In more detail: Heather, 1991, 97–103.

attracting new followers into their spheres.

Too much fluidity, however, should probably not be envisaged. Three generations of the same family monopolized the overall leadership of the Tervingi for the best part of 50 years (between *c.*330 and 376). Some of this dynastic longevity may stem from the nature of their relations with the Roman Empire (see below), and hence be unrepresentative of the Gothic world as a whole. Given, however, that the third-century Gothic migrations were led by warrior leaders (chapter 2), it is a fair guess that the Tervingi as such had first coalesced around a particularly successful commander of this kind. More than that, the obvious strength of Athanaric's dynasty probably also indicates that it was descended precisely from this founder, whoever he may have been. If so, the length of the family's dominion can be pushed back to at least 291, when the Tervingi are first mentioned in literary sources. Athanaric's control was strong enough to survive three years of difficult warfare against the Romans (367–9: see below). It did eventually founder, but only in the course of the Hunnic invasions (chapter 4). Failure in such circumstances is no indication of general weakness. Likewise, the Greuthungi of Ermenaric were sufficiently wedded to the dynastic principle to elect as king Vitheric, the minor son of Vithimer, after the latter's death (AM 31.3.2).

Political competition was not limited to beating off internal rivals. Even if few details are known, groups beyond the Roman frontier were clearly pursuing their own rivalries throughout the fourth century. In 291, for instance, a Roman orator referred to Gothic attacks on Burgundians, and an alliance of Tervingi and Taifali against Vandals and Gepids (*Pan. Lat.* 3[11].17.1). Less trustworthy reports in the *Getica* mention wars with similar foes after Filimer's migration to the Black Sea (89, 96–100, 113–15). An attempt by the Tervingi to move beyond the reach of the Empire in the early 330s, likewise, necessitated war against Sarmatians (*Anon. Val.* 6.31), and Gothic expansion into the hinterland of the Carpathians had involved the expulsion of the Carpic tribes of the region.

The closer such struggles were to the frontiers of the Roman Empire – established since 275 on the right bank of the Danube – the more the shadow of imperial power loomed over them. Goths fought Carpi, but it was the Roman Empire which dismantled the latter's autonomy (p. 47). In the early 330s, similarly, the Tervingi were at first successful in their attack upon the Sarmatians, but an imperial army then intervened to force a Gothic surrender (*Anon. Val.* 6.31). There could be no better demonstration of the power of the Roman Empire, from which the Tervingi had been looking to escape in the first place. For the Tervingi, at least, the foreign power which loomed largest in their minds was the Roman Empire. A deep ambivalence is evident in their relations with this most powerful of contemporary states.

On the one hand, for over 30 years in the mid-fourth century (332–65), relations were close. On three occasions a contingent of perhaps 3,000 Gothic warriors crossed the frontier and marched through Asia Minor to take part in Roman wars against Persia. The survivors no doubt returned home richer men.[9] In these years, the Gothic frontier on the Danube was also completely open for trade, where normal Roman policy was to control cross-border traffic closely, in the interests of security.[10] The physical remains of the Černjachov culture bear testimony to the result. Roman coins particularly of the Emperor Constantius II (337–61) are numerous, and the remains of many Roman wine amphorae have been unearthed both in settlements and cemeteries. Many individual Goths thus enjoyed the fruits of close contact with the Roman state. The Empire may even have played a role in sustaining the ruling dynasty of the Tervingi. As part of the treaty of 332, the son of the then Judge went to Constantinople. A statue was eventually erected in his honour behind the Senate (*Anon. Val.* 6.31; Themistius *Or.* 15, p. 276, 7ff). Annual gifts from Romans to Goths were likewise part of the treaty. If, as was normal Roman policy, they were initially presented to the ruler to be passed on to his followers, they would have helped to strengthen the position of individual Judges.[11]

But Roman support came at a price. The *quid pro quo* for any frontier dynast in receipt of annual gifts was that he should endeavour to keep his unruly followers in line. Extracting royal hostages was likewise an age-old Roman practice. It was designed, not least, to produce future frontier leaders who had already been seduced by Roman civilization. Seen in this broader context, it becomes much less surprising that such a close, and, on the face of it, favourable order of relations from the Goths' point of view (annual gifts and trading privileges), should have actually followed a crushing Roman victory. After taking control of the whole Empire in 324, the Emperor Constantine undertook a general pacification of the whole Danube frontier area, and of his Gothic neighbours in particular. A

[9] 349: Libanius *Or.* 59.89; 360: AM 20.8.1; 363: AM 23.2.7. 3,000 Goths were sent to the usurper Procopius in 365: AM 26.10.3.

[10] Themistius *Or.* 10, p. 205.24ff; Thompson, 1966, 15 n.2.

[11] Themistius *Or.* 10, p. 205.13ff; Klose, 1934, 138; Braund, 1984, 62–3.

bridge was constructed over the river in 327 between Oescus and Sucidava to the north. The strategic point of the bridge (like Constantine's parallel constructions on the Rhine) was to facilitate the movement north of Roman troops and their equipment.[12] Coins celebrating the achievement make its purpose clear, portraying a barbarian tribesman kneeling in submission beside it (plate 3). In response to this and other Roman pressures, the Tervingi decided to move into Sarmatian territories in the uplands of the Carpathians. A Roman army, however, starved them into submission. Given this sequence of events, the ostensibly favourable aspects of the subsequent treaty must be seen as sweeteners, designed to make the Tervingi less resistant to the fact of Roman hegemony. Even the statue to Athanaric's father was placed *behind* the Senate.

Plate 3 Numismatic celebration of Constantine's bridge over the Danube (note the submitting barbarian at the bottom)

The Tervingi proved more than a little resistant, however, to Roman blandishments. Part of the Roman strategy, for instance, seems to have been to Christianize them. Constantius II sponsored Christian activity north of the Danube in the 340s, ordaining as bishop Ulfila, creator of the Gothic Bible. As we shall see, Ulfila's brand of Christianity became, in the fifth and sixth centuries, a distinctive feature of Gothic societies inside the Roman frontier. Sometimes labelled 'Arian' or 'semi-Arian', he actually belonged to a strand of educated Christian opinion which rejected the Nicene definition of faith – that the Son was of one substance (*homoousios*) with the Father – on two grounds. First, it was non-Biblical (the term is nowhere mentioned in the sacred texts), and, secondly, they felt it carried with it the danger of collapsing any real distinction between

[12] Tudor, 1974, 5ff; cf. Heather, 1991, 107ff.

God the Father and God the Son. In the 340s, when Ulfila was at work north of the Danube, it was not clear that the Nicene definition of faith would win out. It had been rejected by the Emperor Constantius II himself, who held to the more traditional positions advocated by Ulfila and his allies.[13] Ulfila's Christianity, then, was mainstream imperial Christianity for its day, and it was this which led different Judges of the Tervingi to try to restrict its influence in their lands.

A first dispute occurred as early as 347/8. Ulfila was ordained bishop to minister to those who were already Christian in Gothic territories. Many of these, like himself, it would seem, were descended from Christian Roman prisoners taken in third-century raids. He also, however, engaged in missionary work, and this may have been the cause of the trouble. Whatever the case, Ulfila was expelled with many other Christians from the lands of the Tervingi. This was not, however, the end of the story. Christians still lived north of the Danube, and maintained close contacts with Christians south of the river inside the Roman Empire. A Gothic Christian priest called Sansalas, for instance, was able to drift across the frontier at will (*Passion of St. Saba* 4.2). It is perhaps not surprising, therefore, that non-Christian leaders of the Tervingi remained hostile to Christians in their lands. When they got their chance after a new treaty in 369, they launched a religious persecution of Gothic Christians which lasted at least until 372. In their view, Christianity was specifically identified with the Roman state, and its spread was disrupting the established community of belief in Gothic lands (Socrates *h.e.* 4.33.7; Ephiphanius Panar. 70). The fact that a formal conversion to Christianity by some of these leaders was part of the price they paid for admission to Roman lands in 376 (chapter 5), confirms the role that religion played in Gotho–Roman relations.

Resistance to Roman hegemony was not limited to religion. From the early 360s at the latest, the Tervingi began to agitate for revisions to the terms of the treaty which Constantine had forced upon them in 332. They started by trying to negotiate (Libanius *Or.* 12.78), but were ready to press the matter to the point of war when the opportunity arose to support the usurper Procopius against the reigning Emperor Valens. No doubt they hoped that a victorious usurper would give them the concessions they required. Maybe so, but Valens won, if only just. The Emperor then turned his attention to the

[13] The two main sources on Ulfila are Philostorgius *h.e.* 2.5 and the letter of Auxentius. Both are translated with commentary in Heather and Matthews, 1991, ch. 5.

Goths who had actively aided his opponent.

Valens launched a three-year campaign against the Tervingi between 367 and 369, but stalemate ensued. The Goths were unable to defeat his assaults, but did avoid a defeat on the scale of 332. In this, their own organization (manifested by a well-organized retreat to the Carpathian uplands which blunted Valens' attack in 367), combined with the emergence of a new threat to the Empire on its Persian front, to make Valens change his mind. The weather had also been against him. In 368, an unusually high spring flood meant that Valens could not get his forces over the Danube quickly enough. In the end, the Emperor decided not to pursue the war to its ultimate military conclusion. Instead, he concluded a new treaty, which ended the Goths' annual gifts and more closely regulated the frontier. He also instituted a major defensive building programme. Apart from these financial losses, the new treaty freed the Goths from much of the substance of Roman hegemony, particularly the requirement that they had to provide military contingents. The persecution of Christians also followed on immediately from the treaty, which suggests that Valens had relinquished any claim to protect Christians north of the river.[14]

Relations between the Tervingi and the Roman Empire were thus close, but liable to strain. Roman policy combined periodic military domination with targeted financial blandishment to turn the Goths into a largely peaceable frontier client state. And this, in many ways, is what they were. The fourth-century Tervingi at least (the extent to which this was true of the other Gothic kingdoms is hard to judge) were part of the Roman imperial system. Gothic soldiers fought in Rome's Persian wars, and Gothic princes were educated in Constantinople. Being part of the system, however, did not imply equality. The huge fortifications of the Danube river bank are a symbol of the Goths' subordinate position within the Roman order.[15] Roman propaganda of the period still referred to them on important ceremonial occasions as 'lesser men' (Themistius *Orr.* 10. p. 212. 1ff; 16. p. 299, 14–15). Likewise, Constantine considered his victories of the 330s to have made the Goths, in legal terms, Roman subjects (i.e., subordinate non-citizens). This is graphically portrayed in a coin issue

[14] Sequence of events: AM 26.6.10–12; 27.5. Persia: AM 27.12. Imperial propaganda: Themistius *Orr.* 8 and 10 charting the imperial change of mind (both trans. with comment in Heather and Matthews, 1991, ch. 2). Full argumentation in Heather, 1991, 115ff with refs.

[15] On these, see, e.g. Scorpan, 1980.

celebrating his victory inscribed with the word *Gothia*, a usage meant to signify the creation of a Roman province out of the Goths.[16]

In practice, however, the relationship was not so one-sided as imperial propaganda liked to claim. The Tervingi could not match the Empire's military power. But on two occasions in the fourth century, the Tervingi intervened in internal Roman politics, supporting one candidate for the imperial throne against another. In 321, they backed Licinius against Constantine (*Anon. Val.* 5.27), and in 365, as we have seen, Procopius against Valens. Neither of these moves was particularly successful. The Tervingi, at least, also had sufficient sense of themselves and their independent identity to resist Roman religious and political hegemony, and sufficient strength and coherence not to fall apart in three years of warfare. At most, then, the Tervingi were an only partly subordinated Roman client state. They had the ability and desire both to attempt to shape imperial politics to their own advantage, and, at times at least, to resist the more overt forms of Roman dominion.

B. Goths in the Germanic Revolution

To judge by the Tervingi, the Gothic kingdoms of the fourth century were a far from negligible force. The structural underpinnings of this strength were the result of a series of transformations which had profoundly affected the entire Germanic world in the first three centuries after Christ. Between them, they created more substantial political entities, such as the Tervingi, capable of resisting, or at least parrying, the intrusions of Roman imperial power.[17]

(i) Political structures

The basic political structure of the Germanic world in the first century emerges clearly from Tacitus' *Germania*, especially if the names are placed on a map (cf. figure 2.1, p. 15). It was a world of small political units. Tacitus names well over 50 such units, some of which gathered together in loosely affiliated cult leagues. Larger-scale alliances, such as that generated by Arminius to fend off the Empire's attempted annexation of land between the Rhine and the Elbe (above p. 30),

[16] Chrysos, 1973; cf. Heather, 1991, 110–15 stressing that Constantine's was a claim to dominance.

[17] I have found myself, via a different route, coming to conclusions very similar to those of Lotte Hedeager. See, in particular, Hedeager, 1992, chs 5–6.

were temporary, confined to particular moments of danger or opportunity. By the fourth century, the picture had altered fundamentally, especially in areas close to the Roman frontier where many smaller units had given way to fewer larger ones.

The transformation is particularly obvious in the west. Here, even the names famous from the pages of Tacitus' *Annals* and *Histories* disappeared in favour of new ones: Saxons, Franks and Alamanni. The fourth-century Alamanni of Rome's Rhine frontier were ruled by a multiplicity of 'kings'. This has been taken to show that processes of amalgamation had advanced little beyond the situation described by Tacitus.[18] But whenever Roman attention was turned away from the Rhine frontier by emergencies elsewhere (particularly on the Persian front), Alamannic society consistently threw up a succession of leaders with pre-eminent power. Men such as Chnodomarius, Vadomarius and Macrianus were ready to mount aggressive wars against the Roman state (AM 16.12.23–6; 21.4.1–6; 27.10.3–4; 28.5.8; 29.4.2ff; 30.3.2–6), and Roman policy was precisely directed towards containing them. Kidnapping them at banquets was a preferred approach. Individual leaders came and went, but the fourth-century Alamanni showed a distinct tendency to act as one group.

Further east, on the Danube, there were differences in detail. More of the political labels known from the first century survived: not just Goth, but Rugi, Burgundian and others. The nature of the units designated by these names, however, had undergone a not dissimilar transformation. The first- and early second-century Goths were one small group among many in northern Poland, in all probability a subordinate member of the Lugian and Vandal cult leagues. By the fourth century, many first-century groups had disappeared, the Goths were now a dominant group, and the territory under the control of groups named as Goths was commensurately larger. Probably half-a-dozen or more Gothic political units existed within this territory, and Roman policy was not the same as on the Rhine. The dynasty of the Tervingi at times received positive support from the Roman state, and there was no attempt to destroy its leading figures. This suggests that the Tervingi, at least, did not pose such a direct threat to the integrity of the Roman frontier as the Alamanni further west. Nevertheless, the Tervingi were, in political terms, powerful, well-organized, and ambitious. Processes of absorption, conquest and migration had created, parallel to the situation in the west, even if matters had not

[18] E.g. James, 1989, 42; after Thompson, 1965, 40.

developed to quite the same extent, a political world of larger and more coherent units.

(ii) Social structures

The social foundations of these new political structures had seen equally profound transformation. By the fourth century, Gothic society was entirely typical of the contemporary Germanic world in having a well-entrenched elite. The *Passion of St. Saba*, a contemporary account of the martyrdom north of the Danube of a Gothic Christian in 372, names two members of it. A certain Atharid plays a leading role in the action, and his father, Rothesteos, is called 'prince' (*βασιλίσκος*). Another document from the same persecution names Winguric as a third.[19] The events of 376 and after provide us with the names of other elite Tervingi, such as Alavivus and Fritigern. Less is known of the Greuthungi, but a powerful, dominant class had probably established itself throughout contemporary Gothic society. Some prominent non-royal Greuthungi are named (Alatheus, Saphrax and Farnobius: AM 31.3.3; 4.12), and a class of such men is a constant feature of Gothic groups met in the fifth and sixth centuries. The Gothic term for such men was perhaps *reiks*. Although a cognate of the Latin for king in the sense of 'monarch' or 'sole ruler' (*rex*), it had the more general meaning of 'leader of men' or 'distinguished'.[20]

This social elite had not always existed. In the first millennium BC, central and northern Europe, the area from which Germanic groups were later to emerge, was characterized by a universal adherence to cremation and a basic uniformity in grave goods. Only in the third century BC did richer burials (often referred to as *Fürstengräber*: 'princely graves') begin to appear, and it was in the so-called Roman Iron Age (first century AD onwards) that strikingly disparate numbers of goods were buried with different members of the same communities. There is no simple correlation between rich burials and increasing social stratification. Really rich graves cluster chronologically, with, broadly speaking, one group at the end of the first century and another at the end of the second (the Lübsow and

[19] *Passion* trans. in Heather and Matthews, 1991, 111–17. Wingurich: Menologium of Basil II: *PG* 117 col. 368, trans. in Heather and Matthews, 1991, 126–7.

[20] Thus Ambrose *De Spiritu Sancto* prol. 17 correctly characterizes Athanaric as the 'Judge of kings' (*iudex regum*).

Leuna-Hassleben groups: figure 3.2). It is hardly likely that elites existed only at these moments. It has been suggested, therefore, that such graves mark moments of intense social competition, when different clans were seeking to emphasize their elite status by showing how much they could afford to bury with their dead. If so, these graves make the very important point that aggregations of wealth had profound implications for the societies involved, and did not go unchallenged.[21]

Two other reflections of this competition are worth singling out. First, settlement patterns can document the emergence of centres from which these new elites exercised power. Sometimes the evidence is ambiguous. At Feddersen Wierde in lower Saxony (figure 3.3), for instance, a large building in one corner of the village came to be marked off by a palisade and a ditch from the second century onwards. This area also contained larger storage pits and extensive craftworking remains. Does it represent the domain of a newly emergent headman (a so-called *Herrenhof*) or was it an area of communal activity? In other cases, interpretation is more straightforward. Excavations on the Runder Berg, for instance, have revealed the kind of dwelling from which members of the Alamannic elite ruled in the fourth century. Germanic settlements of earlier eras have turned up no similar, geographically differentiated elite dwellings.[22]

Secondly, the rise of groups of specialist armed retainers was a social development of the greatest importance. Tacitus reports that, already in the first century, Germanic chiefs possessed retinues of young men of military age, their size varying according to the chief's fame (*Germania* 13). The main body for social enforcement, however, was a public one: the *comitatus*. Its membership was controlled by communal gatherings of full adult male members of the group, and it fulfilled a variety of military, political and judicial functions.[23] By the fourth century, much had changed. In the bulk of so-called Free Germany, the area not conquered by Rome, weapon burials became common from at least the first century AD. This suggests in a general way, perhaps, that military status was

[21] Good introductions are Thompson, 1965, chs 1–2; Todd, 1992, ch. 2. More detailed discussion: Eggers, 1949/50; Gebühr, 1974; Hedeager, 1978, 1988; Hedeager and Kristiansen, 1981; Steuer, 1982, 212ff; Pearson, 1989; Hedeager 1992, chs 2–3.

[22] Evidence: Todd, 1975, ch. 3, Hedeager, 1992, ch. 4; Todd, 1992, ch. 62ff (the Runder Berg is illustrated at p. 210). General comment: Hedeager, 1988.

[23] E.g. Thompson, 1965, 29ff.

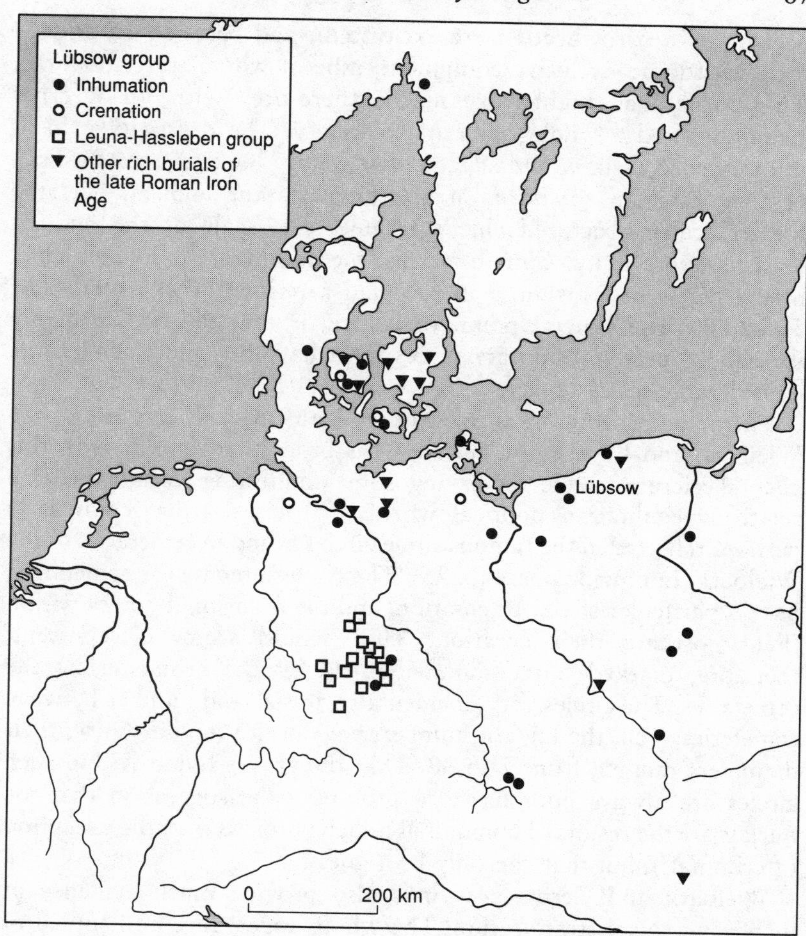

Figure 3.2 Germanic Fürstengräber *of the Roman Iron Age*

gaining in importance. More illuminating are a series of weapon deposits found in Danish bogs, placed there from the later second century onwards. The deposits represent the arms and equipment of large retinues – even whole armies – which were ritually mutilated before being sacrificed (presumably to the gods) by deposition in a bog. At Ejsbøl Mose in southern Jutland, a complete excavation has taken place of one third-century set of weapons, providing a profile of the force to which it belonged. It was actually a small army of 200 men armed with spears, lances and shields (at least 60 of whom also carried swords and knives), an unknown number of archers (675 arrowheads were excavated), and between 12 and 15 men with more exclusive equipment, nine of whom were mounted. This force was highly organized, therefore, with an internal hierarchy, and a whole range of weaponry. The degree of evident military specialism would suggest that we are looking not at a first-century Tacitean *comitatus* of part-time peasant soldiers, but at a hierarchically structured chief's retinue. The scale of the find, at least, is appropriate. Chnodomarius, the dominant Alamannic chief at the battle of Strasbourg in 357 had a retinue of 200 men (AM 16.12.60). The general point, of course, is that the rise of highly specialized personal military forces must have brought their leaders considerable social power.[24]

The material from areas relevant to Goths in these centuries – the Wielbark and Černjachov cultures – is broadly consistent with this general picture, while displaying some interesting variations. The relatively egalitarian political world of Tacitus' tribal councils is perhaps reflected in the famous stone circles found in cemeteries of the Wielbark–Lubowidz phase (p. 25). The circles predate the cemeteries, have a particular stellar orientation, and the occasional graves within them postdate their creation. They would seem to represent, therefore, marked out communal areas for the groups using the cemeteries. The circles vary, incidentally, in size and number between cemeteries. Ten, the highest number, have been found at Odry, their diameters ranging from 7 to 30. That the graves found within such circles are always poor has also prompted the suggestion that the burials are the results of communal judicial process (i.e., the execution of criminals), but that can only be a guess.

Wielbark and Černjachov finds also provide much evidence of increasing social stratification. The whole appearance and spread of inhumation rather than cremation, a central feature in both, represents, of course, one form of social differentiation. Whether differentiation in death reflected social differentiation in life is at this point impossible to know. Other signs of differentiation and social competition are less ambiguous. A few *Fürstengräber* have been unearthed, especially those at Kitki and Rostolty from the Wielbark–Cecele period. For the most part, however, social differentiation manifested itself in death by other means. Competitive monumentalization is a strongly marked feature of second-century

24 Evidence: Ørsnes, 1963, 1968; Ilkjaer and Lonstrup, 1983; Ilkjaer, 1995. Discussion: Hedeager, 1987 with refs. (cf. generally on retinues, Thompson, 1965, 48ff; Todd, 1992, 29ff).

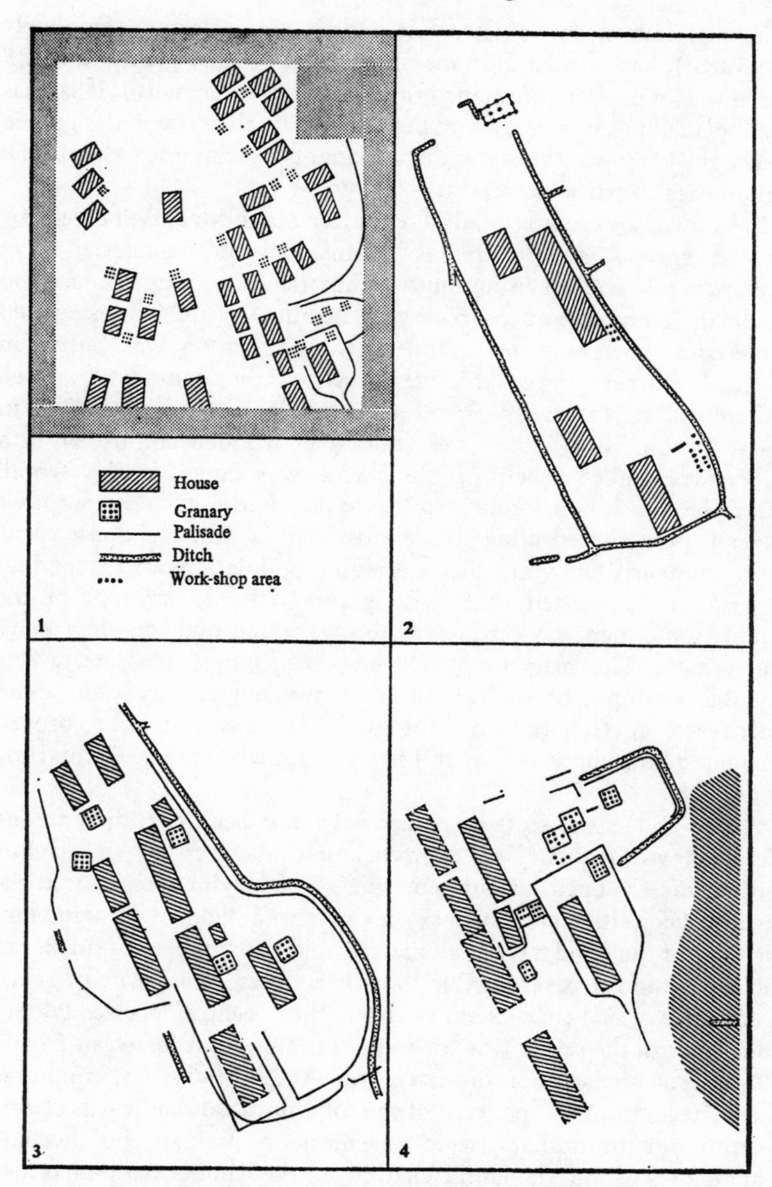

Figure 3.3 The settlement at Feddersen Wierde

Wielbark–Lubowidz cemeteries. In many of these, groups of burials were marked out by piling up stones to create barrows, and individual graves by the erection of standing stones (*stelae*). The classic

Wielbark–Lubowidz cemetery at Odry (now almost completely excavated) has turned up, for instance, 500 flat graves and 29 barrows (some containing one grave, others two or more). If, as has been plausibly suggested, families buried in their own designated zones, the barrows would represent attempts to emphasize the special importance of particular clans.

In Černjachov cemeteries, differentiation manifested itself chiefly by size of grave. In part, this is because all the cemeteries were systematically robbed in antiquity. Thus richer gravegoods have no doubt in many cases been removed. In all the carefully excavated cemeteries, however, one strand of the population was buried in distinctly larger graves than the rest of the community. Such individuals were usually placed in holes $2\frac{1}{2}$ m × 2 m × 2–3 m deep. In some cases, they were buried in wooden coffins, or in a larger wooden chamber, or the corpse was covered with wood. Near the Black Sea, stone tended to be used for these purposes instead, perhaps reflecting the relative lack of trees in those parts. From comparisons with other Germanic populations of the period, it has been suggested that these graves reflect a stratum of the population which was certainly elite, but which ranked below kings and princes. The latter may well have been buried separately. One possible example of such a burial is the single, very rich, tomb uncovered at Concesti in Moldavia.[25] It has not been proved beyond doubt, however, that this is a fourth-century Černjachov grave.

As we have seen, seats of power have also been identified among Černjachov remains. The overwhelming majority of Černjachov settlements are open, unfortified, villages of varying size, so that the few fortified settlements, such as Alexandrovka (figure 3.1), stand out. No sites of this kind have been identified in Wielbark areas further to the north, and it is reasonable to suppose that a new type of social dominance was being exercised from these central places. Pottery finds confirm the point. Roman amphorae amount to between 15 and 40 per cent of sherds on ordinary sites. At Alexandrovka, amphorae sherds account for 72 per cent of the total finds, so that it was clearly a centre of extraordinary (wine) consumption. A single elite dwelling – analogous to the Alamannic example of the Runder Berg – has also been unearthed at Kamenka-Antechrak (figure 3.5). This consisted of four stone buildings with annexes and a courtyard, covering, in total, an area of 3,800 m^2. Its excavators describe it as a villa: the home of a

25 Evidence and discussion: Magomedov, 1995; cf. Bierbrauer, 1989.

Figure 3.4 Mounds and stone circles of the Wielbark Cemetery at Odry

member of the elite and, to judge by its storage facilities, a considerable centre of agricultural production and consumption. Again, Roman pottery, consisting here of both amphorae sherds and fine wares, occur in above average quantities, amounting to over 50 per cent of total finds. At Pietroasa in Romania, the local Gothic elite reused an old Roman fort. Finds of pottery and storage pits likewise suggest that it was a centre of consumption and exploitation.[26] Nothing similar has been found among Wielbark remains.

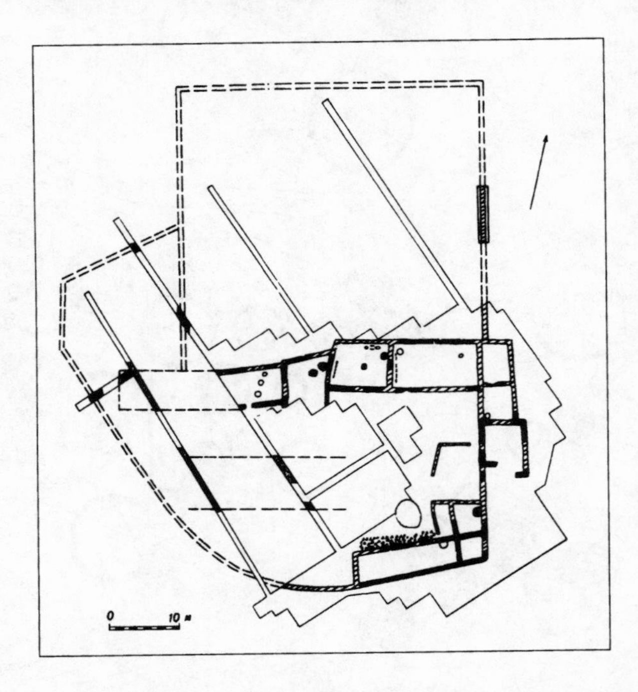

Figure 3.5 Plan of the Černjachov period 'villa' at Kamenka-Antechrak

The question of retinues suggests a similar picture of change over time. A distinguishing feature of the Wielbark and Černjachov cultures was the custom of not burying weapons with dead male members of the community (above p. 23). What beliefs generated this practice are unclear, but a passage in Tacitus' *Germania*, from the same chapter in which he mentions Goths but referring to the Swedes (*Suiones*), is worth consideration. 'Arms are not, as with other

[26] Pietroasa: Diaconu, 1977. Otherwise, Magomedov, 1995; cf. Kazanski, 1991, 47ff.

Germans, at everyone's disposal, but are kept securely locked away or under the guard of a slave ... it is a fact that the exclusion of nobles, free men, and even of freedmen from the control of weapons is very much in the interest of a king' (*Germania* 44.4). Ceasing to bury weapons with the dead may thus have had something to do with limiting the arms supply to prop up the existing social order. Whatever its origins, it did not prevent the rise of armed retainers.

Striking evidence is again provided by the *Passion of St. Saba*. Amongst other things, it describes the way in which one member of the Gothic elite, Atharid, used retainers to enforce the persecution of Christians in a Gothic village. It would also seem that his sway extended over a number of villages, since Atharid appears unfamiliar with local conditions (*Passion* 4.1 ff). Other fourth-century Goths, such as Athanaric and Sarus, also had retinues (Zosimus 4.34.5; 5.34.1 respectively). They were probably supported economically by the surplus agricultural production of villages such as that mentioned in the *Passion*. First-century Germanic chiefs already received impromptu voluntary contributions to support their followers (*Germania* 13). The more structured retinues of the fourth century probably required more systematic exactions, the redistribution of which was perhaps organized from centres such as Alexandrovka, Kamenka-Antechrak and the Runder Berg.

How far had such processes of social development transformed Germanic society by the fourth century? There had certainly been some shift of power to an elite. The persecution of 369 to 372, for instance, is described as a policy imposed by a group of great men. The sources make no reference to formal consultations of a body such as the gatherings of all adult male tribesmen, which Tacitus describes in the first century.[27] Faced with such evidence, and titles such as that of 'prince' accorded Rothesteos (p. 65), it is at first tempting to think of any Gothic elite as a tight-knit, closed nobility of a few families. This, however, would appear to be a mistake.

Even in the sixth century, the politically significant class among the Ostrogoths, at least, remained numerous. It amounted to at least one-fifth (and perhaps rather more) of a total male population of 25,000–30,000. This group should probably be equated, indeed, with something like the freemen class described in Germanic law codes of the early medieval period (see App. 1). It is difficult to believe that fourth-century Gothic society will have been more stratified than that of the sixth. As we shall see, both the Hunnic Empire and the

[27] Cf. Thompson, 1966, 43–55.

creation of successor states to the Roman Empire, introduced new wealth into Gothic society between the fourth and sixth centuries. Social stratification in *c.* AD 350 is most unlikely, therefore, to have been greater than it would become in AD 500. And looked at closely, fourth-century sources do confirm that political participation was not limited to a highly select elite.

Ammianus, for instance, depicts Gothic leaders as frequently unable to control the martial enthusiasm of their followers. Those applying the pressure were numerous, and not a restricted inner circle of nobles. Likewise, while the persecution of Christians among the Tervingi is portrayed as the policy of a few great men, the political processes it let loose involved a far wider social group. This wider group was called upon to make a series of public acts to demonstrate its assent to the policy espoused. The sources mention a variety of mechanisms: public oaths, sacrifices before sacred statues, and participation in public feasts of food previously offered to the gods (*Passion of St. Saba* 3.1–4, 4.1–3; Sozomen *h.e.* 6.37.12–14). Of these, public oaths may have had a more general use in expressing and generating political consensus on important matters. The decision to cross into the Roman Empire in 376, according to one source, was similarly confirmed by an oath.[28]

More generally, the *Passion of St. Saba* warns us not to overestimate the degree of control exercised by fourth-century rulers. Despite orders to persecute, pagans within Saba's village were prepared to protect Christians in their midst both by swearing false oaths and by consuming meat that they had only pretended to offer to idols (3.1–4). The *Passion* explicitly reports that Saba was 'of the Gothic race', so that we are presumably dealing here with a Gothic village. Correspondingly, a local elite exercised considerable authority. When Saba refused to cooperate in the deceptions, threatening the safety of other (presumably Christian) villagers, the elders expelled him (3.2). Atharid, the leading Goth met in this text, was not the only authority among the Goths, nor was his authority very immediate. The larger Černjachov graves perhaps belong, therefore, to such locally important elders.

In each of the fourth-century Gothic kingdoms, as the case of the Tervingi shows, a particular political elite (the class, perhaps of *reiks:* above p. 65) did dominate affairs, to the extent, at least, of making key decisions. They may even have controlled sufficient wealth to render them 'a-nobility-in-the-making'. The dominance of this group

[28] Eunapius fr. 59; discussed at Heather, 1991, 139ff.

was limited, however, by the continued existence of a politically participatory group, which remained substantial in size. Power was not solely the preserve of a very restricted group of families. Indeed, we should not just assume that the distribution of property and wealth was stable. The status of *reiks* may have been more of an informal distinction, acquired in an individual's lifetime, than a legally defined rank passed from generation to generation. Among the Visigoths, the free class was subdivided in legal terms, to acknowledge the existence of distinct nobility, only in the seventh century (chapter 9). Introducing such evidence, of course, begs a number of questions, but the later, so-called barbarian law-codes do provide a model of how we might understand Gothic societies, where a relatively numerous minority still figured in the political process.

All of them describe broadly similar structures across a wide variety of Germanic groups, with societies divided into three broad social groups: free, freed or half-free and slaves. The groups were, notionally at least, closed off from one another by strict laws against intermarriage, and the unfree classes were considerably disadvantaged. Characteristically, they received heavier punishments for the same offence, and lacked legal autonomy. Their evidence counted for little if anything in court, and the law offered them much less protection. Marriages or other sexual liaisons conducted with women of a higher social group were also punished with great severity. Essentially, the codes suggest the existence of symbiotic but separate social castes. For the fourth century, as well as the sixth, we should probably reckon with an elite which consisted of a substantial freemen class with defined privileges and rights, existing alongside an emerging but perhaps still informally, defined nobility.[29]

(iii) Economic structures

Between the birth of Christ and the late Roman period, agricultural practice was transformed throughout central and northern Europe. At the start of the period, an extensive agriculture, of generally low

[29] Many of these codes are now readily available in translation: *Lombard Laws*, *Burgundian Code*, two sets of *Alamannic Laws*, *Bavarian Laws*, and the two Frankish codes: *Salic Law* and *Ripuarian Law* (see Bibliography). Of Visigothic materials, the *Code* is available only in an old (and scarce) translation, and the *Code of Euric* has never been translated into English. Among these, the *Lombard Laws* (643), *Burgundian Code* (*c.* AD 500), *Bavarian Laws* (mid-7th century) and *Visigothic Code* distinguish a more restricted elite within the freeman class.

productivity, prevailed across much of northern and central Europe. Based on the so-called 'Celtic field' system, it alternated short periods of cultivation with long periods of fallow. Little other effort was made to maintain the fertility of cultivated fields. For this reason, it was marked by dispersed, short-lived settlements. The regime was neither productive enough to generate dense settlement patterns, nor capable of maintaining crop yields in any particular area for an extended period.

The available evidence from Wielbark areas fits this pattern exactly. Before the Second World War, few settlements had been identified, and the culture was known primarily from its cemeteries. With advances in archaeological technique, the situation has been reversed. The ratio of settlements to cemeteries is now seven to one and growing. All of these settlements were short-lived, hence their overall numbers, and in none of them did the inhabitants invest much time and effort, hence the original difficulty in tracing them. Even compared to contemporary Przeworsk sites, the settlements of the Wielbark–Lubowidz phase are particularly tatty. This is precisely what we might expect from a society practising an extensive, unstable agriculture. Since they knew that they would shortly move on to pastures (or Celtic fields) new, grand settlements would have been dysfunctional. This might also explain why longer-lived cemetery areas, with public meeting places marked by stone circles, should have been so obviously important to the functioning of society (p. 68).

A little more direct evidence of agricultural technique has also survived. The cemetery at Odry was established on top of an old field system. From underneath one of the barrows there emerged evidence of the ploughing and fertilizing techniques previously employed. Both were rudimentary. Ploughing took the form of narrow, criss-crossed scrapings, and the addition of ash – perhaps reflecting a slash and burn agriculture – the only form of fertilization. Similar evidence has also come to light at Gronowo. Especially on the rather poor soils of northern Poland, the latter would have been insufficient to maintain fertility for any length of time. Studies of so-called 'micro-regions' have suggested, consonant with this, that family groups would occupy a given area for between only two and three generations.

By the late Roman period, much more intensive agricultural regimes had evolved. By the fourth century, larger, longer-lived villages such as Feddersen Wierde and Wijster had evolved in at least some areas of so-called 'Free Germany'. The inhabitants of both these villages practised mixed farming, part arable, part pastoral. The fact that they occupied the same site for several centuries (first to fifth in the case of Wijster, second to fifth in the case of Feddersen Wierde) shows that their inhabitants had developed new techniques for maintaining the fertility of their arable fields. In particular, they were to some extent integrating arable and pastoral production, using manure from their animals, together, probably, with some kind of two-crop rotation to maintain yields. These changes represent a revolution in agricultural productivity. It is now broadly accepted that these changes were associated with a substantial and general increase in population.[30] Another broad indication of the same thing has been provided by pollen diagrams. Between the birth of Christ and the year 500, cereal pollens reached unprecedentedly high percentage values, at the expense of grass pollens, in wide areas of what is now the territory of Poland, the Czech Republic and Germany.

The chronological longevity of Černjachov settlements is unclear (chapter 5). They were, however, more substantial than their Wielbark predecessors. This is obviously true of the central places. It is also true of ordinary, agricultural settlements, although these varied considerably in size. The largest, Budeşty, covered an enormous area of 35 hectares, several others were around 20 hectares (e.g. Zagajkany, Kobuska and Veke). At the other end of the scale, Petrikany was only 2 hectares, and Komrat 4.5 hectares. The populations of these villages derived their subsistence from mixed farming, with a high priority being given to the production of cereals. Indeed, the Černjachov culture as a whole spread eastwards to the point, broadly speaking, where the lack of rainfall makes crop-raising unreliable. To judge from deposits in storage pits, the most important crops were wheat, barley and millet; rye, oats, peas, acorns and hemp were also harvested. At the same time, considerable effort was put into animal husbandry. Cattle were the most numerous animals kept, but there were also sheep and goats, along with pigs and some horses. Whether the agricultural techniques employed in these Černjachov villages matched the sophistication of those of the fourth-century Germanic west is unclear. In ploughing equipment, at least, they did. The iron coulters and ploughshares found in a variety of Černjachov contexts demonstrate that ploughing techniques were far more advanced than those prevalent in the earlier phases of the Wielbark culture.

[30] Some studies specifically devoted to agricultural evolution: Myhre, 1978; Van Es, 1967; Haarnagel, 1979. Further comment: Steuer, 1982, 258ff; Hedeager, 1988; Randsborg, 1991, 72ff; Hedeager, 1992, 193ff; Todd, 1992, ch. 4.

Plate 4 Černjachov glassware

A similar picture emerges from other areas of economic activity, such as specialization and exchange. What evidence there is, such as finds from the so-called Herrenhof at Feddersen Wierde, suggests a picture of increasing economic diversification and specialization in the early centuries ad.[31] Further east, in territories dominated by the Goths, glass was produced in non-Roman Europe for the first time in the fourth century (plate 4). Before this, all the glass found in non-Roman Europe had been exported from the Roman Empire. One production site for the glass has been found at Komarov in the hinterland of the Carpathians. As the distribution map shows, its products were distributed widely across large tracts of central and eastern Europe (figure 3.6).[32] Increasing sophistication is apparent elsewhere. In the later nineteenth century, a hoard of exquisite gold and silver items was found at Pietroasa in Romania. Much of it has proved to be fifth

31 See e.g. Haarnagel, 1979; Todd, 1992, 125ff.
32 Rau, 1972.

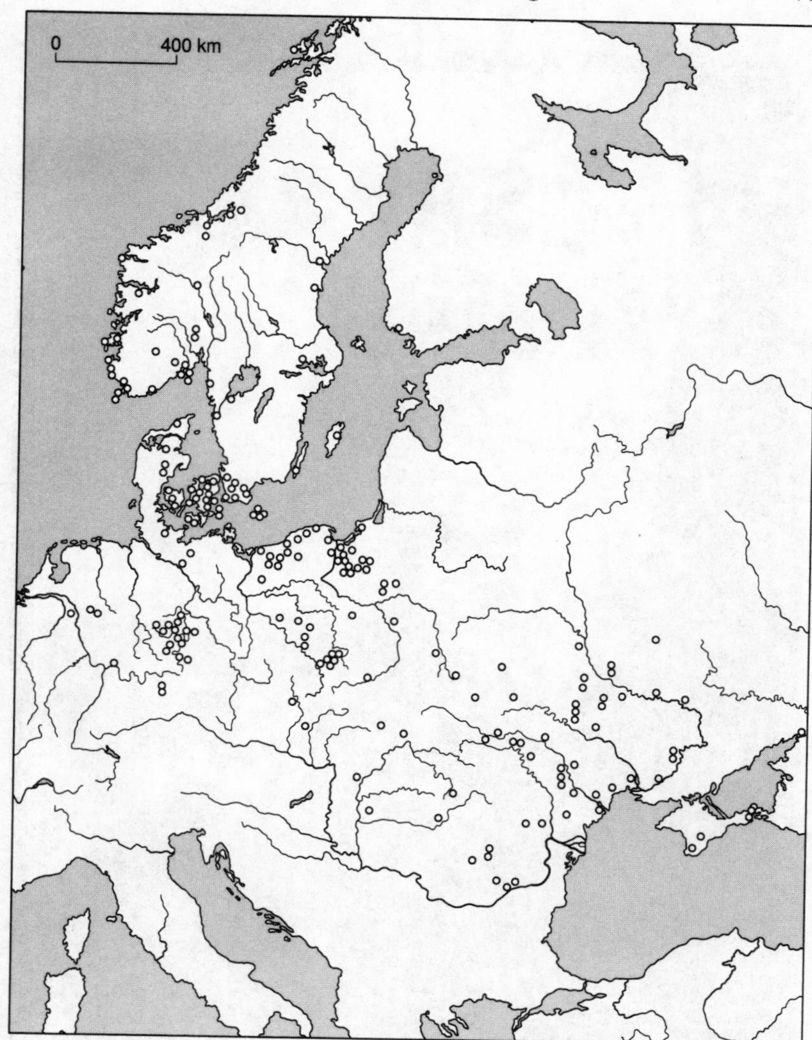

Figure 3.6 Finds of Černjachov glass

century, but one of the silver dishes (plate 5) was probably made in the fourth century, outside the Roman Empire. Moulds for making such products have been found. The working of precious metals would reach a new peak in the Hunnic Empire (chapter 4), but metal-working techniques were already relatively well advanced, as the intricate silver brooches (*fibulae*) of the fourth century confirm.[33]

[33] Harhoiu, 1977.

Plate 5 The Pietroasa Treasure

How some, at least, of this production was organized is suggested by the excavated Černjachov village at Bîrlad-Valea Seacă in Romania. A characteristic Černjachov find, often placed with individuals in graves, is a type of composite bone comb made from

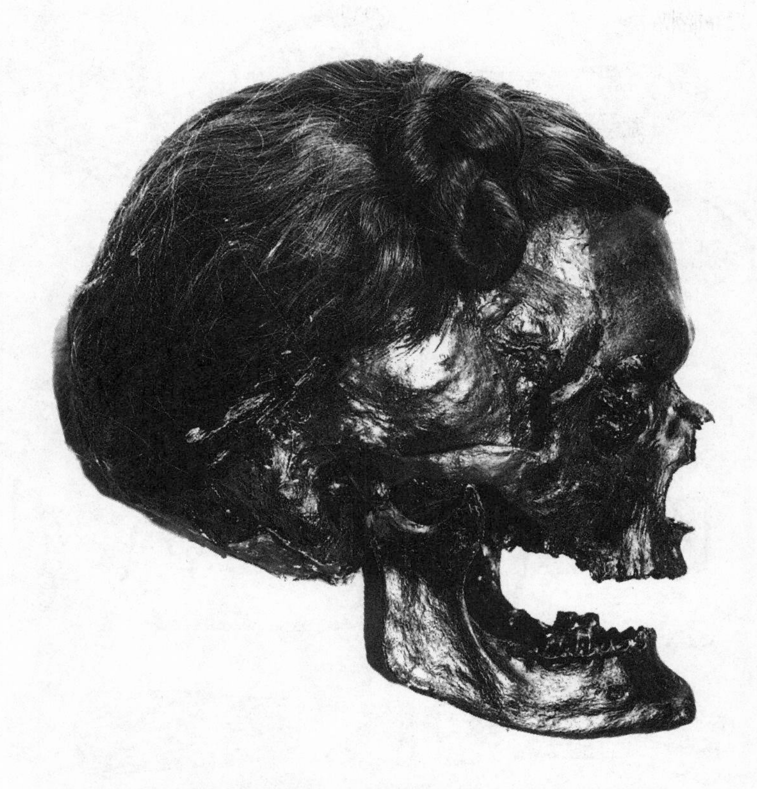

Plate 6 The importance of hairstyles: A Suebian knot (from a peat-bog at Osterby, Schleswig-Holstein)

deer antlers. Hairstyles were used by some Germanic groups to express political affiliations, particularly the famous Suebian knot, of which examples from antiquity have survived (plate 6). The production of Černjachov combs can be comprehensively reconstructed, because excavations at Bîrlad-Valea Seacă have unearthed a large number of huts containing combs and their constituent parts in various stages of production (figure 3.7).[34] Questions, however, still remain. Did the relevant artisans make their living solely from such craftwork, or was it a part-time activity? Either way, it is hard not to see this village as a specialized production centre, making goods for widespread distribution. Glass and silver working proceeded perhaps

[34] E.g. Palade, 1966.

a) Find raw material

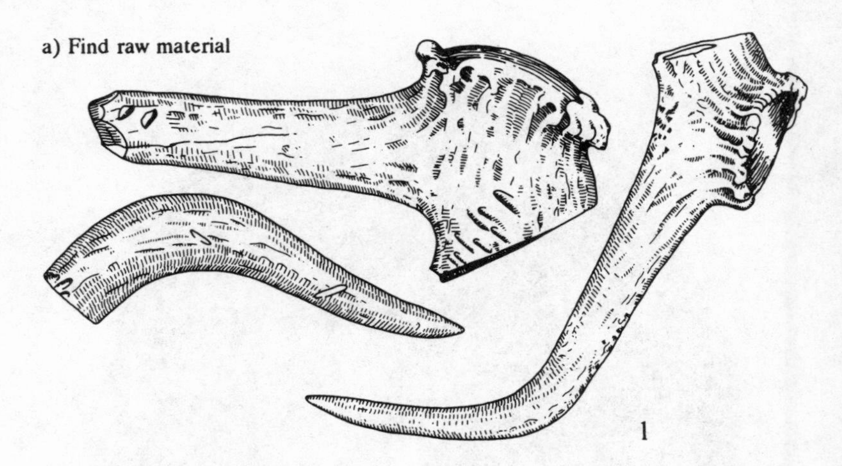

b) Cut horn extensions into short sections and split

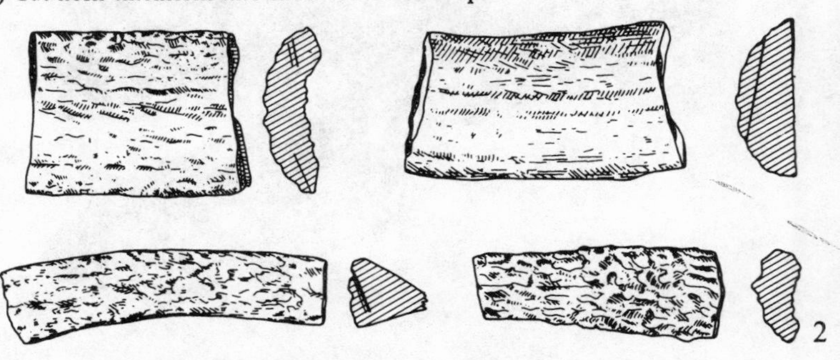

c) Cut away curved surface and trim to create thin, flat, rectangular plates.

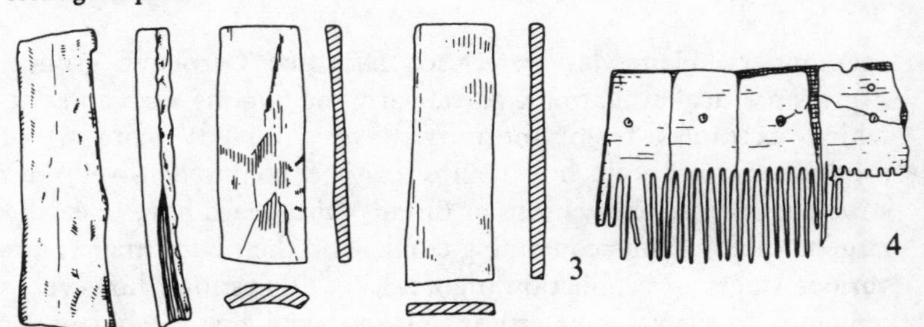

N.B. Those shown are in varying stages of completion; *do not* cut teeth until very end of process

Figure 3.7(a)

d) Take remaining part of horn, split and work into flat, semi-circular shape

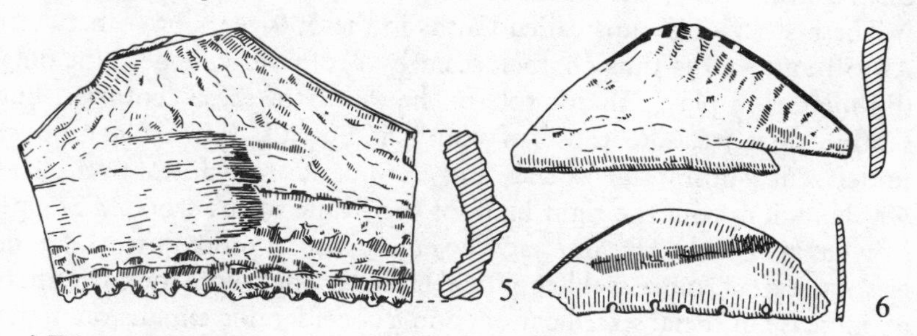

e) Take a series of plates, place semi-circular piece either side and rivet together (copper)

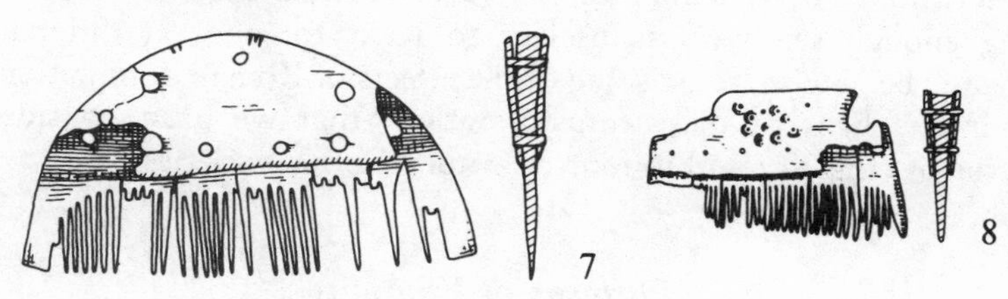

f) Success!

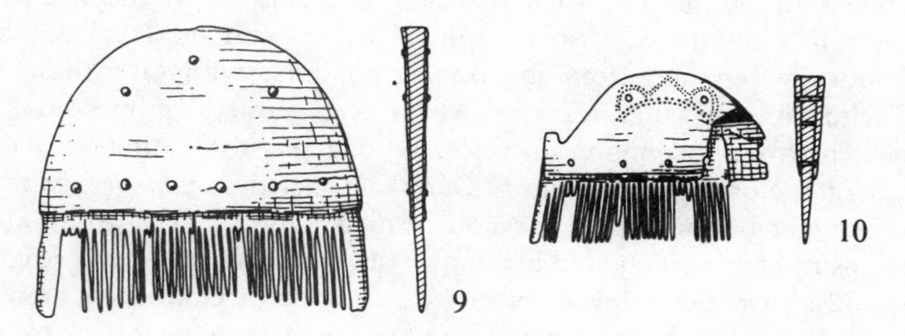

Figure 3.7(b) How to make your own bone comb

in a similarly specialized fashion, but this was not true of all crafts. Another characteristic feature of the culture is its high quality wheel-turned pottery (see below). Enough kilns have been found, however, to suggest that every major settlement had its own potter. There was thus no pottery industry as such. Iron, likewise, was produced and worked, but, again it seems, more after the pattern of the ceramics than the combs. Centres of iron and bronze production have been found, such as that at Sinicy, where 15 or so smithies clustered on the bank of the nearby river. Sinicy is quite small, however, compared to

Iron Age La Tène complexes of the same region from the last centuries BC. Again, most of the studied villages had their own smith.

The history of groups called Goths in the 300 years or so between AD 50 and 350 is thus characterized by profound change. Not only did migration play a major role in the events of these centuries, but Gothic societies, like those of many, if not all, Germanic groups, underwent substantial social and economic transformation. The whole region from the right bank of the Rhine to the wooded Steppe of what is now the Ukraine saw the emergence of more powerful and, to some extent, more stable political entities. They were founded upon an increase in social stratification, and a considerable expansion in the agricultural base of the economy. While their coherence should probably not be overstated, both the Tervingi and the Alamanni had a strong enough sense of themselves to want to, and, at different moments, be able to, resist some of the effects of Roman domination. It is in the light of these transformations that we must consider patterns of ethnicity within fourth-century Gothic societies.

C. *Patterns of Ethnicity*

Somewhere within the Wielbark–Lubowidz culture, we might guess, there first originated a socio-political entity with the label 'Goth'. Politically separate from its near neighbours, with (according to Tacitus) its own kings, it may also have been marked out by a sense of descent from a common ancestor. A long pre-history underlay the emergence of even first-century Germanic societies, however, so that this might be too simple a vision of their nature.[35] The group also seems to have participated in a larger ritual association or cult league (p. 32). How powerful or exclusive any sense of Gothicness among this group might have been, is hard to estimate. If we refer back to the rough checklist cited in chapter 1 (p. 7), the first-century Goths fulfilled only a minority of its criteria. They possessed a self-appointed name and were, up to a point, established on a specific territory. They also had kings, whom they are said to have obeyed. Tacitus' language is ambiguous, however, about whether they had more than one at any given moment (*Germania* 44). Migration, moreover, was a major feature of their existence, and the extent to which they were either a firm population aggregate or had their own distinctive peculiarities of culture and/or language seems rather doubtful. If anything, as we have

[35] Hedeager, 1992, esp. chs 1–2.

seen, the Wielbark culture probably reflects a cult league, in which more than just Goths participated. At the most, then, the first-century Goths were only a half-emerged ethnic group.

By the fourth century, Gothicness had become, at least among the Tervingi, a more powerful, self-assertive, phenomenon. This is most obviously true, as we have seen, in relations with the Roman Empire. In the 360s, imperial political hegemony was thrown off, and the opportunity was immediately seized to crack down on Christianity which was firmly identified with Rome. The sense of identity of the Tervingi even had a territorial dimension, again perhaps generated in opposition to Rome. In 369, Athanaric forced Valens to meet him in a boat in the middle of the Danube, claiming to have sworn an oath not to enter Roman territory. This suggests a reasonably developed sense of what was Gothic land and what was Roman land. In the Goths' conception, the river Danube marked the physical limit of Roman power. A Gothic liturgical text preserves the name *Gutthiuda*: the land of the Goths. Contemporary Alamannic leaders, similarly, saw their kingdoms as physical entities where the rights of Roman intrusion were at least curtailed at a border marked by the Rhine. Alamannic kings, like Athanaric, occasionally met Roman Emperors on boats, and one diplomatic incident was caused by the determination of the Emperor Valentinian, against established practice, to build a fort on the Alamannic side of the river (AM 28.2.5–9; 30.3.4–6).

With Ulfila's translation of the Bible, the Goths even started to possess their own distinctive written language. Writing a language down, especially in sacred books, tends to generate linguistic rigidity. Too little is known of dialectical and linguistic development among Germanic speakers to be sure even of the long-term impact of Ulfila's work, and it is unlikely to have had any major effect before 376. None the less, the fourth-century Goths, or at least one group of them, the Tervingi, were thus much closer to fulfilling the requirements we might expect of a real ethnic group. Comparative studies have stressed, indeed, that conflict – self-identification against outsiders – acts as a critical catalyst in the development of more powerful senses of identity.[36] Established on the frontier, the Tervingi faced formidable competition in the form of the Roman Empire. But the whole process of expansion south and east from the Baltic region had been violent and competitive (chapter 2). The Tervingi are unlikely to have been very different from other fourth-century Gothic groups.

If, by the fourth-century, Gothic entities probably were more self-

[36] E.g. Smith, 1986.

assertive, with a stronger sense of themselves, in another sense, the situation was less clear-cut. For the lands by the Black Sea were not occupied solely by immigrant Goths. The historical sources mention other Germanic and non-Germanic groups (above pp. 43ff), and archaeological remains testify to the fact that the Černjachov culture was not the preserve of one ethnic unit. Many of its features do suggest that it was created around Germanic immigrants (metalwork, hand-made ceramics, female costume and, above all, burial habits). On the other hand, both in technique and range of forms, the distinctive largely grey wheel-turned pottery of the culture is very similar to Roman provincial wares. Likewise, particular sites have produced artefacts (other hand-made ceramics, mirrors, weapons and ornaments) and evidence for the employment of particular customs which had other, non-Wielbark origins: whether Przeworsk, Dacian, Iranian nomad or Slavic. Possibly Slavic forms are a marked feature of the sub-group of the upper Dniester, and Iranian, nomadic ones of the so-called Steppe group (p. 56).

Many attempts have been made at precise ethnic attributions on the basis of individual artefacts. These are doomed to failure, however, because the originally separate strands behind the Černjachov culture quickly coalesced to create a homogeneous whole. Some scholars, for instance, have insisted on a Dacian origin for the wheel-turned pottery, and argued that its appearance on any site means that at least some Dacians lived there.[37] But wheel-made pottery quickly became the norm throughout the culture, and is simply technically superior to its hand-made counterparts. Its use was also spreading in non-Roman Europe in the third century, and there is no reason to suppose that Gothic potters could not have learned how to use the wheel. Any simple equation between pots and people is misconceived, therefore, as grave 36 from the cemetery of Letçani in Romania underlines. This contained an individual buried with large amounts of non-Germanic wheel-turned pottery, but one of the pots was inscribed with Gothic runes. This individual was presumably Gothic, despite the pottery.[38]

More convincing are analyses which work with evidence of variant customs, particularly burial customs, which betray a different set of beliefs from those of the Wielbark/Černjachov norm. Good examples are the occasional, probably Przeworsk, weapon burials (p. 47), and finds of distinctively Sarmatian inhumations, when gravegoods were placed on a shallow shelf of earth at one end of the grave. Divergent

[37] Palade, 1980.
[38] Illustrated in Blosiu, 1975, 267.

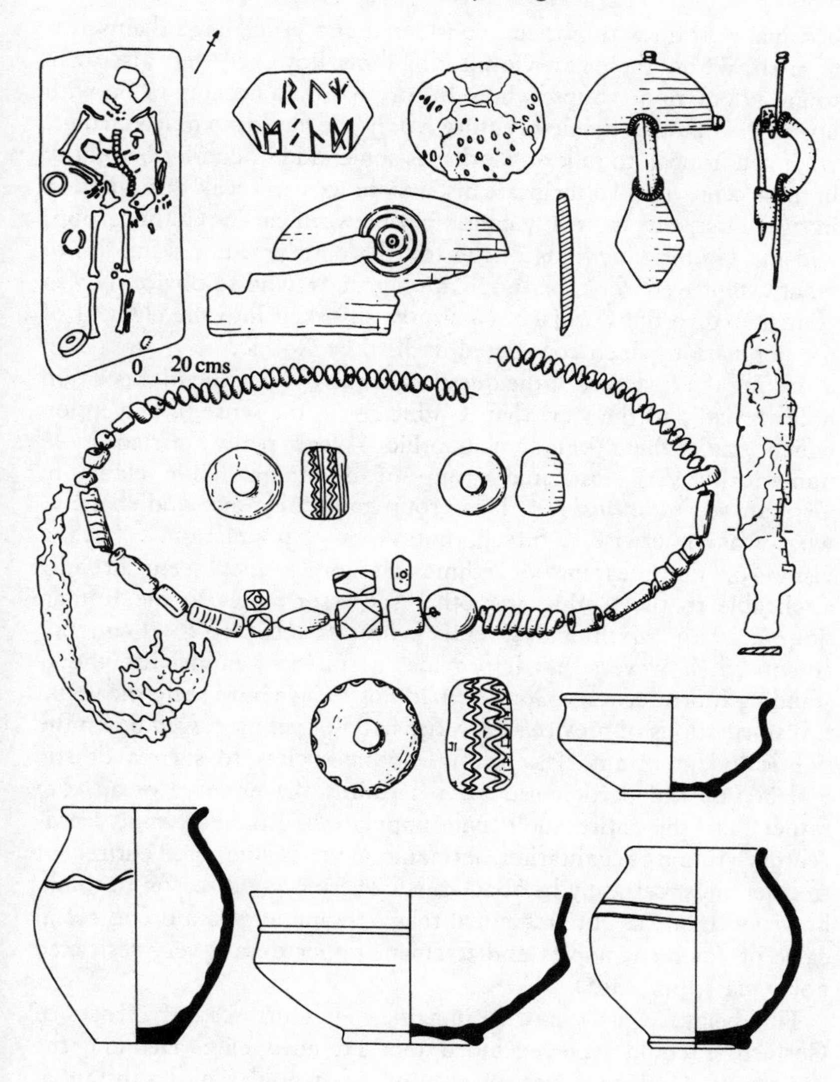

Figure 3.8 Grave 36 from Letçani

burials of this kind are very much the minority, however, and do not advance the analysis very far.

By the fourth century, therefore, the label 'Gothic' no longer designated a simple kind of community. More than one political entity attracted the Gothic label, and these entities were Gothic – and recognized by their Roman neighbours as such – because a politically dominant group within them, considered and proclaimed themselves to be so. Within these new Gothic kingdoms, however, were also to be found population groups, whose history had had nothing to do with northern Poland of the first century AD. In the face of so much change, what can it mean to talk of 'Goths' as some kind of continuous entity in these centuries? To facilitate discussion, we can break this question in two. First, was there any continuity between earlier Gothic groups and the Gothic kingdoms of the fourth century? And, secondly, to what extent were the other population groups, who so obviously also contributed to the Černjachov culture, absorbed into the element of the population which considered itself to be Gothic?

Taking the first part of the question, a currently influential position holds broadly to the view that 'Gothicness' – the sense of perception which made these kingdoms Gothic – was really carried by a numerically very restricted group of dominant noble clans: in German, a *Traditionskern*. This group gave coherence and shape to what was otherwise a mixed, multi-ethnic, population.[39] Such a vision of the meaning of ethnic categories does seem broadly applicable to the Gothic and other successor states to the Roman Empire in the sixth and seventh centuries (chapter 9). I am not convinced, however, that it provides a sufficient model for understanding fourth-century Gothic kingdoms. As we have seen, the social transformations of previous centuries had not yet narrowed down the politically important class within Gothic society to such a drastic extent. Political participation was certainly the preserve of an elite rather than the entire adult male population. Romantic nineteenth-century visions of egalitarian Germanic societies composed entirely of freemen must certainly be abandoned. There is good reason to think, however, that this elite remained relatively numerous: a broad social caste of emergent nobles and freemen, rather than a very restricted noble class (pp. 73–5).

This being so, it is hard to imagine that fourth-century senses of Gothicness could have excluded this extended elite. Defining the bearers of 'Gothicness' as an elite of quasi nobles plus substantial numbers of freemen, also makes better sense of the substantial population movements south and east out of northern and central Poland in the third century. The few figures in the sources, and, more important, the implicit evidence of the range of action undertaken by the migrant groups imply armies to be numbered in a few thousands, not just hundreds (p. 47). Likewise, the continuity in female costume

[39] See in more detail, chapter 6, pp. 169ff.

between Wielbark and Černjachov cultures points to mixed social groups, with significant numbers of women and children, having made the move south (chapter 2). The new realms were probably built up, then, around substantial bodies of Gothic migrants.

The arrival of thousands of immigrants in the third century, of course, does not rule out the mass absorption of new population groups in the fourth: the second part of the question. Literary sources define two ends of a spectrum of possibility. On the one hand, the sixth-century *Strategicon* of the Byzantine Emperor Maurice describes the way in which Slavic tribes of that period were ready, after a given period, to accept prisoners as full and equal members of their tribal groups (11.4). At the other end of the spectrum stands the Hunnic Empire of Attila. Here too, certain individuals were absorbed: most famously the Greek merchant met by Priscus in Attila's camp (fr. 11.2). But, as we shall see, larger groups of non-Huns (Goths, Gepids, Heruli etc.), although incorporated politically into the Hunnic Empire, were kept separate and subordinate, to supply their masters with food, tribute and military manpower (e.g. Priscus fr. 49). In these circumstances, the Huns had every interest in limiting the ability of their subjects to acquire Hunnic, therefore higher, status. Otherwise, the amounts of tribute and service available to them would have drastically declined. Not surprisingly, therefore, the various subject groups maintained their own identity over several generations, to re-emerge after the collapse of Attila's Empire (chapter 4). Where, within this spectrum, should we place the Gothic kingdoms of the fourth century?

Given the limited evidence available, it is hard to know what ethnic transformations occurred during the first expansion of the Wielbark culture into Masovia. Signals are mixed. Some cemeteries suggest the adoption, on the part of Przeworsk populations, of Wielbark ways, i.e. absorption. On the other hand, the economic changes to the Germanic world in these centuries were associated with an increase in population. Likewise, pressure from the north was probably a factor in the Marcomannic war (chapter 2). If some absorption (the Slavic end of the spectrum) is suggested, this was probably not the full story.

In the second phase of expansion leading to the creation of the Černjachov culture, there are, similarly, a number of indications that something other than the Slavic model applied. The establishment of Gothic and other Germanic groups north of the Black Sea involved, as we have seen, competition with powers indigenous to the region. The immigrants did not create multi-ethnic confederations by negotiation, but intruded themselves by force. Amongst others, Dacian Carpi,

Black Sea city-states, and nomadic Sarmatians lost out in the process. The original pattern of the new political units created by these events, the direct ancestors of our fourth-century kingdoms, was, therefore, a mixture of dominant Germanic, especially Gothic, groups and subordinate locals. Viewed from across the frontier, Gothic immigrants were the obviously dominant force in the region after the third-century upheavals. Hence fourth-century Graeco–Roman sources mention only Goths north of the Danube, and the Gothic language of Ulfilas' Bible is certainly Germanic. The fourth-century kingdoms contained an ethnically mixed population, but not in origin an equal one.

This lack of equality is likely to have hindered the degree to which other groups were absorbed with full rights into the dominant and sizeable migrant Gothic groups. The sixth-century Ostrogoths, for instance, remained strongly hierarchical in nature. Somewhere between 50 and 80 per cent of the group's population occupied only subordinate roles (pp. 324f). It is even possible that the division of Gothic society into distinct castes was itself the result of the processes of migration and conquest we have been examining. The conquering migrants, for instance, could have transformed themselves into an elite freeman caste by turning conquered indigenous populations, or elements of them, into subordinates, whether slave or freed. As in the Hunnic Empire, the dominant migrants will have had an interest in maintaining their superiority, and hence a sense of separation. In this context, subordinate locals could easily become Gothic servants, but not so easily fully fledged members of the Gothic elite.

A case in point, which captures the difficulties and ambiguities of the evidence and situation, concerns the descendants of Roman prisoners taken by the Goths in the course of the third-century raids. From this group was descended Ulfila, translator of the Gothic Bible. To judge by his case, such people maintained some memory of their origins well into the fourth century. It was known, for instance, from which Cappadocian village his parents had been taken (Philostorgius *h.e.* 2.5). Captives of this kind may also have remained an identifiable group, if we are right to think that Ulfila was originally ordained bishop to minister to them, and that it was largely people in this category who followed him across the Danube in 347/8 (p. 61). Interestingly, these refugees did not fit back easily into the mainstream of Roman society. Rather than returning to the presumably various places in Asia Minor and the Balkans from which their ancestors had been taken, they formed a separate population enclave close to the Danube frontier, where they survived until the mid-sixth century

(Jordanes *Getica* 267). This group clearly spoke Gothic – Ulfila's name means 'Little Wolf' – and were too Gothicized simply to disappear among the peasant population of the Roman Empire. At the same time, they obviously had not been fully absorbed by the Goths. In addition to Gothic, Ulfila also knew Latin and Greek (his Gothic Bible translated one of the standard Greek Bible texts of the fourth century). He presumably learned these languages while growing up among this captive population.[40] Such Roman prisoners may have been accepted, then, only as Gothic subordinates (freed or slaves), rather than as fully integrated Goths.

A seventh-century text, the *Miracles of St. Demetrius*, describes in more detail what may be an analogous situation. It concerns the experiences of more Roman prisoners, taken this time by nomadic Avars. From various places within the Roman Empire, they were settled together in a way which did not preclude intermarriage with other groups of the Avar Empire. They grew in number over time, and most of them acquired free status. This being so, the Khagan eventually organized them into a semi-autonomous subject group. Some of them had none the less maintained a sense of their Roman origins and language for over 50 years or more, by carefully cultivated oral tradition and adherence to Christianity (285–6). The parallels with Ulfila's circumstances here, and the emphasis on status, are both striking. The passage may even suggest, therefore, a model for understanding the evolution of the group who fled south of the Danube with Ulfila in 347/8. Whether they had already acquired free status, and, with it, semi-autonomy, is impossible to know. Either way, the case of the Avars' prisoners nicely illustrates some of the complex dynamics which were at work in the fourth-century Gothic kingdoms. The prisoners' origins offered them one potential ethnic identity, and intermarriage others. Their options were limited, however, by the socio-political constraints placed upon them by the dominant Avar group. They had no real options at all, until they were made free.

Any simple model of how ethnic structures operated in the fourth-century Gothic kingdoms is likely, therefore, to be insufficient. Ethnic identity is essentially a perception or claim on the part of an individual recognized by peers and/or outsiders. By the fourth century, Gothic groups were at times strongly assertive of their identity, at least against the Roman state. The extent to which the perceptions of identity powering this resistance were shared by all the population of lands dominated by Gothic kingdoms was probably not

40 In more detail, Heather and Matthews, 1991, ch. 5.

fixed. It is certainly not easily predictable on the basis of the available evidence. Simply to conclude from the broad homogeneity of the material remains of the Černjachov culture, that everyone quickly came to participate equally in the political process, is to make an old mistake. Anthropologists no longer count concrete cultural traits on the assumption that, when two originally separate groups have come to share most traits in common, they will have merged (pp. 3–4). Objects and technologies can be passed from one group to another without this affecting perceptions of difference, especially in a context where the different population groups were not politically equal.

There is every reason to suppose that further research will advance our understanding. In particular, the whole question of the pattern of life within the Černjachov culture requires systematic investigation. Did the Goths and other migrants occupy entirely separate settlements from their indigenous subordinates, or were mixed villages established? In later nomadic Empires, for instance, subject groups were to some extent kept geographically apart (pp. 123ff). Černjachov cemeteries contain a minority of burials with no gravegoods: at Kosanovo, for instance, eight inhumations and seven cremations.[41] There are a variety of possible explanations for such burials, and some have thought that they might represent Christians. Just as likely, however, is that they are the remains of a subordinate stratum of the population, the freed or slaves, within ethnically mixed settlements. And of course, both mixed and separate villages could have existed at the same time. For the latter, there is even some evidence. Some Romanian excavations have suggested that certain sites (Costişa-Mănoaia, Botoşana-Suceava and Dodeşti-Vaslui) were occupied continuously by an indigenous population before, during and after the period of Gothic domination.[42] If so, in these cases, the indigenous population retained its own socio-economic structures and probably did no more than pay tribute to dominant Goths.

Thus conclusions can only be provisional. The fourth-century kingdoms were founded on the aggressive intrusion of substantial migrant groups, and the social structures of the resulting kingdoms were considerably stratified. Hence there was plenty of scope for non-migrants to be absorbed into the kingdoms in ways which made clear their subordinate status, either as otherwise autonomous tribute-payers, or as disadvantaged population strata (freed or slaves) in mixed settlements. Either way, they would have been denied full

41 Heather and Matthews, 1991, 62 for other figures.
42 Teodor, 1980, 3ff.

participation in Gothic identity and political processes.

At the same time, in the fluid situation north of the Black Sea in the later third century, individual warband leaders might well have wanted to strengthen their position by recruiting as many supporters, whatever their background, as possible. A good (and documented) analogy might be Totila's war to retain the Italian kingdom in the sixth century. The campaigns overstretched available Gothic manpower, and he consistently offered prisoners generous terms to encourage them to transfer their allegiance to the Goths, and, very occasionally, included former Roman slaves in his armies. This evidence illustrates the capacity of Gothic groups to take on board outsiders, but also the limits of absorption. Apart from a few individuals, and groups who faced punishment because they had killed their Roman commanders, most of the recruits simply transferred back to a Roman allegiance when Narses' army arrived (App. 2). Joining a Gothic army did not necessarily lead individuals or groups to become Goths. Indeed, any leaders' desire for recruits may have been checked by his original, migrant, following. Their rights and advantages were bound up in maintaining a particular status. The resulting ethnic structures are unlikely to have been simple. As late as the sixth century, some 50 to 80 per cent of the population of the migrant Ostrogoths in Italy was composed of subordinated individuals, who did not share in the full rights and privileges of elite freemen. I would likewise argue that a substantial elite of immigrant quasi nobles and freemen lay at the heart of the fourth-century Gothic kingdoms. A significant proportion of their total population did not derive from northern Poland, but that should not be taken to mean that just anyone could become a Goth.

Part II

Goths, Huns and Romans

4

The Hunnic Revolution

The Gothic world of the fourth century was divided into perhaps as many as six or more separate kingdoms. In the last quarter of the fourth century, this political order was completely overturned by a mysterious third party: the Huns. The Huns further fragmented the Gothic world. Between 376 and 406, a number of Gothic groups made separate decisions to move inside the Roman Empire. All were trying to escape the insecurity generated by the Huns. At the same time, other Goths – again in a number of separate groups – made an alternative choice. For them, it seemed better to resist the onset of the Huns directly.

Hunnic power in central Europe grew steadily, however, until, in the middle of the fifth century, it reached its apogee. By *c.*450, most, if not all, of the Goths still north of the Danube had been incorporated into the Empire of the Hunnic leader Attila. Only after Attila's death (453), were some Goths able to reassert their independence: at different moments and in different contexts. Many of these Goths again ended up inside the Roman Empire. From the perspective of the Roman authorities south of the Danube, therefore, Goths had invaded their lands in two waves: one in the last quarter of the fourth century, another in the third quarter of the fifth. While such a vision of events is broadly correct, it does not do justice to the full story of the impact of the Huns upon the Goths.

A. *Goths in the 'Hunnensturm'*

Ammianus reports that the Huns originally came from the north, near the 'ice bound ocean' (31.2.1). Arguments have long raged as to whether this should be taken literally, in which case they might have had Finno–Ugrian roots, like the later Magyars, or whether the Huns were the first known group of Turkic nomads to disturb the frontiers of Europe.[1] For the Roman imperial authorities, a first major consequence of their arrival was the appearance, in 376, of two substantial and separate Gothic groups, Tervingi and Greuthungi, on the banks of the river Danube. They were asking for asylum. That the onset of the Huns prompted this request is certain (e.g. AM 31.2.1). The precise course of the action, and, along with it, the basic nature of the Hunnic assault, has often been misunderstood.

(i) Huns and Goths on the lower Danube

Ammianus' famous digression on their customs and manners portrays the Huns as a group of nomadic tribes lacking an overall ruler (31.2.2–11). There is no reason to disbelieve this basic characterization. That the Huns were nomads, however, in no way explains their sudden intrusion into the fringes of Europe. This was a deliberate decision, not the random extension of established cycles of movement. Unfortunately, no source tells us why the decision was taken, and we can do no more than guess. Population pressure, drought on the Steppes, or the general attraction of the richer grazing lands at the western end of the Eurasian Steppe are all plausible motives.

Rather clearer is the impact of the Huns upon the Goths. Ammianus records that they first subdued the Goths' Alanic neighbours east of the Don (the Alans were Iranian nomads), and then, in alliance with some of them, attacked the Goths. The first assault fell upon the Greuthungi of Ermenaric. After some fighting, Ermenaric died in (what seems to us) mysterious circumstances. Because of the fears inspired in him by the unfolding events, the king 'gave himself up to a voluntary death'. Pagan Germanic kings were sometimes held mystically responsible for the general fortune of their peoples, so that Ermenaric perhaps sacrificed himself voluntarily to the gods to stave off the Hunnic menace. If so, it didn't work. After Ermenaric's death, his successor Vithimer took a more martial approach, even paying some Huns to help him fight his enemies, who

[1] Maenchen-Helfen, 1973, chs 8–9 is in the end inconclusive.

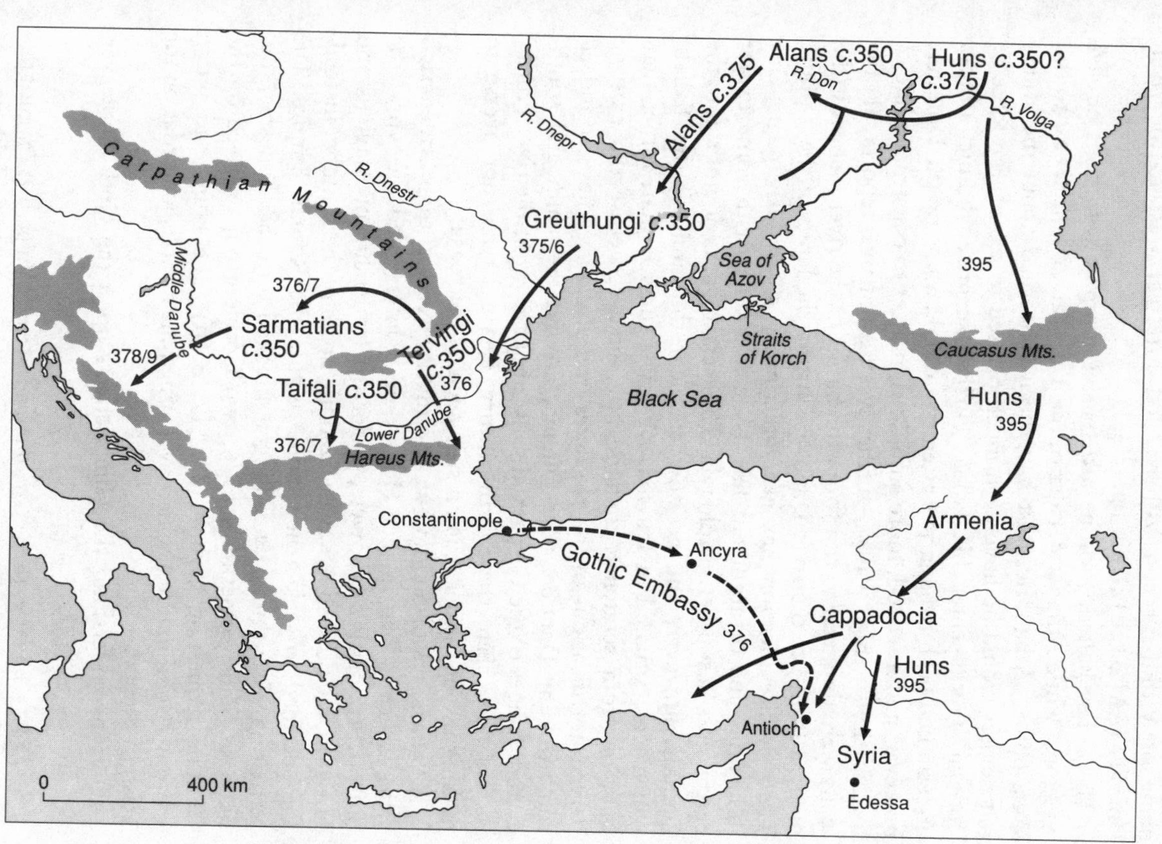

Figure 4.1 The arrival of the Huns (i): the crisis of 376–380

now consisted mostly of Alans. Vithimer was eventually killed in battle, after which a pair of leaders, Alatheus and Saphrax, in the name of Vithimer's son Vitheric, led a retreat west to the river Dniester (AM 31.3.12.1–3; figure 4.1).

There they halted, forming a defensive rampart with their circled waggons, while Athanaric, ruler of the Tervingi, advanced east to the same point.[2] Athanaric must have been concerned about the Huns, but neither would he have been much pleased to see a large force of 'foreign' Goths enter his lands. Further surprise Hunnic attacks undermined both Athanaric's attempts to hold a line on the Dniester, however, and a second, more ambitious, project to construct a line of fortifications – 'high walls' – further west. Ammianus reports that the walls were designed to run 'from the banks of the river Gerasius (the modern Pruth) to the river Danube, skirting the lands of the Taifali'. Their precise location has generated many a scholarly page. One influential line of argument has associated them with some extant earthworks in southern Moldavia. These earthworks do not run to the Danube, however, and go nowhere near the lands of the Taifali, which were situated in Oltenia. My own guess is that, rather than building from scratch, Athanaric attempted to re-use the existing Roman fortifications of the old *limes transalutanus*. These do indeed run from the Danube, near Oltenia, around the south and south-eastern fringes of the Carpathians just about as far as the river Pruth.[3] As we have seen, the fourth-century Tervingi were not averse to making use of former Roman sites such as Pietroasa.

Athanaric's wall-building was no more successful than Ermenaric's self-sacrifice. When further Hunnic raids interrupted the work, the bulk of Athanaric's followers, under the leadership of Alavivus and Fritigern, abandoned Athanaric and life north of the Danube. Instead, they decided to seek a new home within the Roman Empire. The retreating Greuthungi, no longer blocked on the Dniester, did likewise. Thus, sometime in 376, two Gothic groups arrived on the Danube requesting asylum (31.2.12; 3.1ff). The Huns had set in motion a domino effect which overturned the established order on the western Steppe.

Fully to understand the Hun's effects upon the Goths, however,

[2] AM 31.3.4 refers to the *Greuthungorum vallo*. Vulpe, 1957 argued that this should be equated with some earthworks in southern Moldavia. AM 31.15.5 shows that the historian used *vallum* to designate the Goths' circled

[3] AM 31.3.5–8. Moldavian earthworks: Vulpe, 1957. *Limes transalutanus*: Cataniciu, 1981.

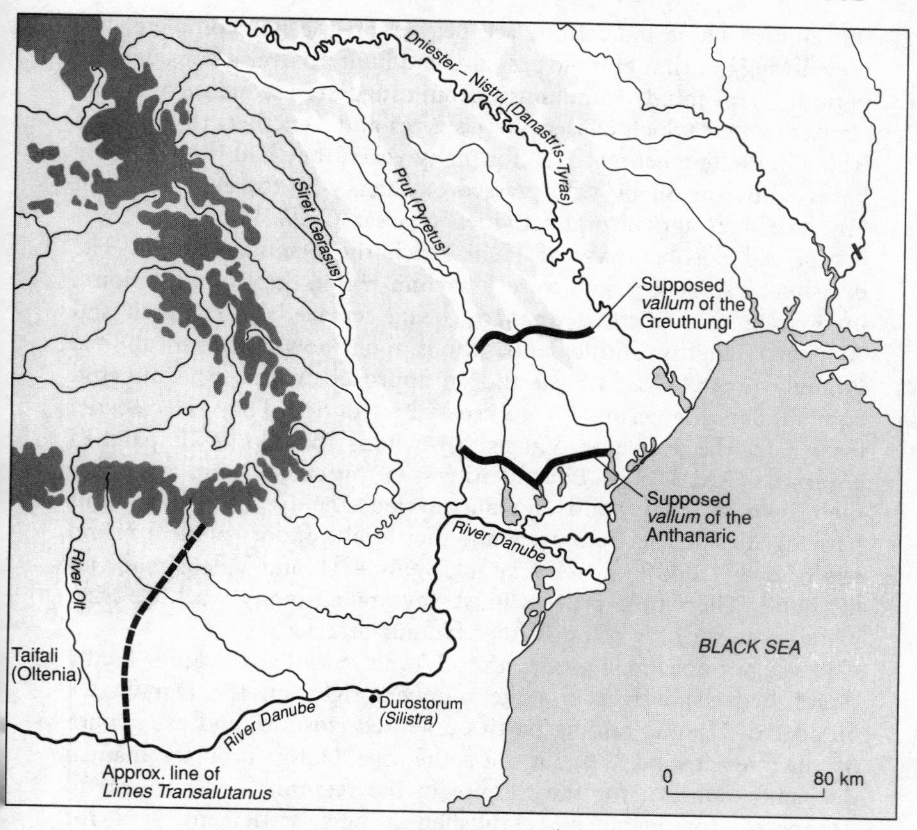

Figure 4.2 Vallums of Moldavia and the Limes Transalutanus

some features of what an older generation of German scholarship so evocatively labelled the *Hunnensturm* require further discussion. On the basis of Ammianus, it is generally thought that, in 376, the Goths were retreating before a solid mass of Huns. The latter are usually portrayed as overturning the hold of the Goths on lands north of the Black Sea rather suddenly, and immediately advancing in large numbers right up to the Danube. In the process, any Goths who had not retreated before them were captured. Such a vision of events seems mistaken.

First, Hunnic pressure seems to have built up on the Goths over some years. Ermenaric resisted them 'for a long time' (*diu*: AM 31.3.1), and Vithimer for 'some time' (*aliquantisper*), fighting 'many engagements' (AM 31.3.2). Troubles further east in the Caucasus region in the early 360s may also have been caused by the Huns.[4] These indications are neither precise nor complete, but they do suggest that Hunnic pressure had built up over a considerable period. To my mind, Ammianus' account suggests a sequence of events similar to that which caused the Usipetes and Tenctheri to cross the Rhine in the first century BC: 'for many years, they had been severely harassed by the Suebi, who pressed on them with force of arms and hindered their agricultural activities' (Caesar *Gallic War* 4.1).[5]

Nor did a solid mass of Huns reach the Danube in 376. The decision of some Tervingi to seek asylum within the Roman Empire, involved a coup d'état (Athanaric being replaced by Fritigern and Alavivus), lengthy Gothic deliberations about how best to escape the Hunnic threat (AM 31.3.8), and an approach to the local imperial commanders for permission to cross the frontier. They referred the matter to the Emperor Valens, to whom the Goths despatched embassies (AM 31.4.1). But Valens was in Antioch, so that, even after their own internal political manoeuvring, the Goths had to wait patiently beside the Danube, while their ambassadors made a round trip of over 1,000 km each way (cf. figure 4.1), and Valens made up his mind. The whole process must have taken many weeks, during which time we hear of no further Hunnic attacks.

It was not until many years after 376, in fact, that the Huns finally established themselves in large numbers right on the Danube. A number of Hunnic raiding parties operated close to, and even south of, the river around 376, but, for some time, Gothic groups remained the major concern for the Empire in the region. Tervingi loyal to Athanaric, for instance, established a new settlement area for themselves in the Carpathians in the late 370s. Athanaric himself was ousted in *c.*380, but the bulk of his former followers remained north of the Danube. This group may or may not be identical with the Gothic kingdom of one Arimer, which is known to have maintained an independent existence north of the Danube into at least the mid-380s. Archaeological evidence from Transylvania may reflect the operations of either or both of these groups, or, indeed, of other Goths. The first Černjachov discoveries in Romania were made at Sîntana de Mureş, actually in Transylvania. The cemetery actually contains a late form of the culture, to be dated *c.*380–400, and further investigations have uncovered a number of analogous sites in the same region. There is no archaeological evidence of a substantial

4 Demougeot, 1979, 383.

5 Standard accounts: e.g. Maenchen-Helfen, 1973, 26–7; Thompson, 1995, ch. 2.

Černjachov presence in the area before *c.*380, so that these sites perhaps reflect refugee Goths seeking safety from the Huns in the Romanian uplands.[6]

In 386, likewise, a second force of Greuthungi, under one Odotheus, attempted to cross south over the river. It was defeated with heavy casualties, and the survivors were resettled in Asia Minor. Odotheus is often characterized as a refugee from Hunnic control, but no source suggests that he was other than an independent Gothic king.[7] Even as late as 405/6, another Gothic king, Radagaisus, broke through the Roman frontier, this time invading Italy. Again, modern commentators have thought that Radagaisus was throwing off Hunnic dominion, but there is not a word of this in the sources. He too was probably an extra-Danubian Gothic king, still independent of the Huns some 30 years after 376.[8]

What we know of the Huns themselves further clarifies the situation. In 395 – nearly 20 years after the Tervingi and Greuthungi made their way to the Danube – the Hunnic centre of gravity was situated not beside the Danube, but much further east. In this year, many Huns crossed the Caucasus mountains. One group moved south and east towards Persia, and another attacked Roman territories in Armenia, Cappadocia and Syria, penetrating as far west as the cities of Antioch, Edessa and Cilicia (figure 4.1). It has often been held that the obviously substantial forces involved in these attacks were Danubian Huns, who had decided to outflank Roman defences by taking an unexpected route. But the distances involved make this exceedingly unlikely. If these were Huns from the Danube, they would surely not have dragged themselves (and their horses) 1,000 km or so around the north and eastern shores of the Black Sea and through a rugged mountain range. All the journey's hardships (for man and beast) would have only reduced their fighting abilities, long before they could even begin to plunder. The bulk of the Huns were thus well to the east of Rome's Danube frontier in 395, probably somewhere in the region of the lower Don and Volga rivers.[9] The

[6] Caucalanda: AM 31.4.13. Arimer and his Goths: Achelis, 1900, 310ff; cf. Wolfram, 1988, 135. Transylvanian Černjachov material: Horedt, 1986, 2–13.

[7] Zosimus 4.35.1, 38–9; Claudian *IV cons. Hon.* 626ff, Cons. Const. s.a. 386 (= *CM* 1, 244).

[8] Refs. as *PLRE* 2, 934. There is some chance that Radagaisus' Goths are the same as those led by Arimer in the 380s.

[9] Best account: Maenchen-Helfen, 1973, 52–9. More detailed argument: Heather, 1995, 7ff.

often aired view that 395 also saw a substantial Hunnic raid across the Danube is based on a misreading of the sources.[10]

While the Goths who came to the Danube in 376 certainly were retreating under Hunnic pressure, these events were only the first act in a slowly unfolding drama. Huns did not arrive en masse on the Danube as the result of a sudden surge in 375–6. Rather, a slow build-up of pressure precipitated, at this point, a crisis among certain Goths. Their retreat westwards provoked a similar response from many of their neighbours. Hence, two distinct Gothic groups arrived on the Danube, and, in addition, the related displacements of some groups of Alans, Taifali and Sarmatians, who all pushed across the Roman frontier in or shortly after 376. As Ambrose of Milan put it (writing in *c.*380): 'The Huns threw themselves upon the Alans, the Alans upon the Goths, and the Goths upon the Taifali and Sarmatae ... and this is not yet the end' (*Expositio Ev. sec. Luc.* 10.10). These groups were not closely pursued, however, by massed Huns. Other substantial Gothic groups maintained their independence north of the Danube for 30 years, and, in 395, the bulk of the Huns were still much closer to the Don and Volga than to the Danube. Only from AD 400, in fact, is there clear evidence of Huns as a permanent presence on or around the Danube frontier. In that year, a Hunnic leader called Uldin announced himself to the imperial authorities in Constantinople by sending them the head of a renegade imperial general, Gainas (below p. 144). But even Uldin's kingdom, established a quarter of a century after the first Goths crossed the Danube, by no means marks the high tide of Hunnic intrusion into eastern and central Europe.

(ii) The road to Hungary

Attila's Hunnic Empire of the 440s and 450s was centred not in the lower Danubian region, where Uldin rose to prominence, but on the Great Hungarian Plain: the Alföld of the middle Danube, west of the Carpathians. This region (in subsequent centuries the heartland of the Empires built by nomadic Avars and Magyars) was the centre of Hunnic power from, at the latest, the 420s. Somewhere between 395 and 420, then, the bulk of the Huns moved from lands north of the Black Sea to what is now Hungary. No source, unfortunately, tells us precisely what happened. It is also very doubtful that archaeology will ever fill the gap, even if maps showing the spread of characteristic

10 The enemy threatening the Balkans in 395 in Claudian *In Ruf.* II.26ff, esp. 36ff is Alaric the Goth, and Philostorgius, *h.e.* 11.8 has been tampered with by the editor: Heather, 1995, 9 n.1.

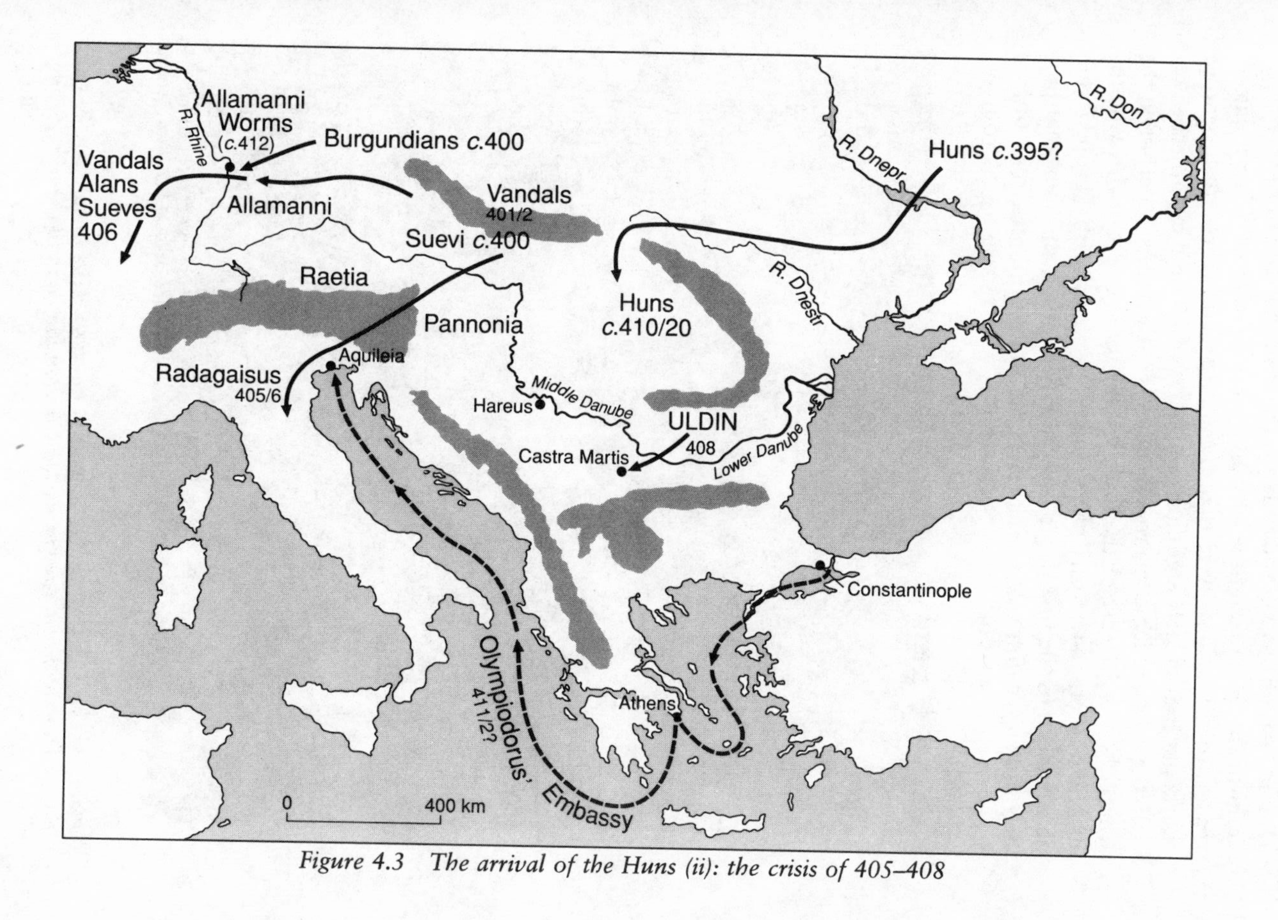

Figure 4.3 The arrival of the Huns (ii): the crisis of 405–408

Hunnic cauldrons, cranial deformations and rich horse burials confirm the general outline of westward movement.[11] There is good reason to think, however, that the first decade of the fifth century marked a particularly significant moment of Hunnic expansion.

In the crisis which came to a head in 376, the Huns undermined the established order east of the Carpathians. One effect of this was the arrival on Roman territory of a number of different tribal groups from that region. In the first decade of the fifth century, the sources report an even larger influx of peoples into the Roman Empire, the result of

Plate 7 The Theodosian Walls: built in the early 410s to counter the rising tide of Hunnic threat, they protected Constantinople until the age of cannon

[11] Werner, 1956; Bona, 1991.

three convulsions affecting virtually the entire length of the Empire's European frontiers. First, the Gothic king Radagaisus invaded Italy in 405/6. Secondly, a host of peoples made the famous Rhine crossing on 31 December 406: particularly the wide-ranging Vandals, Alans and Sueves, but also Burgundians who established a new domain much closer to the river Rhine, near Worms. Finally, the Hunnic leader Uldin threw off the mantle of Roman ally, and, in 408, crossed the Danube with a mixed force of Huns and Sciri. No source describes the causes of these incursions, and Hunnic involvement in the first two has been much debated.

Taken together, however, Radagaisus' invasion and the Rhine crossing represent a large exodus from middle Danubian areas west of the Carpathians (cf. figure 4.3). Radagaisus invaded Italy rather than Thrace, which suggests a middle Danubian origin for his force. Suevi is probably a collective name for the older established tribes of the middle Danube (such as the Quadi and Marcomanni). The Burgundians were certainly from this region. Likewise, while we have no information on the Alans, the Vandals were in the same area in 402 (Claudian, *De Bell. Get.* 363ff). What contemporaries witnessed in 405/6, then, was an outpouring of peoples from the middle Danubian region west of the Carpathian ring. Given that in 376 Hunnic power affected only lands east of the Carpathians, and that in 395 most Huns were still close to the northern Caucasus, it becomes hard not to view 405/6 as a re-run of 376, reflecting this time the intrusion of Hunnic power into central rather than eastern Europe.[12]

While the first unequivocal evidence for massed Huns in the middle Danube region comes from the 420s, there are some indications that they had been there since *c.*410. In 412, the authorities in Constantinople perceived a substantially increased threat to their European possessions in the Balkans. A programme was put in place to strengthen the Danubian fleets (in both the middle and lower regions of the river) in January of that year (*C. Th.*7.17.1; cf. 7.16.2). The great land walls of the capital itself were likewise erected in the following year (plate 7).[13] These have sometimes been taken as a response to Uldin's attack of 408/9, but, in that case, they would be strangely postdated. Uldin had anyway suffered a crushing defeat. I find it very tempting, therefore, to associate these new defensive measures with the closer proximity of the main Hunnic threat. Also,

12 Full argument and references: Heather, 1995, 11ff.
13 Mango, 1990, 46ff.

in 412, the historian Olympiodorus and his parrot went on an embassy to the Huns, leaving Constantinople by ship. After a severe storm, his ship put in at Athens, suggesting that it was travelling west through the Aegean, presumably before heading up the Adriatic (cf. figure 4.3), not east to the Black Sea. This route also suggests Hunnic chiefs established in the middle Danube region.[14] A further westward shift in the Hunnic main body might also explain Uldin's odd change of behaviour in 408, from imperial ally to invader. The arrival of new Hunnic forces perhaps put him under pressure to carve out a new domain. Indeed, just a year later, the western imperial authorities negotiated the assistance of a large Hunnic force (Zosimus 5.50.1). Help had previously been obtained from Uldin, but he had just suffered a major defeat, so that these arrangements were presumably made with some other Hunnic group. The middle Danube, rather than anywhere further east, would have been a convenient region for the authorities in Ravenna to look to for assistance.

For our purposes, it actually matters little whether the mass of the Huns arrived west of the Carpathians in the 410s or a little later, say by the 420s. It was only a generation after 376, even though they were the ultimate cause of the turmoil of that year, that Huns in large numbers even got as far as the lower Danube (Uldin in 400). When we find that the Huns' later appearance west of the Carpathians was preceded, in the same way, by a huge convulsion among the tribal groups of the middle Danubian region, it seems only reasonable to conclude that similar processes were at work in both cases. The large-scale penetrations by outsiders of the Roman frontier in 376 and 405–8 thus represent two phases of the same crisis. Both were prompted by the staged progression of the Huns from the outer fringes of Europe to its heart.

Such a view of the *Hunnensturm* makes it possible to write a fuller account of Gothic fortunes in this period. Hun-inspired crises washed up altogether four major Gothic groups onto the shores of the Roman Empire. Two came in 376 – the Tervingi of Alavivus and Fritigern and the Greuthungi of Alatheus and Saphrax – but two more followed subsequently: the Greuthungi of Odotheus in 386, and the Goths of Radagaisus in 405/6. We will return to these groups in the next chapter. Of the remainder who stayed north of the Danube, some may have fallen under Hunnic hegemony almost immediately after 376, but many, as we have seen, did not. It was another 30 years before Hunnic power established itself fully in central Europe, and, in the

14 Olympiodorus frr. 19, 28; cf. Croke, 1977, 353.

intervening years, there is plenty of evidence for independent Goths. It is to the fortunes of these Goths that the rest of this chapter is devoted.

B. Goths Under Hunnic Domination

The Hunnic Empire, which reached its greatest extent in the time of Attila (*c.*440–53), was created by two basic processes. First, non-Hunnic tribal groups were brought progressively under Hunnic dominion. Some Alans had already been subdued by the time that Hunnic attacks began upon the Goths (AM 31.3.1), and, in the years up to *c.*400, we find not just Huns and Alans, but also Huns and Carpo-Dacai, and Huns and Sciri operating together (Zosimus 4.34.6, Sozomen *h.e.* 9.5). Attila's Hunnic Empire, likewise, incorporated a huge range of subject peoples. Germanic Goths and Gepids find particular mention, but Attila also controlled originally nomadic Iranian Sarmatians and Alans, together with a host of other Germanic groups: Rugi, Heruli and Suevi amongst others.[15] The Huns' moves west onto the Hungarian Plain (where they seem to have established themselves around the river Theiss) had been accompanied, therefore, by the subjugation of many peoples.

Secondly, the Huns themselves underwent a process of political centralization. Ammianus reports that they had no single overall leader in the 370s (31.2.7), and, on a visit to them in 412, Olympiodorus encountered a number of autonomous Hunnic kings (fr. 19), one of whom was known as 'first among the kings of the Huns'. The Byzantine historian Priscus reports a similar phenomenon among another set of contemporary nomads, the Akatziri (fr. 11.2, p. 258). The Akatziri were divided into a number of groups ruled by largely independent chiefs who had, nevertheless, a developed system of internal ranking.[16] Only 30 years after Olympiodorus' visit, however, a single dynasty had achieved a monopoly of political power. The Hunnic king Rua passed on power to his two nephews, Attila and Bleda, and there is no mention of any other, even semi-autonomous, Hunnic kings. Attila's lifetime saw further change. He originally shared power with his brother Bleda, an arrangement which seems to mimic the distribution of power in the previous generation,

[15] Jordanes *Getica* 50. 259ff. See further Pohl, 1980.

[16] Maenchen-Helfen, 1973, 12–13 discounts Ammianus, but see my Afterword in Thompson, 1995 with refs. Nomad power structures: e.g. Cribb, 1991, ch. 4.

where two of the brothers' uncles, Octar and Ruga, had ruled jointly (Jordanes *Getica* 180). Eventually, however, Attila murdered Bleda to rule alone, and, after his own death, political competition was confined to Attila's direct descendants (his sons) with no further participation of collaterals (nephews).

These political transformations were matched by changes in the economic basis of Hunnic society. The Huns were no longer simple Steppe nomads. We know, for instance, that they exploited the agricultural surpluses of their subject peoples (Priscus fr. 49). By definition, nomadic economies require exchange with agriculturalists to acquire foodstuffs (particularly grain) and other items not readily produced by stock rearing. By the time of Attila, these necessary exchanges were taking the form of forced levies. Likewise, the military component of their lifestyles had increased dramatically. Raiding, especially stock rustling, had probably always been a useful source of extra income. By *c.*450, warfare had become a much more valuable form of activity for the Huns than it ever could have been in the depths of the Eurasian Steppes. This was the result of both proximity to the rich Roman Empire, and the much-enhanced war machine which was created by drafting in the manpower of the Huns' conquered subjects. At first, Hunnic troops served a succession of imperial regimes as mercenaries. By the 430s, however, Hunnic power had so increased that war could now be waged independently of, and, indeed, against the Roman state. In this new context, warfare still retained its economic function. The demands and treaties of the Huns in the period of Attila show that not only looting but also the extraction of tribute – protection money – was its central purpose. At the height of his success in 447, Attila received from the Byzantines a single payment of 6,000 pounds of gold, and the promise of further annual tributes of 2,100 pounds.[17]

The effects of all this are clear in the archaeological 'record'. The finds of Attila's time are conspicuous for their richness: everything from gem-encrusted jewellery to gold worked saddlery and bows. Political centralization among the Huns, indeed, could probably not have happened without the wealth extracted from the Roman Empire. Otherwise, no single leader would have been able to attract sufficient support to overturn the established political order. Progressive Hunnic empire-building thus provides the basic context for the history of those Goths who stayed north of the Danube after 376.

[17] See generally, Maenchen-Helfen, 1973, 94ff; Thompson, 1995, chs 4–7. On nomad economics, Khazanov, 1984.

(i) Goths and Huns

As with Gothic origins (chapter 2), modern discussions of the fortunes of the Goths under Hunnic rule have been dominated by the *Getica* of Jordanes. Once again, this unique text purports to provide a coherent narrative of events which are otherwise only spasmodically illuminated. From the relevant passage (*Getica* 48: 246–52), there emerges a clear picture of an ancient royal family, the Amals, which maintained its control over all those Goths who had been conquered by the Huns. Ermenaric was an Amal, it is claimed, and the text and Amal genealogy together portray the descent of power in the Hunnic period through two branches of the family: one stemming from Ermenaric himself, the other his brother Vultuulf. Not without trauma (the death in battle of three kings and a 40-year interregnum), control passed, in the time of Attila, to three Amal brothers: Valamer, Thiudimer and Vidimer. These brothers were the great-great-great-nephews of Ermenaric (cf. table 1). But the *Getica*'s picture of the Goths under Hunnic dominion is highly misleading.

Above all, it displays a tunnel vision of the most dramatic kind. By the *Getica*'s account, the Amal-led Gothic group maintained its existence from the fourth century throughout the period of Hunnic domination, before going on to establish a successor kingdom to the Roman Empire in Italy at the end of the fifth. This, however, is deceptive. The Amal-led group, or most of it, did indeed go on to Italy, but formed only one part of the much larger Gothic group – usually known as the Ostrogoths – which established the new kingdom. The latter was put together in the Roman Balkans only in the 470s and 480s, after the collapse of Attila's Empire (chapter 5).

Nor was this Amal-led group of Goths, contrary to the *Getica*'s implication, the only Gothic force to have been incorporated into Attila's Empire. It was only one of at least six and possibly seven Gothic groups who, definitely or probably, experienced Hunnic domination.

1 One group of Goths was detached from Hunnic hegemony by Roman military action in Pannonia and resettled in Thrace in 421 or 427 (Theophanes *AM* 5931: 94 De Boor). They were possibly the ancestors of group 5 (see below p. 127).
2 Valamer's Amal-led group established their independence of the Huns in the mid-450s.
3 A Gothic king Bigelis – whose following seems entirely unrelated to the Amal group – unsuccessfully invaded the eastern Roman

Empire somewhere between 466 and 471 (Jordanes *Romana* 336).

4 Still more Goths were to be found in the train of Dengizich, son of Attila, who invaded the Empire in the late 460s (Priscus fr. 49).

5 By *c.*470, a further large group of Goths had established itself in Thrace as favoured allies (*foederati*) of the eastern Roman Empire. They were just as numerous as Valamer's Goths (see p. 152).

At least two other Gothic groups had also established themselves at some point close to the Black Sea.

6 The Tetraxitae of the Cimmerian Bosphorus (Procopius *Wars* 8.4.9ff).

7 The Goths of Dory, established in the mountains of the south-western Crimea (Procopius *Buildings* 3.7.13).

The *Getica*'s history of the Goths under Hunnic domination is thus hugely selective. Reflecting the dynastic bias of Theoderic, the Amal king of Italy for whom its Cassiodorian model was written, it tells the story only of the particular group from whom this dynasty emerged. There were at least six others whom it completely ignores. The *Getica*'s monolithic vision of the history of the Goths under Hunnic domination – total conquest followed by total re-emergence – must, therefore, be rejected.

Indeed, just as four Gothic groups are known to have fled from the Huns into the Roman Empire at three different moments (376, 386, 405/6), so is it extremely likely that the other known Gothic groups who remained north of the Danube in the Hunnic orbit – six in all – were not conquered by the Huns at one fell swoop. As we have seen, the Gothic world of the fourth century comprised several independent kingdoms rather than one big one, and the Hunnic invasions took 30 years, rather than one, to engulf eastern and central Europe. And given that we hear of two of these groups (5 and 6) only in the works of the sixth-century historian Procopius, there is also every chance that there had been other Gothic groups of whom we are completely ignorant.

Some Goths may not have come fully under Hunnic sway at all. The Crimean peninsula and adjacent lands around the Sea of Azov fell outside the fourth-century domains of the Černjachov culture. They have turned up archaeological evidence of a Gothic presence only from the fifth century onwards.[18] Our two groups of Pontic Goths –

[18] Kazanski, 1991, 111ff; see further p. 118.

the Tetraxitae and the Goths of Dory – may well have originally taken over these lands, therefore, as refuges from the Huns. In the sixth century, the Tetraxitae used their geographical isolation to maintain a virtual independence of a later set of nomadic neighbours, the Utigurs (Procopius *Wars* 8.5.15 ff).

The point can be generalized. The Hunnic Empire was in large measure a rule over peoples. It possessed little bureaucracy or governmental machinery, so that not all of the groups formally under its dominion faced the same degree of interference and control. Amongst other things, sheer distance from Hunnic core areas (by the 420s, the Great Hungarian Plain) will have increased the likelihood that any particular subject group would have, in practice, enjoyed virtual autonomy. In the analogous sixth-century nomadic Avar Empire, for instance, dominion over subjects ebbed and flowed. Slavs, above all, were difficult to control because of their tendency to occupy forested uplands.[19] Virtually autonomous Pontic Gothic groups would fit such a pattern, since the Crimea is separated from the Hungarian Plain by 1,000 km and the Carpathian mountains. Something of the same is also suggested by the varying fates of the Gothic groups under Hunnic control. As early as the 420s, the east Romans detached one group of their Gothic subjects from the Huns' dominion (group 1).[20] Valamer's Goths (group 2) asserted their independence only in the 450s, however, and other Goths were still firmly under Hunnic sway a decade later (group 3). These different moments of escape underline the contingent nature of Hunnic rule. They perhaps also reflect different degrees of Hunnic dominion.

At most, then, the *Getica* describes the history of no more than one Gothic group – that eventually led by Valamer – of the several who remained north of the Danube after *c.* AD 400. Even given such a limited significance, however, the passage still cannot be taken at face value.

(ii) The Goths of Valamer

The passage opens by describing how, after the death of Ermenaric and the coincident Hunnic conquest of the Goths, the same royal family continued to rule the now subdued Goths. The king was one Vinitharius, whom the *Getica*'s genealogy of the Amal family of

[19] Cf. Avar control of the Slavs: Whitby, 1988, 169ff.

[20] Jordanes *Getica* 166, Marcellinus Comes s.a. 427 (= *CM* 2, 76), with Croke, 1977. This may have something to do with the Thracian Goths: below p. 127.

Theoderic casts as Ermenaric's great-nephew (table 1). Vinitharius was in the first place a subordinate of the Hunnic king Balamber, but, after an unspecified time, rejected Hunnic control. Balamber refused to accept this assertion of independence, however, and, with the help of more Goths under Gesimund, a son of Hunimund, killed Vinitharius. Balamber then married Vinitharius' granddaughter Vadamerca. The dead Vinitharius was succeeded by Ermenaric's son Hunimund, and he in turn by his son, Thorismund. Thorismund died fighting Gepids in the second year of his reign. Unable to bear Hunnic hegemony, Thorismund's son Beremund fled west to Gaul. Meanwhile, the Goths mourned Thorismund's death so deeply that no other king was appointed for 40 years. Finally, Valamer became king with the help of his two brothers, Thiudimer and Vidimer. These three brothers were sons of Vandalarius, and grandsons of Vinitharius. At first, Valamer ruled within Attila's continuing hegemony, but then re-established Gothic independence after the latter's death.

While working with, I believe, genuine materials, the historian who originally put this passage together (probably Cassiodorus) made two major errors. First, he knew Ammianus' account of Ermenaric and his successors (AM 31.3.1–3), and mistakenly equated the Vinitharius who appears there with the Vithimer mentioned by Ammianus (above p. 100). This made him think that the events of this passage covered the entire period from Ermenaric (fl. *c.*370) to Valamir (fl. 450). He adjusted their chronology accordingly, adding the 40-year interregnum between Thorismund and Valamer to make the events fit the time span. Amongst other things, this generated an unresolved problem of why Gesimund son of Hunimund should have helped Balamber defeat and kill Vinitharius, only for Hunimund himself to succeed the dead king. Secondly, writing in Ostrogothic Italy, the author could not conceive of circumstances where one Gothic leader might have fought another. He thus failed to recognize that the 'Balamber' who appears in some of the events was not a king of the Huns, but actually the Gothic leader Valamer himself. What this passage of the *Getica* sees as events covering the entire period *c.*370 to 450, should all, on the basis of Valamer's participation in them, be placed in *c.*450.

Taken together, they describe not Ermenaric's successors, but how Valamer first consolidated his hold over his followers. Rather than inheriting an Amal pre-eminence, which had supposedly remained undiminished through a 40-year interregnum, Valamer overcame a number of rival Gothic dynasties. That of Vinitharius was extinguished by direct military action. Valamer was presumably attempting to conciliate that leader's followers when he married Vinitharius' granddaughter, Vadamerca. This marriage explains why Vinitharius appears where he does in the Amal genealogy (table 1). He was indeed Theoderic's great-grandfather, but ultimately through a maternal, not paternal, line as the genealogy would suggest. Several branches of a third dynasty, that of Hunimund, also appear. Both Hunimund and his son Thorismud would seem to have ruled independently of Valamer, but Gesimund, a second son of Hunimund, explicitly accepted Amal hegemony, presumably after his father's and brother's deaths. A letter of the *Variae* provides separate confirmation that Gesimund had been a separate Gothic king who deliberately abandoned his claims in favour of the Amal family (8.9.8, where the name is spelled 'Gensemund'). Thus Thorismund's son Beremund (another member of the dynasty, and hence another rival for Valamer) probably chose to flee, not because he was fed up with Hunnic dominion, as the *Getica* claims, but because he could not resist growing Amal power.

Instead of an Amal family with unique prestige in *c.*450, therefore, we should envisage a series of competing Gothic groups with their own dynastic lines. Valamer united them partly by military action (Vinitharius killed, Beremud forced to flee), and partly by conciliation (Gensemund accepting Amal rule, Vadamerca an Amal marriage). Rewritten in this way, Valamer's role as Gothic king comes to resemble that of an equally if not more famous contemporary, Clovis, king of the Franks (Gregory of Tours, *HF* 2.40ff). His reign likewise involved destroying the independence of previously separate Frankish ruling lines.[21]

There is no reason to think that the Amal dynasty had ever held such pre-eminent power before Valamer's success. Simply to have competed in these dynastic struggles, it must have been an important family. There is no sign, however, that it had already previously produced a line of kings as the *Getica* maintains. The only king named in the upper reaches of the genealogy whose existence finds independent confirmation elsewhere is Ermenaric. But Ermenaric's name has been falsely added to Amal history from the text of Ammianus (pp. 53ff). Many of the other names are not only unconfirmed in other sources (which, given the gaps in our source material, would not be a great objection), but are arguably, or definitely, of legendary origin. Name-giving (eponymous) kings and

[21] This passage has long been recognized as problematic. For more detailed argument with full refs, see Heather, 1989.

legendary heroes (such as Amal, Ostrogotha, Athal, Hunuil, Hisarnis and Gapt/Gaut) cannot be taken as historical kings, and, without them, the Amal pedigree looks very thin.[22] Given too that information in the *Getica* actually shows Valamer creating rather than inheriting his dominion, nothing suggests that the dynasty had ever previously exercised power on this scale.

Further questions follow. When and where did Valamer unite these Goths? It must have been *c.*450, but did it precede or follow Attila's death (453) and the collapse of the Hunnic Empire? Two sources suggest that Valamer was pre-eminent before Attila's death, but neither inspires much confidence.[23] Of more disinterested sources, Theophanes gives Valamer a leading role only in the time of Attila's sons (*AM* 5977: 131 de Boor). Likewise, a number of smaller Gothic groups under individual leaders – the situation before Valamer – would have been easier for the Huns to control, and the Huns do seem to have been suspicious of leaders with too great a personal following. When Attila conquered the Akatziri, for instance, the existing overall leader was deposed and Attila's son set up in his place (Priscus fr. 11.2). Goths in a Hun-led force of the 460s, similarly, retained their own lower-level leaders, but did not operate as a coherent sub-unit with their own Gothic commander (Priscus fr. 49). Valamer's activities are perhaps more likely to have followed Attila's death, therefore, but the evidence is not conclusive.

As to geography, according to the *Getica*, Valamer's Goths moved west of the Carpathians only when they received lands in Pannonia (modern Hungary west of the middle Danube) from the emperor Marcian (451–7). This followed the defeat of the Huns at the battle of the Nedao (453/4), which had, according to Jordanes, led the Huns to abandon their lands around the Danube in favour of the northern shores of the Black Sea (263–4). The *Getica* thus envisages Valamer's Goths moving west into a vacuum created by the Huns' departure. Again, however, the account is problematic. At least some Huns remained in the Danubian region until the mid-460s, and many Goths had moved out of Russia long before. One group of Goths, detached by Roman action from Hunnic control in the 420s, had already been

[22] Heather, 1989 with refs.

[23] Damascius = Photius *Bibliotheca* 242.64 mentions his special relationship with Attila incidentally, in a passage devoted to the light which Valamer's body used to emit! The second is Jordanes (*Getica* 38.199–200, 48.252–3; cf. *Romana* 331), but his word on matters to do with the Amal dynasty can never be conclusive.

settled by the Huns in Pannonia. In the 440s, Attila again forced both halves of the Empire formally to cede him parts of Pannonia, events perhaps reflected in a rich Hunnic burial recently found at Pannonhalma, within the bounds of the old Roman province.[24] Valamer's Goths could have already been settled in Pannonia by the Huns themselves, therefore, forming, with other subject groups, a protective ring around central Hunnic lands on the middle Theiss (p. 104). If so, the Goths' contacts with Marcian would have concerned Roman recognition for lands the Goths already held. By implication, of course, this would also situate Valamer's unification of the Goths in the middle Danubian region.

Despite its fragmentary nature, and the many problems of the *Getica*'s account, the surviving literary evidence allows us to reconstruct something of the variety of experience of the different Gothic groups caught up in the *Hunnensturm*. Some are likely to have been conquered in or shortly after 376, suffered considerable Hunnic interference in their internal social and political structures (particularly the suppression of important group leaders), and been resettled by the Huns according to the latter's needs. These groups no doubt also endured regular Hunnic exploitation of their agricultural surpluses and military manpower. The Goths still under the control of Dengizich in the late 460s (group 3) perhaps represent this end of the spectrum. Others were probably subdued only in the fifth century, were perhaps less regularly exploited, and, with or without Roman help, escaped more quickly. Their internal political structures had perhaps also been interfered with less, although this is far from certain, even in the case of the Amal-led Pannonian Goths. Some Goths, particularly those finding refuge on the shores of the Pontus, may even have escaped conquest altogether.

(iii) The archaeological evidence

Our general understanding of this variety of Gothic experience can be extended by a review of the archaeological evidence from central and eastern Europe for the period *c.*375–450. Its ability to answer more precise questions is currently limited, however, by a dispute over what is, for our purposes, a central question. Both sides to the argument agree that a later phase of the Černjachov culture, phase D, can be identified which overlaps in some measure with the Hunnic invasions. Both also agree that phase D shows itself in remains both from the outlying Černjachov groups on the Steppe and the upper Dniester, as

[24] Maenchen-Helfen, 108ff, cf. Tomka, 1986.

well as in those from the main homogeneous core of cemeteries in the forest Steppe zone of the Ukraine (Danceny and Malaechty), Moldavia (Bîrlad Valea-Seacă and Izvoare), Muntenia (Pietroasele, Tîrgsor and Independenţa) and Transylvania (Sîntana de Mureş and Tîrgu Mureş) (figure 4.4). Beyond these general points of agreement, however, there are currently two alternative chronologies on offer for phase D of the Černjachov culture.

According to the shorter chronology, the cultural unity wrought by the Goths north of the Black Sea was fundamentally broken by *c.* AD 400. The subsequent survival and continued transformation of Černjachov forms in certain areas peripheral to the fourth century culture (Crimea, the Kuban and the Caucasus) is, it is argued, not to the point. The Černjachov culture had come to an end, and its main legacy to the fifth century lies not in such fragmentary offshoots, but in clearly marked contributions to fifth-century cultural assemblages of middle Danubian area (see below). Amongst other things, proponents of this line of argument have claimed that the archaeological evidence proves that Jordanes is wrong to envisage Goths continuing to occupy lands east of the Carpathians until after the death of Attila.

In the longer chronology, argued for particularly by Kazanski, these Černjachov contributions to central European cultural horizons become an argument that the Černjachov culture was itself still in existence in the fifth century. In his view, these visible influences mark a process of continuous exchange between central and eastern Europe, west and east of the Carpathians, occurring under the auspices of the Hunnic Empire. For Kazanski, the main Černjachov cemeteries continued in use well into the fifth century, the culture occupying much the same geographical spread of territory as it had in the fourth. He would identify not only Černjachov phase D1, but also D1b and D2, taking us down to *c.*450 and the death of Attila. Only at this point did the culture finally break up. Kazanski would thus argue that Jordanes' account of numerous Goths surviving east of the Carpathians down to *c.*450 is substantially correct.[25]

The author of the present volume is not an archaeologist, and not competent to venture an opinion on a technical disagreement between well-informed specialists. But both lines of argument focus strongly on an historical agenda derived from the deeply untrustworthy account of Jordanes. In particular, both chronologies are arranged around the

[25] Shorter: Bierbrauer, 1991, 23–5, after Tejral, 1986, 1988. Longer: Kazanski and Legoux, 1988; Kazanski, 1991.

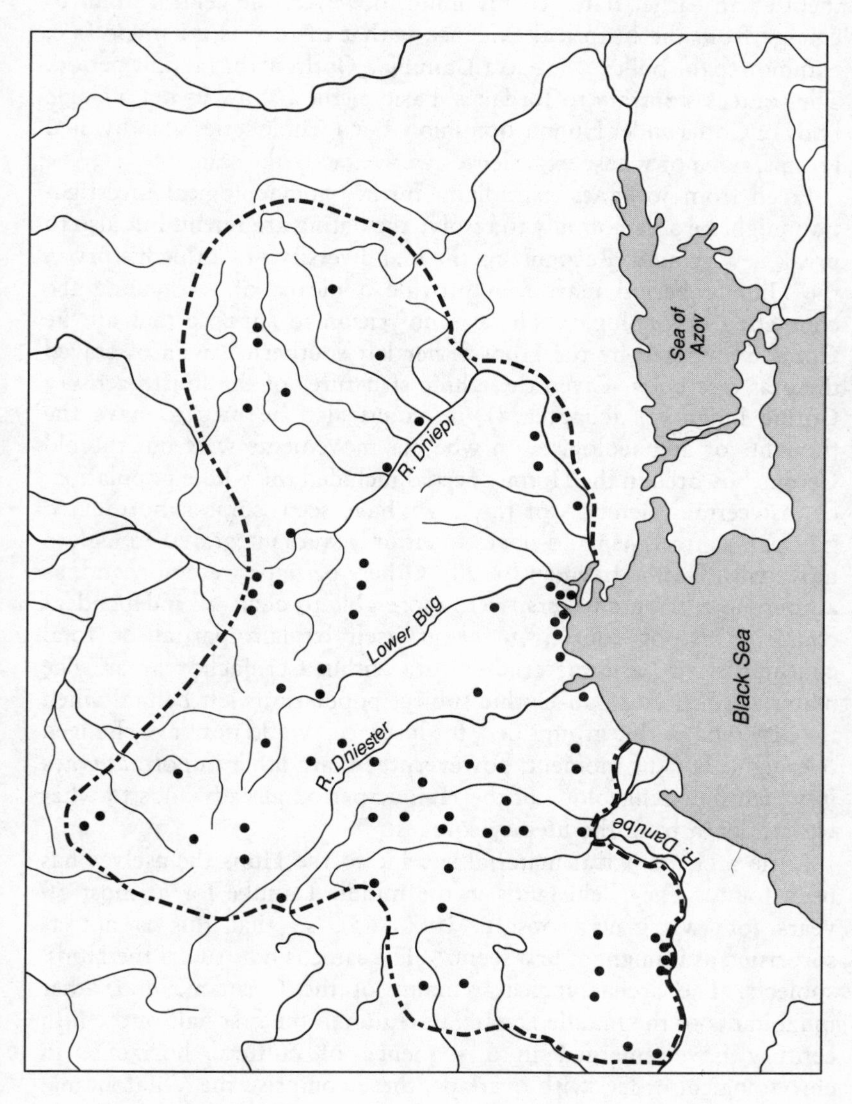

Figure 4.4 Find spots of Černjachov Phase D materials

overall question of whether those Goths who did not flee into the Roman Empire in 376 stayed east of the Carpathians until 450, or moved west of them at an earlier date. To my mind, however, the central point to emerge from the historical evidence is that there was no *single* fate, common to the bulk of the extra-Danubian Goths in the Hunnic period. The sources, contrary to Jordanes' basic picture, show us not a single body of Goths under Hunnic dominion, but a whole series of individual groups, none of whose experiences were exactly the same.

Freed from Jordanes' paradigm, further archaeological investigation might be able not only to resolve the dating argument, but also to break new ground. Recognizing the real diversity of Gothic history in the Hunnic period may even provide a means of reconciling the competing chronologies. There is no reason to suppose that all the Goths dominated by the Huns either left southern Russia or stayed there as one body. Given the ethnic structures of the fourth-century Gothic kingdoms (chapter 3), it would also be nice to have the thoughts of archaeologists on whether movements west out the old Černjachov area in the Hunnic period included the whole population, or just certain elements of it. As we have seen, some subordinated groups – as freedmen and slaves – certainly were integrated enough to move with Gothic freemen (p. 90). Others perhaps were not, and, as autonomous tribute payers, were more able to chart an independent course. This, of course, might in itself explain partial or total continuities of basic material culture within Černjachov areas. The material culture of non-Gothic subject populations left behind when the different Gothic groups fled, for instance, would not have changed overnight. For the moment, however, there are other important ways in which the archaeology of the Hunnic period already adds to what we can learn from the literary sources.

Little archaeological material specific to the Huns themselves has been found. They held lands in the middle Danube for at most 50 years (or two generations: *c*.410/20–65), so that this is not as surprising as it might at first seem.[26] The same is not true of the Huns' subjects. The archaeological remains of the Germanic and other inhabitants of the middle Danubian region in the first half of the fifth century have emerged in a sequence of cultural horizons. In chronological order, with overlaps, these comprise the Villafontana, Untersiebenbrunn and Domolospuszta/Bacsordas horizons.[27] Three

[26] Latest survey: Bona, 1991.

[27] On the Danubian style, see Kazanski, 1991, 66–76, 100–3; Bierbrauer, 1980; Tejral, 1986, 1988.

main features of these finds have particular historical importance. First, they demonstrate the emergence, west of the Carpathians, of the so-called 'Danubian style', known from a whole series of cemeteries typically producing inhumation rather than cremation burials. The Danubian style consists of a number of characteristic objects (large brooches with semi-circular heads, plate buckles, earnings with polyhedric pendants and gold necklaces), characteristic weapons (saddles decorated with metal appliques, long straight swords suitable for cavalry use and particular kinds of arrow), and some new burial habits (cranial deformation and the deposition in burials of broken metallic mirrors). These objects and habits appear in different combinations in various fifth-century burials from the region. A particularly fine example is the double, male and female, burial from Untersiebenbrunn in Austria.

From the literary sources, we know that many different Germanic and other groups occupied this area under Hunnic hegemony. The Danubian style, however, is common to the entire region, and it is quite impossible to distinguish the different subject groups of the Huns on the basis of the archaeological evidence. Ethnic differences may have been signalled in ways which cannot now be read, but the first half of the fifth century is marked by the building of a broad material cultural uniformity across the middle Danubian region. Given that this uniformity manifests itself in rich burials, it is presumably elite Hunnic court culture which is being mirrored in these remains. The Hunnic Empire thus generated a certain unity across its domain.

Secondly, while the majority of burials in the cemeteries contain few grave goods, or none at all, a minority are very richly endowed. These have produced a vast array of gold fittings and ornamentation, particularly the garnet-encrusted jewellery which became the mark of elites in the late- and post-Roman periods. The fifth-century horizons, indeed, are all named after such burials, and their general distribution is illustrated on figure 4.5. As has often been argued, the gold wealth of these burials demonstrates that not only the Huns themselves, but also elites among the Huns' various subjects shared in the wealth generated by the predatory activities of the Hunnic Empire. The gold jewellery may well represent reworked Roman coin and bullion, and when Priscus visited Attila, he came across many prominent courtiers who, to judge by their names, were not themselves Huns.[28] The Hunnic Empire thus

[28] Thompson, 1995, ch. 5.

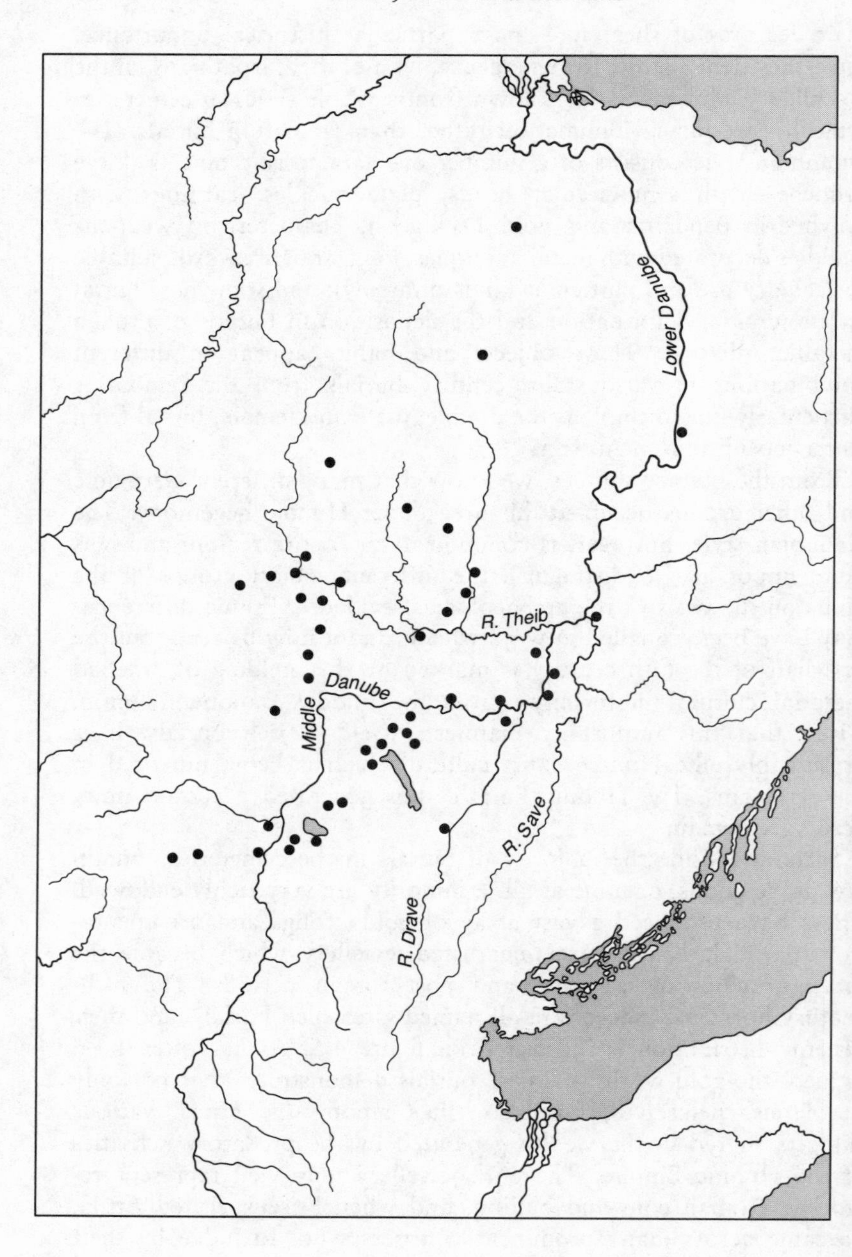

Figure 4.5 Rich burials of the Hunnic period in the Middle Danubian region

operated not only on the basis of intimidating its subjects, but also by redistributing to them some of the profits of its warfare.

The third point follows from what we have already observed, in another context, of the social significance of ostentatious burial. What was true of the second century might be equally true of the fifth. Rich burials in the Germanic world would appear to be a sign of social upheaval, in that they seem to represent would-be elites engaged in a process of competitive display (chapter 3). The broader context suggests that this might also be true of the rich burials of the fifth-century middle Danube. Take, for instance, the Goths. As we have seen, the Huns destroyed the hold of at least two established Gothic dynasties – those represented in *c.*370 by Athanaric and Ermenaric – and seem generally to have suppressed the appearance of pre-eminent overall leaders. New, post-Hunnic dynasts, such as Valamer, had to establish their position by shouldering aside, in a mixture of violence and conciliation, a series of rivals. There is no reason to suppose that such conditions will have applied just to the Goths. In the uncertain political conditions created by the Huns, competitive burial display would have been an entirely appropriate strategy for a whole series of ambitious dynasts to adopt.

As the evolution of the Danubian style underlines, the Hunnic Empire revolutionized the lives of its subjects. The wealth was distributed, no doubt, to and through any of their subjects whom they considered particularly loyal. These individuals may or may not have been those who had previously dominated their respective groups. A whole class of leaders could be created by such manipulations, owing a great deal to their Hunnic overlords. As the struggles of Valamer with the dynasties of Vinitharius and Hunimund demonstrate, and as the burials perhaps reflect, this was a highly competitive era. The Huns destroyed the conditions under which old elites had flourished and offered opportunities for new ones to distinguish themselves. They also set new standards in the display of elite status which, as the undifferentiable rich burials show, were accepted throughout their Empire. The fact that we are now unable, on the basis of these particular archaeological remains, to tell the different subject groups apart, does not mean, however, that contemporaries had lost all sense of difference. On the contrary, after the death of Attila, old divides resurfaced, utterly to extinguish Hunnic power north of the Danube.

C. The End of the Huns

The collapse of Hunnic power after Attila's death (453) was even more dramatic than its rise. Late in the 460s, the two surviving sons of Attila, Dengizich and Hernac, sought permission to resettle their followers within the bounds of the Roman state. They had presumably concluded that they could no longer maintain their independence north of the Danube. In the ensuing fighting, Dengizich was killed and his following dispersed. Hernac eventually came to a peaceful accommodation with Constantinople which saw his followers establish themselves south of the Danube in the Dobrudja (Jordanes *Getica* 266). Within 20 years of Attila's death, the mighty Huns had ceased to exist as an independent force in the non-Roman world.[29]

The general processes underlying this collapse are clear. The Hunnic Empire was created by a combination of centralization among the Huns and the conquest of numerous subject peoples. In the era of its collapse, the cycle went into reverse. Political unity among the core Hunnic tribes fragmented, and the subject peoples reasserted their independence. Attila's last years had seen less than totally successful campaigns in Gaul (451) and Italy (452). In these circumstances, his unexpected death – caused by an excess of alcohol on his latest wedding night – provided a quick acting catalyst. As the *Getica* describes it, Attila's death let loose a struggle for power among his sons, which in turn allowed different subject peoples, particularly the Gepids under Ardaric, to break their bonds. These struggles culminated in a great battle on the river Nedao (unidentified, but placed by Jordanes somewhere in Pannonia), in which one of Attila's sons, Ellac, was killed, and the Gepids reasserted their political independence. As a result, the Huns moved east out of the middle Danubian region, returning to their old homes north of the Black Sea. This in turn allowed the Huns' other subjects, such as Valamer's Goths, to regain their freedom too (259–64).

Some features of this account require qualification. The idea that the Huns suddenly moved out the middle Danube in the mid-450s is problematic. No source directly contradicts Jordanes, but the Huns did remain a force in the Danubian region until the late 460s. At that point, as we have seen, they launched attacks across the lower Danube into the Roman Empire, and in the mid-450s and early 460s, had

[29] Secondary accounts: Macartney, 1934; Maenchen-Helfen, 1973, 165ff; Thompson, 1995, ch. 7.

twice intervened west of the Carpathians against the Goths of Valamer (Priscus fr. 48; Jordanes *Getica* 268–9, 272–3). If defeat at the Nedao did cause them to move off the Great Hungarian Plain, then, the Huns probably moved no further away than the lower Danube. Nor did the Nedao suddenly free all of the Huns' subjects. Indeed, as late as Dengizich's last attack on the Roman Empire in 467, there were still some subject Goths in his train (Priscus fr. 49). Jordanes also describes how he had mobilized a variety of subjects – Ultzinzures, Angisciri, Bittugures and Bardores – earlier in the decade for an attack on Valamer (*Getica* 272). None of this denies that the Nedao was a turning-point, but does indicate that the Huns' subjects were not all set free, nor Hunnic power extinguished, in one fell swoop.

Turning to the Goths, it is hardly surprising to find, once again, a considerable variety of experience. Thanks to Jordanes, we know most about the Pannonian Goths, now successfully united behind the standard of Valamer. The *Getica* records two bouts of warfare between this group and the Huns. In the first, the sons of Attila attacked Valamer's Goths as 'fugitive slaves', but were defeated. News of the Gothic victory, we are told, arrived on the day that Valamer's nephew and future successor, Theoderic the Great, was born, an event which other sources allow us to date to *c*.453/4. More or less at the same time as the Gepids were freeing themselves at the Nedao, then, Valamer's Goths fought off a first Hunnic attempt to reassert hegemony.[30] But Valamer's unification of the Pannonian Goths may also have been a prerequisite for success, in that it created a Gothic force strong enough to resist the Huns. Likewise, by the time that the Huns attacked Valamer's Goths, their own civil wars and the success of the Gepids had substantially weakened their power. The renewed independence of Valamer's Goths was thus a process rather than an event. Divisions among the Huns, defeat by the Gepids, and Gothic unification altered the balance of power, so that when it came to a specific test of strength, the Goths could now prevail. The changing balance of power is even more obvious in a second confrontation of the early 460s. On this occasion, Attila's son Dengizich was not trying to reassert Hunnic hegemony, but hold in check Gothic expansion. Valamer had just attacked a Pannonian group called the Sadagis (*Getica* 272). Again, the Huns were defeated.

But if Valamer threw off Hunnic dominion in the 450s, other Goths did not. Others led by Bigelis attempted to move into the Roman orbit

[30] *Getica* 268–9, with Heather, 1991, 246 n.15 on the date.

in the later 460s (his operations can only be dated broadly between 466 and 471.[31] It is a not unreasonable guess that these Goths had taken the always risky step of moving across the Roman frontier as part of an attempt to escape Hunnic control. Of still other Goths, we are better informed. When Dengizich launched himself for the last time against the Roman Empire in the late 460s, he still retained some Gothic subjects. It is probably no coincidence that these Goths did not have their own overall leader (Priscus fr. 49). They had not managed to create a unified front to resist Hunnic domination, perhaps because Dengizich had never given them the opportunity.

The overturning of Hunnic hegemony in central Europe was thus no simple matter. Valamer's Goths escaped relatively quickly after the death of Attila, others only a decade later, and some not at all. Likewise, there may have been other Gothic groups about whom we hear nothing, and it is quite unclear whether the Pontic Goths had ever been fully subjugated by the Huns at all. With this variety of experience in mind, and the likelihood that the Huns had other Gothic subjects of whom we never hear, we must turn our attention to one last, and highly intriguing problem. What were the origins of a large Gothic group whom the East Roman imperial authorities had established in Thrace sometime before *c*.470?

By *c*.470, these Thracian Goths occupied a very privileged position within the eastern Empire. Formally recognized as allies (Lat. *foederati*), they were closely associated with the imperial general and politician, Aspar, who was murdered on the orders of the Emperor Leo in 471. This act prompted them to rebel, and it is the reporting of this rebellion which provides us with our first explicit reference to their existence.[32] When and how had the Thracian Goths come to occupy their very comfortable niche within the body politic of the East Roman state?

The collapse of the Hunnic Empire is one possible context. In the 450s, many peoples had thrown off Hunnic dominion, and the final crisis of the Hunnic Empire brought more Goths – those still under the control of Dengizich and the group led by Bigelis – into the eastern Empire in the later 460s. Both these sets of Goths met military resistance, rather than a favourable welcome. It remains possible, however, first, that either or both contributed to the manpower of the Thracian Goths, and/or, secondly, that other Gothic groups, of whom we hear nothing, crossed the frontier by agreement in the same era to

31 Jordanes, *Romana* 336; cf. *PLRE* 2, 229.
32 See generally, Heather, 1991, 253–6.

be settled by the Roman state on more favourable terms.

It is worth emphasizing, however, that the Thracian Goths originally consisted of a number of separate groups under individual leaders, rather than a united force under a single king (chapter 5). There may be no need, therefore, to search for one single origin. While the break-up of the Hunnic Empire certainly provides one likely context, the groups who united in rebellion in 471 could have entered the Empire on a number of separate occasions. Indications of two kinds suggest that at least some Goths had settled in Thrace long before the collapse of Attila's Empire.

First, we have information about the military careers of important individual generals. This material seems to reflect a consistent involvement, in the earlier fifth century, of Goths in the army of Thrace. Anagastes, commanding general in Thrace in 469/70, for instance, had a father Arnegisclus who had himself occupied the same position in the 440s. Other Germanic-named officers (Ansila, Arintheus and Ariobindus) were his contemporaries. Of these, Ariobindus was the most distinguished. As *comes foederatorum*, he had commanded allied troops (*foederati*) in the Roman army in the early 420s, before being appointed supreme military commander (*MVM praesentalis*) in 434. Similarly, Fl. Plintha, a Goth and perhaps Aspar's father-in-law, was already an important commander in 418, and supreme commander between 419 and 438.[33]

Secondly, the chronicler Theophanes describes the way in which some Goths were transplanted by the Romans from Pannonia to Thrace in the 420s. The report is not without problems. Theophanes' dating methods mean that the event could have occurred in either 421 or 427, and a chronological error has crept into his report of the Goths' later departure from Thrace.[34] There is no reason, however, to doubt the basic information. Such a settlement might explain the appearance of Gothic officers, including a *comes foederatorum*, associated in part with Thrace from the 420s onwards. If at least some of the Thracian Goths had been part of the Empire since *c.*420, the special relationship they had forged with the Roman state by *c.*470 would also become readily explainable.

[33] Refs. as *PLRE* 2, 151 (Arnegisclus), 145–6 (Ariobindus), 892–3

[34] Theophanes *AM* 5931 (94 de Boor); cf. Procopius *Wars* 3.2.39–40 with Croke, 1977, 360. The Goths are said to have stayed in Thrace for 58 years, but no Gothic exodus is known in either 479 or 485. An emendation to 68 would solve the problem.

As the history of the Thracian Goths underlines, there is much that we do not know about the Goths in the Hunnic period. It could not be clearer, however, that Hunnic expansion marked a watershed in Gothic history. Traditional views of Gothic history in this period, taken directly from the *Getica* of Jordanes, suppose that two Gothic groups – Visigoths and Ostrogoths – already existed in southern Russia before the Hunnic invasions. The Huns merely pushed one group (the Visigoths) across the Roman frontier in 376, and conquered the other (the Ostrogoths). The reality was much more complicated and much more interesting.

The Huns took over 30 years to establish themselves at the heart of Europe. In the course of this period, numerous Gothic groups met varying fates. Some delayed conquest, or perhaps avoided it altogether, by establishing themselves in geographically protected niches in Transylvania or along the Pontic coast. Others were overwhelmed more quickly. But, however long it took, most, if not all, of the Goths who remained north of the Danube ended up under Hunnic control. The Huns' treatment of their various Gothic subjects varied considerably. This is best illustrated, perhaps, by marked differences in the ability of different Gothic groups to reassert their independence after Attila's death. For all, however, the Hunnic invasions had destroyed the prevailing pattern of life. Established political orders were overturned by Hunnic conquest and subsequent interference. Even among the Pannonian Goths, one of the first Gothic groups to throw off Hunnic dominion, an overall leadership had to be recreated via dynastic competition. The Goths' century-old tenure of lands north of the Black Sea was also destroyed. They either fled west of the Carpathians on their own initiative, or were deliberately resettled there by the Huns. Goths, who had been dominant north of the Black Sea in the fourth century, themselves became dominated. As Hunnic subjects, they became a source of agricultural produce and military manpower.

At the same time, at least four major Gothic groups (the Tervingi and Greuthungi of 376, Odotheus' Greuthungi of 386 and the Goths of Radagaisus in 405/6), had, at three different moments, decided that there was a greater chance of finding security and prosperity inside the Roman Empire, beyond reach of the Huns. In this they were matched by numerous other smaller groups and individuals. The Huns thus destroyed the Gothic world of the fourth century. More than that, whether fleeing from Hunnic hegemony before 410, or escaping it after 450, many of the Gothic groups caught up in these events sooner or later found themselves in unprecedentedly close contact with the Roman Empire. As we shall see in the next chapter, these contacts completed the revolution started by the Huns. The Hunnic invasions destroyed one political order in the Gothic world. The need to survive in the face of Roman imperial power generated another.

5

Goths and Romans: Remaking the Gothic World

The Migration Period set in motion by Hunnic expansion, inaugurated an unstable and highly dangerous period in Gothic history. Two waves of Gothic survivors, in a number of separate groups, eventually made their way into the Roman Empire, one before and one after the creation of Attila's Empire. The experience of co-existing with Roman power was to work yet further transformations. In broadest terms, it generated two new groupings, the Visigoths and Ostrogoths. These were larger and more coherent political units than anything that had previously existed in the Gothic world.

A. The Creation of the Visigoths c.376–418

This section takes up the story of the four major Gothic groups who, in the later fourth and early fifth centuries, before the creation of Attila's Hunnic Empire, decided to seek a new home inside the Roman Empire. As we have seen, they arrived on the frontier at three different moments. Some Tervingi and Greuthungi crossed the Danube in 376, more Greuthungi attempted to do so in 386, and still more Goths (not called either Tervingi or Greuthungi), under Radagaisus, invaded Italy in 405/6. By 418, the bulk of three of these groups had coalesced to create a new political unit: the Visigoths.

(i) War and peace on the Danube: 376–382

First to arrive were the Tervingi of Fritigern and Alavivus, and the Greuthungi led by Alatheus and Saphrax, who appeared on the Danube sometime in 376, appealing for asylum from the Huns. Imperial propagandists proclaimed that the Emperor Valens was overjoyed, seeing an opportunity both to expand his armed forces, and to fill the treasury by commuting the usual recruitment tax, normally exacted in the form of actual recruits, into a cash payment.[1] Nevertheless, after much discussion, Valens admitted only one of the two groups. The Tervingi were duly ferried across the Danube. The agreement probably included the stipulation that the Goths would accept the Emperor Valens' non-Nicene Christianity: a definition of faith broadly in line with the teachings of Ulfila.[2] All the remaining imperial troops in the region, however, were posted to keep the Greuthungi north of the river. The local Roman commander Lupicinus then attempted to disrupt the coherence even of the Tervingi. Inviting many of their leaders to dinner in Marcianople, he sprang a trap. Fritigern escaped only with difficulty, Alavivus is never heard of again. Not surprisingly, this intriguing episode sparked off a general revolt among the Goths (AM 31.4–5).

Ammianus implies that the trap was Lupicinus' misplaced initiative, and more generally portrays the Goths' revolt as the result of local incompetence and ill-will. In particular, he blames local commanders for making money out of Goths suffering from food shortages. Individual acts of exploitation surely did take place, but, to my mind, Ammianus' overall account does not quite ring true. A senior local commander (who had carefully referred the matter to Valens before admitting the Tervingi) is hardly likely to have attacked over dinner those whom he knew to be his Emperor's welcome allies. No doubt there was an element of local panic in the events, but hijacking important tribal leaders was a standard feature of Roman frontier policies for containing the build-up of dangerously large confederations.[3] I do not believe that Lupicinus would have acted so aggressively on his own initiative, and there is good reason to believe that Valens was much less pleased to see the arrival of the Goths on the Danube than his propagandists might have suggested.

At the moment the Goths approached the Danube, Valens was already engaged in armed confrontation with Persia over Armenia.

[1] AM 31.4.4; Eunapius fr. 42; Socrates *h.e.* 4.34; Sozomen *h.e.* 6.37.
[2] Heather, 1986.
[3] AM 21.4.1–5, 27.10.3, 29.4.2 ff, 30.1.18–21 (although note 29.6.5 for an authorized attack).

Most of his troops were committed to this theatre, and it took him two years to disentangle them for war in the Balkans (AM 26.4.6; 27.12; 29.1; 30.2). Policy towards the Goths was thus, at least in part, dictated by the non-availability of reinforcements for the Danube frontier. The Roman Empire had, over the centuries, resettled hundreds of thousands of immigrants within its borders, but only on its own terms. The established approach was to subdue them thoroughly first, militarily and politically, and then break them up into small groups which were spread widely over the map. These kinds of policies had been enforced from the early Empire down to the resettlement of Carpi at the turn of the fourth century. The degree of violence and harshness involved varied from case to case. In 376, the Empire was in no position to enforce such policies on the Goths, and probably had just enough troops in the Balkans to attempt to keep one of the two groups out. As soon as there was any trouble with the Tervingi, the troops excluding the Greuthungi had to be moved, and the latter immediately crossed the river. This suggests that the most the Roman authorities could hope for was to keep out one of the two groups. The Tervingi were admitted only because Valens had no other available option. Imperial ideology made it impossible, however, for an Emperor ever to admit that policy towards 'barbarians' had been dictated by events beyond his control. To maintain face, Valens' propaganda had no choice but to pretend that he was happy at the turn of events.[4]

This conclusion is of fundamental importance because much of the subsequent dynamic of Gotho–Roman affairs would be lost if it were thought that the Romans had entered voluntarily into their new relationship with the Goths. The Goths too were hesitant. The Tervingi had reached the decision to seek asylum inside the Roman Empire only after 'long deliberation' (AM 31.3.8), and were clearly suspicious of Roman motives and policy. Even after the Tervingi had been admitted, their leaders remained in contact with the excluded Greuthungi. Alavivus and Fritigern advanced only slowly from the Danube, because they knew that the Greuthungi had forced a crossing and wanted to give them time to catch up (AM 31.5.3–4). Although given preferential treatment, the Tervingi remained interested in at least the possibility of a united Gothic front against the Roman state.[5]

[4] Full discussion and references: Heather, 1991, 128–35; Cesa, 1994, 13ff. I here argue against the prevailing consensus.

[5] According to Eunapius (fr. 59), the Goths may have sworn an oath never to let any Roman blandishment divert them from overthrowing the Empire. Much was made of this by Thompson, 1963, but it is impossible to be certain of its veracity.

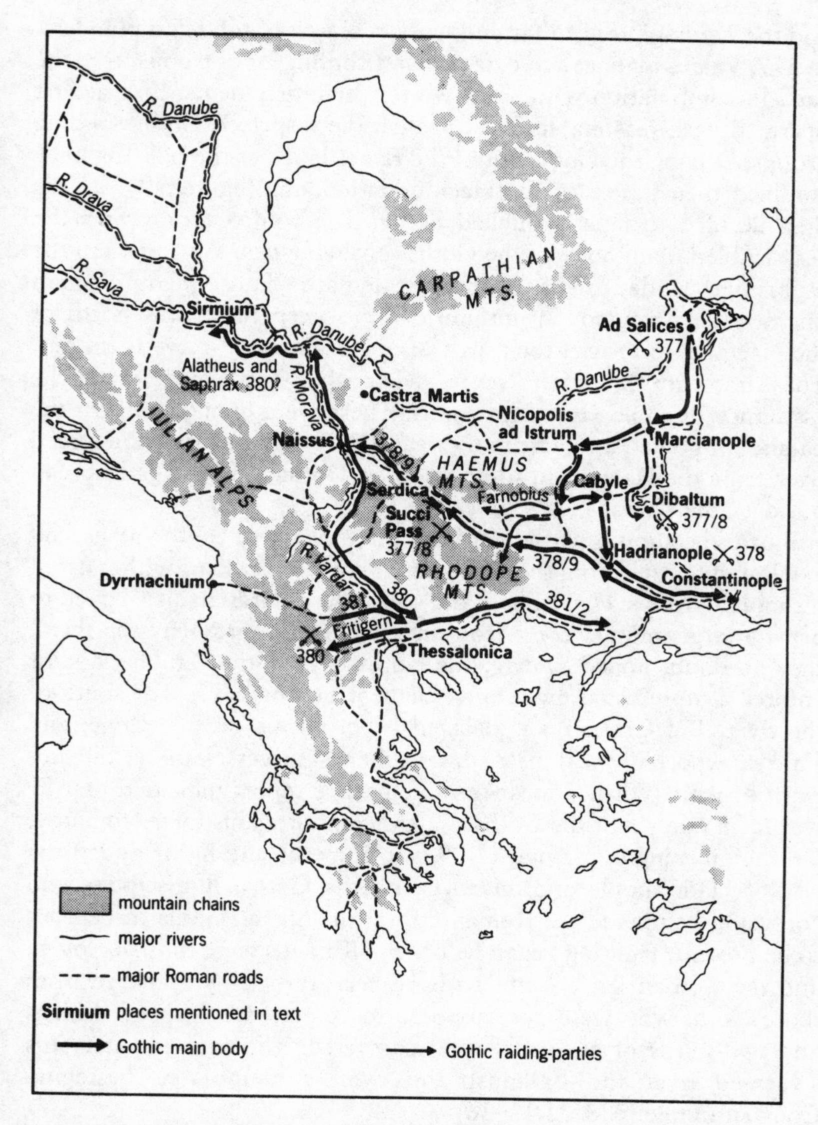

Figure 5.1 The Gothic War from Ad Salices *to the conclusion of peace, 377–382*

Immediately after the revolt, the Roman authorities could do little because of the shortage of available troops. Lupicinus was defeated outside Marcianople, and, for the remainder of 376 into the early part of 377, Gothic raiding parties, probably from both the Greuthungi and the Tervingi, ranged far and wide in search of food and plunder.[6] In 377, Valens managed to detach a first contingent of troops from the east. In combination with some western reinforcements, they at first operated with reasonable effect against the dispersed Gothic raiding groups. Driving the Goths out of the richer lands of the Balkans, they confined them north of the Haemus mountains (figure 5.1). It was then decided to fight a pitched battle. The confrontation with the reassembled main body of the Goths (probably near Ad Salices in the Dobrudja) ended in a bloody stalemate. Subsequent Roman operations attempted, in autumn 377, to keep the Goths north of the Haemus, to restrict their area of operations and starve them out. The stratagem failed, however, when the Goths negotiated the assistance of some Huns and Alans. These were enough to turn the balance of power, and, late in the year, the Roman troops were forced back from the Haemus in some disorder. Gothic raiders again spread out over the Balkans (AM 31.7–10).

By the beginning of the campaigning season of 378, Valens had extricated himself from the east, and entered the Balkans with most of his mobile troops. His nephew and co-Emperor Gratian also agreed to bring a large military force from the western Empire. Between them, they no doubt hoped to drive the Goths beyond the Danube, and/or enforce a more usual mode of settlement on any Goths left south of the river. But Gratian was delayed by problems on the Rhine, and Valens, reportedly jealous of his nephew's successes there, did not want to wait. When a mistaken intelligence report indicated that he was facing only half the Goths, Valens committed his forces to battle. On the morning of 9 August 378, the Emperor and his army left the city of Hadrianople and advanced on the Goths. Ill-discipline and confusion hampered the Roman effort, and all the Goths turned out to be present. Fighting began before the Romans were fully deployed, and the Roman flank seems to have been turned by a charge from those Goths who were not supposed to be present. Trapped, Valens and two-thirds of his army were massacred. The triumphant Goths swarmed over the Balkans, and even contemplated besieging Constantinople (AM 31.11–16).

The Goths had won their greatest victory ever over the Roman state. Ammianus compared it to that most cataclysmic of ancient Roman reverses: Hannibal's victory at the battle of Cannae. The extent of Roman losses has stimulated much discussion, because

[6] Ammianus does not say when the Greuthungi joined in revolt: I suspect it was at this point. See further Heather, 1991, 144–5.

Ammianus says only that two-thirds of Valen's army fell. Some have argued that there were losses of between 20,000 and 25,000 men. On the first day of the Somme, however, when serried ranks of infantry walked forward into massed machine gun fire, the British lost no more than 21,000 dead. I do not believe that Hadrianople could have been more destructive of human life, and suspect, as have others, that Roman losses were more in the region of 10,000–15,000 men.[7]

Perhaps not surprisingly, given the extent of the disaster, Gratian seems to have made no further moves against the Goths in 378. Only in January 379 did he promote Theodosius to be eastern Emperor, and gave him command of the Gothic war. Establishing himself in Thessalonica, Theodosius' first concern was to rebuild the eastern army. Deserters were rounded up, new recruits (Roman and barbarian) drafted, and veteran regiments transferred to the Balkans from the east. In the meantime, the Goths had moved west out of Thrace, probably because of food shortages, into Dacia and upper Moesia in Illyricum (figure 5.1). In 380, again perhaps driven by hunger, they divided. The Greuthungi of Alatheus and Saphrax moved northwest into Pannonia, while Fritigern moved southwest towards Thessalonica and Theodosius' restructured army. The fate of the Greuthungi is unclear. It has long been argued that Gratian settled them in Pannonia, but the evidence for this is highly ambiguous, and they may actually have been defeated by him. Further south, Theodosius' new army fell apart in battle. The Goths had inflicted a second major defeat upon the Empire. Ceding control of operations to Gratian, Theodosius retreated to Constantinople, which he nevertheless entered in triumph in November 380. In 381, Gratian's troops conducted an effective series of operations. They drove Fritigern's Goths, perhaps together with refugee Greuthungi, east from Illyricum. Subsequent and clearly lengthy negotiations culminated in an agreement formalized on 3 October 382.[8] The peace was as much Gratian's as Theodosius', and was probably made with all the Goths, Greuthungi and Tervingi, who had survived the six years of warfare.

The terms of the peace reflected a rough military balance. The Romans had been unable to defeat the Goths in all-out battle. The Goths, however, had suffered heavy casualties and were forced to curb

[7] Discussion and refs: Heather, 1991, 146–7.

[8] The main source is Zosimus 4.24–34 (after Eunapius): a better account than is usually thought: Heather, 147–56, App. B. I there argue (and still would) against the consensus view, which considers Gratian to have made a separate peace with the Greuthungi in 380. See, for instance, Cesa, 1994, 30–6.

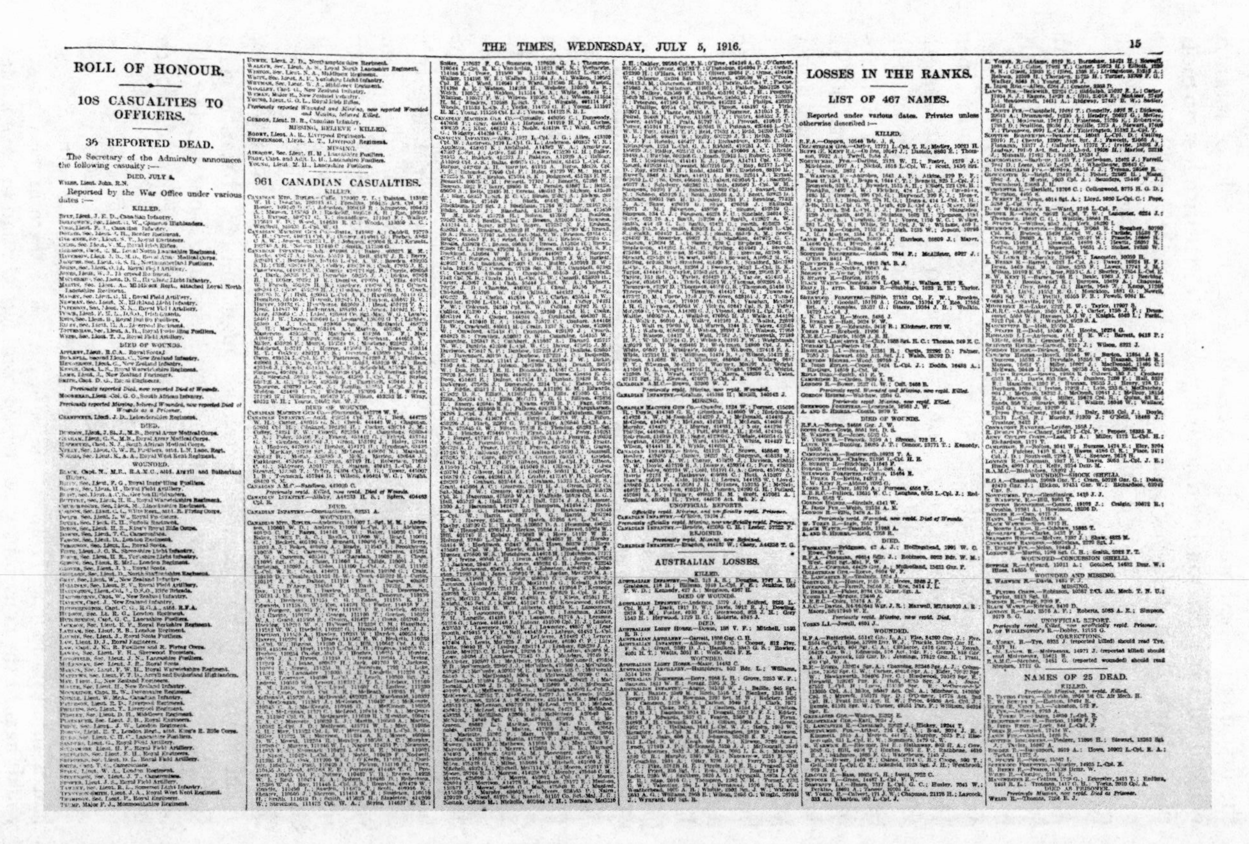

THE TIMES, WEDNESDAY, JULY 5, 1916. 15

ROLL OF HONOUR.

108 CASUALTIES TO OFFICERS.

36 REPORTED DEAD.

The Secretary of the Admiralty announces the following casualty:—

DIED, JULY 4.

Reported by the War Office under various dates:—

KILLED.

DIED OF WOUNDS.

DIED.

WOUNDED.

961 CANADIAN CASUALTIES.

KILLED.

AUSTRALIAN LOSSES.

LOSSES IN THE RANKS.

LIST OF 467 NAMES.

Reported under various dates. Privates unless otherwise described:—

KILLED.

NAMES OF 25 DEAD.

KILLED.

Plate 8 A grim reflection of the Somme: according to some estimates, the battle of Hadrianople was as destructive of

any ambitions for an independent kingdom of their own on Roman territory. Fritigern had expressed such a demand in an open letter to Valens on the eve of Hadrianople, but seems himself to have been aware that such a dramatic concession was unlikely to be granted. Along with the demand, he had also sent a secret message that, given a suitably impressive Roman military demonstration, he would be able to persuade his men to accept something rather less (AM 31.12.8–9). The demonstration was not forthcoming at Hadrianople, of course, but, over the next four years, the point was made. Despite two major defeats, Roman armies kept appearing and the Goths were subdued. In 382, the Roman state granted the Goths land for farming, and allowed them to maintain their own laws. To this extent, the agreement broke with tradition by giving the Goths considerable communal autonomy within the imperial frontier. In return, the Goths would undertake military service for the Roman state. This probably involved an initial draft of recruits, and agreeing in principle to occasional mass military service when required. The Emperors also refused to recognize any particular individual as overall leader of the Goths. Again, Fritigern had shown such an ambition. In the secret message before Hadrianople, he had also asked Valens to recognize him, should he deliver a deal with the Goths, as friend (*amicus*) and ally (*socius*) (AM 31.12.9). This sounds vague enough at first sight, but *rex socius et amicus* was the traditional title accorded fully recognized allied kings, as Fritigern surely knew. His ambitions came to nothing. Fritigern's exact fate is unclear, but he is not mentioned after 380 (nor, indeed, are Alatheus and Saphrax). Even if Fritigern had still been alive, the Romans would not have been ready, in 382, to grant honours to the victor of Hadrianople.

Roman face had been saved, but only to a certain extent, and public opinion required further reassurance. As in 370 (above p. 62), the orator Themistius attempted to make the best of the situation. A series of orations between 381 and 383 gradually built up the case that it was better to conquer the Goths by friendship than by violence. Again, Themistius' oration on the actual peace agreement claimed that Theodosius could have utterly defeated the Goths if he had wanted to (*Or.* 16). This should not be believed, but shows how carefully imperial policy had to be presented to fit the expectations of its audience. Themistius also looked forward to the time when the Goths would be totally absorbed into Roman provincial society.[9] Six

[9] Themistius *Orr.* 14–16. They are translated in Moncur and Heather 1996. On the peace more generally, Cesa, 1994, 36ff.; Heather, 1991, ch. 5; Wolfram, 1988, 131ff.

years of determined warfare had enabled two Gothic groups to constrain the Roman Empire into accepting (at least temporarily) their autonomous existence upon Roman soil. Wider pretentions to an independent kingdom or a recognized client kingship, had been curtailed, but even such a limited reversal of traditional Roman policy was no mean achievement.

The treaty marked no general shift, however, in imperial policy towards immigrant groups. Four years later, a third major Gothic group approached the Danube, the Greuthungi of Odotheus. Their attempt to cross the Danube met fierce resistance. The group suffered heavy casualties, and its leader was killed. The survivors, described as 'captives' in the sources, were resettled on Roman terms in Phrygia in Asia Minor. Some were drafted into the Roman army, while others were turned into agricultural labourers. It is specifically recorded that they had to live under Roman laws. Any sense of independent community among them was thus deliberately dismantled.[10] The changes to normal imperial policy enshrined in the treaty of 382 had not been made voluntarily. Nor did they apply to any but the Tervingi and Greuthungi who had fought for six years to establish their right to an independent existence.

(ii) The revolt of Alaric

The new treaty held firm, more or less, until the death of the Emperor Theodosius in 395. In one incident, a crowd lynched a Goth in Constantinople (Libanius *Or.* 19.22), in another a regular garrison unit on the Danube seems to have attacked a force of Goths. Its commander was disciplined, presumably to forestall a general Gothic uprising (Zosimus 4.40). The Emperor also invited Gothic leaders regularly to dine with him (Eunapius fr. 59): a channel of communication to ease away the difficulties of co-existence. This period of reasonable calm was first punctuated, and then brought to an end by two major Gothic revolts. Chronologically, and, I suspect, causally, they were associated with the two occasions on which Theodosius obtained large-scale military service from the Goths settled under the treaty of 382.

In 387, Theodosius declared war on a usurping western Emperor, Maximus, who had murdered Gratian in 382. As part of his preparations, Theodosius mobilized the Goths en masse. Some rebelled even before the campaign began (suborned, it is said, by

[10] Zosimus 4.35, 38–9, Cons. Const. s.a. 386 (= *CM* 1, 244). *captivi*: Claudian *In Eut.* 2.582. *coloni*: *ibid.* 205.

Maximus), but a much larger revolt followed the Goths' return to the Balkans after Theodosius' victory. The trouble was eventually brought to an end by negotiation, but the events of a second campaign, in 392/3, against a second western usurper, Eugenius, suggest its root cause. Again mobilized en masse, the Goths found themselves, in the summer of 393, in the front line at the battle of the river Frigidus, where the armies of Theodosius and Eugenius entered upon pitched battle. The Goths suffered heavy casualties in fierce fighting; reportedly as many as 10,000 Goths died. The historian Orosius commented that Theodosius had won two victories for the Roman state: the first over a usurper, the second over his Gothic 'allies' (7.35.19). Where such attitudes prevailed, the Goths had every reason to be suspicious of Roman motives in the longer term. Already on the Maximus campaign, they had probably realized that casualties incurred in Roman civil wars threatened their continued independence. As we have seen, the Roman state tolerated Gothic autonomy only because it had no choice. Should Gothic military manpower be witted away, that necessity would disappear.[11] Whether Theodosius had it in mind deliberately to erode Gothic manpower is impossible to be sure.

Soon after the Eugenius campaign, therefore, this time under the leadership of Alaric, the Goths again revolted. Theodosius' death, in January 395, had presented them with the perfect opportunity. Alaric is a mysterious figure. He had played some role in the revolt which followed the Maximus campaign, but it has recently been doubted that, in 395, he was really leading a general revolt of the Goths previously settled under the treaty of 382. In 395, he demanded 'command of an army' rather than just barbarians (Zosimus 5.5.4). This, it has been suggested, better fits a man wanting a career in the Roman army rather than a would-be Gothic king: a successor, for instance, for Fritigern. Such an alternative career path had been followed by a number of known Gothic nobles: Gainas, Fravittas, Munderic and Modares. Rather than the new leader of the Goths of 382, he should be seen, it is argued, as the commander of a mutinous regiment of Goths in the Roman army. Around him a large, but essentially disparate, following eventually gathered. To my mind, however, such a view takes insufficient account both of the general situation, and of the pattern of surviving source material.

[11] The connection between military service and both revolts is established by Heather, 1991, 183–8. Other accounts: Liebeschuetz, 1990, 51ff; Wolfram, 1988, 136ff.

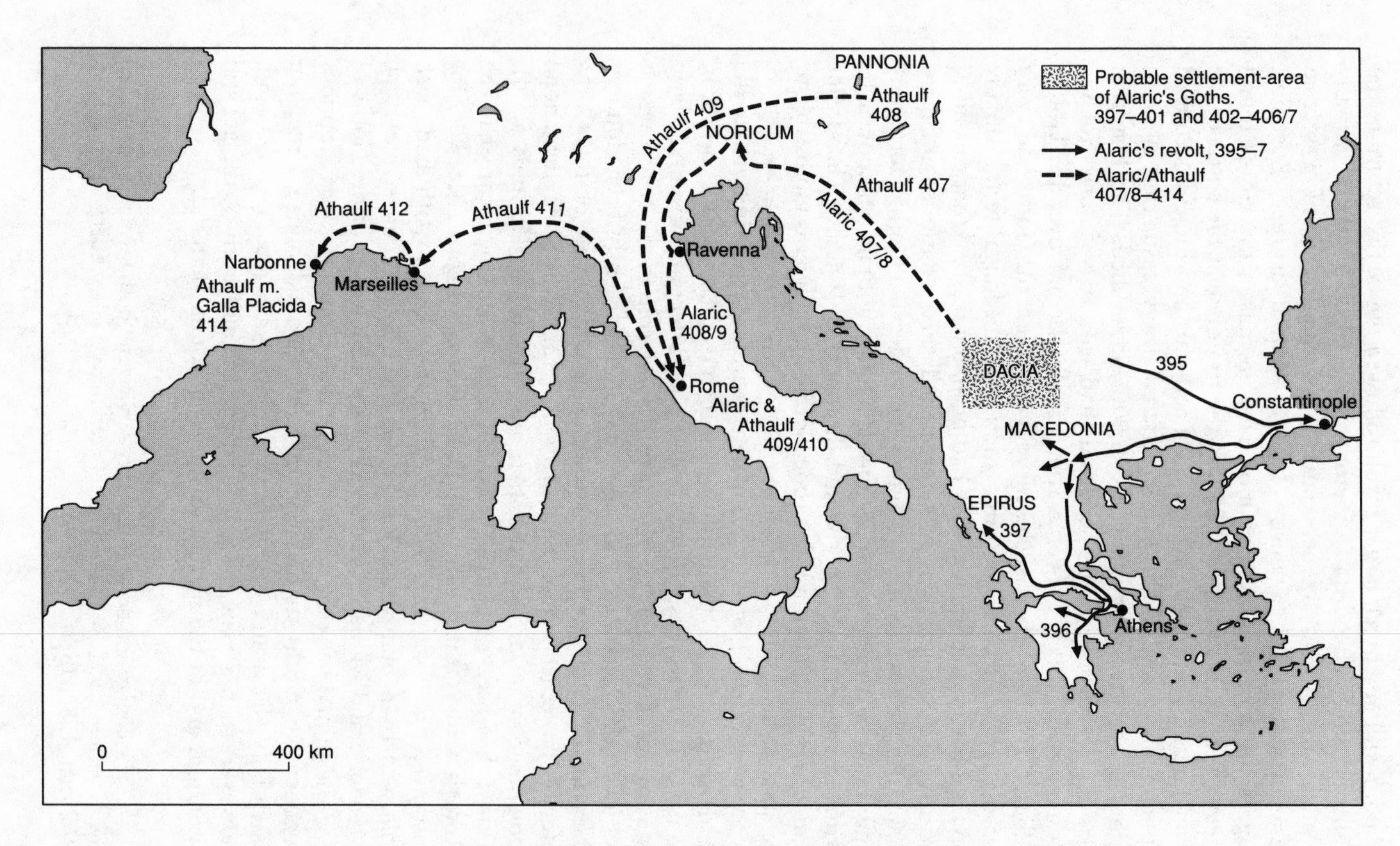

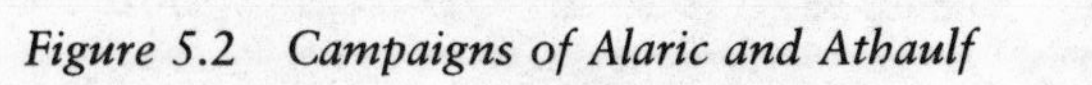
Figure 5.2 Campaigns of Alaric and Athaulf

The battle of the Frigidus had provided the Goths with a general reason to revolt. More than that, our sources for the years 395 to 399 are very fragmentary, giving no real information about the composition of Alaric's force. The first available characterizations of Alaric's activities date from 399, and, as soon as they begin, contemporary Romans of both east and west explicitly and consistently describe Alaric as the leader of a general revolt of the Goths who had treated with Theodosius in 382.[12] No source ever portrays him as anything else. Alaric had also had sufficient followers to stand up to major Roman field armies commanded by Stilicho, *de facto* ruler of the western Empire, in both 395 and 397. Alaric's supporters clearly comprised, then, even in the beginning, far more than a mutinous regiment.

As to the military command, Alaric was to demand a Roman generalship at intervals throughout the rest of his career. Even after 408, when he certainly commanded a large force of Goths, Alaric continued to make this demand. Such a command cannot have been incompatible with kingship of the Goths, therefore, and was probably designed to strengthen Alaric's hold over his followers. From 405, when we have more details, the demand for a generalship was associated with a large annual payment in gold for his followers, notionally, perhaps, their pay. By the 440s, this kind of arrangement was used to disguise tribute payments to Attila, and was also applied to Goths in the eastern Empire in the 470s and 480s (below p. 153). It was perhaps first invented to provide a more palatable gloss to the deals done with Alaric. A generalship also implied Roman recognition of Alaric as the overall ruler of the Goths: something denied any leading Goth in 382.[13]

Even in 395, therefore, Alaric is best understood as the most powerful leader of the Goths settled under the treaty of 382, and probably already controlled most of the Tervingi and Greuthungi. Only Ammianus distinguishes between these originally separate groups, and most writers of the 390s and 400s talk as if only one group of Goths crossed the Danube in 376. This reflects a transformation of fundamental importance. In the years after 376, Tervingi and Greuthungi had become one. As early as the Hadrianople campaign, they were already cooperating in the face of

[12] Claudian *De Bell. Get.* 166ff, 610ff, dating from 402, and Synesius, *De Regno* ed. Terzaghi 19–21, in 399, both characterize Alaric as the leader of a general revolt of the treaty Goths. See further Heather, 1988.

[13] Revisionary view of Alaric: Liebeschuetz, 1990, 51ff. More detailed counter-argument: Heather, 1991, 193ff.

Plate 9 Stilicho as portrayed in his consular dyptych

Roman power, not least in circumventing Valens' attempt to divide them, by admitting one and not the other in 376. Their established ruling dynasties had also failed to survive the crisis years. The *Hunnensturm* destroyed one set of leaders from each group, even before they reached the Danube (Athanaric of the Tervingi, Ermenaric and Vithimer of the Greuthungi: chapter 3). Another set had been ousted by 382 (respectively Fritigern, and Alatheus and Saphrax), probably by a combination of direct and indirect Roman action. The dynasties around whom the Tervingi and Greuthungi had originally stabilized, and whose interests might have kept the groups apart, were thus swept away. The way was open for a new generation of leaders to stake their claim to control of all the Goths.

The full story of this political process cannot be recovered, but Alaric was not the only contender. He had played some role in the earlier revolt of *c.*390/91 (p. 139), and this must have helped his cause. His rise to power can only have been furthered, moreover, by a struggle between two other potential leaders, Eriulph and Fravittas. In 392, their incipient hostility spilled over into violence at a dinner party. It ended in Eriulph's death and the enforced flight from Gothic society of Fravittas, to escape the workings of feud. Two possible contenders disappeared in one fell swoop.[14] Even so, Alaric and his brother-in-law and successor Athaulf still had to pursue a long drawn out rivalry with two brothers named Sarus and Sergeric. Sarus, like Fravittas, eventually fled to Roman service, but Sergeric perhaps organized Athaulf's murder, certainly killed his children, and briefly succeeded him as king. Sarus and Sergeric would appear to have been a rival dynasty disputing the overall leadership of the newly united Goths.[15]

Most of Alaric's 15-year reign was spent attempting to renegotiate the terms of the treaty of 382. Between 395 and 400, his manoeuvrings were assisted by internal Roman disunity. Theodosius left only minor sons: Honorius in the west ruled by Stilicho, Arcadius in the east ruled by first Rufinus and then Eutropius. Stilicho had designs on the whole Empire, however, and, in both 395 and 397, intervened in the east, ostensibly against Alaric, but with the real aim of securing power in Constantinople. Hence, in 397, Eutropius preferred to negotiate with Alaric than to submit to Stilicho. The full terms of their agreement are unknown, but Alaric did get his coveted generalship, perhaps a regional command in Illyricum (*MVM per*

[14] Eunapius fr. 59; Zosimus 4.55.3–56. 1 (on the date, Wolfram, 1988, 147). Significance: Heather, 1991, 186ff.

[15] Refs as *PLRE* 2, 978–9, 987.

Illyricum). The agreement no doubt included other, especially financial, benefits for his followers, and marks a crucially important moment. The Goths had dragged further concessions out of at least one half of the Roman Empire. Not surprisingly, the agreement attracted considerable criticism from contemporary Roman observers, particularly because Alaric had spent 395 and 396 conducting an extended booty raid through Greece and Macedonia. Arresting images of Alaric, as general in Illyricum, administering justice to those whom his forces had just pillaged and raped, were put out by Eutropius' enemies to stir up opinion among the political classes in Constantinople.[16]

They were all the more effective because the concessions stimulated a further Gothic revolt, this time among the survivors of Odotheus' Greuthungi. They, as we have seen, had been settled in Phrygia on traditionally harsh terms in 386 (p. 138). In the spring of 399, Tribigild, commander of a military unit seemingly drawn from these Greuthungi, left Constantinople for Phrygia feeling that he should have received greater rewards. Our sources indicate that it was the comparison with Alaric's recent successes which made Tribigild so disgruntled. Back in Phrygia he raised the standard of revolt. Amongst others, survivors of Odotheus' force flocked to his side. Tribigild and his men then raided through Phrygia and Pisidia and defeated an imperial army sent out against them. At this point, an imperial general of Gothic origins, Gainas, decided to use Tribigild's revolt as a means of overthrowing Eutropius. Claiming that he could not control Tribigild unless Eutropius was deposed, Gainas forced Eutropius' exile in the summer of 399. Moving on Constantinople, Gainas proceeded to oust his other political rivals in April 400. He clearly had it in mind to emulate in the east, the position of politically dominant generalissimo occupied by Stilicho in the west. In July 400, however, his former political ally, Caesarius, organized a counter-putsch. Gainas fled from Constantinople on the eve of a massacre of the city's Gothic population (7,000 were killed). Still another Goth, Fravittas, then arrived with elements of the eastern army to compound Gainas' defeat. The victory was commemorated on the column of Arcadius (plate 10). Left with no other option, Gainas attempted to carve out a niche for himself north of the Danube, having killed the last of his Roman supporters. He was eventually killed by the Hunnic chieftain Uldin, who sent his head back to

16 See generally, Cameron, 1970, chs 4 and 6. The treaty: Claudian *Eutr.* 2.211ff, *Get.* 533ff, Synesius *De Regno* 19–21.

Plate 10 *The defeat of Gainas. Renaissance drawing from the (now collapsed) column of Arcadius*

Constantinople (Zosimus 5.21–2).[17]

Alaric did not intervene directly in the events unfolding around Constantinople, but, in autumn 401, moved his followers to Italy. That Alaric should have abandoned the Balkans and the eastern political establishment where he had enjoyed particular success in 397, is very suggestive. After suppressing the revolts of Tribigild and Gainas, Caesarius' regime had probably taken what would by now have been a popular stand on Gothic policy, and refused to honour the concessions granted to Alaric in 397. This policy was already being advocated in 399 by those hostile to Eutropius. Hence Alaric moved his supporters into the sphere of the western Empire and tried instead to extract a deal from Stilicho. Again, he was unsuccessful. Crossing the Dinaric Alps in autumn 401, Alaric fought two battles against Stilicho in the following year: Verona and Pollentia. Both were drawn, but this was sufficient; Stilicho had only to parry the Goths' assault long enough for logistic problems to force their withdrawal. By 403, Alaric found himself back in the Balkans, an outlaw rejected by both halves of the Empire.[18]

(iii) Alaric, Stilicho and Radagaisus

The Goths were rescued from this precarious position by a sequence of events over which they had little control. Stilicho, effective ruler of the west, fell out with Caesarius' successor in the east, Anthemius, and sought to wrest from him legal control of eastern Illyricum. To this end, he negotiated a joint campaign with Alaric, agreeing that Alaric would receive in return his coveted generalship and his followers a large annual subsidy. The alliance with Alaric might even have been the central point of the campaign. The Goths had been occupying eastern Illyricum illegally since their expulsion from Italy, and securing its legal control may have been the price they demanded of Stilicho. The alliance was made in 404/5, on the eve of the second great wave of incursions generated by the Hunnic invasions (Chapter 4). Stilicho perhaps foresaw that he would need extra troops.[19]

The incursions began, however, before the projected campaign.

[17] Most recent account: Cameron et al., 1993. Gainas has been seen by Liebeschuetz, 1990, 100ff as potentially an alternative Alaric, but should rather be seen as a would-be Stilicho.

[18] The main sources are two poems of Claudian: *VI Cons. Hon.* and *Get.*; further commentary, Heather, 1991, 208–10; Cesa, 1994, ch. 3.

[19] Main source: Sozomen *h.e.* 8.25.3–4. Commentary: Liebeschuetz, 1990, 65–6; Heather, 1991, 211–12.

Radagaisus invaded Italy in 405/6, and on 31 December 406 there occurred the famous Rhine crossing by Vandals, Alans and Sueves. The first demands our particular attention. In Zosimus' account, Radagaisus is the leader of a multi-national force. Other, more contemporary sources describe him as a Gothic king, however, and Zosimus has probably confused Radagaisus' incursion with that of the Rhine invaders, which was indeed a multi-national force.[20] To deal with Radagaisus, Stilicho mobilized 30 army units and drafted in Hunnic auxiliaries. The army thus assembled was equal to the task. Radagaisus was trapped, captured and executed, his force dispersed. According to one source, 12,000 of Radagaisus' defeated force were drafted by Stilicho into the Roman army (Olympiodorus fr. 9), but others were less fortunate. According to Orosius, so many were sold into slavery that the bottom dropped out of the market (7.37.13ff). This disparity in treatment suggests that those drafted into the army had done a deal with Stilicho.

Stilicho's victory proved only a fleeting triumph. Not only was it quickly followed by the Rhine crossing, whose participants caused much more damage to Roman territories than had the forces of Radagaisus, but the Rhine crossing itself provoked a series of damaging usurpations. Starting in Britain, they quickly spread to the larger army of the Rhine. By 408, Constantine III, the most successful of the pretenders, had extended his power to the Alps and Pyrenees. Constantine's successes broke Stilicho's hold on Honorius. There followed a coup – accepted, if not organized, by Honorius – in which Stilicho and his son were arrested and killed in the summer of 408.[21]

These unexpected events prompted a further change of tack from Alaric. The collapse of political unity in the western Empire had allowed him to move, even before Stilicho's death, safely towards Italy. This was a repeat of the strategy he had adopted in 401/2, but this time the western Empire needed a deal, and his negotiating position was much stronger. More than that, after Stilicho's death, Alaric not only moved into Italy itself, but also received substantial reinforcements. First, in the coup which deposed Stilicho, the families of barbarian soldiers in the Roman army of Italy, quartered in various Italian cities, were massacred. This caused their menfolk to join Alaric. Many of this obviously distinct group within the Roman military are likely to have been the former supporters of Radagaisus drafted in large numbers into the army only two years previously.

[20] Zosimus 5.26.3; other refs as *PLRE* 2, 934.
[21] Main source: Zosimus 5.29–34. Commentary: Matthews, 1975, ch. 10.

Secondly, while Alaric's Goths sat outside Rome for 18 months from early 409 to the summer of 410, large numbers of slaves joined his forces. I strongly suspect that most of these were again former followers of Radagaisus, those who had been sold into slavery. The numbers given for these reinforcements are problematic, but Alaric's original force of *c.*20,000 men had perhaps doubled in size by the summer of 410.[22]

In the meantime, events had been following a set pattern. Alaric sat outside Rome and threatened to sack it, unless the imperial authorities in Ravenna negotiated with him. His demands at this point are well documented. At most, he offered a military alliance with the Roman state, demanding, in return, a generalship for himself, a large annual payment in gold, substantial corn supplies, and his troops to be settled in the Venetias and Raetia. Such a position would have allowed the Goths to control Ravenna and routes over the Alps (Zosimus 5.48.3). The level of ambition here is remarkable. His personal honours and the envisaged proximity of Alaric's forces to its political heart would have effectively established a Gothic protectorate over the western Empire. When these demands were rejected, and despite the fact that the Roman position was no stronger, Alaric offered an alliance in return for just a land settlement in Noricum (well away from the political heart of the Empire), and as much corn each year as the Romans saw fit to grant him (Zosimus 5.50.3). Even contemporaries found his moderation at this juncture surprising. It suggests that Alaric expected the current political and military weakness of the western Empire, the combined effect of invasion and usurpation, to be temporary.

Nevertheless, no agreement followed. Honorius, the western Emperor, was willing to sacrifice Rome rather than negotiate. In disgust, Alaric finally sacked the city on 24 August 410. In a straightforward way, the sack of Rome represents a Gothic failure: the frustration of Alaric's desires to carve out for himself a new role at the heart of the Empire. Alaric failed, indeed, to achieve any settlement of Gotho–Roman affairs before his death. Shortly after the sack of Rome, he died from disease, and control of the Goths passed, in 411, to his brother-in-law and successor Athaulf. In the meantime, the Goths had moved back and forth the length of Italy, and failed to force their way to Africa. Running short of food, Athaulf adopted a new stratagem, leading the Goths into Gaul. There he tried the familiar mixture of force and persuasion to obtain advantageous

22 Zosimus 5.35.5–6, 45.3; cf. Heather, 1991, 213–14.

terms. Suppressing one usurper, Jovinus, he then set up another of his own: the Roman senator Attalus (Alaric had earlier done the same outside Rome). His last move was to marry Honorius' sister Galla Placidia, whom he had captured in the sack of Rome. Their marriage was celebrated in Roman splendour in a villa at Narbonne, and, when they had a son, they named him Theodosius (Olympiodorus frr. 18, 22, 24, 26). Honorius had no children, and the new Theodosius was the grandson of one Emperor by that name and first cousin to another (Arcadius had been succeeded by his son Theodosius II in 408). Athaulf thus had it in mind to become the power behind the imperial throne, very much the same level of ambition shown earlier by Alaric, pursued by another route. Such was also the tenor of Athaulf's famous alleged remark that he had first thought to replace the Roman Empire – *Romania* – with *Gothia*, but then decided instead to use Gothic arms to uphold Roman rule (Orosius 7.43.2–3).

But Honorius' leading general, Fl. Constantius, had other ideas. He first defeated the usurpers to reunite the western army under central control, and then turned on the Goths, subduing them by blockade and starvation. This aroused discontent among the Goths, which expressed itself in hostility to Athaulf's leadership. The king suffered a mortal wound in an assassination attempt made, according to one source (*Getica* 163), by the aptly named Dubius. At this point, Sergeric, member of a rival dynasty (p. 143), mounted a coup, killing in the process Athaulf's brother and children. Sergeric himself, however, lasted only seven days, before another coup replaced him with Vallia, a man seemingly unrelated to the previous kings. In the face of increased Roman pressure, instability had returned to Gothic politics.[23]

As we have seen, Alaric had united elements from at least three previously separate Gothic groups: the Tervingi and Greuthungi of 376, and many of Radagaisus' followers. His command of this new group rested essentially on his own ability. There was no established dynastic tradition to exploit, and many a potential heir for Alaric's mantle. After his early death, seemingly from natural causes, Vallia was succeeded by Theoderic I in 417/8. It was thanks only to Theoderic's longevity and fertility that a ruling dynasty eventually established itself, whose control was to last uninterrupted until 507. A huge revolution in Gothic society, started some 50 years earlier by the Huns, had come to fruition. Out of the chaos had emerged a new

[23] On Fl. Constantius and the imperial revival, see Matthews, 1975, chs 12–13.

political unit – the Visigoths – headed by a new royal dynasty.[24]

Theoderic I was also responsible for restoring order to Gotho–Roman relations. Allowing unsubdued Goths into the Empire in 376 had been an involuntary break with tradition, and subsequent years saw both Gothic leaders and Roman Emperors improvise policy as they attempted to establish a new paradigm for their evolving relationship. Fritigern, before Hadrianople, had alternately demanded that Thrace be handed over to the Goths as an independent kingdom, and offered to make himself a Roman client. The treaty of 382 had granted the Goths some autonomy, but recognized no Gothic client king. In response to losses suffered in Roman civil wars, Alaric then demanded a greater degree of recognition via a generalship and annual monetary payments. These demands mushroomed in particular contexts. Thus Alaric in Italy and Athaulf in Gaul had it in mind, at different moments, to establish virtually a Gothic protectorate over the western Empire. The imperial collapse which prompted such thoughts, however, was temporary. The campaigns of Fl. Constantius made Vallia in 416, and Theoderic in 418 accept a much less revolutionary settlement of Gotho–Roman affairs. The details of the treaty will be discussed later (chapter 7), but the Goths were established in the Garonne valley between Toulouse and Bourdeaux. No payments in gold seem to have been made to them, and neither Vallia nor Theoderic received a generalship. The agreement also renewed the military alliance between the Empire and the Goths.

The more grandiose schemes of Alaric and Athaulf had been restrained, but, compared to the treaty of 382, the Goths had still extracted considerable concessions. The Empire had been forced to recognize the leadership of a Gothic king, and even sent hostages to his court after 418 (Sid. Ap. *Carm.* 7.215–20). Nor is there any sign after 418 that hopes lingered on in imperial circles of snuffing out Gothic independence, as they had after 382. The new Gothic unit, created by Alaric and sustained by his successors, was much larger than anything previously seen, and that much more difficult to defeat. After the Rhine crossing of 406, moreover, the Goths were no longer the only tribal group on Roman territory, and Romans clearly preferred the Goths to the newer arrivals. From 416, Goths and Romans cooperated militarily in Spain, attacking the survivors of the Rhine crossing. For the Empire, the Goths had become the lesser evil,

[24] The process: Heather, 1991, 28–33, 220–1. Subsequent dynastic events: Wolfram, 1988, 173ff.

and the Goths' autonomous settlement within the Roman frontier more acceptable than it had been in 382.

B. The Creation of the Ostrogoths c.450–484

The emergence of the Ostrogoths likewise represented the generation of a new Gothic political unit of greater size and coherence than anything previously attested in reliable sources. Two separate Gothic groups, the Pannonian Goths and the Thracian allies (*foederati*), united, after much rivalry and even open conflict, behind the rule of the Amal dynasty, in the person of Valamer's nephew, Theoderic the Great. The new Gothic 'supergroup' eventually carved out a kingdom for itself in Italy, at the heart of the old Roman Empire.

(i) Background

The Pannonian Goths had probably been settled by the Huns in the ex-Roman province in a series of separate groups firmly under Hunnic control. Unity and independence came only when Valamer alternately extinguished and conciliated members of at least two other rival dynasties. This created a united force of sufficient strength to throw off Hunnic hegemony in the aftermath of Attila's death (chapter 4). The newly united force numbered somewhere between 10,000 and 15,000 fighting men, which would imply a total for the group, including women and children, of perhaps 50,000. Farming remained for them a central concern. The Huns exploited the agricultural surpluses of their Gothic and other subjects, and negotiations between this group and the Roman state after 473 focused, amongst other things, on the possession of good quality agricultural land. This the Goths were clearly to farm for themselves, since the 'lack of inhabitants' in an area was held to be part of its attraction. It was also a basic assumption in many of the diplomatic exchanges that, in the normal course of events, the Pannonian Goths would grow their own food.[25]

But agriculture was not the sole focus of their lives. As the Hunnic Empire collapsed, intense rivalries were let loose among their former subjects, especially in the middle Danube region, where Goths, Gepids, Sarmatians, Suevi, Sciri and Heruli all jockeyed for position. The end of the Huns' virtually annual campaigns against the Roman state also meant that supplies of booty ceased, and that the Huns'

[25] Agricultural interests: Heather, 1991, 244–5 commenting esp. on Malchus fr. 18.3, p. 430, 5ff; fr. 20, p. 438, 55ff; p. 446, 199ff. Numbers: Heather, 1991, 248–9.

highly militarized former subjects were left unoccupied during the summer months. The end result was an intense competition for pre-eminence and the fruits of victory. For the nearly 20 years between the collapse of Hunnic power and the Pannonian Goths' decision to shift the focus of their activities into the eastern Empire (*c.*455–73), our only connected narrative of events is supplied, once again, by Jordanes' *Getica*. According to this account, the Pannonian Goths – led by the Amal family – were both usually victorious against their neighbours, and particularly favoured allies of Constantinople (*Getica* 268–82). The latter claim, at least, is untrue. Valamer's nephew Theoderic did spend ten years as a hostage in Constantinople after 461, but only as a result of a treaty which followed wide-ranging Gothic campaigns in the Roman Balkans. In this treaty, the Goths also extracted an annual subsidy of 300 pounds of gold. They were not so much favoured allies, as particularly aggressive neighbours. Hence, the eastern Empire looked to undermine the Goths' power as and when it could. When war subsequently broke out between the Goths and the Sciri, for instance, the Empire backed the latter (Priscus frr. 37, 45).

In their struggles with the Huns' other former subjects, the Pannonian Goths were not always successful. In a first battle against the Sciri, Valamer was killed, but the Goths, the *Getica* reports, took ferocious revenge. Jordanes' account of the post-Hunnic period as a whole builds up to a climax at the battle of the river Bolia where the Pannonian Goths triumphed over a coalition of their enemies: Suevi, Sciri, Sarmatians, Gepids and Rugi (*Getica* 274ff). We have no means of verifying this account. If the Goths really did defeat their opponents so soundly, it is slightly surprising that soon after their victory they should have moved into the eastern Roman Empire. But perhaps they had exhausted the available spoils. And, once united with the Thracian Goths at least, they really were a dominant force in post-Hunnic politics (chapter 8).

The history of the Thracian Goths was very different. Once again, we have good indications that, in total, the Thracian Goths numbered between 10,000 and 15,000 fighting men. They were thus similar in power to the Pannonian Goths. This is what the historical narrative would anyway suggest. After 473, the leaderships of the two groups maintained an intense rivalry for over a decade. Such a protracted struggle could not have occurred had one side or the other held a preponderance of strength.[26]

[26] Heather, 1991, 253–4, 256 commenting esp. on Malchus fr. 2, p. 408, 22ff; 18.4, p. 434, 12ff.

As we have seen, their origins and early history are obscure, but by 470 the Thracian Goths held a deeply privileged position within the east Roman state. Recognized allies (*foederati*), they performed military service as regular imperial troops in return for appropriate remuneration. In 473, for instance, their pay and ration allowances were together worth 2,000 pounds of gold per annum (Malchus fr. 2, p. 408. 22ff): seven times the subsidy extracted by their Pannonian rivals in the early 460s. The privileged position of the Thracian Goths was also visible in other ways. The evidence is not so explicit as for the Pannonian Goths, but a number of indications clearly imply that the Thracian Goths, or some of them, held and farmed agricultural land. These lands seem to have been located on the Thracian Plain itself, inside the ring of the Haemus mountains, and relatively close to the imperial capital. Most other imperial allies we know of were settled further away.[27]

Their political contacts inside Constantinople were equally good. They supplied, we know, some of the palace guard. Likewise, Theoderic Strabo ('the squinter'), the son of Triarius, who had become their overall ruler by 473, was connected by marriage to Aspar, the imperial generalissimo who had dominated the eastern court since the 420s. Strabo also owned property in Constantinople, and a series of political contacts kept him closely informed of developments in the city, even when he himself was out of favour (Malchus fr. 15).[28] When the Emperor Leo, who had allied with Isaurian elements in the army to limit Aspar's influence, had Aspar and his son Ardaburius murdered in 471, the Goths could not but see this as a direct threat to their own position. Goths in Constantinople under the command of one Ostrys attempted to storm the palace, and, when forced back, fled to Thrace where a general uprising of the 'federates' (*foederati*) followed (Malalas, ed. Bonn, 371–2, *de Insidiis* 31). By 473, the federates had rallied to the banner of Theoderic Strabo, who proceeded to act as their king.

His pre-eminence was newly established. Before the revolt, there is no sign that the Thracian Goths had one overall leader. Several Gothic-named Roman military commanders seem to have been associated with the Thracian Goths: Theoderic Strabo himself, of course, Ostrys, Ullibus and Anagastes. I suspect that Ostrys is none other than 'Triarius', Theoderic Strabo's father (on the grounds that Ostrys and Triarius could well be alternative transcriptions of the

27 Full argumentation: Heather, 1991, 257–9.
28 For Aspar and Strabo, refs as *PLRE* 2, 164ff, 1073ff.

same Gothic name). Ullibus and Anagastes, however, were certainly separate leaders who rose independently in revolt. Ullibus was eventually killed by Anagastes. If Ostrys was Strabo's father, he may simply have died. After killing Ullibus, however, Anagastes himself disappears from our texts, quite likely eliminated in turn by Theoderic Strabo. The unification of the Thracian Goths was thus the end result of a Darwinian power struggle, similar in character to that by which Valamer had first united the Pannonian Goths.[29]

This sheds additional light on how the Thracian Goths had been incorporated into the eastern Empire. A distinct body of favoured allies, they were not allowed to operate as a kind of Gothic client state. Rather, they had been settled under a series of independent military-cum-political leaders. The right kind of historical parallel might be the separate contingents of Turkish troops brought into the Abbasid Caliphate in the ninth century. And, just like the Caliph's Turks, they united when they felt deeply threatened by moves to establish alternative powerbases. Thus in 471, their fear of Leo's Isaurian allies, whose pre-eminent leader was Zeno, prompted the Thracian Goths to revolt. At that point, they created or renewed an old political unity among themselves, to protect their privileged position within the east Roman state.

(ii) The struggle for mastery in the Balkans 473–479

In 473, the Pannonian Goths, led since Valamer's death by his brother Thiudimer, advanced into the Roman Balkans, moving their military forces, non-combatants and livestock by two main routes south, to converge on Thessalonica (*Getica* 283ff: Figure 5.3). The decision to move could not have been taken lightly. Whatever its momentary troubles (the Thracian Gothic revolt had been underway since 471), the eastern Empire was the most powerful state of its day. What prompted tens of thousands of people to pick up their movable possessions and undertake this trek?

For one thing, an internal political agenda was at work. Even after Valamer's unifying activities, the Pannonian Goths had continued to live in three separate groups, under Valamer and his two brothers, Thiudimer and Vidimer (*Getica* 268). When Valamer was killed in battle, Thiudimer inherited the status of overall leader, and then exploited subsequent events to undermine the third brother's position. First, he raised his own son Theoderic to royal status upon the latter's

[29] Refs and fuller discussion: Heather, 1991, 260–1.

return from Constantinople in 471. Secondly, Vidimer and his body of close personal followers decided to move west rather than take part in the advance upon Thessalonica (*Getica* 276-8, 282-3). The *Getica* presents this as a voluntary separation effected by the casting of lots, but it seems likely both that Vidimer would have preferred to have remained with the main Gothic body, and that Thiudimer would have wanted as large a body of Gothic manpower as possible. The move south thus completed, and was probably in part designed to complete, the process by which one segment of the new ruling dynasty of the Pannonian Goths achieved a monopoly of power.[30]

Thiudimer also had it in mind to usurp the privileged position of the Thracian Goths. The Thracian *foederati* were in receipt of annual payments worth seven times the subsidy granted the Pannonian Goths by the Emperor Leo. Their leaders also enjoyed high court honours. The Byzantine historian Malchus reports that the Pannonian Goths had entered the Empire to be able 'to measure gold out by the bushel' (fr. 18.2). Thus Thiudimer surely had it in mind to share in these benefits. In subsequent years, the two Gothic groups would refer explicitly, in messages to Constantinople, to their mutual rivalry, and it was already implicit in Thiudimer's first move. The extended revolt in Thrace gave the Pannonian Goths the opportunity to persuade Leo that they would make better allies than the Thracian *foederati*.[31]

The inherent complexity of the situation created by the move is already visible in the events of 473. Leo responded by sending an army and a representative to confront the Pannonian Goths near Thessalonica. It was subsequently arranged that they should be resettled in the nearby Macedonian canton of Eordaia (*Getica* 285–7). There is no sign that Thiudimer's Goths received larger annual payments at this point, nor their leadership Roman court honours. The very fact of their appearance in the western Balkans, however, shifted forces away from the east – Thrace – where the revolt of the *foederati* was under way. It was probably as a direct result of the Pannonians' arrival, therefore, that the Thracian Goths were able, in 473, to attack, without resistance, two major Thracian cities, Arcadiopolis and Philippopolis. As a result, a new agreement was also reached in 473 between the Emperor Leo and Theoderic Strabo. Leo no doubt wanted to protect his Thracian cities, and Strabo's followers, unsupported now by the state for two years, were short of food. Strabo's willingness to compromise can probably also be

30 Similar is Wolfram, 1988, 260, 267–8.
31 *Getica* 281–2, with Heather, 1991, 246 on the date.

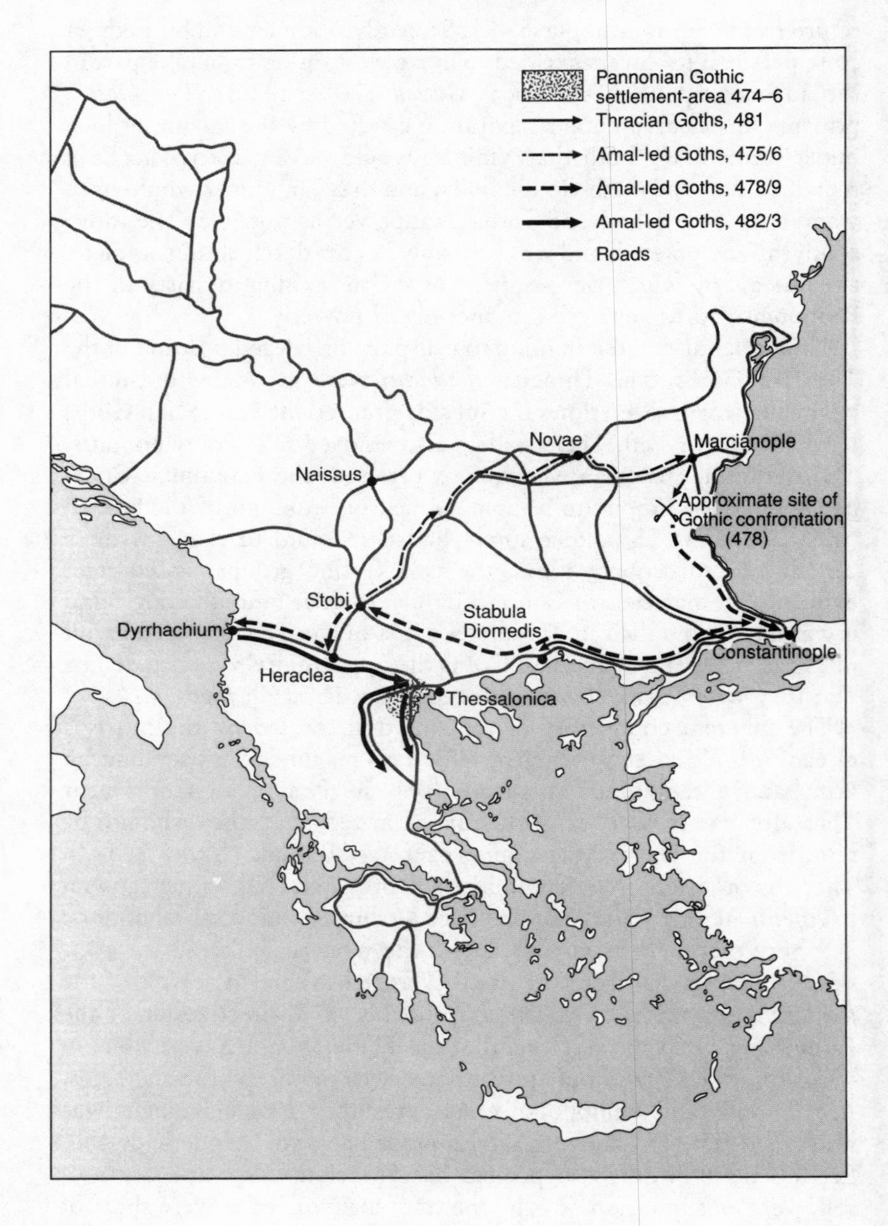

Figure 5.3 The Pannonian and Thracian Goths in the Balkans, 476–484

explained by the appearance of Thiudimer and a dawning realization that there was now competition for the comfortable niche occupied by the Thracian Goths.

The treaty rewarded Strabo's new followers for their loyalty to him, guaranteeing them 2,000 pounds of gold per annum. It also heralded Strabo's return to court. He was appointed to the senior military command in the eastern Empire (*MVM Praesentalis*), reflecting a previous demand that he should inherit the position and titles of Aspar. The treaty also acknowledged Strabo as 'sole ruler' (autocrat: *αὐτοκράτωρ*) of the Goths, and Leo promised not to receive into his service 'any Goths who wished to serve him' (Malchus fr. 2). It is hard not to see these latter clauses as directed at least in part at the Pannonian Goths. They guaranteed Strabo's status as 'chief Goth' and 'most important ally', reinforcing his position precisely where Thiudimer's move threatened it most. Already in 473, the Pannonian parvenus were perceived as a direct threat to the Thracian Goths' position.

It is most unlikely that matters could have rested for long where they stood at the end of 473. The Pannonian Goths had established themselves within the Empire's frontiers, but their expectations were otherwise unsatisfied. As it was, Leo died in January 474, being succeeded by his seven-year-old grandson, Leo II, who was also the son of Zeno, the leading Isaurian general. Events in Constantinople moved quickly. Zeno had himself declared co-Emperor on 9 February 474, and became sole ruler when his son died the following November. Once again, Isaurian dominance at court was threatening the Thracian Goths. Hence, late in 474, Theoderic Strabo threw his weight behind a coup organized by the Empress Verina, widow of Leo I, and her brother, the general Basiliscus. Zeno fled the capital, hurrying back to his Isaurian base, as his supporters in the city were massacred. Basiliscus assumed the throne and ruled in Constantinople from January 475 to August 476.[32]

Under Basiliscus, Strabo continued to hold his generalship and cut an important political figure, even if, as the sources report, he was both frustrated in attempts to move his soldiers into the capital, and resented the promotion of Basiliscus' nephew Armatus.[33] Zeno, however, was not just an imperial general. He was also an Isaurian chieftain with resources of his own. Despite fleeing the capital, he was far from beaten. Back in Isauria, Zeno rebuilt his forces, and, in

[32] The best guide to the internal politics of Zeno's reign is still Brooks, 1893.

[33] Malchus fr. 15, *Suda* A 3970 trans. in Blockley, 1983, 477.

particular, won over to his cause another Isaurian general, Illus, who had previously supported Basiliscus. Illus had managed to capture Zeno's brother, Longinus, and, for that reason, it seems, felt sure of wielding powerful influence over a restored Zeno. Together, the Isaurians advanced on Constantinople in the summer of 476. When Armatus, commanding Basiliscus' remaining troops in Asia Minor, also changed sides, the usurper was doomed.

In the meantime, the Pannonian Goths had not been idle. Thiudimer died in Macedonia, shortly after the settlement (*Getica* 288: probably in 474). When we next hear of his followers, in 476, they had already made their way, under the leadership of Theoderic, to Novae in Moesia Secunda (figure 5.3). Theoderic made this move on his own initiative. It was only in Novae that he opened negotiations with Zeno, who was at this point still in Isauria (*Anon. Val.* 9.42). The direction of the Pannonians' move suggests its purpose. Novae was a heavily fortified military centre on the Danube, which sat astride numerous north-south routes through the Haemus mountains. The passes through the eastern Haemus are also too gentle to be easily blocked against an invader. Theoderic had provided his followers with a defensible base, and put himself in a perfect position to intervene militarily on the Thracian plain. The move thus advanced further the strategy of 473. It presented Zeno with an open invitation to use the former Pannonian Goths against their Thracian counterparts. As Theoderic later put it to Zeno's representative in 479 (Malchus fr. 20, p. 444. 172ff), 'staying [in Novae] I thought that I should trouble no one, yet from there I should be ready to obey whatever the Emperor commanded'.

Desperate to return to power, Zeno responded positively to the invitation. Under their subsequent agreement, Theoderic was to receive his Thracian namesake's generalship, and his followers the payments previously directed at the Thracian Goths. Quite explicitly, the *quid pro quo* for these benefits was that the former Pannonian Goths should, by themselves, attack the Thracian *foederati*.[34] This, indeed, may well explain why Theoderic Strabo was not in Constantinople in the summer of 476 to defend Basiliscus from Zeno. His forces were probably already deployed against the menace from the north posed by Theoderic the Amal. Thanks to the upheavals at court, the two Gothic groups were now in direct competition, as Thiudimer had always intended they should be, for the same benefits. The competition was all the more intense, because the funds were not

[34] Malchus fr. 18.2, p. 426, 4–5; fr. 18.3, p. 432, 18–19.

available (or so Zeno got the Senate of Constantinople formally to declare) to pay both groups at the same time (Malchus fr. 15).

In 477, little changed. Some fighting occurred, in the course of which the Pannonian Goths moved on to Marcianople, and Theoderic Strabo attracted some of their number into his own camp. Strabo also made an attempt to mend his fences with Zeno. He offered the Emperor an alliance on minimal terms (no generalship, and no gold payments) in a message which is striking for the clarity of its references to Gothic rivalry (Malchus fr. 15, p. 420. 1–9). Strabo 'asked the Emperor to consider how little harm the son of Triarius [i.e. himself], though an enemy, had done to the Romans and how much damage Theoderic the son of Valamer [*sic*] had done to the cities. Zeno ought not now to look to old hatreds but rather to how he might most advance the common good'. Strabo was thus well aware that, to win back his position, he had to make his case in terms of why Zeno should prefer him to his Amal rival. Zeno rejected the embassy, and, in winter 477/8, the Empire remained formally in alliance with the Pannonian Goths.

But the switch in support between the two Gothic leaders had clearly begun to make Zeno feel uneasy. In the course of the winter, he started to play a double game. While continuing to urge Theoderic the Amal to make good on promises to attack the Thracian Goths, he put out diplomatic feelers towards Strabo, proposing peace on the terms that Strabo had himself previously offered. Now more confident, Strabo rebuffed the offer on the grounds that, since he had more followers, his forces would require greater financial support. Zeno responded to this rejection by pursuing again his alliance with Theoderic the Amal. He drew up with him plans for a joint campaign against the Thracian Goths. In addition to the 10,000–15,000 men who followed the Amal, 2,000 cavalry and 10,000 infantry of the imperial army of Thrace, and a further 6,000 cavalry and 20,000 infantry from the central imperial field armies were to be committed to the campaign (Malchus fr. 18.1–2). A combined force of nearly 50,000 was thus to fight the 10,000–15,000 men of Theoderic Strabo. The envisaged aim of the campaign was surely the destruction of Strabo's power.

As it proved, none of the promised imperial troops showed up. Zeno's guides led the Amal along an odd route through the Haemus mountains, at the end of which he found not an imperial army, but his Thracian namesake. The Thracian Goths were not in the locality envisaged in the plan, even though Zeno must have known where they were; he had had diplomatic dealings with them throughout the previous winter. I can only echo Theoderic the Amal's conclusion at the turn of events. Zeno had drawn up the plan for the joint campaign in bad faith. His intention had never been to support the Amal, but to engineer a clash between the two Gothic groups. As Malchus has Strabo say: 'while remaining at peace, [the Romans] wish the Goths to wear each other down. Whichever of us falls, they will be the winners with none of the effort, and whichever of us destroys the other side will ... be left with diminished numbers to face Roman treachery'. After the Goths had fought, the imperial forces, which Zeno had indeed mobilized, were no doubt to intervene. Zeno probably hoped either to expel the remaining Goths, or to break them down into groups of a less threatening size.[35]

Perhaps not surprisingly, the Goths saw through Zeno's deceptions and agreed among themselves a non-aggression pact. Both Theoderics subsequently sent embassies to Constantinople, and, in considerable and natural anger, the Amal advanced on the imperial capital, reaching the Long Walls: an arc of fortifications about 50 miles outside the city. Here there was some fighting. This outcome must always have been possible, but any fall-back plan Zeno might have had was wrecked by internal political feuding. In 478, in the middle of the campaign, a supporter of Zeno organized an assassination attempt on Illus, the Isaurian general who was holding Zeno's brother hostage. As a result, Illus abandoned Constantinople for Isauria. This put in doubt the loyalty of the central field armies, which Illus was to lead, so that Zeno was forced to disband them. Left with no army and two hostile Gothic groups in the vicinity of his capital, Zeno was in serious trouble.

A series of attempts to bribe the Amal to return to his commitment to fight the Thracian Goths failed. This being so, Zeno had no choice but to make peace with Theoderic Strabo on whatever terms he could get. Strabo drove a hard bargain. He regained his generalship and large-scale economic support for his followers. He also used the diplomatic exchanges to emphasize that the Emperor had to choose between the two Gothic groups, and to claim that he was the much more trustworthy ally (Malchus fr. 18.4, p. 434. 1ff). Zeno would probably not have agreed, but needed a breathing space. The treaty was duly ratified before the end of 478.[36]

In the meantime, Theoderic the Amal had fought his way through

[35] Full reconstruction and argumentation, Heather, 1991, 278ff. Strabo's speech: Malchus fr. 18.2, p. 428, 34ff.

[36] Malchus fr. 18. 3–4 with Heather, 1991, 280ff.

the Rhodope mountains as far west as the city of Stobi, which he reached and sacked sometime in 479 (figure 5.3). In response, Zeno decided to make peace to prevent further damage, and this, indeed, may have been the central point of Theoderic's aggression. While negotiations were underway, the Pannonian Goths withdrew west to Heraclea, whose inhabitants, seemingly under orders from Constantinople, provided them with supplies. After much deliberation, Zeno offered the Goths a settlement area around the city of Pautalia, whose advantages, according to the Emperor, lay in its combination of rich, fertile land and lack of inhabitants. The Amal, however, had his eyes on a stronger bargaining counter, and moved instead on Epidamnus, a fortified city on the Adriatic coast. With help from a supporter, Sidimund, who had estates in the area, and taking with him his swiftest forces, Theoderic seized the city without opposition, and held it as a fortified base from which to await developments.

His renewed sense of security is evident in a subsequent interview with Adamantius, an ambassador sent by Zeno. Theoderic made it clear that he had no intention of leaving the city in the coming winter (479/80), but did offer to contribute 6,000 picked troops to an imperial army which, he suggested, could be used either to reconquer Italy (lost to the Empire since 476), or to destroy the Thracian Goths. Theoderic must have known, however, that neither of these projects would much appeal to Zeno, and the main point of taking Epidamnus was to enable him to sit tight and await a good opportunity to advance his position (Malchus fr. 20).

In the three years since the overthrow of Basiliscus, Theoderic the Amal had learned much of imperial duplicity. After their brief understanding in 478, the rivalry between the two Gothic dynasties had also reasserted itself. Both Theoderics still continued to negotiate with Zeno in terms of why he should be in alliance with the one rather than the other. Indeed, the events of 478 had forced both Gothic groups to confront the fact that Zeno would rather not deal with either of them. The result was an alliance, which, however brief, presaged a much longer-lived union to come.

(iii) Gothic unification

Strabo had extracted a favourable settlement from Zeno in 478. Their previous rivalries meant, however, that he could not rely on it to survive once the immediate circumstances constraining the Emperor – particularly his quarrel with Illus – ceased to apply. The two Isaurians healed their rift at the end of 478; when Zeno handed over to Illus the

Empress Verina (widow of Leo I): held to be the root cause of the trouble. When a new opportunity for political meddling offered itself in 479, therefore, Strabo grasped it with both hands. Late in the year, yet another coup was launched against Zeno, this time by Marcian, grandson of the eastern Emperor Marcian, son of the western Emperor Anthemius, and husband of a younger daughter of Leo I. His imperial credentials could hardly have been better, and Strabo presumably calculated that he stood a better chance of establishing a stable relationship with this pretender, than with the present incumbent.

On hearing that the plotters had made their move inside the city, Strabo advanced on Constantinople from Thrace. Illus' Isaurians, however, quickly put down the uprising, and captured Marcian. At this point, Strabo claimed that he had actually come to save Zeno. A further temporary accord followed, but Zeno was not taken in for a moment. Indeed, Strabo continued to show his disaffection by giving a safe haven to some of the plotters (Malchus fr. 22). It can have come as no surprise, then, when Zeno removed Strabo's generalship and paid some Bulgars to harass the Thracian Goths from across the Danube in the summer of 480 (John of Antioch fr. 211.4). He used Bulgars because, late in 479, his general in the western Balkans, Sabinianus, had ambushed Theoderic the Amal's slow-moving baggage train before it could reach Epidamnus. In this action, he captured 2,000 waggons and 5,000 prisoners together with considerable booty. This success prompted Zeno not to make peace with the Amal, but to pursue a military option (Malchus fr. 20). In the summer of 480, therefore, the Emperor's main forces were conducting operations in the western Balkans.

The Bulgar stratagem worked well enough in 480, but the imperial troops did not manage to force home any advantage over the Amal, safely tucked in behind the walls of Epidamnus in the west. In 481, consequently, Strabo was free to mount his own operations further east in Thrace. Again, his forces advanced on the imperial capital, and this time they attacked it. The first assault fell on the main gates of the city, but was beaten off by Illus' troops. The Goths then renewed operations from Sycae across the Golden Horn. Finally, they moved to Near Hestiae and Sosthenium beside the Bosporos in an attempt to cross to Bithynia. The aim was perhaps to mount a third attack from Chalcedon, but the imperial navy forced Strabo to abandon the idea.[37] While all these attacks were beaten off, their intent is clear enough. Strabo had

[37] John of Antioch fr. 211.5; other refs, *PLRE* 2, 1076.

decided that a meaningful political accommodation with Zeno was impossible, and was trying to destroy him entirely. He probably had it in mind to place one of Marcian's brothers on the throne.

When his attacks on Constantinople failed, Strabo moved his forces towards Greece, but was killed when his horse threw him on to a spear-rack at Stabula Diomedis on the Via Egnatia (between Philippi and Maximianopolis).[38] At the western end of the Via Egnatia lay Epidamnus, base of Theoderic the Amal since 479, so that some further military cooperation between the Goths may have been planned (cf. John of Antioch fr. 211.4). Strabo's death frustrated whatever plans had been laid, however, and also paved the way towards Gothic unification. Succession among the Thracian Goths first passed jointly to Strabo's son Recitach and his two (anonymous) uncles, but Recitach later murdered them to rule by himself (John of Antioch fr. 211.5). This must have strained loyalties within the Thracian Goths, but the uncles may also have been plotting, of course, to oust Recitach. A fairly close parallel is provided by Theoderic the Amal's relations with his uncle Vidimer, only in that case, as we have seen, Theoderic's father was alive to help him dispose of the uncle in question (pp. 154f). Securing his position at the head of the group had to be the first priority for any new Gothic leader.

This particular round of dynastic instability had profound consequences. In 482 the Amal broke out of Epidamnus and ravaged much of the south-west Balkans. This perhaps indicates that Zeno had turned his troops east, once again, towards the Thracian Goths. Theoderic's successes forced Zeno, in 483, to grant him an unprecedentedly favourable agreement. The former Pannonian Goths received land in Dacia Ripensis and lower Moesia, and Theoderic himself was appointed senior imperial general (*MVM praesentalis*) and consul for 484. To be consul was a totally unheard of distinction for a man whose political prominence stemmed from his position as barbarian king.[39] Strabo's son Recitach was also subsequently murdered, in late 483 or early 484, by agents of the Amal, at Zeno's instigation. He was on his way from a bath to a feast, in Bonophatianae, probably a suburb of Constantinople.[40]

[38] John of Antioch fr. 211.5 (the best account); Marcellinus Comes s.a. 481 (= *CM* 2, 92); Theophanes *AM* 5970 (126 de Boor); Jordanes *Romana* 346; cf. *PLRE* 2, 1076.

[39] Marcellinus Comes s.a. 483 (= *CM* 2, 92).

[40] John of Antioch fr. 214.3: Usually dated 484, because it reports Recitach's jealousy of the Amal's consulship (484). But the nomination would have been announced in autumn 483.

With Recitach's death, the line of Strabo ceased to exist as an effective political force, and the majority of the Thracian Goths attached themselves to Theoderic the Amal. We have no explicit statement to this effect, and some Thracian Goths did prefer to give their allegiance to Zeno.[41] But no large Gothic group remained in the Balkans after Theoderic left for Italy in 488/9. Likewise, the army of Ostrogothic Italy in the 530s and 540s consisted of *c.*25,000–30,000 men.[42] This is precisely the order of magnitude we should expect from a unification of the Pannonian and Thracian Goths, both of which numbered 10,000–15,000 men (above pp. 151f). The murder of Recitach thus enabled the Amal to unite the majority of Goths in the Balkan peninsula, either immediately, or in the course of the revolts which presaged his departure for Italy (see chapter 8). In the process, Theoderic approximately doubled the military power of his following.[43]

On one level, unification had been brought about by the accidental death of Theoderic Strabo and resultant dynastic mayhem. This is, however, an insufficient explanation. Even on Recitach's death, the Thracian Goths did not have to attach themselves to the Amal bandwagon, and some chose not to. To my mind, therefore, of equal, if not greater, importance was the increasing contacts that had grown up between the two groups. The process began, at the latest, in 477, when, as we have seen, some of the Amal-led Goths joined Theoderic Strabo. Apart from perceptions of which leader was likely to do better, a further reason for such switches of allegiance emerges from the events of 478. The confrontation engineered by Zeno underlined the risks which open conflict between the two Gothic groups posed to long-term survival. The thoughts which Malchus gives to Theoderic Strabo must have occurred to all. If the Goths fought, then only the Romans would gain. This thought had a logical extension. Although their leaders were in competition, the mass of the Goths stood to do much better, in the face of the powerful eastern Roman Empire, as a united force. Two separate forces were smaller, and could always be played off against one another. The bulk of the Goths were willing to accept unification as the natural outcome of Recitach's assassination, only because they had come to realize that unity rather than conflict best served their interests. For the Goths as a whole, the Empire, rather than any rival leadership line, had become the main danger.

[41] E.g. Bessas and Godidisclus: Procopius *Wars* 1.8.3; cf. 5.5.3; 5.16.2; cf. Wolfram, 1988, 279 n.162.
[42] Hannestad, 1960, 136ff.
[43] Further argumentation: Heather, 1991, 302–3.

As we shall see, Gothic unification created further serious problems for Zeno, whose eventual solution would involve establishing a Gothic state in Italy (chapter 8). For the moment, however, we can leave Theoderic the Amal savouring his moment of triumph. Consul and imperial general, distributor of large annual payments to his followers, he had achieved all the aims for which he and his father had left Pannonia a decade previously. Theoderic had indeed ousted the Thracian Goths from their particular niche within the eastern Empire. More than that, he had subsumed the bulk of them within the ranks of his own followers. An even greater level of ambition beckoned.

6

The Transformation of the Goths 376–484

The period of Hunnic ascendency wrought huge changes among the Goths. Many Goths, at different moments and in different circumstances, decided, or were forced by the Huns, to leave their homes north of the Black Sea. They took with them large numbers of subordinates, who, as slaves or freedmen in permanent dependence, actually comprised a majority of the population, at least among the sixth-century Ostrogoths. The prevailing socio-political order was also destroyed. Some Gothic fragments sought asylum in enclaves around the Pontus. Others, in varying circumstances, thought that the Roman Empire offered the best chance of future success. Still others fell under Hunnic sway. In the process, established dynasties (Athanaric, Ermenaric, Vithimer) fell by the wayside, either in battle against the Huns, or because their followers – under enormous stress – refused to accept their continued guidance. The Huns also deliberately dismantled the overall leadership of at least some of the Gothic groups they conquered (chapter 4).

A. *The Supergroups*

Some of these fragments came together, inside the Roman Empire, to create two new Gothic 'supergroups'. Precise circumstances varied, but there are important similarities between the creation of the Ostrogoths in the late fifth century, and that of the Visigoths some

75 years before. In both cases, a number of previously separate groups united to create a Gothic entity of unprecedented size, amidst a cacophony of dynastic competition. Alaric and Athaulf fought Sarus and Sergeric for control of the Visigoths; Valamer and his nephew Theoderic overcame a series of rivals, familial and non-familial, to head the Ostrogoths. Both were also created inside the Roman Empire, which played a critical role in the process on two levels.

First, the Empire was pre-eminently powerful and had, over the centuries, developed tried and trusted methods for undermining the independence of even welcome immigrants. Part of the Empire's ideological vision of itself also portrayed outsiders as straightforwardly inferior. Faced with such power and such attitudes, many Goths were well aware, or became so, of good reasons, whatever their past divisions, to operate together in the face of the Roman state. Tervingi and Greuthungi cooperated together as early as 376, as Valens attempted to divide and rule them by allowing just the former across the Danube. Those of the former followers of Radagaisus who had been sold into slavery, or seen their wives and children massacred in Italian cities, quickly grasped the logic of attaching themselves to Alaric's following. The followers of the two Theoderics, likewise, refused to countenance the mutual destruction planned for them by Zeno in 478. The dangers of the Migration Period taught all these groups the virtues of cooperation. Others should have followed their example.

Before 376, numerous Goths (not just Ermenaric and Vithimer) were killed in 'many engagements' against the Huns (AM 31.3.2–3; Eunapius fr. 42). Many more died in six further years of warfare against the Roman state between 376 and 382. To the losses in the major battles – Ad Salices and Hadrianople – we must add those who died in the costly siege of the city of Hadrianople (AM 31.15). Three whole Gothic subgroups had also been destroyed by different imperial commanders, and Gothic hostages massacred.[1] Many more Goths were killed trying to cross the Danube in 386 under Odotheus, and in the course of Radagaisus' adventure in 405/6. Similarly, the Hunnic empire of Attila and his sons caused innumerable Gothic fatalities, whether in fighting for it at the Catalaunian Plains and afterwards (*Getica* 192ff; Priscus fr. 49), in attempting to establish independence from it (*Getica* 268–9, 272–3), or in trying to escape from it into the eastern Empire under Bigelis (Jordanes, *Romana* 336). Still more

[1] Frigeridus (AM 31.9), Sebastianus (AM 31.11), and Modares (Zosimus 4.25). Hostages: AM 31.16.8ff.

Goths died in the Balkans in the 470s and 480s. The Goths' overall experience in the Hunnic period was extremely violent. Amidst upheavals on this scale, there was safety in numbers.

Secondly, the Roman Empire operated very powerful redistributive financial mechanisms. This quality was exploited enthusiastically by adventurous Goths who were able to make the Empire, more or less willingly, recognize them as allies. Thiudimer decided to move into the Empire's Balkan possessions in 473 to share in the financial success of the Thracian Gothic *foederati* (p. 153). Such financial support could be extracted, however, only when the relevant Goths were already too numerous for the Empire to enforce its traditional policy of dismantling immigrant autonomy. This is well illustrated after 376. The Gothic groups who became the Visigoths, in the first place united to survive, and only later, in the reign of Alaric (395–410), were able to extend their range of financial and political demands. The Roman Empire thus provided both cogent reasons for Goths to put aside previous divisions, and wealth to finance the new socio-political enterprises.

The inherent logic of the exciting, but dangerous, world of the Migration Period, was felt by others too. The Vandal coalition which seized north Africa was composed of two previously separate Vandal groups (Hasdings and Silings) and a large number of Alans.[2] The career of Clovis, creator of the Frankish kingdom in Gaul, likewise consisted in no small measure of uniting a series of previously separate Frankish groups (Gregory of Tours *Histories* 2.40ff). The precise admixture of fear and anticipated profit varied from case to case. In the general circumstances of the late fourth and fifth centuries, however, a heady cocktail of fear combined with unprecedented opportunities for cashing in on the Roman Empire's financial sophistication, applied to all. But for every group which survived and prospered, there was another which experienced defeat and destruction. The Siling Vandals were destroyed in Spain in the 410s, Belisarius completing the process of Vandal genocide in North Africa a century later.[3] The Burgundians, likewise, were savaged by the Huns and resettled inside the Empire in the 430s,[4] and the Rugi suffered such a defeat at the hands of Odovacar that they voluntarily attached themselves to the Ostrogoths (John of Antioch fr. 214.7).

[2] See generally, Courtois, 1955.

[3] Hydatius 59–60 [67–8]; Procopius *Wars* 3–4 with further comments and parallels below at chapter 7.

[4] Refs conveniently collected by O'Flynn, 1983, 89 n.4.

B. Peoples and Armies

Of extreme importance in themselves, these patterns of historical transformation raise again the question met before in the context of the later second and third centuries. Given all the changes, was there any real continuity between the Goths of *c.*350 and the two supergroups of the fifth century? The picture of total continuity found in the pages of Jordanes held sway for a very long time indeed. Many, even recent, books have talked as though Ostrogoths and Visigoths already existed in the fourth century. This, as we have seen, is deeply misleading. Visigoths and Ostrogoths were new creations of the later fourth and fifth centuries.

In a necessary reaction, some recent work has argued, on the contrary, that there was relatively little continuity in the meaning of the term Goth between *c.* AD 350 and 500. In particular, one influential view regards a limited number of royal or noble families, such as the Amal and Balth dynasties, as the real binding force – *Traditionskern* – in Gothic society. This approach to the question was pioneered by the German historian Reinhard Wenskus, in a revolutionary work of the early 1960s. Its general vision of ethnicity has since been applied to a number of case studies, including the Goths, by scholars working particularly in Vienna.[5] Different commentators have understood this *Traditionskern* as encompassing greater or smaller numbers of families, and as either a genuine dynastic continuity, or the myth of continuity, which was available for any successful Gothic leader to exploit. The reality behind this legitimizing façade, it has come to be argued, was the Gothic military kingship. This was a highly flexible institution which allowed anyone, whatever their origin, to become a Goth by accepting the rule of one of these dynasties, and incorporation into the armies that followed them. It has been suggested, correspondingly, that groups labelled Gothic in this period behave more like armies than peoples. Fluctuating greatly in size, they demanded gold and food supplies rather than grants of land. Tending to be predominantly male, they were composed of a wide mixture of ethnic elements, not just Goths.[6] There is something to all of these points. But such an overall vision of 'Gothic' history in the Hunnic period does not, it seems to me, do full justice to the evidence.

Once inside the Roman Empire, the average military component of

[5] Wenskus, 1961; cf. Wolfram, 1988; Pohl, 1988.

[6] Military kingship: Wolfram, 1988. Armies: Rouché, 1986; Liebeschuetz, 1990, 1992.

the lives of individual Goths surely increased. They had to fight to survive, and the basic *quid pro quo* in Gothic agreements with the Empire always consisted in performing military service in return for economic benefit. Life on the march, likewise, is likely to have taken a higher toll on the old, the young and possibly womenfolk too.[7] Thus increasing militarization was a major consequence of the Migration Period, and Gothic units carving out a niche for themselves in the Roman Empire are likely to have contained an abnormal proportion of men. Neither militarization nor unusual population ratios, however, mean that the Ostrogoths and Visigoths were essentially armies.

Neither the Amal and Balth families, the great royal houses of the successor states, nor even a myth concerning them, it must be stressed, provide any germ of continuity. As we have seen, both generated their pre-eminence in the course of building up around themselves their respective following. Contrary to the picture in Jordanes' *Getica*, the Balthi emerged only in Gaul from the 410s, and the Amals in the Balkans from the 450s. Both defeated a large number of potential rivals. The idea that they came from ancient ruling traditions is a phantasm created by their own, later, dynastic propaganda. The appearance of the label 'Goth' cannot be explained merely by the persistence of these families and their traditions.[8] Indeed, there are distinct signs of alternative memories and traditions which did not coincide with the claims of these dynasties to a monopoly of political power (p. 239). Likewise, one Gothic group within the Hunnic Empire preserved its identity despite having no overall leader at all (Priscus fr. 49). Correspondingly, the politically enfranchised class of 'notables' in Ostrogothic Italy consisted not just of a few leading clans, but of several thousand adult males (App. 1). This body of individuals cannot, it seems to me, be excluded from our vision of Gothic ethnicity. There is also plenty of evidence that the Gothic supergroups were rather more than just armies.

First, at least some Gothic groups of the Migration Period were mixed social units, not just gatherings of young men. Graeco–Roman sources, it must be stressed, had no interest in providing a broad survey of the social composition of Gothic groups moving over the frontier, but were basically concerned to chronicle their effects upon the Empire. That women and children are often not mentioned, therefore, is only a weak argument from silence. In some cases, we can anyway be more positive. In 479, for instance, Theoderic the Amal offered to leave the

[7] Kazanski, 1991, 65–6.
[8] See further; Heather, 1991, chs 1–2; Heather, 1995b.

Plate 11 A non-Gothic waggon train (for Western lovers, it is the Red River in the background)

'unarmed multitude' within his following in a city of Zeno's choice, while he campaigned with 6,000 chosen warriors (Malchus fr. 18.4, p. 446, 213). If not women, children and the old, it is hard to know who else this multitude might be. Theoderic's force also carried along with it herds, seed grain and a huge baggage train. In 479, Zeno's general Sabinianus captured 2,000 Gothic waggons; there may well have been more. In a single line, 2,000 waggons would have stretched out over ten miles or more.[9] The Rugi who later attached themselves to Theoderic in 487 likewise came with their womenfolk, mentioned both in Ennodius' *Life of Epiphanius* (118–19) and Procopius (*Wars* 7.2.1ff). Procopius also mentions women, children and waggons following Theoderic to Italy.[10] This evidence makes it very difficult not to see Theoderic's

[9] Discussing Alaric, Hall, 1988, 253 cites the Great Trek of the Boers and western expansion in the USA. In these cases, there was a waggon for approximately every six people, and 460 waggons stretched out over three miles.

[10] Procopius *Wars* 5.1.12; cf. Ennodius *Life of Epiphanius* 111–12.

following as a broadly based social group engaged in a large-scale migration of more or less the traditionally envisaged kind.

Of the constituent parts of the Visigoths, the same would seem to be true of the Tervingi and Greuthungi who crossed the Danube in 376. The sources make various (if rhetorical) references to the women and children in their ranks. Likewise, the followers of Radagaisus drafted into the Roman army by Stilicho later joined Alaric because their women and children, quartered in Italian cities, had been massacred (Zosimus 5.37.5). For the core of Alaric's group operating in the Balkans in 395, we have no such explicit evidence. But there is every reason to view them as the Goths of 382 (and hence those of 376) in general revolt (p. 141), and the poet Claudian does in passing refer to Gothic womenfolk enjoying the fruits of their husbands' success (*Eut.* 2.198–9). Overall, the evidence is certainly not comprehensive, but it is sufficient in the case of Theoderic's Ostrogoths to contradict a contrary argument from silence. This suggests, more generally, that, in the other cases where women and children are not mentioned so explicitly, too much weight should probably not be placed upon the silence of our sources.

Secondly, too much, to my mind, has been made of fluctuating numbers. Recent studies of Alaric's Visigoths have seen him as the commander of a single mutinous regiment in 395, and put great emphasis on the poet Claudian's description of his forces melting away from him in Italy (*VI Cons. Hon.* 127ff, 252ff). But Claudian actually worked for Stilicho, Alaric's opponent at this point. Given that Stilicho was not displaying the Goth's head on a pole (as he later did with that of Radagaisus), Claudian had to find some other way to maximize his employer's achievements. And after retreating from Italy, Alaric showed no signs of having suffered a major defeat. He re-established his position in the Balkans, and, within three years, was being courted by Stilicho because of his military strength (p. 146). Claudian's highly partial account will not bear much weight. Indeed, the better evidence, as we have seen, suggests that Alaric was in fact a Gothic noble-turned-king, leading, already in 395, a mass revolt of the Goths settled under the 382 treaty. In 409/10, he then added to his group substantial numbers of recruits from one major additional source: the former followers of Radagaisus.

Some population elements certainly came and went. As the Visigoths were forming, for instance, Gothic nobles found their way into Roman employ. Only five, however, are known to have made the switch: Munderich, Modares, Fravittas, Sarus and Gainas. Four of these were defeated candidates for the overall leadership of the Goths, or their associates. Munderich and Modares were associates of the ousted Athanaric,[11] Fravittas was driven out of Gothic society by the operation of feud , and Sarus belonged to a line which competed with that of Alaric (p. 143). These men had to leave or die, therefore, and provide no good evidence of incoherence in the Gothic main body.[12] Of larger comings and goings, some Huns had become part of Alaric's force by 408 (Zosimus 5.37.1). But these may be the same Huns, or their descendants, who had fought at Hadrianople. We hear of only one significant departure, in *c.*414, of a group of Alans in Gaul. They were perhaps a recent addition to Gothic strength, since numerous Alanic groups had invaded Gaul in 406 (Paulinus of Pella *Euch.* 372ff). Given the eventual size of Alaric's following and the dramatic events unfolding around them, the evidence does not amount, to my mind at least, to a picture of great fluctuation.

The Ostrogothic pattern is similar. Dynastic rivalries again caused upheaval and desertion. Beremud and Vidimer both left for the west rather than accept increasingly centralized Amal dynastic rule over the Pannonian Goths. Otherwise, apart from one exchange of population in 477 (p. 159), the Pannonian and Thracian Goths seem to have operated as discrete groups who then united. Although some of the latter chose not to follow Theoderic to Italy, only two are mentioned by name, both officers in the Byzantine army. This level of social distinction suggests that they may have belonged to the top echelon of the Thracian Goths. If so, then, as close associates of a defeated dynasty, it was perhaps again too dangerous for them to remain in Gothic society. The sources also record the comings and goings of some groups. The largest of these was clearly the Rugi, who played a very independent hand in Theoderic's conquest of Italy (chapter 8). They, however, had only been recruited in 487, and had previously run their own independent kingdom. Such a group is hardly typical of the bulk of Theoderic's following. Otherwise we hear of some Gepids, Bittigur Huns and others within the Italian kingdom, to whom we should probably add heterogeneous contingents added after the defeat of Odovacar.[13] There is no sign,

11 Munderich: AM 31.3.5. Zosimus 4.25.2: Modares was a 'member of the Scythian royal family' (= Athanaric's family: p. 57).

12 *Contra* Thompson, 1963. For a similar critique, see Rousseau, 1992. Of the origins of Gainas, we know nothing. I have not included Tribigild as he was presumably forced into the Roman army in the aftermath of Odotheus' defeat: above p. 138.

13 Huns: Agathias 2.13.1ff; Jordanes, *Getica* 272. See generally: Wolfram, 1988, 300ff.

however, that any of these contingents was very large. The basic pattern for both Ostrogoths and Visigoths was not one of constant flux.

Thirdly, the evidence of Gothic demands is more complicated than the army hypothesis might suggest. In 376 and 382, the first Goths to move into the Empire wanted, and eventually received, land to farm, even if, at their most ambitious, they wanted much else besides (pp. 135ff). Of Alaric's demands, we are ill-informed until his forces were sitting outside Rome in 409 and 410. At that point, he was certainly interested in grain and gold, as the army hypothesis would suggest, but he also wanted a place to 'dwell' or 'settle'. By 418, this meant farmland (chapter 7). Indeed, without their own food-producing lands, the vulnerability of Goths to blockade and food shortages was extreme (p. 148). In the case of Theoderic the Amal, in the 470s, there is no doubt that land for farming was as much a part of the deals being negotiated as were food supplies and gold payments. As we have seen, the Thracian Goths had probably been established on farmland too (p. 151). The fact that Goths wanted to profit as much as possible from the Empire, and hence were not above demanding gold from it when they could, should not confuse the discussion. They also wanted lands to hold and farm.

While the lives of male Goths increasingly revolved around military activity, this does not make it helpful to view the Gothic groups coming within the orbit of the Empire simply as armies. To my mind, the evidence suggests that we are dealing with mixed social groups, which, given the circumstances, showed perhaps surprising coherence. The demands they made of the Roman state, likewise, varied according to circumstance. Stakes increased when bargaining positions were stronger, but the Goths consistently demanded land to farm, as well as money and food supplies from the Roman state. As in the third century, we would seem to be dealing with the large-scale movement of mixed social groups: 'proper' migration.

C. *Ethnicity*

None of this necessarily means, of course, that the new Gothic supergroups were not also multi-ethnic. It is simply a fact that the Visigoths and Ostrogoths were not composed entirely of Goths. Huns and Alans were more or less permanently incorporated into the former, and, among the Ostrogoths in Italy, there were Rugi and

Gepids, and perhaps also Bittigur Huns. Indeed, some of the new units of the Migration Period, particularly the force controlled by Odovacar in Italy, were amalgamations from such a multiplicity of ethnic groups, that the sources disagree over how to label them. Should we envisage Visigoths and Ostrogoths as ethnically random collections of pre-existing groups, or was there a more substantial reason for the fact that our sources designate them as Gothic?

In a very important sense, the fourth-century Gothic kingdoms were already multi-ethnic. As we have seen, they probably consisted of a defining migrant elite of quasi-nobles and freemen, the basic carriers of 'Gothicness'. These migrants coexisted, however, with a whole series of subordinates, and boundaries between the groups were liable to fluctuation (chapter 3). The real question, therefore, is not so much whether there were any non-Goths among the fifth-century supergroups, but the degree to which new non-Gothic outsiders and old non-Gothic subordinates were absorbed into the defining political elites of the new groups.

The fact that survival and profit in the face of Roman power provided a huge impetus to the creation of the new supergroups in part argues against the importance of any pre-existing Gothic ethnicity. Belonging to a large group was what really mattered, not its composition. We might also expect the shared experiences of the Migration Period to have generated a degree of homogenization, i.e. the absorption of subordinates into the elite. Groups needed to stick together to survive.

But not all the non-Gothic recruits into the Visigoths and Ostrogoths were so absorbed. The Rugi, for instance, who attached themselves to the Ostrogoths, retained a sense of separate identity for the best part of 50 years. Some Alans, likewise, who had attached themselves to the Visigoths, were quick to leave when a better opportunity presented itself. More generally, the Ostrogoths remained strongly hierarchical in nature, with a defining political elite consisting of between one-fifth and one-half of the adult male population.[14] The shared dangers of the Migration Period did not iron out social difference within this group.

Moreover, most of the main component parts of the two new supergroups were themselves Gothic. In the case of the Visigoths, the Tervingi and Greuthungi who crossed the Danube in 376 were both, according to Ammianus, straightforwardly Gothic. A smaller group of Huns and Alans joined them in 377, fought at

[14] Appendix 1, cf. p. 325.

Hadrianople, and was probably also settled under the treaty of 382.[15] That Athaulf led a mixed force of Goths and Huns in 408 may reflect the continued existence, within Alaric's force, of this group, or the addition of some more outsiders. The greatest source of non-Goths among the Visigoths is likely to have been the further recruits Alaric gained from Stilicho's federate troops after the latter's murder, and runaway slaves as the Goths sat outside Rome. As we have seen, some of these may well have been Alans and Taifali, but many were former followers of the Gothic king Radagaisus (above p. 147). While certainly incorporating non-Goths, the bulk of the defining Visigothic elite probably did stem, therefore, from groups which were already Gothic.

In similar vein, the Pannonian and Thracian groups, the major sources of manpower for the Ostrogoths, are individually labelled Goths in a variety of independent sources. Visigoths and Ostrogoths would seem to have been Gothic, therefore, because their elites – to judge by the Ostrogoths, a substantial social caste – were largely composed of people who both considered themselves Goths, and were considered so by others. Where no single ethnic group was dominant in a new political unit, titulature was capable of expressing this fact. The Hasding rulers of North Africa called themselves *reges Vandalorum et Alannorum*: 'kings of the Vandals and Alans'.

No confusion or ambiguity attends the Visigoths and Ostrogoths. No contemporary ever thought of these groups as a whole, or indeed of their main constituent elements, as anything other than Gothic. Not everyone, however, had an equal claim to 'Gothicness'. This was the preserve of a defining elite, into which some of the non-Goths bound up with the Visigoths and Ostrogoths will have been recruited, but not enough to change the elite's self-image. The new supergroups were, indeed, very large. The Ostrogoths could field 25,000–30,000 fighting men, and the Visigoths were probably similar in order of magnitude. This would imply total populations in the region of 100,000 people, and a defining elite of 4,000–5,000. If so, each group could incorporate large numbers of non-Goths (perhaps 10,000 or even 20,000), especially in subordinate roles, while still remaining 'Gothic'.

Not, of course, that a pre-existing sense of Gothic identity shaped the behaviour of every individual Goth. In the fourth century, Gothic

[15] Alatheus and Saphrax are sometimes held to have led a 'polyethnic' confederation of Goths, Huns and Alans, but this has no basis in the sources: Heather, 1991, 144–5.

groups established a number of separate kingdoms. One powerful effect of the Hunnic invasions was to fragment the Gothic world still further. Different groups chose or were forced to take different options in the face of new instability. As the supergroups were generated, individual Goths had the choice of joining them or not, and these options could find expression in a single career. A case in point is one Sidimund. A Goth of high status, he would seem to have originated among the Pannonian Goths. He is said, at least, to have had some connection to Theoderic the Amal. We first find him enjoying service (and its rewards) in the east Roman Empire. As circumstances changed, he decided to throw in his lot with Theoderic, assisting him in the capture of Epidamnus, where he had previously been rewarded with imperial estates (Malchus fr. 18.4, p. 438, 64ff). Sidimund clearly required some convincing, and not all elite Goths – either as individuals or in groups – necessarily saw the logic of joining the new supergroups. In particular, those who had most invested in the old order, or were excluded from the new (such as the defeated would-be contenders for the new groups' overall leadership), tended to seek alternative niches. Other Goths remained totally independent. The Pontic Goths saw no need to leave the Black Sea region, maintaining their independence there into the sixth century.

It was only in certain situations, therefore, that some Gothic groups were ready to lay aside histories of separation from, and competition with, one another. This tended to happen where the threat of Roman power was a major factor, since the logic of cooperating to survive in such circumstances was both powerful and immediate. Without such an external stimulus, the similarities that Goths may have shared (on which, see chapter 10) would not have been enough to overcome the competitive rivalries opened up by processes of kingdom formation in the third and fourth centuries. Ostrogoths and Visigoths were Gothic, because their defining elite caste – much more than a few noble clans – was composed largely of Goths. This does not make them, however, anything other than situational constructs. Their existence is inconceivable outside the frontiers of the Roman Empire. Without the threat of Roman power, and the availability of hard Roman cash, Gothic freemen and nobles would not have been ready to put aside a history of separate development.

This leaves one further question. Once this critical external stimulus was applied, did the fact that groups were already Gothic make them more likely to join up with similarly Gothic groups, rather than with others of different backgrounds? As we have seen, most of the constituent parts of the two supergroups already attracted a 'Gothic' label before they united to create the Visigoths and Ostrogoths. This suggests that the answer to the question might be 'yes', but clearly not exclusively so. Rugi, Alans, Gepids and others could and did attach themselves to Ostrogoths and Visigoths as well. While there was seemingly a preferential tendency for Goths to unite with one another, this did not extend to the point of totally excluding non-Goths, and the point should not be pressed.

That even a tendency to work preferentially with other Goths should have existed, is not, perhaps, surprising. As we have seen, fourth-century Goths had already evolved a substantial sense of their own separate identity, and were erecting and enforcing barriers to maintain it, especially against the Roman state. Whether, at this point, the different Gothic kingdoms all had a sense of sharing something against outsiders (as the contemporary Alamanni did: p. 64) is impossible to judge. It seems more likely that they were as much in competition with one another as with outsiders.

Nevertheless these kingdoms had been created by a process of migration and expansion out of northern Poland. Thus the tendency of Gothic freemen to act together against outside threats in the later fourth and fifth centuries may well have had a basis in a heritage of shared beliefs and values from the first, second and third centuries. This was, however, no more than a tendency, and, for many Goths, it took the harsh experience of the Migration Period to break down powerful traditions of separate action. I think it likely, therefore, that there was a layer of common Gothic identity within Gothic individuals of the fourth century who enjoyed the crucial social status of freemen. It was submerged, however, beneath other layers of identity of a more particular and separate kind (Tervingi, Greuthungi etc.). Only when Huns and Romans had, between them, destroyed these outer layers, could a more general sense of Gothicness, given added point by circumstances of danger and opportunity, be utilized to help create the new supergroups. Even so, Gothicness was not such an exclusive concept that other would-be recruits were refused. The 'Gothicness' of the new supergroups was thus a complicated mixture of claimed and recognized social status, pre-existing similarity, and the overriding press of circumstance.

Part III

The Kingdoms of the Goths

7

The First Gothic Successor State

The early fifth-century *History Against the Pagans* of Paulus Orosius ends in *c.*416 with the Gothic king Vallia's wars in Spain against the Alans and Vandals. Orosius refers to a Gothic people (*gens Gothorum*), and to their king (*rex*), but never to a Gothic kingdom (*regnum*). *Regnum*, as applied to the Gallic Goths, appears in sources only in the time of king Euric (466–84).[1] There is a real point here. The Visigothic kingdom of the later fifth century was a very different entity from the immigrant Goths established in south-western Gaul in the 410s.

A. *Creating a Kingdom*

(i) The settlement of 418 and after

The new order in Gotho–Roman affairs seems to have been dictated by two separate peace treaties: one between Fl. Constantius and Vallia in 416, the second with Theoderic I in 418.[2] As a result, the Goths were established in the Garonne valley between Toulouse and Bordeaux. Hostages, it seems, were exchanged. Theodorus, a friend of the future Emperor Avitus, was a Roman hostage at the court of Theoderic I (Sid. Ap. *Carm.* 7. 213ff). There was also a military alliance; the Goths promised to furnish troops for Roman campaigns.

1 Teillet, 1984, 146–9, 20ff, 242ff.
2 See e.g. Wolfram, 1988, 172ff; the relevant essays in Drinkwater and Elton, 1992; Cesa, 1994, ch. 4.

Much ink has been expended on which military campaigns Fl. Constantius might have had in mind.[3]

The best indicator of at least his immediate plans for them, however, must surely be the use to which they were put. Under Vallia, Goths, combined with Roman forces, destroyed Siling Vandal and Alan power in Spain (Hyd. 59–60 [67–8]). After a brief pause, they returned to Spain in the early 420s, attempting to mete out the same treatment to the Hasding Vandals (Hyd. 69 [77]). Given that the Garonne valley was conveniently placed for passes over the Pyrenees into Spain, there seems little doubt that restoring the situation in Spain was the Romans' main objective. This makes sense on two counts. Spain was a rich, tax-producing area. Likewise, the Hasding Vandals, together with the other remnants of the 406 Rhine crossing, were now the main barbarian force left unsubdued within the Empire.

The settlement also provided for the Goths' economic needs. The old view – the so-called *hospitalitas* system – was that, by an extension of army billeting rules, actual land was made available to them, which they then exploited to produce their own food. More recently, essentially on the basis of evidence from Ostrogothic Italy, it has been argued that in all cases the Roman state handed over tax revenues rather than actual land when settling barbarian immigrants in any given area.[4] This is not the place for a detailed discussion, but, as we shall see, the Ostrogoths do seem to have been given original land grants in Italy (chapter 8). Likewise, the one specific piece of evidence we have for the 418 settlement reports that the Goths were given 'land for farming'. The statement is preserved only in a late epitome, but derives from a detailed contemporary source, and I see no reason to disbelieve it. That actual land was handed over, at some point, is also implied by some later Visigothic legal texts.[5]

Ideally, archaeological evidence would be called upon to resolve the question, but the archaeological invisibility of the Goths in Aquitaine is famous. No Gothic cemeteries or other substantial physical remains have so far been identified. But before we conclude that the Gothic settlement left no trace, it must be remembered that Aquitaine has been relatively little investigated. More cemeteries have been excavated in just the Pas de Calais than in the whole of the region south of the Loire.

[3] Wallace-Hadrill, 1961 argued that the Goths were meant to defend Aquitaine against Saxon pirates; Thompson, 1956 Gallic landowners against rebellious peasant *Bacaudae* (bandits).

[4] Goffart, 1980, 103ff; Durliat, 1988.

[5] Philostorgius *h.e.* 12.4–5 (= Olympiodorus fr. 26.2). Full discussion and refs: Liebeschuetz, 1990, 73–4; Cesa, 1994, 167ff. On the legal evidence, see p. 284.

And when researchers say that no 'Gothic' cemeteries have been found in Aquitaine, what they have in mind is large 'row grave' (*Reihengräber*) cemeteries, full of rich burials. This form of cemetery is held to be characteristically 'Germanic', on the basis of finds in the Rhine area above all, but also, as we shall see, in Visigothic Spain. Later Černjachov and Danubian cemeteries suggest, however, that Gothic burial rites were evolving towards inhumation with few or no gravegoods. Only a few elite burials were being equipped with striking inventories by the mid-fifth century. 'Real' Gothic graves in Aquitaine, therefore, are likely to have been much less visible: not rowgrave cemeteries, but inhumations with few goods. The current lack of Gothic burials from Aquitaine does not mean, therefore, that Goths were not present there in large numbers, nor that further investigation will not bring their remains to light. There is no doubt, for instance, that the Ostrogoths were present in large numbers in Italy (20,000–30,000 adult males), but the standard modern archaeological monograph identifies only 126 graves with some claim to be Gothic.

Indeed, striking archaeological evidence of quite different kinds is already available. Fifth-century Aquitaine was extremely prosperous, in so far as prosperity can be measured by artistic production for its elite: mosaics and decorated marble sarcophagi (plate 13). Over 300 villas with fifth-century mosaics have been unearthed, more than in any other area of the western Empire. The famous Aquitainian sarcophagus series also began in the fifth century. This elite prosperity must reflect at least the general conditions created by the Visigothic settlement, and perhaps, more directly, the buying power of the area's new Gothic elite, as much as that of indigenous Gallo-Roman landowners. By 418, the Goths, or some of them, were Christian, rich and attuned to the pleasures of Roman culture. Vandals, for instance, are known to have liked Roman mosaics, and Gothic kings would later patronize Roman culture (see below). Four genuinely Černjachov objects have also been found in the Garonne: three combs at Beaucaire-sur-Baise, Seviac and Bapteste, and a crossbow fibula at Le Canet. All four were found in villas. The argument cannot be pressed, but the available archaeological picture is certainly consonant with landowning Goths spread over, and enjoying the fruits of, the Aquitainian countryside.[6]

Whether the Roman state gave the Visigothic king Theoderic I any official administrative powers over the region is unclear, but, to my mind, unlikely. Imitations of official Roman coins issued in Gaul

[6] See generally, Kazanski, 1991, 89ff, with James, 1991 and refs.

Plate 12 An Aquitanian sarcophagus

before *c*.450 have sometimes been ascribed to the Goths, but not on the basis of any evidence.[7] That Theoderic I issued laws has also sometimes been inferred from a passage in Sidonius Apollinaris (*Ep.* 2.1.3), and a reference, in the surviving part of a law code traditionally ascribed to king Euric, to 'laws of my father' (*CE* 277: Euric's father was Theoderic I). But Sidonius was punning – comparing the Roman laws of Theodosius (i.e. the *Theodosian Code*) with the illegal Gothic ones of Theoderic – and it is highly doubtful that the latter really existed. Likewise, many now argue that the *Code of Euric* was actually issued by Alaric II (484–507), Euric's son. In this case, the 'father' would be Euric himself.[8]

[7] King, 1992.
[8] See Nehlsen's article in *RgA* 5, 42ff with refs.

The evidence for taxation paints, I think, a similar picture. Salvian, a priest of Marseilles, described at great length how, because of their tax burdens, rich and poor Romans alike had fled to the Goths (*De Gub. Dei* 5). Some have concluded from this that, by the early 440s, Theoderic was running an autonomous entity, beyond the reach of Roman tax assessors. Salvian was complaining, however, not about tax rates *per se*, but about the inequitable distribution of the burden. He never actually says that tax rates were lower in the Visigothic area. Rather, rich Romans had been forcing their neighbours to pay beyond their share, which is not the same thing as saying that Theoderic had the power to set the tax rates of Romans within his own defined domain. While there is every reason to suppose that Theoderic exercised a steadily increasing *de facto* influence over all aspects of life within the region, I very much doubt that in 418 he was given autonomous administrative power over the Garonne.

Up to *c*.450, the subsequent history of the Gothic settlement is illustrated by little more than a few chronicle entries. These show the Goths active in two directions. On the one hand, they are found in Spain, usually on the orders of the Roman state. Fighting the invaders of 406 was part of Vallia's original agreement with Fl. Constantius, and Goths continued, on occasion, to be employed in Spain to the same end. In 422 – the four-year gap perhaps reflects the complexity of installing the Goths on estates across the Garonne – they took part in a further expedition to Baetica under the imperial general Castinus. This targeted the Hasding Vandals. A decade of instability within the Empire and a lengthy Gothic revolt (see below) both brought the campaign to a halt, and delayed any repetition of the strategy until the 440s. In 446, under the general Vitus, a Gothic force again moved through Carthaginiensis and Baetica, this time directed against the Suevi. The campaigns had mixed results. Those of the 410s, as we have seen, were highly successful, but the later ones of 422 and 446 failed. Our jaded Spanish source blames the failures on Gothic treachery, which may or may not be correct.[9]

The Goths' second area of activity was southern Gaul. Here their aims were overtly expansionary. Taking advantage of every bout of political instability within the western Empire, the Goths attacked Arles in both 425 and 430 (Prosp. 1290 a 425; Hyd. 82 [92]). Between 436 and 439, moreover, they sustained a longer and more serious confrontation with the Roman state. Arles was attacked and

[9] Hyd. 69 [77], 126 [134]. On the conditions which prevented campaigns between the 420s and 440s, see Heather, 1995.

Narbonne besieged in 436/7, but the Goths were then driven back to Toulouse by the imperial commander Litorius and his largely Hunnic forces. When Litorius was captured, an agreement restored peace, and we hear of no further trouble before 451.[10] This marked willingness to confront the Empire makes it unsurprising that Theoderic at times also pursued his own agenda in Spain. In 431, a Goth called Vetto went to the Suevi 'with treacherous intentions' (Hyd. 87 [97]). This could mean several things, but it is perhaps most likely that Theoderic had it in mind to reach some kind of independent agreement with the Suevi. For, somewhere between 446 and 448, the Gothic king abandoned the policies pursued by the central imperial authorities and made a separate peace with the Suevic king Rechiarius. Theoderic's daughter married Rechiarius and he presented his son-in-law with a gift of arms: a formal sign of recognition (Hyd. 132 [140]).

What did the Goths want from these confrontations? Merobaudes' second panegyric on Aetius, probably delivered on 1 January 446, implies that the major revolt of the 430s, at least, was designed to win extra territory. Aetius is described as having re-established the boundaries between Roman and Goth.[11] The events seem to confirm Merobaudes' account, since, in 436, the Goths opened hostilities by attempting to capture Narbonne. They would later annex the city (see below), and several plausible motives suggest themselves for this design. The city and its dependent territory were rich, and the Goths probably wanted to control its wealth. Narbonne also had strategic importance. It gave access to the Mediterranean, and, perhaps more significant given later events, its control also opened up routes around the eastern Pyrenees into Spain.

The fact that they also attacked Arles does not mean, however, that their aim was always to capture that city too. Arles was the capital of the Gallic Prefecture, and, in threatening it, the Goths may have aimed to pose a threat to the jugular of Roman administration which would force the Empire to concede their demands. This had been Alaric's strategy in attacking Rome (chapter 4), and the latter's demands also suggest additional motivations beyond a desire for territory. The treaty of 418 authorized no generalship for Theoderic I, no annual gold payments (as far as we know) for his followers, and a land settlement only on the periphery of the Empire. As such, it was much closer to Alaric's minimum demands than his maximum (above p. 148). Apart from extra land, the Goths' agenda may well have

10 See e.g. Wolfram, 1988, 175f.
11 Ed. Clover, p. 13.19–22 (text); 50f and 56–8 (commentary).

included annual subsidies, and the opportunity to exercise real influence on the running of the Empire. If so, they were largely frustrated, for until *c.*450, Theoderic I remained without a generalship, perched on the edge of Roman territory beside the Atlantic ocean.

(ii) From settlement to kingdom (c.450–476)

This situation was transformed, after 450, by momentous events which originated largely outside of south-western Gaul. The three Gothic groups united by Alaric were only part of a much larger historical phenomenon, which saw a whole series of foreign groups thrown across the Roman frontier as a result of Hunnic action in eastern and central Europe. At the same time as the Goths were settling and periodically revolting in southern Gaul, Suevi were expanding, when they could, in Spain (particularly in the 440s). The Vandals had likewise seized the richest territories of the western Empire in North Africa (439), and the ambitions of Franks and Burgundians threatened north-eastern and south-eastern Gaul, again particularly in the 430s. To counter these invaders, the Roman general Aetius, paradoxically, drew on the military power of the Huns. He used them extensively in Gaul in the 430s, to savage Burgundians, and, particularly under Litorius, to check the Goths.[12]

This (none too solid) strategic balancing act was destroyed in the early 440s when the Hunnic Empire reached the apogee of its power under Attila and (at first) his brother Bleda (chapter 4). With the greater strength at their disposal, Hunnic leaders widened their ambitions. The policy of using them against unwanted immigrants in the west collapsed, as the Huns launched a series of attacks on the Roman Balkans in the 440s, and then turned to Gaul in 451.[13] This forced Aetius to reverse his previous approach, and put together a defensive alliance against Attila. Burgundians and Franks also played their part, but the central role was played by the Visigoths. Battle was joined against the Huns in late June or early July 451 on the Catalaunian Plains in the Champagne, where the Goths' now veteran king, Theoderic I, died gloriously in battle (*Getica* 191–215). Hunnic ambitions received a decisive check, and Attila retreated to the Hungarian Plain.

The real significance of these events lies not so much in the Huns'

[12] Hunnic allies also kept him in power in 425 and 433. For more detail, and refs, see Heather, 1995.

[13] Thompson, 1995, chs 4–6; Maenchen-Helfen, 1973, 94ff.

defeat, but in the fact that they ushered the Goths back into the centre-stage of imperial politics and thanks to Attila's death in 453, they stayed there. For the subsequent collapse of the Hunnic Empire made it impossible to continue Aetius' policy of the 430s. Huns could no longer be employed to contain the immigrant groups already established in Roman western Europe. As a direct result, a fundamental change followed in the pattern of political activity within the western Empire. Since the immigrants could no longer be contained by use of an outside force, the only viable alternative was to include all or some of them within the body politic of the western Empire. The Goths and Burgundians of southern Gaul subsequently advanced their claims for political inclusion, but so too did the Vandals of North Africa.[14]

In the reigns of Petronius Maximus (March to May 455), Avitus (455–6) and Majorian (457–61), the Goths, now ruled by Theoderic II (son of Theoderic I), made no territorial gains. They did succeed, however, in staking a claim to be considered one of the major players in the political game for control of the western Empire. Petronius Maximus was the first to approach them (Sid. Ap. *Carm.* 7.392ff), they were major sponsors of Avitus (ibid. 508ff), and Majorian felt it necessary to integrate them into his regime.[15] Their reward was the right to intervene ever more freely in Spain. From 455 onwards, seemingly still in cooperation with the Empire (Hydatius records armies with joint commanders: one Goth, one Roman), the Goths destroyed the previously stable kingdom of the Suevi, and conducted widespread and profitable warfare.[16]

The reign of Libius Severus (461–5) saw further expansion. In return for their support, the Goths gained Narbonne in 462/3 (Hyd. 212 [217]). As we have seen, its wealth and geographical situation had attracted them before. Indeed, from this point on, Theoderic II took direct control, it seems, of policy towards the still rebellious Suevi. He may have replaced the imperial commander in the area, Nepotianus, with his own man Arborius (Hyd. 208 [213]: although the text is a little ambiguous). He certainly sent a flurry of ambassadors to the Suevi, who likewise sent their deputations directly back to him (e.g. Hyd. 215 [219]). Severus' decision to cede Narbonne also seems to have caused the Gallic army under Aegidius to revolt, which afforded Theoderic yet more opportunities. Despite

14 Clover 1978; Heather 1995.
15 Mathisen, 1979, 618–20.
16 Hyd. 166–79 [173–186]; see further p. 200.

initial setbacks, including the death of his brother Frederic, the Goths extended their power into the Loire region after Aegidius' death.[17] Through their willingness to cooperate with a whole series of imperial regimes in the decade after 455, the Goths not only gained wealth and territory, but significant control over events in Spain.

But the Goths were not the only group within the western Roman Empire busy acquiring such rewards. After participating in one of the Spanish campaigns, for instance, the Burgundians received new and better lands in Savoy, removing another prosperous agricultural area from central imperial control.[18] After 454, there thus built up a vicious circle within the western Empire, with too many groups dividing up and squabbling over a shrinking financial base. In such circumstances, the weakened Empire was also unable to prevent the rise of other forces on its periphery. Particularly ominous in this respect was the expansion of the Amoricans, and, above all, the Franks in Northern Gaul from the 460s.[19] With the number of players increasing rather than diminishing, and the Empire's financial base decreasing, the idea of Empire quickly became meaningless, since the centre no longer controlled anything that anyone wanted. In consequence, one group after another came to the realization, from the later 460s, that the western Empire was no longer a prize worth fighting for.

The first to grasp the point was Euric, who murdered and succeeded his brother Theoderic II as king of the Visigoths in 466. He trod carefully until Anthemius' regime was emasculated by the defeat of its Vandal expedition in 468, but then dropped all pretence of obedience.[20] From 469, he launched a series of campaigns to extend his dominions. A striking description of his decision is preserved in Jordanes, 'Becoming aware of the frequent changes of [western] Roman Emperor, Euric, king of the Visigoths, pressed forward to seize Gaul on his own authority' (*Getica* 237). This captures rather well what it must have been like suddenly to realize that, after 400 years, the western Empire was a spent force, and that the time had come to pursue one's own aims with total independence.

Euric's campaigns achieved swift success (figure 7.1). Between 471 and 476, he acquired most of southern Gaul. Having captured the great imperial centres of Provence – Arles and Marseilles – by 475, he

17 Wolfram, 1988, 180f.

18 Mar. Avent. ad a. 456.2 (= *CM* 2, 232), with Wood, 1990, 65–9.

19 See generally, James, 1988, 64ff.

20 Victory in North Africa would certainly have extended the life of the western Empire: Heather, 1995.

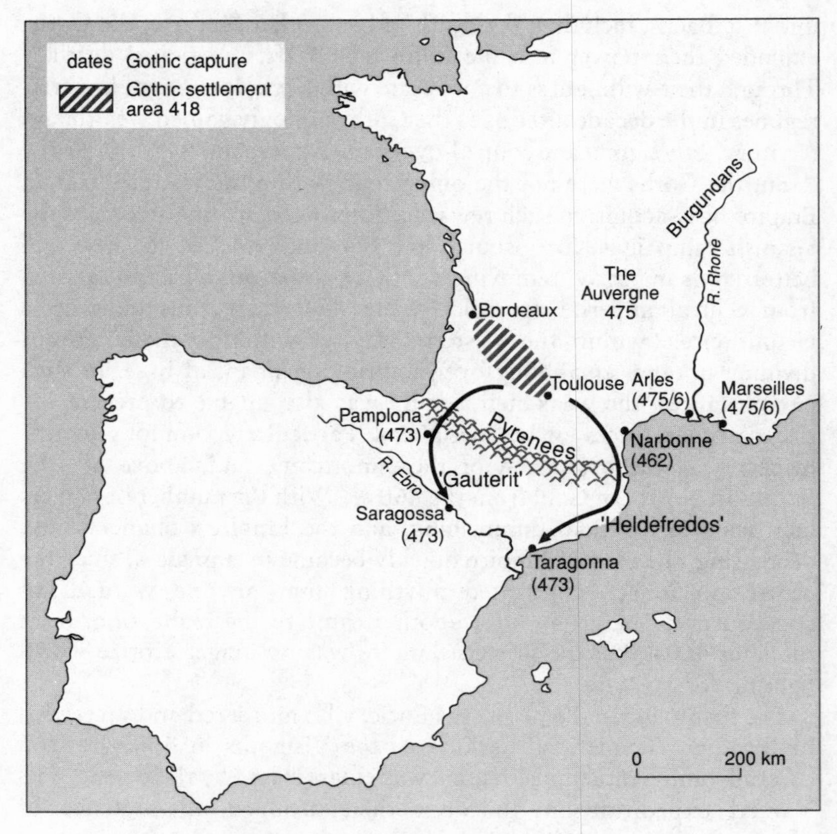

Figure 7.1 The conquests of Euric

exchanged them in that year for the Auvergne, much to the annoyance of one of its more vocal inhabitants, Sidonius Apollinaris (see below). Further campaigns in 476, however, restored the cities to his control. At the same time, his armies were annexing most of Spain. In 473, he unleashed a two-pronged assault. The *comes* Gauterit advanced with one force through the western Pyrenees and down the valley of the river Ebro. He received the formal capitulation of the great cities of the region: particularly Pamplona and Zaragossa (Caesaraugusta). A second force, led by Heldefredus, besieged Tarragona and captured the coastal cities of Tarraconensis. By the 480s, Euric's control extended over all of the Spanish peninsula, except for the Suevic kingdom in the north west.[21]

21 In more detail: Wolfram, 1988, 181ff.

These events did not occur in a vacuum. Others, especially the Franks, were also establishing their own independent political units on former Roman territory. Thus the end of the Roman state in western Europe quickly followed, as its main supporters, particularly the east Romans and the Burgundians, ceased in the early 470s to sustain it. Fittingly, it was the army of Italy which was the last to give up. In 475, Orestes, its Roman commander, proclaimed his own son Romulus Emperor, but, within a year, lost control of his soldiers. Not surprisingly, given all the resources which had by this time been seized by others, it was shortage of money which caused the unrest. Exploiting this discontent, Odovacar organized a putsch, murdered Orestes, and deposed Romulus Augustulus. He then sent an embassy to Constantinople which merely stated the obvious: there was no longer any need for an Emperor in the west (Malchus fr. 14).[22]

With this act, the Roman Empire in western Europe ceased to exist, and in its downfall – if by design only from the time of Euric onwards – the Visigoths had played a major part. Military action, to establish and extend political boundaries, was only one element, however, in transforming the settlement of 418 into a kingdom. Of equal importance was securing the allegiance of Roman elites, the group most able to fashion and run a working governmental machine in this new territorial unit carved out by Gothic arms.

(iii) Gothic kings and Roman elites

The landowning Roman elite of the late imperial period had a deep conviction of its own cultural superiority over outsiders: 'barbarians'. Where Roman individuals and their society were rational, barbarians were held to be controlled by their physical passions. They were thus (to Roman eyes) faithless and inconstant, a prey to their every bodily whim, particularly those to do with sex, violence and alcohol.[23] Against this backdrop, the rapprochement of Gothic kings and Gallo-Roman elite in the fifth century is a historical phenomenon of the greatest interest.

Up to *c.*450, a variety of motivations pushed Goths and Romans together. Some members of the Gallo-Roman elite sought to use the Goths as a weapon in political disputes with the central imperial authorities. Thus the 'Gothic usurper' Attalus, when his cause was revived by Athaulf in the 410s, attracted the support of a section of the Gallo-Roman aristocracy. Men such as Paulinus of Pella saw the

[22] On all this, see in more detail Heather, 1995.
[23] In more detail, below pp. 222ff.

Goths as a bulwark for a regime that would propel them into power, although mixed motives surely operated. Paulinus of Pella is not necessarily lying when he claims that he became involved with Attalus because he thought that peace with the Goths was the best line of policy to pursue (*Euch.* 290ff). After 418, economic reasons also dictated that any Gallo-Roman with estates in the Garonne had either to enter into relations with the Goths or leave the area. Many of Paulinus of Pella's estates, for instance, were situated around Bordeaux, which perhaps explains why his two sons migrated to the Visigothic court (*Euch.* 499ff). The unexpected arrival of payment from a Goth for one of Paulinus' former farms some years after the settlement may have been the result of some successful lobbying (ibid. 570ff, cf. 514–15). A third kind of involvement was involuntary. As we have seen, one Theodorus ended up as a hostage at the Visigothic court. Indeed, his predicament is symbolic of the whole situation in south-western Gaul. Whether local Gallo-Romans liked it or not, Goths had been planted upon them by the central imperial authorities, and they had to preserve themselves in this new situation.

Between 418 and 450, therefore, relationships began to grow up of necessity between Gothic king and landowning Romans. We do not hear, however, of important Romans acting as the king's close advisers, or serving him in military capacities, as they were to do later. Sidonius Apollinaris' description of Theoderic II's court in *c.*455, for instance, does not even hint at a major Roman presence there (*Ep.* 1.2), and the men who would later figure prominently at the Visigothic court in the 460s and 470s – notably Leo of Narbonne and the poet Lampridius – were still active in imperial Roman circles in the 450s.[24] This is not the place for a full discussion, but I suspect that relations between Gallo-Romans and Goths went no further than a limited rapprochement before 450, because of a new, or rather renewed, imperial institution. In 418, just as the Goths were settled in Aquitaine, the annual council of the Gallic provinces was reinstituted by Ravenna.[25] This was surely no chronological coincidence. The details of the settlement were perhaps thrashed out (or publicized) in the first council, and, more generally, it functioned in subsequent years as a forum of contact between central imperial government and local Roman elites. To my mind, it was specifically designed to counter the new kind of centrifugal force generated by potential

[24] Sid. Ap. *Carm.* 23.446; Mathisen, 1979, 611ff respectively.

[25] Matthews, 1975, 333 ff provinces and individual cities had to send delegates from classes of governors, decisions and ex-officials on pain of heavy fines.

political alliances between Roman and Goth, such as Attalus' regime.

After 450, however, circumstances changed dramatically. The writings of Sidonius Apollinaris show an ever wider section of the Roman landowning elite of southern Gaul being drawn into the Gothic orbit. From *c.*470, for instance, we find Romans holding military offices to which they had been appointed by Gothic kings (Vincentius, by 477 Euric's *dux Hispaniae*; Victorius, Euric's commander in Gaul in the early 470s; Calminius and Namatius). Disaffected Roman officials were also entering into negotiations with the Goths. In 468, Arvandus, although newly reappointed Praetorian Prefect, supreme civilian administrator in Gaul, wrote to Euric telling him to throw off the rule of Anthemius – the 'Greekling' – and divide up the provinces of Gaul with the Burgundians (Sid. Ap. *Ep.* 1.7.5). Shortly afterwards, Sidonius' correspondence records even greater outrage at the close relations between Euric and Seronatus, possibly deputy (vicar) to the Gallic Prefect (ibid. 2.1: Seronatus was tried and executed before 475). And as Euric's campaigns gathered momentum, Romans came to hold high civilian office under his rule. The first known case is that of Leo of Narbonne, who was Euric's chief adviser by the mid-470s. A wonderful vignette in *The Life of Epiphanius* describes the reception of an Italian embassy at the Visigothic court (85). Leo is pictured doing all the negotiating, with Euric muttering in Gothic in the background.

The brief reign of Avitus (453–4), acted here as a crucial catalyst. Avitus had negotiated the Goths' participation in the war against Attila in 451, and in 453 was at the Gothic court on behalf of the Emperor Petronius Maximus. The latter was killed in the Vandal sack of Rome while Avitus was still negotiating, and Avitus' subsequent elevation to the purple took place first among the Goths. Only later was it confirmed by the Gallo-Roman council at Arles on 9 July 455. As this suggests, Avitus' regime was essentially an alliance of Goths and Gallo-Roman aristocrats. Sidonius penned a description of Theoderic II and his court at this point, which is worth dwelling on for a moment (*Ep.* 1.2; cf. *Carm.* 7). It portrays a king educated in Roman law and literature, who presided over an ordered court, where unruly behaviour, especially drunkenness, was not tolerated. Set against traditional Roman prejudices about 'barbarians', there is no doubt that Sidonius was signalling to his fellow Roman landowners that the Gothic king was a worthy political ally, who had entered the world of Roman civilization. It reminds me forcefully of Mrs Thatcher's summing-up of her first meeting with President Gorbachev of the former Soviet Union, 'We can do business with this man'. Thus the regime of Avitus brought Goth and Gallo-Roman together in political alliance for the first time since the 410s, and graced this alliance with a coherent ideological legitimation. As subsequent imperial regimes bought further Gothic support, they continued to advance the process of legitimation. Majorian sanctioned joint campaigns with the Goths, and Libius Severus ceded them Narbonne. All of this greatly eased the transition of Romans into Gothic service. It even became natural for Roman landowners to look to the Goths for assistance in their disputes. Theoderic II's brother Frederic wrote to the Pope over the disputed election to the episcopal seat of Narbonne, on behalf of one Roman group within the town.[26]

Such processes of political redefinition, however, were far from smooth. While some Gallo-Romans were willing to work with Gothic kings, others were not, especially if the Goths threw off their allegiance to the Empire. Sidonius himself was happy to cooperate with the Goths and even praise them when they were the main plank of Avitus' regime. He was also willing to accept Gothic territorial extensions, such as the ceding of Narbonne, if they were sanctioned by the imperial authority. When the Goths took over southern Gaul without authorization, however, he resisted.[27] Roman aristocrats of southern Gaul – even Sidonius himself after a period of exile – were willing to accommodate themselves to Gothic power if they had to. This transformation in political orientation was of huge importance, marking the break up of the coalition of interests on which the western Empire was founded. It was, however, neither swift nor smooth. If they wanted to retain their elite status, western landowners had no real choice but to adapt. The expansionary ambitions of Goths and other immigrant groups had undermined the ability of the Roman Empire to exercise a centralizing influence in western Europe. In the process, the first Gothic successor state was born: a combination of Gothic arms and the social and political muscle of the Roman elite of south-western Gaul.

B. *The Kingdom of the Goths*

The basic system of government in the new kingdom closely but not exactly followed Roman imperial precedent. Central bureaucracy was much reduced. Gothic kings possessed nothing on the scale of the

[26] Harries, 1994, 135–6.
[27] See most recently, Harries, 1994, ch. 11. Sidonius' chief collaborators were Ecdicius, son of Avitus, and Eucherius.

central palatine ministries of the Roman state (*scrinia, agentes in rebus, res privata* and *sacrae largitiones*). In provincial administration, they retained, in the first instance, the old imperial chief civilian official, the Praetorian Prefect, at least for their Spanish provinces. This officer is referred to in the *Breviary of Alaric*, and one holder of the post, Stephanus, named elsewhere (*PLRE* 3, 1183). Whether, the Gallic provinces were also run by a Prefect before 507 is unclear. Otherwise, provinces functioned as before. Each seems to have had its *rector* or *iudex* (governor or judge), who employed bureaucratic assistants organized in *officia*.[28]

Roman tax gathering also continued, if in simplified form. The land tax, customs tolls and *collatio lustralis* continued to be levied, but the province, rather than the city, was (or quickly became) the focus of money raising. There is no way of knowing how soon the patterns it describes evolved, but the so-called *de fisco Barcinonense* sheds great light on Visigothic tax gathering at the end of the sixth century. By 592, Barcelona had become the centre of a financial district comprising Tarragona, Egara, Gerona and Ampurias. Two royal accountants (*numerarii*) were responsible for setting tax rates and making valuations. In each city, a local counterpart (also called a *numerarius*), elected by the citizen body, was responsible for collecting the money. It is usually supposed that Goths within the new kingdom were not taxed. Romans, the vast majority of the population, certainly were. Acts of manumission into Roman citizenship, for instance, customarily involved inscribing the name of the given individual onto the tax registers.[29]

In the field of law too, the imperial inheritance was marked. In 506, the *Breviary of Alaric* (or *lex Romana Visigothorum*) was issued in the name of Euric's son, Alaric II. As a legal text, it is closely modelled on the *Theodosian Code*. Redundant legislation was omitted, and interpretations were added to specific laws in the language of provincial, rather than imperial court lawyers. Selections of material both from imperial legislation subsequent to the *Theodosian Code*, and from the earlier writings of the jurisconsults, were also included. Much of the actual legislation, the legal practice, and the legal principles of the *Breviary* were quite indistinguishable, therefore, from established Roman norms.

In the main, therefore, it would seem likely that the *Breviary* was

[28] Jones, 1964, 257–9.
[29] King, 1972, 69–70; Thompson, 1969, 130–1, after *Formulae Visigothicae* 2–6 (= Gil, 1972, 72–7).

aimed at the Roman population of the Visigothic kingdom – especially given its political context (p. 214) – but matters such as property law may have governed the dealings of both Roman and Goth. Alongside it, there also grew up a second body of written law, the rulings of successive Gothic kings on a wide variety of subjects. By the seventh century, these rulings had been collected into the so-called *Visigothic Code*. Itself regularly updated to include new royal rulings, some examples of different editions of the Code survive intact from the time of Reccesuinth (649–72) onward. There also survives, in fragmentary palimpsest, a small part of an earlier manifestation of the same tradition, the so-called *Code of Euric*. For present purposes, there are two points of particular interest. First, was the *Code of Euric* applicable to the entire population of the kingdom, Roman and Goth, or just the latter? In legal jargon, was it territorial or personal law? Learned opinion differs greatly. No one doubts that it was meant to apply to Goths, but some would claim that its rulings, where relevant, were also applicable to Romans. My own view is broadly in favour of the latter. The second point follows from the first. Gothic kings of the fourth century and earlier had not governed their Gothic subjects by written edict. This was a Roman habit. Its persistence under Visigothic kings, as much as the survival of any specifically Roman legislation, is a good indicator of the degree to which the new kingdom was continuing along paths established by the fallen Empire.[30]

While the boundaries of the Visigothic kingdom were established by Gothic force of arms, the territories so annexed were run using a governmental system which was recognizably Roman in origin. Bureaucratic officers and their assistants, a tax system based on meticulous written records, and written law were all foreign to the Goths. The origin of these sophisticated tools of government was Roman, and, in the first place, Romans operated them for Gothic kings. We have already seen how the landowning elites of southern Gaul – more or less willingly – made their accommodations with the Goths. In the next generation, their successors continued along the same lines. The preface to the *Breviary* mentions the roles played in its formulation by Timotheus and Anianus, presumably provincial Roman lawyers, the kind of men who wrote the interpretations added to the *Theodosian Code*. Ruricius of Limoges also wrote letters

[30] Useful introductions: King, 1972, 10–11; Nehlsen in *RgA* 5, 42ff (both in favour of personal law); Collins, 1983, 24ff (territorial law). My views on the general nature of Visigothic legislation are similar to those of Amory, 1993 on the different Burgundian codes. For thoughts on law-giving: Wormald, 1977.

to various Romans of influence within the Visigothic kingdom after *c*.480 (e.g. Elaphius, Praesidius, Rusticus and Eudomius: *Epp*.2.7, 2.12. 2.20, 2.39 – cf. *Ep. ad Ruric.* 7). As *iudices* and *rectores*, such men provided administrative know-how for Gothic kings.

Plate 13 The Roman bridge over the Guadiana at Merida, repaired by Euric

As a result, the character of Gothic kingship continued to evolve. In issuing written rulings as part of a living Roman legal system, Gothic kings added an entirely new function to their office. A similar pattern is visible elsewhere. A famous building inscription of 483 commemorates Euric's role in repairing the main bridge over the river Guadiana at Merida in Spain (Vives, 363; plate 13). Public building was a traditional function of Roman Emperors. In ideological terms, too, Gothic rulers approximated themselves increasingly to their Roman counterparts. The rule of written law was seen, in the self-defining ideology of the Roman elite, as the basic guarantor of a civilized, ordered way of life (*civilitas*: p. 222). Issuing the *Breviary of Alaric* thus had overt ideological overtones. Amongst other things, it signalled that the Visigothic state would continue the God-ordained civil order which had prevailed under the Empire.

Despite their non-Catholic religion, Visigothic kings acted in accordance with such a view of their kingship. Alaric II claimed in theory, and took in practice, some responsibility for the running of the Catholic Church. In 506, he called, in the city of Agde, a general council of the Catholic bishops from his Gallic provinces. The surviving correspondence of Bishop Caesarius of Arles makes it clear that this was meant to be the first of a series. Plans had already been drawn up for a general council of Gallic and Spanish bishops to take place in the following year (*Ep*. 3). Since the time of Constantine, the Church had become increasingly a state institution within the Roman Empire. Emperors claimed an ever closer relationship to God, intervened in episcopal appointments and presided in person, or through their officials, over Church synods. The response of the Catholic Church to the religious activities of a non-Catholic Christian king will be considered in more detail below. For the moment, it is enough to note that in ideology, as well as institutionally, the fledgling Visigothic state can be characterized as a simplified version of the Roman imperial model. This tells, however, only part of the story. The interaction of Roman and Goth did not come to a sudden end with the creation of the new kingdom in the mid-470s. Roles and functions within the kingdom continued to evolve. As they did, the lives of the both parties were further transformed.

(i) Goths in the Visigothic kingdom

The Visigoths who settled in the Garonne in 418 were an amalgam of parts of three previously independent Gothic groups: Tervingi, Greuthungi and the force which Radagasius had led to Italy in 405/6 (chapter 5). There was no direct continuity between the leaderships of any of these major groups, and the dynasty which came to rule in Gaul. Alaric I and his brother-in-law Athaulf stabilized matters in part. But, in 415, Sergeric murdered Athaulf, along with his brother and children. He was killed in turn after a seven-day rule. The next king, Vallia, died within two years, and it was only the 33-year reign of Theoderic I which finally established a ruling dynasty. He seems to have married Alaric's daughter (*PLRE* 2, 1070), but there is no reason to think that this was why he was elected king.

Against this background, it is no surprise to find a lack of stability among the Visigoths after 418. Some Goths accompanied the Vandals to North Africa (Possidius *Life of Augustine* 28.4). These may well have been Visigoths, who decided that life with the Vandals looked more promising. The Goths of Anaolsus, rampaging in the vicinity of Arles in 430 (Hyd. 82 [92]), may also have been breaking away from Theoderic's control. We also hear of one Vetericus, quite possibly a Goth, who fought with the Romans against Theoderic I in the 430s (Prosp. 1337 a 439 = *CM* 1, 477). As we have seen, one major reason for Gothic nobles to appear in Roman ranks was that they had been forced to flee after coming second in leadership contests. This was true before 418 (above p. 143), and continued to be so afterwards. Aetius' wife was of Gothic royal stock, but her son was 'barred from the Gothic throne'.[31] This may also explain why the leading imperial general from the mid-450s, Ricimer, pursued an entirely Roman career, even though he was the grandson of the Visigothic king Vallia (Sid. Ap. *Carm.* 2.361–2).

Correspondingly, the fact that Theoderic I reigned for an exceptional period and passed on power to three of his sons in turn – Thorismud, Theoderic II and Euric – must not mislead us into thinking that Gothic politics were anything other than unruly. The sons succeeded by murdering one another, and this reflects something more fundamental than a familial tendency to fratricidal rivalry. In the sixth- and seventh-century Spanish kingdom, the main cause of political instability would be a powerful Gothic nobility (chapter 9). In the fifth century, non-royal Goths led armies (e.g. Suniericus, Heldefredus and Gauterit), and are found, as we might expect, being consulted by the king and exercising patronage in their own right (Sid. Ap. *Carm.* 7.441ff; *Ep.* 1.2.9). Behind the murders of Thorismud and Theoderic II, lay the factional divisions, rivalries and ambitions of great men such as these.[32] Regimes were built on the ability of particular monarchs to improvise working coalitions amongst their powerful and turbulent subjects.

The political experiment of Theoderic II, who gave his brother a recognized share of power, is a case in point.[33] This was surely an attempt to forestall any fraternal resentment, which might have offered dissident nobles the opportunity of gathering behind a royal figurehead. It is probably no accident that Frederic's death in battle

[31] Sid. Ap. *Carm.* 5.203–4; cf. Merobaudes, ed. Clover 29–32.
[32] See generally Claude, 1971, 38–9, 50–2.
[33] E.g. Sid. Ap. *Carm.* 7.431ff; cf. Wolfram, 1988, 178–9.

preceded Theoderic's own murder, breaking up an established balance of forces. In this light, I would also read the executions, by Alaric II's son Gesalic, of two leading nobles, Goiaric and Veila, in 510 and 511 (*Chron. Caesaraug.* s.a. 510, 511 = *CM* 2, 223). A number of political alternatives were open to Visigothic nobles in these years (p. 232), and Gesalic probably suspected them of disloyalty. If Theoderic I had not had so many sons, opposition would have taken the form, as it did subsequently, of more direct challenges to the dynasty. Against this background of dispute, division and competition, we must also consider the most dramatic transformation of the pattern of life for the Gothic population of the kingdom after 418: the transfer of substantial numbers of them to Spain.

Our prime source of information is the *Chronicle of Saragossa* (Caesaraugusta). Its one-line entries record the entry of Goths into Spain under the year 494, and their physical settlement there three years later (*Gotthi intra Hispanias sedes acceperunt* (*CM* 2, 222). What form did this settlement take? And why, 20 years after the campaigns which had brought Spain under Euric's control, did a substantial Gothic population remove itself to Spain?

The evidence is not as full as one would like, but, on the face of it, the language of the Chronicle, *sedes*, implies that Visigoths received actual land. The same is suggested by some Visigothic legislation. Most of it is preserved only in the seventh-century *Visigothic Code*, but was clearly issued long before. This material explicitly refers to an original division of economic resources between Gothic immigrants and indigenous Hispano-Romans. I see no reason not to take this evidence at face value, and would only note that land represented real economic capital in this world, and tax revenues mere interest on that capital. I find it very hard to believe that Gothic conquerors would have been satisfied with anything less than actual land as the reward for their loyalty to their leaders over many years of warfare.[34]

By the 490s, life in Aquitaine had acquired one obvious drawback. Frankish power north of the Loire had waxed ever stronger under the leadership of Clovis, and, by the 490s, was looming threateningly over Visigothic holdings in the Garonne valley. In 496, Frankish forces penetrated as far south as Saintes, and in 498 even captured the city of Bourdeaux along with its Gothic *dux*. A peace treaty followed

[34] Refs. to current debates: above note 5. The relevant codes are *LV* 9.1.8–9; 9.1.16; 10.2.1 (all marked *antiqua*), and note too the much earlier *CE* 277.

in either 500 or 502, but this may have led the Goths to pay tribute, and Frankish power continued to grow. The early years of the sixth century saw the Franks extend their hegemony over Alamannic, Thuringian and Burgundian territories.[35] The rise of the Franks was one reason for Goths to seek new lands in Spain. The history of the Visigothic kingdom suggests another.

In 418, the Goths were settled in the relatively restricted area of the Garonne valley. They probably received land, but under the close supervision of the Roman state. An important element in the subsequent creation of a kingdom was the attraction of Gallo-Roman elites to the Gothic cause, and, as we have seen, Gothic kings put much effort into winning them over. Like the circumstances of the original settlement, this must have placed limits on the amount of land and other wealth that individual Goths could acquire. To attract Roman landowning support, much of the letter of Roman law had to be observed. We have already encountered Paulinus of Pella's surprise when a Goth sent him money through the post for a piece of land which he had simply written off.

The more recent acquisitions in Spain were much larger than the old territories in the Garonne, and offered much more opportunity for land-grabbing. Spain had also been conquered by force, at a point when the Roman Empire ceased to pose a direct threat. While government in the new provinces would work more effectively with the cooperation of local Hispano-Roman elites, the need to attract Roman landowning support was not as imperative as it had been in Gaul. I suspect, therefore, that Goths were attracted to Spain because it offered not just greater security, but also richer pickings.

In particular, a substantial element of the local Spanish population had responded to the circumstances of the fifth century by arming and protecting itself. These initiatives took a number of forms: everything from local, cooperative self-defence forces, to armed bands predatory upon their neighbours. Thus some of the groups were labelled *bacaudae* (bandits) by the Roman state, and others found themselves in ambiguous situations. Resisting the intrusion of Gothic allies of the Empire, for instance, was, even if sensible, tantamount to rebellion. Not surprisingly, many of these groups were based on cities or forts (e.g. Hyd. 81 [91]). Cities, of course, were both sources of revenue and, via their walls, of protection. After the Visigothic conquest, local self-assertion remained a significant phenomenon. *Bacaudae* operated in Tarragona and Aracelli (Hyd. 117 [125], 120 [128], 133 [141], 150 [158]), and the so-called

[35] See generally, Wolfram, 1988, 190–3; Wood, 1994, 41ff.

tyrants Burdunelus and Peter were executed at Toledo in 496 and Tortosa in 506 respectively (*Chron. Caesaraug.* s.a. 496–7, 507 = *CM* 2, 222–3). Given its chronology, it is tempting to think of Burdunelus' enterprise in particular as a direct response to the arrival of the Visigoths, a negative anticipation of the demands they might make. Be that as it may, the suppression of local political independence, at the point where they were moving into the peninsula in large numbers, offered the Goths plenty of opportunity for seizing assets.[36]

Where did the Goths settle? It is usually argued that archaeological evidence answers this question. Primarily on the Meseta, in Old and New Castille, about 70 large 'row-grave' cemeteries (German *Reihengräber*) have long been identified (figure 7.2). Several have been excavated. This basic form of cemetery organization is considered Germanic, on the basis of analogous cemeteries in northern Gaul and the Rhineland, which date from the Migration Period. The attribution of the Spanish examples to the Visigoths is also based on the contents and dating of the graves. Finds from the enormous cemetery at Duraton, containing some 666 burials and about 1,000 bodies, are representative of the rest in character if not scale. There is nothing specifically Gothic, Roman or otherwise about the male burials. For one extended period when these cemeteries were in use, however, some of the women, amounting to about 20 per cent of all the corpses, were buried with their clothing arranged in typical Gothic fashion. This consisted, very much after the Danubian style (p. 121), of a cloak held with a pair of fibula brooches at each shoulder, and a large plated belt buckle around the waist. Not only does this match the standard Gothic pattern from the Wielbark culture onwards, but the brooches and buckles have a genuinely Germanic character. Their forms and decorations are again evolutions of the Danubian style: the norm for Germanic groups of the middle Danube in the fifth century. There is some dispute over chronological detail, but all agree that the Gothic style female burials should be dated between about AD 480/90 and 560/80. The form of the cemeteries, their date and the actual objects, it has been argued, all indicate that the Spanish *Reihengräber* reflect the migration of Visigoths into Spain.[37]

The dates are just about right. Compared to the literary record, the

[36] The modern Spanish historiographic tradition rightly emphasizes the degree to which central imperial control broke down in the peninsula in the fifth century: e.g. Diaz, 1994, with refs.

[37] Basic information: Molinero Perez, 1948, 1971; Zeiss, 1948; Ripoll Lopez, 1985. Commentary: e.g., De Palol and Ripoll Lopez, 1990; Bierbrauer, 1991; *RgA* 6, 284ff; Kazanski, 1991, 95ff.

burials perhaps begin a little early.[38] Some of the objects are more reminiscent of Danubian analogies with dates closer to *c*.450 than *c*.480. The *Chronicle of Saragossa* provides no circumstantial detail about the moves, however, and it is not unreasonable to argue that there were earlier movements of Visigoths which the Chronicle does not record. As we have seen, the Goths had a marked interest in Spain from the 450s. The overall form of the cemeteries, however, is a much more serious problem.

It was a dogma of the early part of this century that the Gallic *Reihengräber* are the remains of Germanic immigrants to that region, so that, when *Reihengräber* were also found in Spain, it was natural to identify them with Goths. But, however Goths were being buried in the Garonne valley after 418, it was certainly not in *Reihengräber* cemeteries. This area in particular, and Aquitaine in general, contains no such cemeteries (p. 182). To suppose that the Spanish *Reihengräber* are the remains of Goths, then, poses a very difficult question. Why did the Goths suddenly adopt such a mode of burial upon their arrival in Spain, when they had not utilized it in Aquitaine? No satisfactory answer has ever been offered to this question, nor has any other type of cemetery been found on the Meseta. If the *Reihengräber* reflect Goths, and just Goths, then this would mean that all the local population had been expelled to make room for them. This is most implausible. The idea that the Meseta cemeteries reflect the arrival of Goths in Spain in a straightforward manner, is thus unconvincing.[39]

On the other hand, the burials began more or less as the Goths arrived in the peninsula, and some of their contents have an obviously Germanic form. There really should be some connection, therefore, between the burials and the arrival of the Goths. Two basic possibilities come to mind. The first is suggested by a famous aphorism of Theoderic the Ostrogoth, 'The poor Roman imitates the Goth, the well-to-do Goth the Roman' (*Anon. Val.* 61). Taking this as our guide, the Spanish *Reihengräber* might represent the response of Hispano-Romans to Gothic hegemony. Rather than those of actual Goths, the burials would become those of 'would-be Goths', those seeking to imitate the new masters of the land. In line with this, some have recently argued that the Gallic *Reihengräber* actually represent an evolution of local Gallo-Roman society.[40]

38 Hübener, 1970, 1973.

39 Cf. Kazanski, 1991, 95ff.

40 Would-be Goths: Kazanski, 1991, 101. On Gallic *Reihengräber*, see now Halsall, 1992.

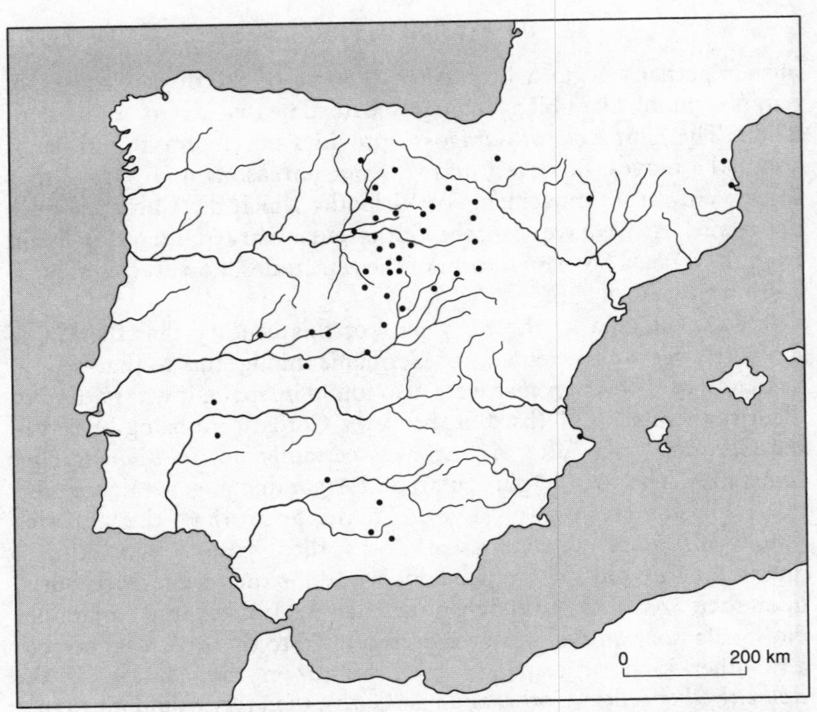

Figure 7.2 Visigothic period Reihengräber *(row-grave) cemeteries in Spain*

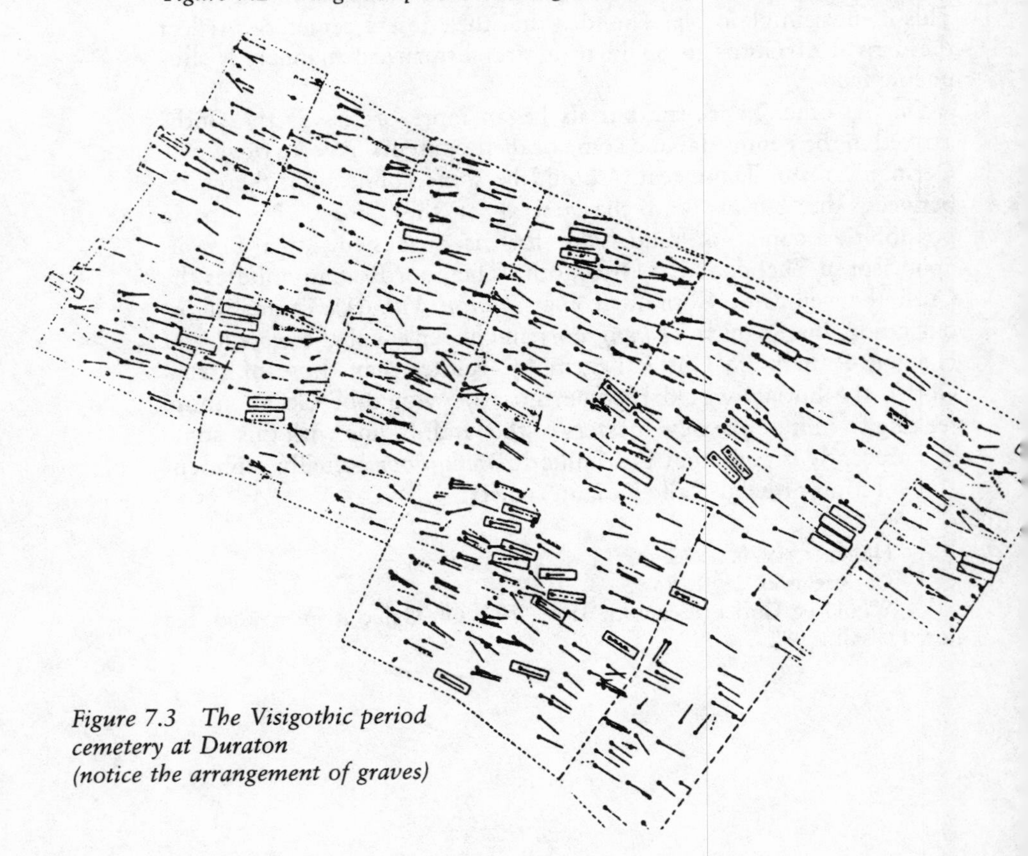

Figure 7.3 The Visigothic period cemetery at Duraton (notice the arrangement of graves)

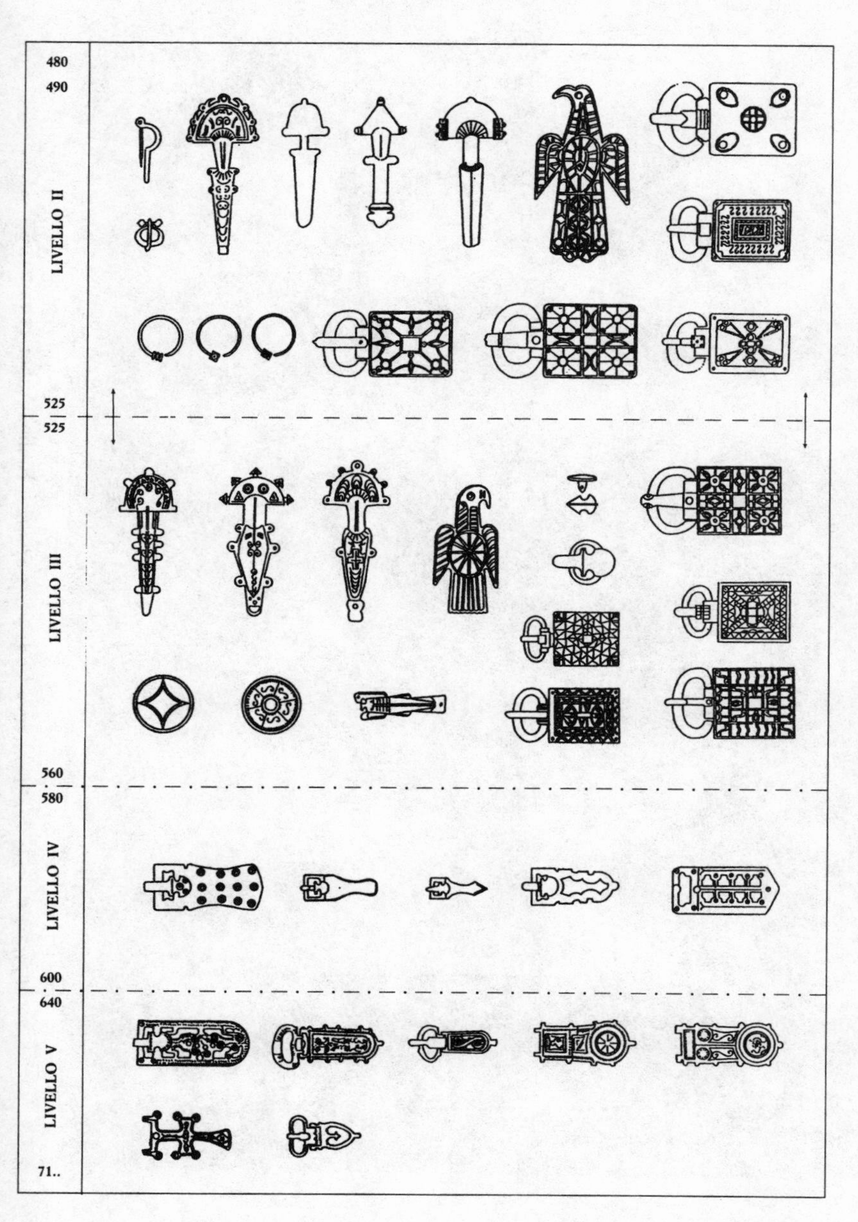

Figure 7.4 *The chronological evolution of* Reihengräber *finds*

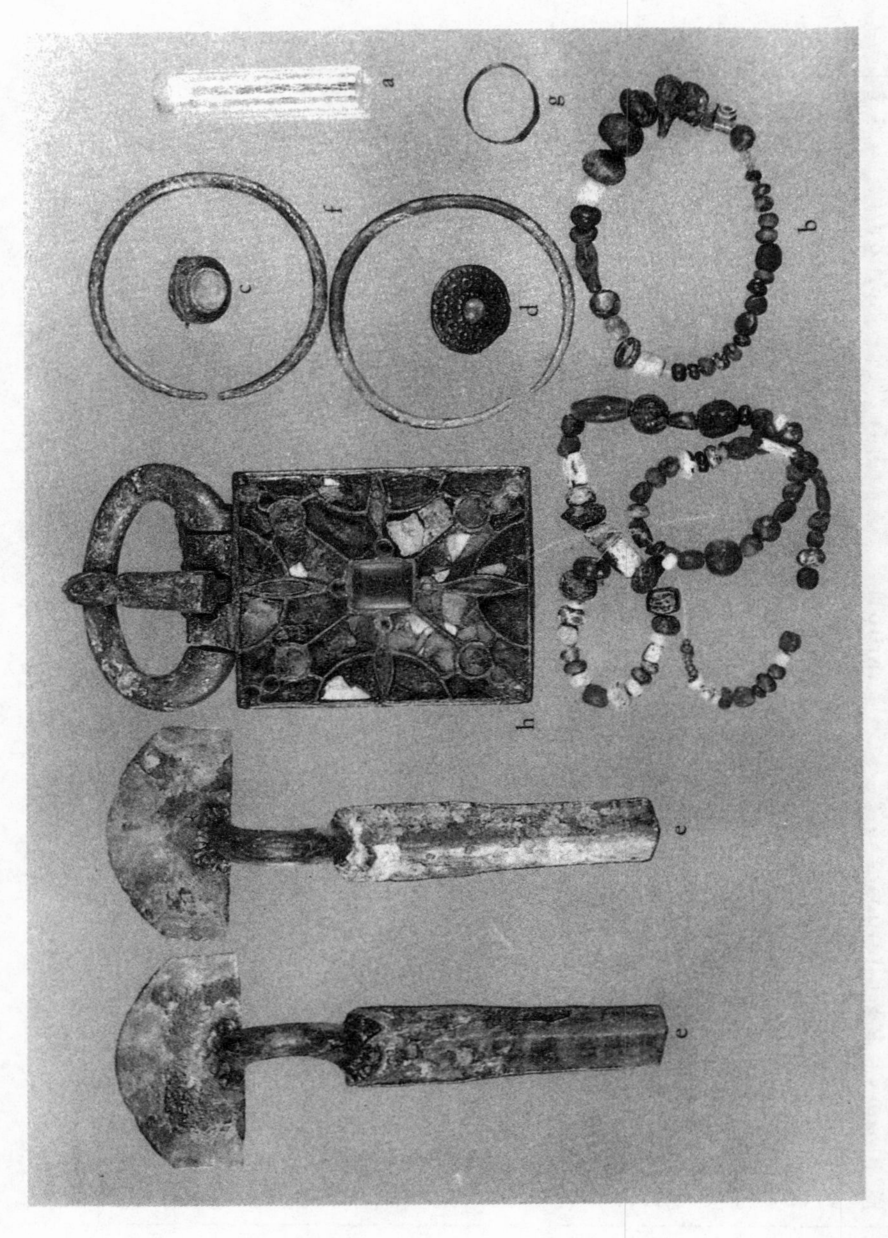

Plate 14 'Gothic' cemetery finds from Spanish Reihengräber *cemeteries*

These arguments have not yet run their course, however, and there is another possible, and perhaps more likely, view of the relationship between the Goths and the *Reihengräber*. The one completely excavated cemetery whose remains have been subject to careful recent re-examination is El Carpio de Tajo. This turned up 285 burials deposited over about 150 years, or five to six human generations. It was the burial place, therefore, of a rural community composed, at any one time, of between 50 and 60 people. While no really rich burials were discovered, the contents of the graves suggest marked differences in status among the population. Of the 285 corpses, only 90 individuals were buried with personal adornments with them to the grave. The other cemeteries show similar patterns. Of the 1,000 or so burials at Duraton, only about 200 produced any gravegoods. The populations using these cemeteries were thus to some extent socially stratified, which suggests an alternative possible relationship between the *Reihengräber* and the Goths.

The cemeteries might actually be those of mixed communities, created by the arrival in new territories of a dominant Gothic elite. The Gothic conquerors of the peninsula will hardly have wanted to till the soil personally, even if they are likely to have wanted to own land (pp. 182f). The cemeteries might well reflect, therefore, a mixture of Gothic landlords and local peasants.[41] The former might well have been keen, in the first instance at least, to demonstrate their Gothicness, since it was the source of their social superiority, perhaps reinforced by tax-free status (p. 284). Hence they maintained customary ritual when it came to burying their female dead. The disjuncture in cemetery form from Aquitaine to the Meseta makes it impossible to see the *Reihengräber* as the result of the implantation in Spain of whole communities composed entirely of Goths. Indeed, associated with the cemetery at Duraton is a fourth-century church, and it would appear that the arrival of Gothic immigrants in the area did not cause a complete break. The cemeteries may well reflect Visigothic land-grabbing, then, but in a slightly less direct way than has been traditionally supposed.

A further guide to centres of Gothic settlement is provided by the sees occupied by non-Catholic, so-called Arian bishops in the sixth century. Nothing suggests that the Goths' religion ever spread very far into the Hispano-Roman population. Hence, one might expect non-Catholic bishops to have been established only where there was a significant concentration of non-Catholics, i.e. Goths. The picture is complicated, however, because most of our information comes from

[41] Cf., with different arguments, Ripoll Lopez, 1993–4.

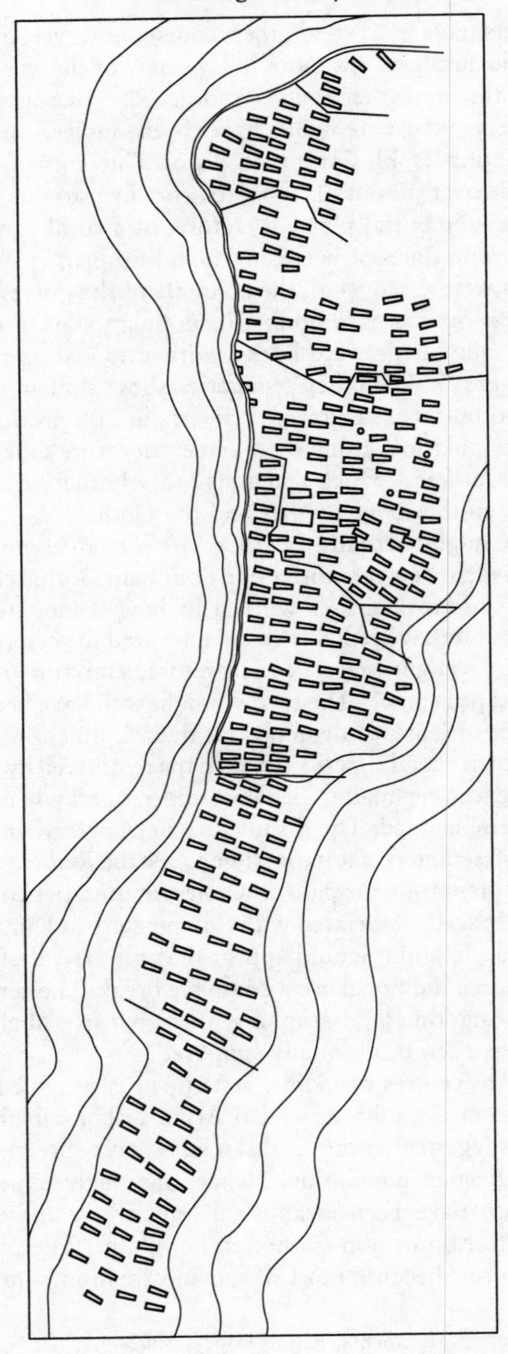

Figure 7.5 The Visigothic period cemetery at Carpio de Tajo

the moment when the Goths actually converted to Catholicism – the third Council of Toledo in 589 – and the last non-Catholic king, Leovigild, made a major effort to undermine Catholic dominance in the peninsula (chapter 9). This included ordaining Arian bishops to new sees.

Eleven non-Catholic sees are definitely attested in the later sixth century (figure 7.6). Four clustered in the old Suevic territories of Gallaecia in the north-west (Viseu, Tuy, Lugo and Oporto), and hence probably reflect Suevic settlement (the Suevi were also non-Nicene Christians) rather than Goths. Of the other seven, two were established in major political centres (Merida and, probably, Toledo), another group ran along the strategic north-east Mediterranean coast (Narbonne, Barcelona, Valencia and Tortosa). The other securely attested see was Palentia in the middle of the Meseta. In addition, a good case has been made for there having been an Arian see at Elvira (Avila), again in the Meseta, and a less strong one (based on the fact that they had no Catholic bishop in 589, and their position in the Meseta) for Osma and Alcala de Henares. Estimates of the density of Gothic settlement on the Meseta would vary substantially, of course, according to whether one accepted these last three as additional Arian sees or not.[42]

We should also note place-names showing Germanic influence. One cluster comes from Septimania around Narbonne, north of the Pyrenees. This area remained in Gothic hands throughout the sixth and seventh centuries. Another has been identified in Catalonia, around Gerona, and a third in eastern Andalusia around the cities of Italica, Cordoba and Seville. Such evidence is problematic, however, because Germanic names continued in use into much later periods.[43] Taken together, the archaeological, religious and place-name evidence paints a suggestive, but hardly definitive picture. There would appear to have been fairly strong concentrations of Gothic settlement in the north-east of the peninsula, either side of the Pyrenees. A further string of Gothic communities ran along the east coast, with more clustered in the Meseta of central northern Spain. The pattern was supplemented with more isolated groups in the major centres of the south and west. The latter were perhaps military garrisons, a phenomenon found in the Ostrogothic kingdom (chapter 8).

Strategic concerns dictated some of this. Holding both sides of the Pyrenees and the east coast were obvious priorities. Likewise, it was

42 Kampers, 1979, 175ff; Mikat, 1984, 12ff.

43 Gamillscheg, 1934, 350ff; Kampers, 1979, 173ff; Billy 1992.

Figure 7.6 Arian episcopal sees

necessary to establish a substantial presence in the vicinity of the Suevic kingdom (which continued to exist independently for much of the sixth century). Nor could the peninsula have been governed without controlling important centres elsewhere. At the same time, the amount of extra space available in Spain, compared to the Garonne, is obvious, and there is every reason to suppose that the settlement brought individual Goths extra material rewards. To maintain his position which, as we have seen, was always liable to attack, any Gothic king needed to channel pressure for rewards from below in such a way as to meet, at the same time, some of his own priorities. The pattern of Gothic settlement in Spain suggests, indeed, such a mixture of enrichment and strategic control.

(ii) Romans, Franks, and the destruction of the kingdom

The Roman population of the Visigothic kingdom, particularly its landowning elite, was also undergoing a series of important transformations. The late Roman landowning elite was a civilian elite, which acquired educational distinctions to gain access to rewarding careers in the imperial bureaucracy. Careers tended to be cyclical. A period in office at the centre brought honours, privileges, money and connections, which allowed the individual to occupy a dominant position in local society, after any period in central office came to an end. In particular, senatorial rank became the basic reward and aim of service at the centre. The disappearance of central governmental institutions in the Visigothic kingdom brought this pattern to an end, and the senatorial order was dissolved by the Visigothic state. Change was not sudden. No doubt the ability of the central imperial bureaucracy to suck local elites into its web had been fading in the west throughout the fifth century. Nor did all administrative posts disappear overnight. Some jobs existed at the Visigothic court for educated Romans like Leo of Narbonne, and rather more within the province and city: *iudex*, *defensor*, *cancellarius*, *numerarius* (all but the first elected by the local citizen body). None the less, control of the distribution of power was no longer concentrated in the ramifications of a bureaucratic state.[44]

This ushered in a fundamental change in the lifestyle of the landed elite of western Europe, which was to last for the best part of a millennium. In so far as there is one, the established orthodoxy is that, faced with the dismantling of the western Empire, surviving members of the Roman elite turned for consolation to episcopal office and their libraries. There are plenty of individual examples of such responses, not least that of Sidonius Apollinaris. But, numerically at least, a more important response was to abandon the bureau for the battlefield. By the sixth century, Roman-descended landowning elites were participating en masse, via city-based militias, in the armies of the Franks. This merely paralleled a development that had occurred in the Visigothic kingdom by the first decade of the century. Gallo-Roman senators, including Sidonius' son Apollinaris, fought and died for Alaric II in 507 at the battle of Vouillé (Gregory of Tours *Histories* 2.37).

The details of this participation are unclear. By the seventh century, the same military obligations were being imposed by Visigothic kings upon all their subjects, whatever their descent. All freemen, together with a percentage of their dependants, were required to answer the call to arms. Whether this was already true in 507 is unknown, but not unlikely. Individual Romans are attested serving in different

[44] Imperial period: Heather, 1994b. *The Breviary of Alaric* shows the dissolution of the senatorial order, although special mechanisms were left in place for the trial of particularly grand individuals. See generally, Thompson, 1969, 114ff.

capacities in Visigothic armies from the time of Theoderic II onwards (p. 188). The *Breviary of Alaric* omitted the old imperial legislation on recruiting, which suggests that military participation had already been re-established on a different footing. In the highly competitive post-Roman world, military manpower was at a premium, and kings of the successor states are unlikely to have delayed for long recruiting from the largest sector of their populations. If, by 507, a general military levy was not already in operation throughout the Visigothic kingdom, matters were heading firmly in that direction.[45]

The lifestyle of the Roman population of the Visigothic kingdom was already approximating quite closely, then, to that of the Goths. Overall, a general process of fusion had begun. Not, of course, that, within two generations of the kingdom's foundation, it was complete. The *Breviary of Alaric* envisages parallel civilian and military administrative structures, usually (and probably, in broad terms, correctly) seen as encompassing respectively the Roman and Gothic elements of the population.[46] Likewise, there was a formal ban on intermarriage between Roman and Goth, which was only lifted in the last quarter of the sixth century (chapter 9).[47] None the less, contact between the two groups could not be prevented. The *Breviary* laid down procedures for dealing with military-civilian (i.e. Gotho-Roman) disputes, and the *Code of Euric* regulated against Romans who tried to use a relationship with a powerful Goth to win legal disputes (*CE* 312). More generally, Goths held and farmed land side-by-side with Romans both in the Garonne valley and in Spain, and, under the new military provisions, fought side-by-side in the same armies. It is hardly surprising, then, to find individual instances of intermarriage (e.g. Theudis: p. 239), and more general evidence of cultural assimilation. As we have seen, Gothic remains are probably not immediately visible in the Garonne valley precisely because they had already adopted many Roman tastes.

This much is uncontroversial. There is one area, however, where it is usual to conceive of a more entrenched division between Roman and Goth: religion. The Goths were non-Nicene, so-called Arian Christians, where the bulk of the Roman population was Catholic (i.e. Nicene). There clearly was some religious tension as the kingdom was created.

[45] Note particularly the omission of almost all of *C.Th.* 7 from the *Breviary*. Seventh-century situation: *LV* 9.2.8–9; cf. in general Sanchez, 1989.

[46] Cf. Thompson, 1969, chs 5–6.

[47] *LV* 3.1.1 probably revising a lost provision of the *Code of Euric* rather than *C.Th.* 3.14.1.

Euric held religious debates at his court, and, while establishing his power in the 470s, exiled a number of bishops. Sidonius, bishop of Clermont, spent a period in exile (in Bordeaux: *Epp*. 4.10, 22), as did Simplicius of Bourges and one Crocus (from an unknown see). Sidonius also complained about sees which were lying empty because Euric had refused to sanction new elections (Bordeaux, Perigueux, Rodez, Limoges and Auch: *Ep*. 7.6.4). This tension is generally supposed to have acquired an extra dimension in the reign of Alaric II, because the rise of Frankish power was accompanied by the conversion of the Frankish king Clovis to Catholic Christianity. Writing about 70 years later, Gregory of Tours placed Clovis' baptism as early as 496, and reports that, because of it, many Gallo-Romans were anxious to have the Franks, rather than heretic Goths, as their rulers (*HF* 2.35–6).

But neither Gregory's account nor his overall judgement can be accepted at face value. For one thing, Euric's initial measures do not reflect any general anti-Catholic policy. There was no attempt to convert Catholics, and Sidonius' exile seems to have had political rather than religious reasons; as we have seen, Sidonius had organized Provençale resistance to Euric in the early 470s (p. 194). The non-appointment of bishops may also have been a product of the same political circumstances, as the king worked out who was likely to cooperate with the new order he was trying to create. After this initial period, there is little evidence for a generally suspicious or hostile approach on the part of the Visigothic monarchy to the Catholic Church. Alaric II gave his approval for sees to be filled, considered himself a God-appointed monarch and called councils for the general health of the Church within his kingdom.

Gregory has also introduced distortions into his account of Clovis' career precisely to present it as the triumphant crusade of a Catholic king. He was certainly baptised later than 496, perhaps even after the victorious campaign of 507 against the heretic Goths. More contemporary sources than Gregory report that the campaign was really to do with money, and it was mounted jointly with Burgundians, who were just as non-Catholic as the Visigoths. On the eve of the campaign, however, Clovis did issue an edict promising his protection to Catholic religious foundations. Baptised or not, he made some attempt to undercut the loyalty of the Catholic population of the Visigothic kingdom.[48] Did he succeed?

Clovis certainly did enough to raise doubts in Alaric's mind. Two metropolitan bishops, whose ecclesiastical jurisdictions ran beyond

[48] On Gregory and Clovis, see Wood, 1985.

the boundaries of the Visigothic kingdom into Frankish and Burgundian territory respectively, Verus of Tours (*c.*505) and Caesarius of Arles (504/5), were exiled from their sees in the early 500s as tension mounted.[49] There is no sign, however, of any general Catholic hostility towards their non-Catholic king. Caesarius, indeed, was soon reconciled to him. He quickly returned from exile in Bordeaux to play a major role in the Council of Agde, and in preparations for the putative 'national' Visigothic Church council planned for the following year.[50] While in exile, (according to his *vita* at least) Caesarius preached against the King's religion, but carefully asserted – in line with Alaric's own view of himself (p. 198) – that worldly authority was God-ordained and should therefore command allegiance.[51]

Indeed, Alaric responded to Clovis' manoeuvres not by persecuting his Catholic subjects, but by mounting a charm offensive of his own. It was in the run up to the 507 campaign, for instance, that Alaric issued his *Breviary*. Amongst other things, its contents reconfirmed stability in such basic points of Roman elite life as property and testamentary rights. The right to hold land and pass it on to the heir of one's choice were the basis, of course, of the secular dominance of the Gallo-Roman elite.[52] He also reinforced their religion by inaugurating a new pattern of Catholic Church councils, the synod of Gallic bishops at Agde in 506, and the 'national' council of Gallic and Spanish bishops planned for 507. Sometimes seen as purely internal measures, both surely reflect the pressure being applied by Clovis. In the face of Frankish power, Alaric was seeking to generate internal unity within his kingdom. As far as we can tell, he succeeded. Above all, when the chips were down, Gallo-Roman landowners turned up to fight and die in battle against the Frankish king at Vouillé in 507. Even after Clovis' stunning victory, they continued to resist. The city of Arles was defended tenaciously by a mixed force of Goths and Catholic Gallo-Romans throughout the winter of 507/8 (Cassiodorus *Variae* 3.32), as was Carcassone (Procopius *Wars* 5.12.41 ff).

With hindsight, Clovis' career would be seen as a God-directed

[49] Gregory also places the exiles of Bishops Volusianus of Tours and Quintianus of Rodez at this point, but this is mistaken; Volusianus had been exiled in the 490s, and Quintianus only later in the 510s.

[50] On these, see Schaferdiek, 1967, 55ff, 243–7.

[51] Wood, 1994, 46ff; Klingshirn, 1994, ch. 4.

[52] Note particularly the wholesale inclusion of *C.Th.* books 2–4 in the *Breviary*.

crusade which culminated in the liberation of the Catholics of southern Gaul. Contemporary reality was somewhat different. Gallo-Roman landowners fought for their Arian Visigothic king, Catholic bishops prayed for him, and, even after his death, stout resistance continued. The first Gothic successor state to the Roman Empire was thrown into disarray not by religious divisions, but by the death of its king in battle. It was to be saved from total destruction by the intervention of a second Gothic power: the Italian kingdom of the Ostrogoths.

8

Ostrogothic Italy: Kingdom and Empire

Under Euric, the Visigothic kingdom became a major force in post-imperial western Europe. More powerful still was the kingdom created by a second Gothic king, Theoderic, and the Ostrogoths whom he led to Italy. Marked for much of its course by unparalleled success, Theoderic's reign, none the less, ended in failure. His successes and failures provide the subject matter for this chapter.

A. The Road to Ravenna

As we saw in chapter 5, the Emperor Zeno granted Theoderic unprecedented honours in 483. But this agreement had been preceded by four years of conflict (478–82), and its underlying causes had been merely put to one side. The first signs of renewed tension appeared in the middle of a joint campaign fought against Zeno's great Isaurian rival, Illus, in Asia Minor. A contingent of Theoderic's Goths fought on until Illus fled to the mountain fortress of Papiris in the autumn of 484. Theoderic himself, however, was recalled at an earlier stage when Zeno began to doubt his loyalty. The recall led to no immediate break between them, but, in 486, Theoderic rebelled against Zeno and ravaged Thrace. No doubt he was trying to apply pressure on the Emperor. In 487, Theoderic raised the stakes by advancing on Constantinople. Encamped at Rhegium, his forces harried the city's suburbs and even cut a major aqueduct. This was enough to make

Zeno negotiate. It had become clear that a radical solution was required to break the deadlocked relationship of Emperor and Goth. Both agreed that Theoderic should take his people to Italy.[1]

The underlying cause of the deadlock is clear enough. Zeno had struggled throughout his reign to retain both his throne and his political independence. He was surely afraid that Theoderic would use the expanded power-base he had created by unifying the Goths, to try to become the power behind the imperial throne. For his part, Theoderic had enough experience to know (or at least suspect) that Zeno would not, in the long term, tolerate his independent power. When Theoderic rebelled in 485, we are told, he had in mind Zeno's treatment of Armatus. Armatus defected from Basiliscus to Zeno in 476, and was made senior imperial general for life. Within a year, Zeno had had him assassinated.[2]

A clash of interests had become manifest, which there was no obvious way of resolving while the Goths remained in the eastern Empire. By damaging Thrace or the outskirts of Constantinople, Theoderic could force Zeno to negotiate, but this would not solve the problem. In anything but the short term, Zeno would not allow a Gothic general the kind of influence that the size of his army and understandable personal ambitions made inevitable. The decision to send Theoderic's Goths to Italy was thus primarily designed to break an impasse. How it was reached is uncertain. Western sources – Ennodius' *Panegyric on Theoderic* and the *Getica* (again probably following Cassiodorus' *History*) – stress Theoderic's initiative in the matter, and ignore Zeno. Stemming directly or indirectly from the Ostrogothic court at Ravenna, these works had every interest in suppressing the Emperor's role. This does not mean, however, that all the running was made by Zeno. While the Emperor must have played an important part in events, as eastern sources maintain, Theoderic also needed to break the deadlock. As early as 479 he had aired the suggestion that, in alliance with imperial forces, he might intervene in Italy to restore a deposed western Emperor (p. 161). Italy did not lie beyond the Goth's vision, and both parties must have considered the agreement of 487/8 a reasonable solution to their problems.[3]

[1] Main source: John of Antioch fr. 214.4–9. Other sources and commentary: Heather, 1991, 304–5.

[2] John Malalas, p. 212.

[3] Western sources: Ennodius, *Pan.* 14, 25 (cf. *Life of Epiphanius* 109); Jordanes, *Getica* 57.289ff. Eastern sources: Procopius *Wars* 5.1.9–12; Theophanes *AM* 5977 (131 de Boor); Jordanes, *Romana* 348. For commentary, see Moorhead, 1984, 262–3.

No authoritative account survives of the terms agreed. The sources again differ as we might expect. Western writers, especially those with some connection to the Ostrogothic court, stress that Theoderic was to rule Italy in his own right; their eastern counterparts report that he held authority only as Zeno's deputy. The historiographical difficulty in reconstructing Theoderic's relations with Constantinople is easy to explain. The sources report four major moments of diplomatic contact between Theoderic and the eastern Empire:

1 with Zeno while the Goths were still in the Balkans (487/8);
2 with Zeno again after Theoderic's victory in Italy (491);
3 with the Emperor Anastasius soon after his accession (492);
4 with Anastasius again (498).

None of these negotiations is described in any detail, so that it is difficult to know where to assign the miscellaneous information about Gotho–Roman affairs which appears piecemeal in a variety of sources. Some of the sources are also letters from one or other of the protagonists. It is not always clear, therefore, whether they are describing things formally agreed, or merely represent the assertions of one side or the other.

The pattern of contacts between Theoderic and Zeno from 487 to 491 (the first two negotiations) is as follows. An agreement was drawn up before Theoderic left the Balkans. Theoderic then defeated Odovacar in an extended campaign (see below), after which he was proclaimed 'king' (*Anon. Val.* 12.57). This proclamation was followed by a second round of contacts with Zeno. The most obvious interpretation of these events is that the second contact was necessitated by Theoderic's declaration as king. Our source does indeed say that the declaration was made without waiting for Zeno's command. This would suggest that Zeno had not agreed in 487/8 that Theoderic should be king; he was perhaps sent to Italy, therefore, as imperial general and Patrician, but no more.[4] However one interprets the contact in 491, the main point of the negotiations in 487/8 was to remove the Goths from the Balkans. Therefore, in the autumn and winter of 488/9, Theoderic, ostensibly, perhaps, as Patrician and imperial general, set out with his followers to create a Gothic kingdom in the rich and famous lands of Italy.[5]

[4] See e.g. Jones, 1962; Claude, 1980. Prostko-Prostynski, 1994, ch. 1 argues that 491 saw no more than a formal confirmation of an earlier agreement that Theoderic was to be king. This is possible.

[5] On what follows, see e.g. Wolfram, 1988, 278 ff; Moorhead, 1992, ch. 1.

Other powers, however, had different ideas. Near the modern city of Vukovar, where the river Vuka reaches the Danube, a force of Gepids under their king Trapstila barred the way. After a hard struggle, the Goths got across the river. Theoderic is said to have shown great personal courage in the battle, and the Gepid king was killed. The Goths may also have been harried on their journey by some Sarmatians of the middle Danube. Their principal enemy was Odovacar, however, and battle with him was soon joined.

The Goths moved into Italy by the Vipava valley, the main route through the Julian Alps. At Pons Isontii, Odovacar's army was waiting, but was driven back into Italy after defeat on 28 August 489. A second engagement followed near Verona on 30 September. Theoderic was again successful, and Odovacar fled to Ravenna, made virtually impregnable by its marshes and walls. One of Odovacar's leading generals, Tufa, promptly deserted to Theoderic, and a quick Gothic victory seemed likely. On being sent to Ravenna, however, Tufa changed sides again (before the end of 489), massacring an elite body of Goths which had been sent with him. As a result, Odovacar could return to the offensive, and, in 490, it was Theoderic's turn to retreat to a fortified redoubt: Pavia. From this precarious position he was rescued by the arrival of some Visigoths. On 11 August 490, battle was rejoined where the road from Lodi to Cremona crossed the river Adda. Heavily defeated once more, Odovacar returned to Ravenna.

Tufa, however, was still at large in the Adige valley around Trent, and, as the siege of Ravenna dragged on, disagreement within Theoderic's ranks brought Odovacar and Tufa further recruits. On being criticized by Theoderic for their behaviour towards the local Italo-Roman population, the Rugi in his ranks, under the control of Fredericus, joined Tufa in 491. The next year, 492, proved decisive. In August, Theoderic established a sea blockade of Ravenna from the nearby port of Rimini. Tufa's force was also finally neutralized; the Rugi changed sides a second time and destroyed it in battle. Unity had been restored to Theoderic's ranks, and Odovacar isolated inside Ravenna with his few remaining troops. The strength of the city's defences was unshaken, however, so, in the end, Theoderic was willing to treat.

Negotiations opened on 25 February 493, and, on 5 March, Theoderic entered the city. Ostensibly, he had agreed to share power, but, ten days later, he murdered Odovacar at a banquet, reportedly with his own hand. He is said to have declared, as his sword cut Odovacar in half, that he 'didn't have a bone in his body' (John of

Antioch fr. 214a). On the same day, Odovacar's surviving supporters and their families were massacred, wherever they could be found. One long march, three major battles, and a host of minor engagements later, Theoderic's forces had conquered Italy.

In the aftermath of victory, the army declared Theoderic king, a declaration accompanied, as we have seen, by a flurry of diplomatic activity. A first embassy went to Zeno. Theoderic's actions had either gone beyond the terms of their initial agreement, or the Emperor's formal approval had to be given for the agreement to be enacted (p. 218). A second embassy soon followed, in 492, to the new eastern Emperor, Anastasius I. Theoderic no doubt wanted Anastasius' recognition, particularly if he had recently demanded better terms from Zeno than those originally agreed. The second embassy was unsuccessful. Not until 497 or 498 did a formal agreement follow with Anastasius, as a result of which Theoderic received from Constantinople royal clothing and palace ornaments (*Anon. Val.* 12.64). At this point, Anastasius clearly granted Theoderic his recognition. Can we be more specific about what it implied?

In 536, further diplomatic negotiations between Theodahad, one of Theoderic's successors, and the eastern Emperor Justinian centred on an intriguingly specific set of issues. Trying to stave off war, Theodahad agreed to the following. First, a practical matter: he would have no authority to execute senators or Catholic priests and confiscate their property, unless the Emperor first agreed. Secondly, only the Emperor, and not Theodahad, would have the right, henceforth, to grant Italians top imperial distinctions: Patrician or senatorial rank. On ceremonial occasions, the Emperor's name was now to be shouted first, before that of the Gothic king, and an imperial statue was always to stand on the right (the position of honour) of the Gothic king's statue (Procopius *Wars* 5.6.2–5). Since recognizing the eastern Emperor's legal and ceremonial rights in these areas featured in the discussions of 536 as Gothic concessions, they had presumably not been recognized by Gothic kings prior to this date. In other words, Theoderic and his immediate successors had placed their own statues on the right and asserted full dominion over the lives and property of Roman senators and Catholic clergy.

That this was true of Theoderic himself seems certain. In 499, a Roman synod acclaimed the king in imperial fashion without bothering to mention Anastasius (p. 225). In a letter of 510, likewise, he stated, in a letter to Anastasius, that it was his own choice that Felix should be consul, and asked the Emperor for no more than confirmation (Cassiodorus, *Variae* 2.1). And in the 520s, as we shall see, Theoderic executed certain senators and confiscated their lands. Whether, as has recently been argued, Anastasius actually agreed, in the negotiations of 497/8, that Theoderic could assert his independence and equality in these ways, is rather less clear.[6] Such a combination of rights and ceremonies stressed the independence and equality, compared to the Roman Emperors in Constantinople, of the Ostrogothic kings of Italy: a huge dent in the image of world hegemony which the east Romans continued to assert.

In 497/8, Anastasius had just secured his own position by defeating an extended Isaurian revolt. There is no obvious reason, therefore, why he should have felt pressed into making such dramatic concessions to the Gothic king of Italy at this date. Unambiguous evidence for Anastasius' recognition of Theoderic's rights over Roman citizens and the distribution of Roman honours, comes only after a further round of diplomatic sparring between the two in the year 508, when, as we shall see, Theoderic greatly strengthened his position (pp. 232f). I strongly suspect, therefore, that while Anastasius certainly recognized Theoderic's legitimacy in 497/8, he did not acknowledge the Gothic king's right to present himself, in ceremonial contexts, as a ruler on a par with the ruler of Constantinople. These further concessions came only later. But why should Theoderic, a king of the Goths, have wanted to use such Roman imperial ceremonial forms in the first place, let alone have his rights to them recognized by the eastern Empire?

B. *Theoderic Augustus?*

Ostrogothic Italy was the most conspicuously Roman of the successor states to the western Roman Empire. It was also overtly deferential to the eastern Empire. Few text books fail to quote Theoderic's letter to the Emperor Anastasius, which Cassiodorus made the first of his *Variae* collection:

> You [Anastasius] are the fairest ornament of all realms, you are the healthful defence of the whole world, to which all other rulers rightfully look up with reverence. We [Theoderic] above all, who by Divine help learned in Your Republic the art of governing Romans with equity ... Our royalty is an imitation of yours, modelled on your good purpose, a copy of the only Empire. (*Variae* 1.1)

[6] Prostko-Prostynski, 1994, 131ff.

But Theoderic's Roman-ness was a consciously adopted pose, and his deference to Constantinople a sham.

(i) Portrait of a king

Ideas of what it meant to be 'Roman' did not exist in a vacuum. As so often with self-definitions, it required a second party to display the inverse of the qualities claimed by Romans: the 'barbarians'. The Late Roman state identified a number of related concepts which differentiated the two. A central contention was that the population of the Roman Empire (or at least its elite) was made more rational by the classical literature in which it was customarily educated. Rationality was defined as the individual's ability to control bodily passions by exercise of the intellect. Immersion in classical literature exposed the individual to accumulated *exempla* of virtue and vice, which, if properly digested, enabled the body to be controlled.[7] Barbarians, by contrast, were prey to their every passion, quite unable to steer a sensible course, and particularly given to gratifying the desires of the flesh. For Roman society as a whole, the greater rationality of its individual members meant that they were prepared to subordinate their immediate desires to the rule of written law: the guarantee of an ordered society. Thus for Romans the rule of law – encapsulated, in the late imperial period in the concept of *civilitas* – became the great distinguishing feature of their society (cf. p. 198).

Christianity gave this sense of superiority a further dimension. The Roman educated elite identified an underlying order in the cosmos, whose structure reflected, throughout, the one organizing principle which had shaped it from primeval chaos. Thus in a view descending from Pythagoras and Ptolemy, distances from earth to the planets mirrored harmonic ratios and exact proportionality.[8] The Christian Roman Empire, following the strong lead of pagan Emperors, claimed that there was a political dimension to cosmological order. No earthly ruler, it was claimed, could hold power unless the Divinity so ordered. This idea was developed still further to support the claim that the Roman Empire was the particular agent of Divine power for perfecting humanity. Thus Eusebius of Caesarea argued that it was no accident that Christ should have been born in the reign of Augustus. It was part of the Divine Plan that the founders of Christianity and the Roman Empire had co-existed. More generally,

[7] See most recently, Kaster, 1988, esp. 12–19.
[8] See esp. Sorabji, 1983, esp. chs 13, 20.

Christian Emperors abrogated for themselves the role of Christ's vice-gerent on earth. Imperial ceremonial was held to echo the majesty of heaven, and an aura of Christian sacrality surrounded the imperial person and his officers.[9] A proper classical education thus led the individual to appreciate the benefits of the Roman way of life, and its historical importance within the Divine scheme of things.[10]

Theoderic's regime seized upon this vision of *Romanitas*, not least the claim to be part of a Divinely inspired order for the world. In his letter to Anastasius, for instance, Theoderic noted that it was God's help which allowed him to rule Romans properly. Likewise, the mosaics of St Apollinare Nuovo originally portrayed Theoderic enthroned in majesty, surrounded by his court in the new palace in Ravenna. Opposite him was displayed Christ the Pantocrator and the majesty of heaven. The greater authority (Heaven) was shown directly sustaining the lesser (Theoderic).[11] Theoderic's Italian palaces (that of Ravenna is best known, but two others were built at Pavia and Verona) seem to have imitated the architectural pattern of the imperial palace in Constantinople. Theoderic, of course, knew it well, having spent ten years there as a hostage. Theoderic not only built 'imperial' palaces, he also deployed in them the imperial cult of the sacred ruler. Great public occasions such as his *adventus* into Rome in the year 500 were designed to proclaim, after the Constantinopolitan pattern, the sanctity and Divinely inspired nature of his rule.[12]

This is a particularly striking element in Theoderic's self-presentation because he was himself a non-Nicene Christian. Given that he was ruling Italy, the land of the papacy, the chief defender of Nicene Orthodoxy, one might think that this should have been a divisive claim. Not so. For the vast majority of his reign, Theoderic and the Catholic establishment treated one another with the greatest respect. On his entry into Rome, for instance, Theoderic greeted the Pope 'as if he were St Peter himself' (*Anon. Val.* 12.65). In similar vein, the *Life of Caesarius* records the very warm welcome that this leading Gallic bishop received from the king in 513. Theoderic also played a major role in securing for Caesarius the new role of Papal

[9] The classic study of political theory is Dvornik, 1966, chs 8, 10–12.
[10] On all this, see further Heather 1993, 1994.
[11] MacCormack, 1981, 236–9.
[12] On Theoderic's palaces, see most recently, Johnson, 1988. Cf. more generally, Ward-Perkins, 1984.

Plate 15 Theoderic, king of the Goths. This head was uncovered in building works in Theoderic's great church at Ravenna, St Apollinare Nuovo. Restored as the Emperor Justinian (none of the lettering is ancient), it almost certainly originally portrayed Theoderic

vicar for the whole of Gaul, which he received in the course of the same trip.[13] Recent reconsiderations have also underlined the care Theoderic

13 *Life of Caesarius* 1.36–43; cf. Klingshirn, 1994, 124ff. with below, p. 258.

took to reach, and be seen to reach, a consensual solution to the fierce dispute for control of the papacy (the so-called Laurentian schism) which came to a head in 501–2.[14]

Catholic churchmen responded in kind. It was such men, of course, who had appealed to Theoderic to settle the disputed papal election in the first place. A similar recognition was granted him in formal Church assemblies. The official minutes of a Roman synod of March 499 have survived and make fascinating reading. At its opening, the assembled churchmen jumped to their feet and shouted, 'Hear us Christ. Long live Theoderic.' They repeated it 30 times. Such repeated acclamations were a standard part of imperial ceremonial, but the churchmen made not the slightest mention of the eastern Emperor.[15] Likewise, many individual churchmen were ready to serve him. While still a deacon, Ennodius pronounced a public panegyric before the king in 507, for instance, which explained how God had brought Theoderic to Italy to subdue the demon-possessed Odovacar.[16] And when approaches were made by successive imperial regimes in the 510s to end a dispute between the Catholic Churches of east and west (the so-called Acacian schism), Theoderic was again deeply involved. Not only was he kept thoroughly informed, but he also gave his approval to the reconciliation which followed.[17] Such was the nature of his relationship with the Catholic Church in his domains, therefore, that the thought of religious reunion between the eastern Empire and the papacy did not fill the king with dread. Notwithstanding his own particular creed, Theoderic thus claimed Divine inspiration for his rule, acted accordingly in all Church matters, and received an appropriate response from the churchmen of his day.

The propaganda and public acts of his regime also showed great awareness of the other essential elements of *Romanitas*. Theoderic was particularly aware of the ideological importance of written law, and of being seen to further individual human rationality via education in the classics. Ennodius' panegyric observed that *ius* and *civilitas* presided in Theoderic's palace, *ius* designating the fundamentals of Roman law.[18] Closely related to this was the concept of true freedom (*libertas*), attained by those who obeyed this law (*Variae* 12.5; cf. 11.13). Many of the letters written for Theoderic by

[14] Moorhead, 1992, ch. 4.
[15] *Acta synh. habit. Romae*, I, p. 405.
[16] Ed. Hartel, p. 267–8; cf. id., *Life of Epiphanius* 97.35.
[17] Moorhead, 1992, 194ff.
[18] Barnish, 1992, pp. xxiv–xxv; cf. *Variae* 1.27; 2.24; 6.5; 8.33; 9.18.

Cassiodorus demanded respect for Roman law, reflected upon its fundamental correctness, or even cited it.[19] It is perhaps of a piece with this approach that Theoderic and his successors (unlike their Frankish, Burgundian and Visigothic counterparts) refused to issue a formal law code in their own names. Instead, they confined themselves instead to *edicta*, which Roman magistrates had always been allowed to issue.[20]

For the king's recognition of the importance of education, Ennodius' panegyric is again a prime piece of evidence. Amongst other things, it stressed the importance of the Greek education Theoderic had received in Constantinople (ed. Hartel, p. 264, 13ff). In his letter to Anastasius, Theoderic claimed, as we have seen, that it was precisely this education which had taught him to govern Romans. Through a classical education, therefore, Theoderic claimed to have grasped the importance of doing things the divinely ordained Roman

Plate 16 Theoderic's palace at Ravenna (from the St Apollinare Nuovo mosaics)

19 *Variae* 2.7; 3.17 (cf. 18); 4.22; 5.40; 10.5. Cross-references to jurists, the *Theodosian Code* and later imperial novels are cited by Fridh in his edition at pp. 281–3.

20 *Edict of Theoderic*, cf. *Variae* 9.18 (edict of Athalaric). See Procopius *Wars* 5.1.27–8 and *Anon. Val.* 12.60 on the deliberate point of this approach.

way, and a number of *Variae* underline the attention he devoted to it. He proclaimed education, for instance, the key to morality. Through it, he noted, the individual learns self-control, without which obedience to Roman law is impossible. Likewise, the individual who lacks self-control cannot be trusted to govern others. For the maintainance of good social order – *civilitas* – education had to function properly (*Variae* 3.13, 8.15, 8.31). Not for nothing did Theoderic's family like to be seen subsidizing the pay of grammarians (*Variae* 9.21).

A whole battery of means was deployed, then, to get over the central message that Theoderic's regime was 'Roman' and in tune with God's plans. Panegyrics, official letters, coinage (some of Theoderic's coins proclaimed *invicta Roma*), visual representation, and buildings were all used to sustain this claim and its main supporting pillars: reverence for Roman law and classical education. The fullest and clearest expression of all this is to be found in the *Variae* of Cassiodorus, but the claim that he was ruling a Roman state ordained by God was a phenomenon general to Theoderic's rule. In later years, Cassiodorus liked to present himself as the chief architect of Theoderic's *Romanitas*.[21] But Cassiodorus entered office only in 507, and retained it for relatively brief periods in Theoderic's lifetime (507 to 511, and 523 to 526). By 507, the ideology of the regime was fully established, and all the ideas which surface in the *Variae* are found elsewhere. The basic stance of the Ostrogothic regime was set not by Cassiodorus but by Theoderic himself.

(ii) The importance of being Roman

Why did Theoderic go to such deliberate and determined lengths to portray his new kingdom as 'the Roman Empire continued'? It has sometimes been ascribed to a sentimental attachment to things imperial. But Theoderic had always been ready in the Balkans, when necessary, to confront the Emperor Zeno head on, and was under no illusion as to how the authorities in Constantinople regarded his rule in Italy. Nor does such a view do justice to the obvious calculation with which Theoderic framed his public statements and acts. His almost obsessive appropriation of *Romanitas* rather reflects a strategy designed both to make his new realm governable and to mask and justify a foreign policy which quickly became, maybe always had

[21] *Variae* 9.24.1–8; taken at pretty much face value by, amongst many others, Momigliano, 1955, 216–7.

been, thoroughly expansionary.

Theoderic's *Romanitas* was partly designed for the consumption of elite groups, clerical and lay, of Italy. The careful recycling of imperial ideological claims to Divine inspiration, and of imperial traditions of behaviour with regard to the Catholic Church, made it much easier for popes and bishops to be seen cooperating with a non-Nicene king. The problems of a diametrically opposite course of action are well illustrated in Vandal Africa. There, successive kings, of the same religious persuasion as Theoderic, persecuted the Catholic Church. This made the Church a focus of resistance and dissidence.[22]

Theoderic's treatment of the secular Roman elite mirrored his policy towards the Church. This elite comprised a set of families, relatively few in number, who controlled the reservoirs of financial power in the kingdom. They dominated local administration and landowning, and their willingness to pay and raise tax sustained the whole edifice. A militarily dominant ruler could compel payment to an extent, but taxation is a political issue, and successful taxation requires some element of consent.[23] The presentation of Theoderic's regime in the clothes of the old Empire rendered it acceptable, and encouraged the participation in the new order of those who had dominated the old. Theoderic's overt *Romanitas* and the continuation of Roman law amounted to a guarantee to the elite that their basic pattern of life and their landed fortunes would survive into the new political era. The *Breviary of Alaric* was a comparable approach to the same problem in the Visigothic kingdom (p. 214). To the same end, he also maintained (where his Visigothic counterparts had not), the established imperial pattern of senatorial dignities, and the bureaucratic offices to which they were tied.[24]

These policies, it must be stressed, were deliberate, not the result of mere inertia. During his struggle with Odovacar, Theoderic had threatened to cancel the testamentary powers of all Roman landowners who had not actively supported his cause. Those affected would have lost the right to leave their landed fortunes to the heirs of their choice. If pushed through, such a policy would have meant social revolution. Theoderic acceded, however, to the request of an embassy, led by Bishop Epiphanius of Milan, to cancel the order (Ennodius, *Life of Epiphanius* 122–35). I doubt that Theoderic ever really meant

22 See Courtois, 1955, 289–310.

23 Families: Barnish, 1988, and, above all, Schäfer, 1991. Taxation: Wickham, 1984.

24 Schäfer, 1991, 1ff.

to implement the policy in full, but its threat was a salutary reminder of what the new king could do if he wanted to. Making and then withdrawing the threat would have made crystal clear, to Italian landowners, the substantial virtues of the Ostrogothic regime, and of active participation in its structures.

Theoderic's appropriation of *Romanitas* had further implications for foreign policy. Above all, it involved a particular stance towards the eastern half of the Roman Empire. At first sight, Theoderic's attitude to Constantinople seems highly deferential, not least as reflected in certain passages of the first letter of the *Variae* collection (p. 221). The deference is superficial. An iron fist is evident within the letter's velvet glove. Beyond the passage quoted above, the letter continues:

> Our royalty is an imitation of yours, modelled on your good purpose a copy of the only Empire; and in so far as we follow you do we excel all other nations ... We think you will not suffer that any discord should remain between two Republics, which are declared to have ever formed one body under their ancient princes, and which ought not to be joined by a mere sentiment of love, but actively to aid one another with all their powers. Let there be always one will, one purpose in the Roman Kingdom. (*Variae* 1.1.2–5; trans. Hodgkin)

The letter was written in 508 when 8,000 east Roman troops in 100 warships and 100 troopships were harrying (or about to harry) the coast of Italy. They were acting on an alliance which the eastern Emperor had forged with the Frankish king Clovis, who was intent on expanding his kingdom at the expense of the Visigoths (pp. 200f). Set in this context, the letter is actually a demand note. Theoderic used his own Roman-ness to rebuke Anastasius on two counts. First, there should be peace, not conflict, between the two Roman states. Secondly, since Ostrogothic Italy is the only legitimately Roman state in the west ('in so far as we follow you do we excel all other nations'), Anastasius should not be concocting alliances with others. Theoderic obviously has the Franks in mind. A further sting in the letter's seemingly respectful tail is its allusion to the 'Divine help' which had sustained Theoderic's attempts to govern Romans. This amounted to a claim that Theoderic's 'Roman-ness' was as much part of God's order as the eastern 'Roman-ness' of Constantinople. It had its own, separate, legitimacy.[25] Beneath the surface deference, Theoderic claimed virtual parity of status with the eastern Empire.

[25] Cf. Claude, 1978, 42–4.

This claim to quasi-imperial status also appears in some of Theoderic's communications to other western successor states. A good example is his letter to King Gundobad of the Burgundians (like Anastasius an ally of the Franks), on the eve of the same crisis. Again, but superficially, the letter suggests friendship, since Theoderic sent Gundobad two time pieces (a sun dial and a waterclock). But the letter presented these offerings as gifts from Graeco–Roman civilization to help bring the Burgundians to a more rational, fully human way of life (*Variae* 1.46):

> [2] Under your [Gundobad's] rule, let Burgundy learn to scrutinise devices of the highest ingenuity, and to praise the inventions of the ancients. Through you it lays aside its tribal way of life ... Let it [by the clocks] fix the hours with precision. [3] The order of life (*Ordo vitae*) becomes confused if this separation is not truly known. Indeed, it is the habit of beasts to feel the hours by their bellies' hunger, and to be unsure of something obviously granted for human purposes.

Theoderic thus presented himself as controlling the monopoly of surviving Roman wisdom in western Europe, with rights to distribute the benefits of classical civilization as he saw fit. The Burgundians, by contrast, are placed on a much lower level of human evolution, still closer to beasts than rational human beings.

Theoderic's pretentions have become clear. Claiming virtual equality with the east Roman Empire, by the same token he asserted a cultural hegemony over the other western successor states. Although interesting, this self-portrait could none the less represent so much hot air. The ancient world, like the modern, is rife with the grandiose claims and self-delusions of dictators. What gives Theoderic's claims real point, however, is that, during his reign, steadily expansionary policies gradually brought reality substantially into line with his rhetorical posturings.

(iii) Empire reborn

The central thrust of Theoderic's foreign policy is often seen as the construction of a defensive alliance against Frankish expansion. He made, for instance, a series of strategic marriage alliances in the late 490s and early 500s, when Clovis had his eyes on the Visigothic kingdom (chapter 7). Theoderic himself married Clovis' sister, and married off various of his female relatives to the royal families of the Visigothic, Vandal and Burgundian kingdoms. We also have a series of letters from the king on the eve of the Vouillé campaign. In these, Theoderic urged restraint on both Clovis and Alaric, and attempted to win over surrounding kings to the same point of view. Thus Theoderic's aim was at that point, perhaps, to resist Frankish expansion. But he also had other aims, and resisting the Franks may be an insufficient interpretation of his manoeuvres even in the run up to Vouillé.

The first of Theoderic's neighbours to feel his power was Vandal Africa. In 491, a Vandal force was heavily defeated by the Goths in Sicily, and the Vandals renounced the annual payments they had previously received from Odovacar. In about AD 500, there followed a marriage alliance between the two kingdoms. It was not an equal match. A handsome dowry went to the Vandal king Thrasamund along with his new bride, Theoderic's sister Amalafrida, but the Ostrogothic princess was also accompanied by a military force of 5,000 men (Procopius *Wars* 3.8.12). These men, or some of them, stayed on in Carthage and were later killed when Thrasamund's successor threw off the Ostrogothic alliance in the 520s (see below). Such a significant Ostrogothic military presence at the heart of the Vandal kingdom clearly betokens a degree of Gothic hegemony. It was reinforced by subsequent events.

In 504/5, Theoderic next expanded his kingdom's holdings in the middle Danubian region. He had inherited from Odovacar parts of Dalmatia and the province of Savia. In 504/5, he defeated the Gepids of Trasericus in a well-directed campaign, and gained the province of Pannonia II, along with its main city, the old imperial capital of Sirmium. This campaign also involved the defeat of an imperial force, consisting mostly of Bulgar mercenaries, led by Sabinianus the younger.[26] The defeat may well explain Anastasius' subsequent support of Clovis, which produced from Theoderic the coded rebuke of *Variae* 1.1.

So far, then, the evidence shows Theoderic asserting hegemony over the Vandals, and adding new territories to his kingdom. On the face of it, in 506/7 he took a different line, attempting to preserve the status quo. But the actual tone of the letter he wrote to the Burgundians was, as we have seen, somewhat at variance with its contents. Haughty and patronizing, it was perhaps more likely to have provoked Gundobad than pacified him. Likewise, while Theoderic was polite enough when writing directly to Clovis, his comments about him to others were inflammatory. The letter to the kings of the Heruli, Warni and Thuringians, for instance, refers to Clovis' 'pride . . . hateful to God', his 'contempt for truth', his

[26] Wolfram, 1988, 320ff.

'arrogance' and his unlawful actions (*Variae* 3.3.1–2). Even in 506/7, then, Theoderic's diplomacy may have been more aggressive than is usually supposed.

Either way, Theoderic emerged the principal winner. In 507, Ostrogothic forces failed to arrive in Gaul in time, and Clovis destroyed the Visigothic army at Vouillé. Byzantine ships raided the coast of Italy in 508, and the threat of something similar is usually seen as the cause of this non-appearance. This may well be so. Theoderic's aggressive diplomacy in 506 and actions subsequent to the Visigothic defeat make it just possible, however, that the failure to show up was deliberate. For when Theoderic's armies, commanded by Ibba, did appear north of the Alps in 508, not only did they relieve the Burgundian siege of Arles and the Frankish siege of Carcassonne, they also went on to take control of the entire Visigothic kingdom.

Immediately after Vouillé, Gesalic, Alaric II's adult son from an earlier liaison, became king of the Visigoths. More recently, however, Alaric had married Theoderic's sister Theodegotha, a marriage which had also produced a son, Amalaric, who was still a minor. Initially, Theoderic supported Gesalic (cf. *Variae* 5.43.2), but, by 511, Ibba had driven Gesalic out of Spain.[27] Two important Visigothic nobles were executed by Gesalic between 508 and 511 (Goiaric and Veila: p. 200), so that Theoderic may have halted his forces in 508 only long enough to recruit political support among the Visigothic nobility. Gesalic briefly found sanctuary with the Vandal king Thrasamund, but was forced to leave when Theoderic applied pressure upon his brother-in-law (*Variae* 5.43–4), a nice demonstration of his hegemony over the Vandal kingdom (cf. above). Gesalic attempted to regain his throne but was captured and executed, probably in 513. In the meantime, Theoderic directly controlled the Visigothic kingdom. The Visigothic royal treasure was taken to Ravenna, and Visigothic taxes were controlled from Italy, along with the annual payments made to Gothic troops (Procopius *Wars* 5.12.47–8). Garrisons and administrators were sent from from Italy to Spain (ibid.), and practical administrative questions were referred to Theoderic in Ravenna (*Variae* 5.39).

In the crisis of 506–8, Clovis gained much of Aquitaine. From 511, however, Theoderic ruled as one kingdom not only Italy, but also substantial parts of both the Balkans and southern Gaul, and most of the Iberian Peninsula. In addition, he confirmed his hegemony over

[27] Ibid., 309–11.

the Vandal kingdom and other smaller nations (particularly the Thuringi), and brought the Burgundians to a similar degree of dependence. They had probably been detached from their Frankish alliance immediately after the defeats of 508. Gesalic was actually apprehended in Burgundian territory, and a marriage alliance followed between Theoderic's daughter Ostrogotha and Sigismund, heir to the Burgundian throne. As we shall see, there is no doubt that the Burgundians saw this marriage as a symbol of domination (p. 248). By 511, the realities of Theoderic's power substantially matched the imperial posturings of his rhetoric and public ceremonial. He had put back together a third or more of the old western Empire, and made other parts of it (Vandal North Africa and Burgundian Gaul) recognize his pre-eminence.

There is every reason to suppose that Theoderic was well aware of the significance of his achievement. Writing in the early 520s, Cassiodorus, in his lost Gothic history, linked the take-over of Spain to a notional 2,000th anniversary of the creation of the Gothic kingdom. In particular, he stressed that this act reunited the Gothic people. This emphasis would suggest that Theoderic did see the incorporation of the Visigoths as the major achievement of his reign. In the summer of 513, moreover, Bishop Caesarius of Arles came to Italy and was made Papal vicar for Spain and the whole of Gaul by Pope Symmachus. Given the relationship that prevailed between the papacy and Theoderic, and the fact Caesarius first visited the king in Ravenna, Theoderic must have had a hand in the vicariate. Its scale, indeed, precisely matched Theoderic's pretentions to hegemony in western Europe.[28] How the Franks may have felt about Caesarius' new rank is not recorded.

Perhaps, above all, Theoderic's succession *plans* indicate that he meant to hand on his newly united kingdom to a single successor. In formal letters, Theoderic declared that his dynasty, the Amal family, was not just another Germanic royal family, but an imperial dynasty attuned to the purple (*Variae* 4.1; 9.1; 10.1–4; cf. more generally 8.2; 8.5; 10.11). Such pretentious claims suggest that Theoderic had grand plans for his heirs, and his actual choice of successor underlines the point. By *c.*515, more than one wife having produced only a series of daughters, Theoderic had given up hope of a son of his own. Instead, a Goth called Eutharic was brought to Italy from Spain to marry another of Theoderic's daughters, Amalasuentha. Theoderic's claims for the imperial status of his own Amal family meant that Eutharic had also to

[28] Anniversary: Heather, 1987. Vicariate: Klingshirn, 1994, 127ff.

Plate 17 The Senigallia Medallion

become, at least notionally, a member of the dynasty. This was achieved by Cassiodorus, who added Ermenaric to the Amal family tree from the pages of Ammianus, and attached Eutharic's line to this king (above p. 53). Presented as an Amal, married to Theoderic's daughter, and formally declared his successor, Eutharic clearly stood a good chance of exercising authority in Italy after Theoderic's death. In addition, Theoderic had deliberately imported him from Visigothic Spain, where his family had been prominent at court (*Getica* 33.174–5). Theoderic surely had it in mind, therefore, that Eutharic would also be able to maintain control in Spain. In all probability, the young Amalaric was not destined, at least in the first instance, to succeed to the Visigothic throne. Theoderic conceived of his united Gothic kingdom as a single entity to be passed on to one designated successor.

After 511, Theoderic's quasi-imperial posturing was matched by a realm which he could with justification claim to be the western Roman Empire reconstituted. In certain formal contexts, Theoderic drew back from declaring himself a new Roman Emperor, but not very far. The eastern Empire remained the most powerful state of its day, and Theoderic probably did not want to antagonize it unduly. We shall see below what difficulties a hostile Empire would cause him in the 520s, even without invading Italy. Thus his formal title was always king, not Emperor; his coinage usually carried the Emperor's bust, and he forbore from issuing gold coins: an imperial prerogative. The latter was very much a constitutional nicety, however, and, on occasion, the mask slipped. One chance survival – the Senigallia Medallion (plate 17) – shows that Theoderic did occasionally issue gold coins. The reverse inscription describes Theoderic as 'conqueror of peoples' (*victor gentium*). The medallion was perhaps issued, therefore, precisely to commemorate Theoderic's great victories in Gaul and Spain.[29] Neither, as we have seen, did Theoderic place imperial statues to the right of his own, nor include the Emperor's name before his own (p. 220). There was thus deliberate ambiguity in Theoderic's stance. He presented himself as a Roman imperial ruler, without quite declaring himself Emperor, and the reality of his power made this self-presentation far from ridiculous. Theoderic deliberately allowed those who wished to, to see him as the first in a new line of western Emperors.[30] Thus, in a famous inscription, the Roman senator Caecina Mavortius Basilius Decius was responding to more than a hint on Theoderic's part when he styled his king 'forever Augustus' (*semper Augustus*): a uniquely imperial title (*ILS* 827).

C. *King of the Goths*

The authors of our two main sources for the internal workings of the Italian kingdom, Ennodius and Cassiodorus, were both Romans. Both were also loyal to Theoderic. Their writings thus reflect the central ideological conceit of his reign, that his rule represented the direct continuation of the Roman order of civilized life: *civilitas*. They also provide only minimal coverage of internal Gothic matters. Moreover, as the king's romanophile rule attracted new supporters, there naturally followed some erosion of boundaries between Roman and Goth. Procopius' account of the Byzantine conquest of Italy from the 530s does not suggest, however, that this boundary had been fundamentally redefined by this date. The vast majority of the

[29] Cf. Grierson, 1985.

[30] In 540, the Goths of Italy also offered Belisarius rule of the western Empire (p. 266), confirming that this is how they regarded their kings.

fighting against the armies of Belisarius and Narses was carried out by Goths, and, as we shall see, the 'first men' of the Goths remained a distinct political force within the kingdom. Belisarius was also able specifically to target the Gothic population of the peninsula, suggesting that they remained a very distinctive group (chapter 9). Looked at closely, the sources document some of the innovative measures by which Theoderic integrated his Gothic followers into the Italian landscape.

(i) The problem

By the time they entered Italy, the Ostrogoths probably numbered around 100,000 men, women and children (p. 164). The sheer numbers involved meant that Theoderic could not have hoped to exercise much direct power over their everyday lives. Indeed, after the defeat of Odovacar, Theoderic settled his followers over more than 1,000 km^2 of Italian countryside (see below), and distance compounded problems of government (cf. *Variae* 6.22). Gothic kingship became even more difficult after 511 when he took direct control of the Visigothic kingdom, perhaps further doubling the number of Goths under his command to *c.*200,000.

It is thus hardly surprising that Theoderic required numerous subordinates to help govern his united kingdom of Spain, southern Gaul and Italy. Men such as Anstat, Invila and Soas had already served as generals in the Balkans. In Italy, likewise, Pitzias led the assault on Sirmium, and Ibba commanded the army which intervened in Gaul and Spain. After 493, Theoderic also required non-military assistance. His administration depended upon a whole series of Goths, who commanded districts of varying importance as counts (*comites*). Some held almost independent sway in frontier regions, others ruled single cities. All the Gothic kings of Italy were also involved in the formulation of policy, a group variously styled the 'first men' or 'most notable' of the Goths. Theoderic used them when trying to deal with Theudis (see below), while Wittigis and his successors deferred to them in war and diplomacy (e.g. Procopius *Wars* 5.17.29; 6.22.13ff; 7.8.12ff). The Emperor Justinian even wrote to them separately on the eve of the Gothic war (*Wars* 5.7.21–4).

Subordinate leaders were not, it seems, appointed merely at Theoderic's whim. When the Goths of Rieti and Nursia in central Italy decided that their leader (called a *prior*) was to be Quidila son of Sibia, this choice was only confirmed by Theoderic. The king then died almost immediately, so that they had to write again to his successor, Athalaric (*Variae* 8.26). This exchange is totally unique in the surviving sources, but probably reflects, in its implied balance between local and central power, a general truth about the origins of these intermediate leaders. The Goths of different areas chose their own leaders, but had to obtain the king's approval.

In similar vein, important Goths had local power-bases which were not under close royal control. Early in the Gothic war, Pitzas surrendered to Belisarius with half the Goths of Samnium (*Wars* 5.15.1–2). These men would seem to have been loyal to Pitzas first. Likewise, when Wittigis surrendered, one Gothic group in Venetia, under Ildebad, refused to give in (*Wars* 6.29.41 (cf. 30.16ff); 7.1.25ff). Similarly, the Goths of the Cottian Alps preferred to follow the advice of Sisigis (commander of the garrisons in the region) although this contradicted royal policy (*Wars* 6.28.28ff). Likewise, Goths of different localities sometimes formulated policy separately. After the defeat of Teias, Goths north of the river Po quickly negotiated with the Franks, while those south of it were much more cautious (Agathias 1.5.1–2). The common denominator seems to be a local cohesion that went beyond more general allegiance to the Ostrogoths as a whole.

Some of these local ties were older than the particular group's acceptance of Amal kingship. The Rugi, for instance, joined Theoderic in 487, but, as late as 541, still maintained an independent identity and their own sub-leader (*Wars* 7.2.1ff). After resigning his own claims in favour of the Amals, likewise, Gensemund continued to lead an at least semi-independent military force on Valamer's behalf (*Variae* 8.9; cf. *Getica* 246). Indeed, the pattern of settlement in Italy probably in part reflected the constituent groups out of whom the Ostrogoths had been formed. Garrisons were established in the south of Rome, and the main Alpine passes were held in strength. Others were settled in an arc around Italy in Dalmatia, Savia and (after 508) Provence. Most Goths, however, were spread across northern and central Italy: Samnium, the Adriatic coast from Picenum up to and beyond Ravenna, Liguria and the Venetias.[31] This pattern obviously reflects strategic concerns. Relatively dense settlement of the Adriatic coast was a response to the potential threat from Constantinople, and the arc of garrisons in and beyond the Alps needs no further explanation. But there is a further point. For a group such as the Rugi

[31] Bierbrauer, 1975, 23–39. The information is essentially provided by Procopius; only 126 graves with some claim to be Gothic have been found in Italy.

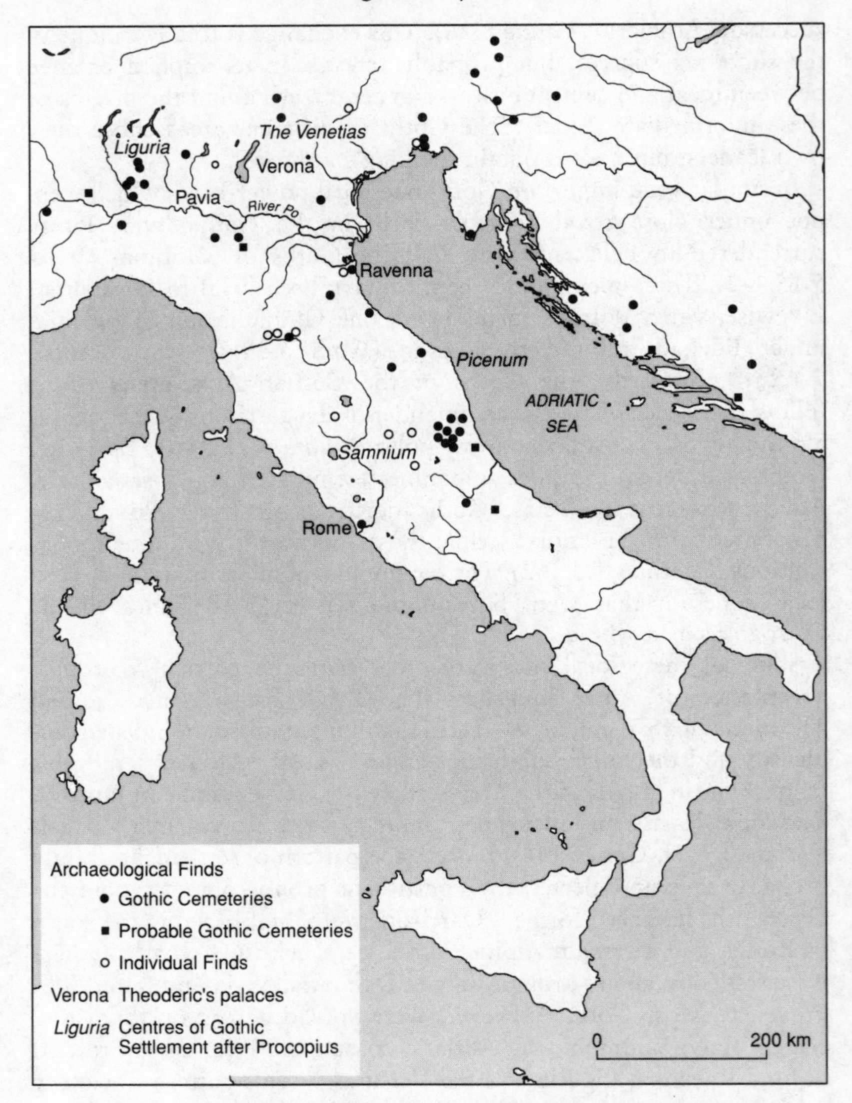

Figure 8.1 Cemeteries containing Ostrogothic gravegoods in Italy

to have maintained its sense of identity, it must have been settled together in one area (precisely which area is unknowable). There is no reason to think them unique in this.

Recent excavations in northern Italy have brought one of the settlements to life. Monte Barro is a prominent, steeply sloped Alpine foothill, 900 m high, which stands between lakes Como and Olignata.

It was a Roman military site in the fifth century, with a wall and fortress. At the end of the century, it was taken over by Goths, and excavations have turned up a series of dwellings and one main building. The latter covers an area of 1700 m^2, enclosing three sides of a courtyard. The central building consisted in part of large audience hall, and, among smaller finds, was unearthed a hanging crown: a symbol of authority. The Goths of this region thus opted for a highly defensible site, but lived in some style, and no doubt enjoyed the wonderful view (plates 18–19).[32]

As Gothic leader, then, Theoderic had to deal with powerful subordinates, some of whom drew on well-established traditions of association. As this suggests, some of these groups had their own internal hierarchies and political traditions, forming alternative centres of power and memory, beyond the control of the royal court in Ravenna. This could have very practical effects. Theoderic's propaganda liked to present his family as a uniquely imperial Gothic ruling dynasty (p. 233), and this has often been taken to reflect the rank and file Gothic view of the matter. As we shall see, however, the Goths did not hesitate to remove the last member of the dynasty from office when he failed to provide effective leadership in the 530s (chapter 9). The new king, Wittigis, stressed that he belonged to Theoderic's dynasty not by blood, but because his deeds were of similar stature (*Variae* 10.31). While Theoderic tried to make kingship the preserve of one family, others held to an older, pragmatic tradition. This, I think, is not surprising. Only just over 40 years separated Theoderic's own death in 526 from that of his great Thracian rival and namesake in the Balkans. Any Italian Goth aged 50 or above will have remembered Theoderic's real origins and the struggles in the Balkans which established his rule, whatever his later, imperial, pretensions.

Distance, numbers, alternative memories and traditions put distinct limitations on Theoderic's power. Even after all his successes, leaders with too great a power-base could still be threatening. A case in point is Theudis. Originally one of Theoderic's bodyguard, he started as a trusted henchman, whom Theoderic made commander in Spain. Once there, however, he married a rich Hispano-Roman, and gathered a sufficiently large personal following (2,000 strong) to make himself effectively independent. Although he never rebelled in Theoderic's lifetime, the king was unable to compel Theudis to come to Ravenna in later

[32] Brogiolo and Castelletti, 1991.

Plate 18 Monte Barro

Plate 19 The central building at Monte Barro: reconstruction

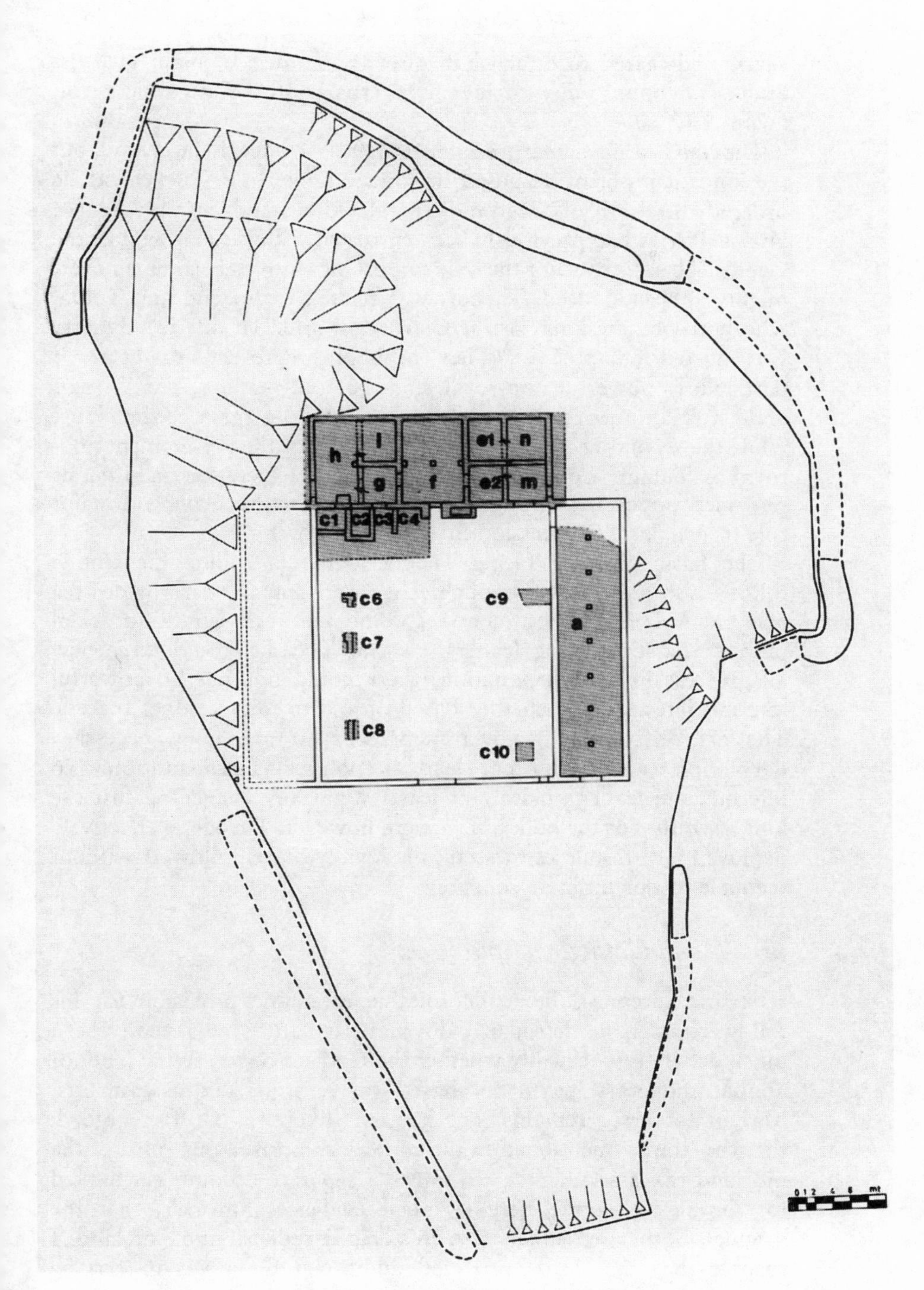

Figure 8.2 The central building at Monte Barro: plan

years, and feared to attack him directly, because it might give the Franks an opportunity to invade, or spark off a Visigothic revolt (*Wars* 5.12.50–4).

Theudis was particularly successful (and particularly far away), but the kind of problem he posed was not unique. In *c.*500, Theoderic ordered the death of a certain general Odoin, and, in 514, that of Pitzias. Pitzias had previously been entrusted with the war against the Gepids. Theudis was not the only important Goth to become an over-mighty subject. Indeed, Theudis was related to Ildebad and Totila, who both became kings of the Ostrogoths after Theoderic's dynasty was ousted (chapter 9). They probably represent, therefore, a particularly powerful non-royal clan. So too, perhaps, did Wittigis and Urais, another related pair, the first of whom again became king, while the second nearly did. A final example of the pre-eminent non-royal is Tuluin. Commander of the Gallic expedition in 508, he remained important throughout Theoderic's reign, playing a major role in Athalaric's succession in 526 (see below).

The basic problem facing Theoderic in controlling his Gothic followers in Italy is clear enough. They were spread over a wide area and old well-established identities combined with significant social mobility, so that rising leaders, such as Theudis, could forge new allegiances. In such a situation, there could not but be powerful intermediate leaders, whether based on old ties or personal success. The art of successful government was so managing necessary devolution that it did not lead to political fragmentation. No intermediate leader (in Italy at least) stood any chance against the king's wrath. For the bulk of his reign, however, Theoderic effectively deployed new resources to retain the loyalty of his followers without recourse to this ultimate sanction.

(ii) Manipulating new resources

First and foremost, he made suitable economic provision for his followers after the defeat of Odovacar. Its nature has recently been much debated, specifically whether the Goths received actual land, or annual monetary payments based on existing tax assessments. Margin for error remains, but it seems likely, as Goffart argued, that the 'thirds' mentioned in the sources comprised one third of the old land tax assessment, paid under a separate account earmarked for Gothic soldiers. There is much evidence, however, that the original Gothic settlement also involved a redistribution of land. I suspect that the thirds provided additional donatives to serving soldiers rather than the total income of all Goths.[33] For our purposes, however, the central point is not the particular way in which the Goths benefited from their move to Italy, but the basic fact that they did. One third of the annual tax assessment of Italy, probably supplementing initial land grants, represents a major pay-off to the Gothic rank and file. Gothic followers were liable to seek alternative leaders if they felt dissatisfied. Theoderic had to reward – and in line with their own expectations – those who had trekked with him from Pannonia to the central Balkans, and from the Balkans into Italy.

As we have seen, Theoderic retained some rights to intervene in local politics. They perhaps amounted to a veto. The wealth of Italy also opened up new types of patronage which he could use to build greater loyalty among his following. He established, for instance, parallel administrative systems where Gothic counts operated alongside Roman provincial officials to administer taxation and justice. The formula for appointing the count of Naples (*Variae* 6.23) refers explicitly to the 'liberal crop of official salaries' that came with such posts. These were paid for by taxation, so that Italian wealth allowed the king to create new ways of rewarding his leading followers: additional reasons for them to seek his favour. The relevant formulae all stress that appointments were initially for one year, but could be extended if the count performed his duties to the king's satisfaction (*Variae* 6.23, 24; 7.1).

Theoderic also made his power felt directly, in one area at least, among the Gothic rank and file. All male Goths of military age received each year a monetary payment (donative) in return for which they were liable for military service (Procopius *Wars* 5.12.47–8). Since the money was paid out from the centre, his administration must have kept some kind of register of all Goths entitled to receive such payments. Retirement from the army involved losing the donative, and Cassiodorus preserves one example of a written honourable discharge (*Variae* 5.36). How this might have worked to give individual Goths reason to establish themselves in royal favour, is illustrated by an order to the Goths of Samnium and Picenum.[34] In this, Theoderic declared that the appearance of these Goths in Ravenna to receive their donatives will enable him to investigate the behaviour of each soldier, so that the brave might be properly rewarded and cowards learn to tremble. A lord distributing

33 See esp. Goffart, 1980, ch. 3 and Barnish, 1986, but debate continues.
34 *Variae* 5.26–7, clearly referring (despite much scholarly debate) to all serving soldiers from these areas.

due reward to the brave is straight out of Germanic heroic poetry, and not in itself an innovation. The novelty lies in the use of Roman administrative methods – lists and written orders – to facilitate the exercise of traditional patronage under new conditions. While the order is a unique survival, the event it mentions is likely to have been a regular occurrence. Military musters, for the purposes of reward and contact, probably continued in Italy a practice which had long been standard. Jordanes *Getica*, for instance, repeatedly refers to annual gifts or customary payments received by Goths from the Romans. There may thus have been a long-standing annual occasion where Gothic leaders passed on their cut of the year's gifts to the rank and file.

Deciding where to cast his vote in local politics, or which Gothic soldiers to reward, demanded Theoderic's close involvement in the activities of his followers. This would not have been easy at the best of times, but became much more difficult once his followers were geographically dispersed across the Italian landscape. One possibility suggests itself, however, as to how Theoderic counteracted the problems of distance.

The sources make much of the imperially inspired ostentation of Theoderic's main royal palaces at Ravenna, Verona and Pavia. As we have seen, these buildings were designed to show that civilized Roman order had not been interrupted. It is striking, however, that there should have been three of them, rather than one. From what we know, all three were designed to function as full royal centres. They were also supplemented by other royal residences: a renovated palace at Abona, a summer palace at Monza and at least one magnificent hunting lodge.[35]

A possible explanation for this multiplicity of palaces emerges when their geographical locations are compared to the spread of Gothic settlement in Italy. While garrisons were dotted around more generally, actual Gothic settlements were concentrated in Samnium, Picenum, Liguria and the Venetias. Comparing settlements and palaces, there is one royal centre for each concentration. We have already seen that the Goths of Samnium and Picenum were on occasion summoned to Ravenna. Pavia was convenient for the settlements in Liguria, and Verona for those in the Venetias (cf. figure 8.1). The sources provide no direct evidence for a regular cycle of movement between the royal centres, but neither do they deny it. Few of the letters in the *Variae* collection give any indication of

[35] Ward-Perkins, 1984, 158–66; Johnson, 1988, 77–80.

where they were composed, and most could have been written in any of Theoderic's residences. Although we have only occasional references to use of centres other than Ravenna,[36] so much time and effort would hardly have been lavished on three royal centres, unless the king was contemplating the regular display of his power in each. Regular royal progresses between the three major palaces of northern Italy may have been undertaken, therefore, to counter the effects of widespread Gothic settlement.

The dispersed Goths were probably also held together by their non-Nicene religion. Catholic Goths, and Goths making gifts to Catholic institutions are known, but some interesting evidence has survived the suppression of Gothic 'Arianism' which followed the Byzantine conquest of Italy. In sixth-century papyri from Ravenna, Arianism is referred to as 'the law of the Goths' (*lex Gothorum*), and Theoderic, when addressing some Catholic bishops in Rome in 502, mentioned, in passing, 'your religion and ours'. This suggests, as we might expect, that the Goths' particular Christianity acted as a defining force. In Ravenna, at least, the religion was plentifully supplied with buildings. The cathedral of St Anastasia and a beautifully decorated Arian baptistry survive. At least some, and perhaps all, of the liturgy was conducted in the Gothic language. Apart from fragments of Gothic Bibles, a small piece of an Ostrogothic liturgical calendar (in a Milanese palimpsest) can still be read. A wonderful papyrus of 551 also lists St Anastasia's clerical establishment. Those who could, signed their own names: 19 individuals are listed, 15 with Gothic names (four of whom signed in Gothic characters) including two priests, a deacon and sub-deacon, two *clerici*, a *defensor* (who probably had financial responsibilities), a seven-man writing office and five *ostiarii* (porters). The latter were illiterate. In Theoderic's time, there would also have been an Arian bishop, who was presumably deposed (or fled) when the east Romans captured Ravenna in 540. Whether the other main centres at Pavia and Verona were similarly endowed with buildings, clergy and texts is unclear, but not unlikely.[37]

[36] *Variae* 2.20 transmits an order to move any provision ships at Ravenna to Liguria; the court was presumably at this point in Pavia. *Variae* 4.45 reports travel expenses given to Heruli to go from Pavia to Ravenna, suggesting that they had expected to find the king at Pavia. Theoderic was at Verona during the indictment of Boethius: *Anon. Val.* 14.81–3.

[37] *Lex Gothorum*: Tjäder, 1982, 268 n.3; cf. Moorhead, 1992, 95. Gothic texts: Heather and Matthews, 1991, 129–30, ch. 6. Clergy of St Anastasia: Tjäder, 1972. Cf. generally, Moorhead, 1992, 89–97 with refs.

Plate 20 Ceiling mosaic from the Arian baptistry at Ravenna

INCIP· LIB· VI

confectuscodexinstatione magistri uiliaric antiquarii
orapromescribtore sicdnm habeasprotectorem

Plate 21 Viliaric's signature in Gothic [and those of other Arian Gothic clergy of St Anastasia] in the papyrus of 551

Other aspects of Theoderic's administration which helped him govern Romans, also facilitated his continued control of Goths. Most of our evidence for the royal court (*comitatus*), for instance, illustrates its role in relations between king and Roman senatorial aristocracy. The court also had importance for the king's Gothic subjects. Children of important nobles seem to have been retained there. The ostensible purpose of this may have been educational. Cassiodorus records that Cyprian's sons learned the arts of war among the Goths at court (*Variae* 8.22). Under different circumstances, such children also made convenient hostages (cf. Procopius *Wars* 6.28.41). A similar policy was also applied to Roman children (*Variae* 1.39; 2.22), and it was no bad idea for the king to impress his influence at an early age on those destined to become important within the kingdom. The next stage for important young Goths seems to have been an appointment within the royal bodyguard (Latin *armiger*). Wittigis and Theudis, senior members of the two clans who dominated the throne after the Amal dynasty had been ousted, both passed through its ranks.[38]

More generally, the court functioned as a centre of patronage and legal appeal as much for Goths as for Romans. Any Goth desiring a lucrative countship was no doubt well-advised to press his suit at court, and access to it was controlled.[39] The king also tried to have some say in the settlement of inter-Gothic disputes. The formula for appointing a *Comes Gothorum* stresses that he was to settle them by the king's edict (*Variae* 7.3), and the *Variae* document a few purely Gothic cases (5.29, 30, 32–3). In all probability, a stream of such cases found their way to the king. The *comitatus* was so besieged with petitioners that Theoderic settled cases on horseback (*Variae* 2.20; 5.41).[40]

But royal justice also had limitations, and nicely illustrates what Theoderic could, and could not, achieve. A case had first actually to reach him. Specialist officials provided the king with a summary of the arguments involved in any appeal (*Variae* 5.40–1), so that a sympathetic hearing from the summarizer was a major advantage. The letters of Ennodius make it clear, as we might anyway expect, that for Romans – and there is no reason to suppose it was different for Goths – friends at court were crucial in obtaining a successful outcome.[41] And after a favourable decision had been obtained, it still

[38] Cf. Ensslin, 1947, 169.

[39] *Variae* 7.34–6; cf. individual invitations: 3.21, 22, 28.

[40] Cf. Ennodius' *Epp.* 2.23; 3.20; 6.5 for appeals against the decisions of local Gothic judges.

[41] Ennodius' relatives turned to him because he had access to Faustus Niger: Moorhead, 1992, 156–8.

had to be enforced. One royal lady, Theodagunda, was warned, for instance, to show prompt obedience to royal commands, and, in similar vein, Theoderic wrote to his nephew Theodahad in harsh terms to make him cooperate (*Variae* 4.37, 39; 5.12). One particularly intractable case was even transferred to Theodahad, presumably because it involved people over whom he had more influence than the king himself (*Variae* 3.15; cf. 10.5). These letters all went to different members of the royal family, but each intermediate level of leadership between king and Gothic rank and file probably presented similar obstacles to effective royal justice. In the honourable discharge, for instance, Theoderic specifically stated that the individual retained the king's legal protection (*Variae* 5.36). This would suggest that access to royal justice was valuable but far from automatic.

We should be wary, then, of accepting at face value the impression of a centralized and very Romanized administration transmitted by the *Variae* collection. Theoderic had still to manipulate a complicated Gothic world to maintain control of the military power-base upon which his rule in Italy was ultimately based. In many ways, his reign was a juggling act, consisting of keeping Goths happy while attracting the support of Roman landowning elites. It has long been traditional to hold that, eventually, the act failed to work. In the king's final years, harmony between Goth and Roman collapsed into conflict. As we shall see, there is no doubt that the king's last years did represent an anti-climax. In precisely what ways, however, did the king fail, and to what extent did this failure undermine the integrated kingdom he had struggled to create?

D. The Extent of Failure

On the face of it, failure would seem almost complete. In quick succession, the early 520s saw the Burgundians attempt to throw off Ostrogothic hegemony, and the Vandals succeed in doing so. In 522, the Burgundian king Sigismund executed his son and heir Sergeric. Sergeric was Sigismund's son by Theoderic's daughter Ostrogotha who had just died. In 523, after the death of king Thrasamund, the new Visigothic king Hilderic killed the Gothic soldiers who had been sent to North Africa with Theoderic's daughter, Amalafrida, and had her arrested. She eventually died in jail. Both Sigismund and Hilderic simultaneously sought new political alliances with Constantinople. At much the same time, the eastern Empire began to persecute non-Nicene Christians within its borders, a policy which Theoderic saw as a personal slight and threatened counter-measures against Italian Catholics. Inside Italy, two leading members of the landed Roman elite, Boethius and Symmachus, were arrested and eventually executed, and, just before his own death, Theoderic had Pope John thrown into prison on the latter's return from an embassy to Constantinople. On Theoderic's death, Italy and Spain were divided between two grandsons, Athalaric (the son of Amalasuentha and Eutharic) and Amalaric. The consent of Roman landowners, religious tolerance, and the king's ambitious foreign policy would all appear to have collapsed.[42] On closer inspection, however, it becomes rather less clear that these difficulties exposed a fatal flaw in the structure of Theoderic's kingdom.

The executions of Boethius and Symmachus have acquired particular significance because of a famous article by Arnaldo Momigliano. In it, he portrayed them as representing an important strand of Roman senatorial opinion, which refused to have anything to do with Theoderic's regime at Ravenna. Because of their attested interest in classical studies, he argued that they were highly traditional in outlook, and that, in political orientation, this made them strongly in favour of a renewal of imperial rule from Constantinople. Given Theoderic's presentation of himself as a determinedly Roman ruler and patron of classical culture, it is very unclear, however, that Momigliano was correct to see classical interests as an expression of political dissidence. At least some of Symmachus' studies were actually conducted at Ravenna (although it is impossible to know whether this was under Odovacar or Theoderic). Likewise, in 506, Boethius received a graceful letter from Theoderic which showed that the king had taken the trouble to acquaint himself with the nature of Boethius' studies (*Variae* 1.45). The contrast with a former British Prime Minister who, when she was told that someone was studying Anglo-Saxon, exclaimed 'What a luxury', is too tempting to omit.

Nor were Boethius and Symmachus scholastic recluses. Symmachus held no administrative office under Theoderic, but he was heavily involved in public life. Our knowledge of Ostrogothic Italy depends largely on Cassiodorus' *Variae*, and it is easy to forget their limited time-span. Before the fall of Symmachus and Boethius, they cover only four years, 507–11, during which both men were deeply immersed in public affairs. Symmachus brought actions in the Senate

42 See in more detail, Wolfram, 1988, 308–9, 312–13; Moorhead, 1992, ch. 7.

(*Variae* 1.23), tried a case of parricide (2.14), and was one of five senators appointed by Theoderic to aid Argolicus in a trial of senators accused of magic (4.22). All these actions involved contacts with the court, so that, at this date, Symmachus was very much *persona grata* in Ravenna. Hence Theoderic's choice of him to supervise the education of some senatorial children, not to mention the king's praise and reimbursement of his restoration of the theatre of Pompey (*Variae* 4.6, 51). The same is true of Boethius. He was made consul by Theoderic for the year 510 (because of his intellectual achievements and his eloquence[43]), and the *Variae* provide other evidence of his proximity to court circles between 507 and 511. He headed an inquiry into the pay of some army officers (*Variae* 1.10), and two famous letters invited him to find clocks for Gundobad, and a lyre player for Clovis (1.45; 2.40). The gap in the *Variae* means that we hear little of relations between Symmachus and Boethius and the court after 511, but in 522 Boethius became Theoderic's *Magister Officiorum*. Such high office is most unlikely to have come out of the blue, so that Boethius had probably remained publicly active in the meantime. He was certainly involved in ending the Acacian schism in the later 510s, a move which was encouraged, as we have seen, by the king.

It is a considerable misrepresentation, therefore, to declare, with Momigliano, that Boethius and Symmachus 'studied and wrote to forget ... their Gothic masters'. Rather than the result of a long-term rift, their fall in the 520s looks much more like a sudden falling out. Boethius, in particular, went from high favour to disaster. Not only was he *Magister Officiorum*, but his two sons had just been made consuls for the year 522.[44] And Theoderic's last years did see, indeed, the emergence of an issue of sufficient divisiveness and importance to explain political dramas on this scale.

Theoderic's succession plans eventually devolved onto Eutharic (p. 233). Unfortunately for Theoderic, Eutharic predeceased him in 522 or 523.[45] Subsequently, Theoderic's choice fell on his eight-year-old grandson, Athalaric, offspring of Eutharic and Amalasuentha. But this choice was far from unanimously received, and Boethius had close links with one of the other candidates, Theoderic's nephew Theodahad. Rather than issuing an unlikely invitation for Byzantium to invade (Momigliano's explanation), it is much more likely that

[43] Cf. *PLRE*, 2, 234.
[44] Momigliano, 1955, the quotation is from p. 216. For the counter-argument in more detail, Heather, 1993, 332ff.
[45] See further Schmidt, 1933, 353–4.

Plates 22 and 23 Theoderic's mausoleum and sarcophagus at Ravenna

Boethius fell from grace because he found himself on the wrong side of a succession dispute. His fall thus marked no great falling out between Gothic king and Roman landowning elite, and many prominent Romans (including particularly Cassiodorus) continued to serve the regime after the executions. Indeed, Boethius counted Romans as well as Goths among his enemies, and it was the Roman Senate which issued his final condemnation.[46]

A similar suddenness attended the foreign policy problems of Theoderic's final years. In part, this was due to biological accident. The deaths of Thrasamund and Sigismund's Amal wife were unpredictable. They only assumed the importance they did, however, because two subordinated allies exploited them as an opportunity to move out of Theoderic's sphere, and into that of Constantinople. The role of the eastern Empire in stirring up trouble for Theoderic is thus of extreme importance, since, in addition to encouraging the Vandals and Burgundians, the Empire was also making an issue out of religious difference at exactly the same time (p. 249). Renewed east Roman hostility towards Theoderic's kingdom was as sudden an event as Boethius' fall.

After the overt clashes of 508, the 510s saw considerable rapprochement between Constantinople and Ravenna. In 513, a serious revolt broke out among the east Roman armies of the Balkans. It was led by the general Vitalian, who, amongst other things, wanted to end the religious conflict which had divided the eastern Church from Rome (the Acacian schism).[47] The Emperor Anastasius responded by courting the Pope. But, as we have seen, the Pope deferred to Theoderic in such matters, so that the Emperor had to alter his stance towards the Gothic king. Overt hostility between Constantinople and Ravenna had ended by 511, when they agreed over the choice of Felix as consul. And, from 516, there survives a startling letter from Anastasius, which explicitly refers to the 'two [Roman] republics' and paired Theoderic (called a 'most glorious' and 'lofty' king) with the Pope: the one enjoying secular authority, the other religious. This amounts to an admission of virtually everything Theoderic had claimed about himself in *Variae* 1.1 of 507/8, that he did indeed rule the other fully legitimate Roman state of the contemporary world (p. 229). Instead of raiding the coasts of

[46] Boethius and Theodahad: Barnish, 1990; cf. more generally, Moorhead, 1992, ch. 7.

[47] Main source: John of Antioch fr. 214e 1–17, cf., with other refs, *PLRE* 2, 1171–6.

Theoderic's kingdom, the eastern Empire was now paying formal public homage to the idea that the Goth was a God-ordained (the parallel with the Pope) Roman ruler.[48]

Anastasius died in 518, but the next imperial regime, that of Justin, was even more anxious for rapprochement with the Pope. Its attitude to Theoderic was correspondingly conciliatory. In 520, Justin referred to Theoderic as 'pre-eminent king' (*praecelsum regum*: *Coll. Av.* 199), and a chronicle written in Justin's reign labelled Anastasius' raid of 508 as a 'piratical venture against fellow Romans'.[49] More practically, Justin went out of his way to support Theoderic's choice of heir. He accepted Eutharic as co-consul in 519, ceding to him, in fact, the senior position. He also adopted Eutharic as son-at-arms, a device used by Emperors to express their recognition of a neighbour's choice of heir.[50] In *c.* 520, relations with Constantinople could not have been better. This explains why subsequent Byzantine hostility should have angered Theoderic so much, but not why Justin should have reversed east Roman policy so shortly afterwards.

Two observations, to my mind, are of key importance. First, the eastern Empire had never acquiesced willingly in Theoderic's pretentions. Conflict had preceded Theoderic's departure for Italy, and six years of negotiations (492–7/8) were required before Anastasius accepted the new order which the Goth had erected in Italy. Likewise, the rapprochement after 508, and particularly the formal recognition of Eutharic, were the products of the eastern Empire's overriding desire for reconciliation with the Pope. There is not the slightest reason to suppose that the eastern Empire welcomed the creation of Theoderic's Gothic super-state cum western-Empire-revived.

Secondly, the death of Eutharic caused disarray inside Theoderic's kingdom. Much of the best recent work in medieval history has re-emphasized the importance and difficulty of succession. Once a king was thought to be dying, especially if he left no unchallenged adult male heir, his control was likely to face innumerable challenges. The contemporary transatlantic image of the lame-duck presidency comes firmly to mind. And this was precisely the position Theoderic found himself in the early 520s. Seventy years old, with his adult male heir

48 *Coll. Av.* 113. Prostko-Prostynski, 1994, 151ff. argues that the letter marked no important shift of attitude since 497/8. To my mind, this pays insufficient attention to the effect on policy of changes to the balance of power.

49 Marcellinus Comes ad a. 508 (= *CM* 2, 64).

50 *Variae* 8.1.3; cf. Claude, 1989, 25–56.

dead, he was trying to win acceptance for the candidacy of an at most seven-year-old grandson.

We have already seen that the fall of Beothius and Symmachus should probably be linked to the jockeying for position which followed Eutharic's death, and particularly to intrigues in favour of Theoderic's nephew, Theodahad. According to Procopius, Theodahad was lazy and academic, but he was an Amal male of majority age, the only one in Italy. He also received a considerable pay-off at the beginning of Athalaric's reign, because he had been 'obedient' (*Variae* 8.23). The same letter expressed the hope that Theodahad would prove to have deserved it. This surely signals that Theodahad had posed a potentially serious threat to Athalaric's succession. There had also, it seems, been support for elevating a senior Gothic noble, Tuluin. He had enjoyed a distinguished military career, which culminated in 523, when he took retributive action against the Burgundians. He defeated Sigismund and extended the Gallic boundaries of the Ostrogothic kingdom north of the river Durance. One of the *Variae* specifically compares him to a hero of an earlier time, Gensemund, who had refused the Gothic crown in favour of the Amals. Like Theodahad, Tuluin also received very special rewards for supporting Athalaric's succession. He was made *Patricius Praesentalis* and hence a senator, the first Italian Goth to receive such a distinction.[51] Despite Theoderic's choice of Athalaric, succession was still being disputed at the time of his death. Cassiodorus took up a military command at this time (*Variae* 9.25.9), and there was a disturbance in Liguria, perhaps a demonstration in favour of one of the other candidates (ibid 8.16).

In Spain, too, Theoderic faced serious trouble. It was towards the end of the reign that Theudis made himself *de facto* independent of the king. Theudis never rebelled in Theoderic's lifetime, but refused a summons to Ravenna (Procopius *Wars* 5.12.51). We are not told what prompted Theudis' rebellious behaviour, but there is good reason to link it to Eutharic's death and the quarrels over succession. After Theoderic's death, Spain and Italy split apart. This had not been arranged by the old king, but was organized inpromptu by the supporters of Athalaric, who received Italy, and Amalaric, who received Spain (*Wars* 5.13.4 ff). Since Theudis was *de facto* ruler in Spain before Theoderic's death, he must have been behind Amalaric's elevation. He presumably supported Amalaric to ensure the

[51] *Variae* 8.9–11. *Variae* 8.3 likewise refers to the possible succession of a non-Amal (*externus heres impertii*).

continuation of his own pre-eminence, and subsequently succeeded him as king in 531, which confirms the point. Theudis probably saw an opportunity in Eutharic's death to secure his own position by resurrecting the cause of Amalaric.

Disarray in Theoderic's kingdom after the death of his heir thus offered the east Roman authorities the opportunity to cut down to size their grandiose Gothic neighbour. One of the *Variae*, written to the Emperor Justin shortly after Athalaric's succession, complained that, unlike his father Eutharic, he had not been adopted as son-at-arms. It also expressed the hope that relations between Ravenna and Constantinople would continue to be good. This suggests that Justin had deliberately withheld acknowledgement of Theoderic's new heir, even though he had previously acknowledged Eutharic.[52] This adds a further dimension to worsening relations between Ravenna and Constantinople.

What did the Byzantines hope to achieve by these manoeuvres? There is no sign that they wanted to invade Italy at this point. More likely, they wished to curb Ostrogothic power by less direct methods. Detaching other states such as the Vandals and Burgundians from its sphere of influence was one obvious gambit, and this, to a degree, they achieved. I also suspect that, in refusing to recognize Theoderic's succession plans, they had it in mind to bring about precisely what happened: the separation of Italy and Spain. At a stroke, this cut the power of the Gothic kingdom by a greater extent than any other single act could possibly have done. Theoderic had taken over Spain by force, and hostility remained. He hesitated to attack Theudis, for instance, for fear of sparking off a Visigothic revolt. Forced to court Theoderic to get to the papacy in the 510s, the east Romans did not hesitate to revert to type in the 520s. The death of Eutharic provided the perfect opportunity of reviving an underlying hostility to the Gothic Empire of the west.

These events were very dramatic, but the extent of Theoderic's failure in the last years of his reign should not be overstated. Thanks to the failure of his succession plans (which were anyway ambitious, since some Visigoths continued to be hostile to a united kingdom), Italy and Gaul broke apart, and the Vandals and Burgundians threw off (or attempted to) Ostrogothic hegemony. Theoderic's most ambitious imperial plans thus came to grief, but the Ostrogothic kingdom was not completely incapacitated. Before the king's death, revenge was taken on the Burgundians. A fleet was also being readied

[52] *Variae* 8.1.3; cf. above footnote 50 at p.253 on its significance.

for a move against the Vandals, when preparations were interrupted by the king's death.

However, critically important relationships inside the kingdom were not irreparably damaged. Despite the fall of Boethius and Symmachus, many Romans continued to play an active part at court. In subsequent years, an Italo-Roman poet would even poke fun at Boethius' presentation of himself in the *Consolation of Philosophy*, written while he was in jail awaiting execution, as the philosopher disillusioned with politics.[53] Cooperation between Goths and Romans at the elite level was already too far advanced to be undermined by the fall of just two politicians, however prominent.

Unlike the Visigothic kingdom, elite integration in Italy does not seem to have been advanced by the militarization *en masse* of Italo-Romans. Indeed, it was part of the official ideology of the kingdom to proclaim a separation of roles. Goths fought, Romans remained at peace.[54] This ideology encompassed only part of the truth. There is no sign of Romans serving *en masse* in the Gothic field armies which fought the Byzantines after 536. Italo-Romans were regularly used, however, for garrison duties, both in cities (p. 273), and frontier provinces. Two Romans, the *comes* Colosseus and the *dux* Servatus, presided respectively over the provinces of Pannonia II and Raetia.[55] Individual Romans did also serve in field armies, particularly Boethius' enemy Cyprian (*Variae* 8.21.3; cf. 9.23.3).

The ideology of separation was a shorthand political slogan, therefore, not an exact description, and interaction occurred on many other levels besides. A few Goths made their way into the Senate. How many is disputed, and Theoderic may well have attempted to forestall dissent on the part of the old families, by keeping the Senate essentially for the Romans.[56] The main route into the Senate was appointment to a major bureaucratic office, all of which were in the king's gift. Theoderic could thus not only control membership of the Senate, but had in his hands a major source of patronage which would encourage members of the Roman land-owning elite to seek his favour (p. 228). On the legal front too,

[53] Barnish, 1990.
[54] E.g. *Variae* 12.5.4; 6.1.5; 7.3.3; 7.4.3; 8.3.4; 9.14.18; cf. Moorhead, 1992, 71.
[55] Moorhead, 1992, 71–2.
[56] Cf. Schäfer, 1991, 286, Gothic *viri illustri*, with the one exception of Tuluin were kept out of the Senate. For a different view, Moorhead, 1992, 73–5.

interaction was the order of the day. Officially, as we have seen, the Italian kingdom maintained one legal system and one body of Roman law. On a practical level, however, the king acknowledged the different origins of his subjects by appointing, where required, two judges: one Gothic, the other Roman. Disputes with Goths will have regularly led Romans before Gothic judges, therefore, and, on occasion, this even happened where two Romans were quarrelling, although Gildilas, the count of Syracuse, was heavily reprimanded for hearing purely Roman cases.[57]

The practical realities of co-existence also brought Roman and Goth together on a whole series of less formal levels. Theoderic's pay-off to his followers catapulted many Goths, particularly those of the free class, into the landowning elite of Italy (pp. 242f). As such, they could not but impress themselves upon Roman society. The *Variae* contain many references to Goths looking to advance their economic position still further. Leading Gothic nobles were courted by Romans because they had influence with the king. Amongst others, Ennodius wrote for help to a series of important Goths: Tancila, Alico, Trasimund and Gudilevus. Intermarriage, too, seems to have been common, as was cultural intermixing of a more general kind. Some Goths adopted Roman ways of burying their dead, setting up inscribed gravestones. Many Goths also knew Latin, although this had probably been true since the fourth century. And some Romans, especially the famous case of the sons of Cyprian, learned Gothic.[58] Theoderic's famous aphorism has often been quoted, but certainly bears repetition. Looking at his realm, the king is said to have declared, 'A poor Roman plays the Goth, a rich Goth the Roman' (*Anon. Val.* 12.61). By the time of Theoderic's death, the migrant and indigenous populations were still distinguishable (p. 273), but a process of cultural fusion was well underway.

Likewise, although Pope John died in prison, this does not seem to have poisoned relations more generally between Gothic monarchy and Catholic churchmen. I suspect, although no one tells us, that the Pope's embassy – the cause of the trouble – may have been designed to win Justin's recognition for Athalaric. Justin treated the Pope with great courtesy, but clearly sent him back to Italy empty-handed. It may not have been a religious issue, therefore, which caused the trouble. After Theoderic's death, subsequent popes continued to defer

57 *Variae* 9.14; cf. Moorhead, 1992, 74ff.

58 See generally, Moorhead, 1992, 73–4, 77–9, 83–7, Bierbrauer, 1980, 102–4.

to Gothic kings, and the papacy never became a focus for dissent. Likewise, Tuluin's Burgundian campaigns reunited the ecclesiastical province of Arles for the first time since the end of the western Empire. This coincidence was cheerfully exploited by its Catholic metropolitan, Caesarius of Arles, who launched a series of important reforming councils, the first in June 524, well before Theoderic's death. This could not have happened without the king's permission, so one established royal/episcopal alliance continued to flourish, despite the difficulties of the king's last years.[59] And even with Constantinople, fences could be mended. In 532, the Ostrogothic kingdom provided important logistic support for Belisarius' invasion of the Vandal kingdom, and relations between Amalasuentha and the east were generally good (chapter 9).

A balance must be maintained, then, when evaluating Theoderic's successes and failures. Plans for recreating the western Empire proved ephemeral. Balancing the competing claims of all the politically important groups within the Italian kingdom, likewise, was never easy. Theoderic passed on to his successors, however, no poisoned chalice. Succession, not deep-seated Gotho–Roman antagonism, underlay the setbacks of his final years. In the course of his long reign the foundation had been set for a successful integration of Goth and Roman. How and why this beginning failed, in the longer term, to bear fruit, is the subject of the next chapter.

[59] On the *Anonymous*, see esp. Barnish, 1983. Caesarius: Klingshirn, 1994, 137ff.

9

Sixth-Century Crises and Beyond

Several independent Gothic units continued to exist in the sixth century. In the Pontus, the Goths of Doru (Procopius *Buildings* 3.1.13) and the Tetraxitae (*Wars* 8.4.9ff) successfully maintained autonomy down to at least the middle of the century. Some of their descendents may even have preserved their linguistic traditions into the early modern period. Between 1560 and 1562, a Flemish ambassador to Constantinople named Busbecq recorded something of the language of a Germanic-speaking group in the Crimea. Some of it is closely related to Gothic.[1] The Gothic groups of the Pontus, however, were small. Most people who thought of themselves as Goths belonged, by the sixth century, to one of two main kingdoms: the Ostrogothic kingdom of Italy, and the Visigothic of southern Gaul and Spain. The second half of the century was a period of intense crisis for both. It ended with the total destruction of one kingdom, and the wholesale transformation of the other.

A. *The Destruction of Ostrogothic Italy*

Within 30 years of his death, Theoderic's kingdom was brought to destruction by the forces of the eastern Emperor Justinian. Hence hindsight tends to set the historical agenda, and accounts of Theoderic's successors largely concern themselves with how subsequent reigns led to disaster. As we shall see, they were marked by considerable turmoil, even before the outbreak of the war with

[1] Relevant section reprinted in Streitberg, 1920, 280ff.

Constantinople. It is not the case, however, that Justinian's intervention merely finished off a kingdom which was already engaged in self-destruction.

(i) Athalaric, Amalasuentha and the outbreak of war

The political situation created in Italy by Theoderic's death in 526 was not ideal. Power was wielded in the name of his minor grandson Athalaric (born in either 516 or 518, therefore aged eight or ten[2] by the boy's mother, Theoderic's daughter, Amalasuentha. In general, women were not expected to wield monarchical power, so that such situations were always fraught with difficulty, and often ended nastily. One Frankish queen-regnant, Brunhild, was eventually torn apart between wild horses, having been made the scapegoat for a series of dynastic conflicts played out over 30 years. There is more than a hint that her anomalous status as a female ruler made her a convenient target.[3] The fate of Amalasuentha is only marginally less alarming.

Amalasuentha's period of power saw two – related – political crises. The first was a struggle for control of Athalaric. As described by Procopius (*Wars* 5.2), conflict was precipitated by Athalaric's education. Like his mother, the young king was at least in part given a Roman education: a process traditionally accompanied by a generous use of the cane. Fearing that Amalasuentha meant to remove Athalaric and marry a second husband, a group of leading Goths argued that a Roman-style training was inappropriate:

> They said that Theoderic would never allow any of the Goths to send their children to school; for he used to say to them all that, if fear of the cane once came over them, they would never have the resolution to despise sword or spear. (*Wars* 5.2.14–15).

Concerned that Amalasuentha would remarry and banish them to the political margins, the leading Goths emphasized that Athalaric was under their care too. That this dispute also represented a more general rejection, on the part of leading Goths, of Theoderic's plans for the peaceful co-existence of Roman and Goth is most unlikely. 'Too much Roman education' or 'A return to Gothic values' are likely enough rallying cries in the particular context. But the real issue was clearly political control of the kingdom, not whether Romans and Goths should live together peacefully.

Amalasuentha eventually won out, but only by drastic measures.

2 *PLRE* 2, 175.
3 Nelson, 1978.

She got her three leading opponents away from court by appointing them to senior frontier commands, and then had them murdered. In Procopius' account, they are anonymous (*Wars* 5.2.23ff). One of the three was perhaps Tuluin who held large estates in Provence (i.e. a frontier command) and who disappeared from the sources shortly after 526.[4] Another may have been Osuin. He was sent to Dalmatia, another frontier command, early in Athalaric's reign, and is not heard of again (*Variae* 9.8–9). The identity of the third is completely obscure. Amalasuentha survived, but only just. At one point, she had even loaded a ship with treasure and sent it to the eastern Empire, in case she needed to cut and run.

Plate 24 Sixth-century ships in port at Ravenna. Amalasuentha had one loaded with treasure in case she needed to flee to Constantinople

The murders provided only a temporary solution. Early in 534, Athalaric's health went into decline, the result, according to Procopius, of too much loose living. As soon as the decline was perceived to be terminal, and particularly on Athalaric's death in

[4] See *PLRE* 2, 1132–3; Cassiodorus *Variae* 8.25 of *c.*527 is the last dated reference to him; so too Wolfram, 1988, 336.

October 534, the question of who should control the kingdom reasserted itself (*Wars* 5.3.10ff). Without a son to legitimize her position, Amalasuentha was in great difficulty. To maintain control, she elevated Theodahad, her cousin and Theoderic's nephew, to the throne, making him swear to follow her commands (*Wars* 5.4.4ff; cf. *Variae* 10.1–4). But Theodahad was an Amal male of majority age, who had probably figured in the succession debate of the 520s (chapter 8). Not surprisingly, therefore, he had his own ideas, so that the new arrangement proved far from secure. The relatives of the three murdered men – according to Procopius, 'numerous and of very high standing' – plotted with Theodahad to remove Amalasuentha from power. They imprisoned her on an island in Lake Bolsena in Tuscany in December 534, and later killed in her bath, on 30 April 535.[5] The second crisis was thus an extension of the first; the issue remained the distribution of power.

None of this by itself threatened the alliance of Roman and Goth, the cornerstone of Theoderic's Italian kingdom. Prominent Romans, such as Cassiodorus and Liberius, served Amalasuentha and Theodahad in turn. What really made these court disputes dangerous was the range of opportunity they presented to predatory neighbours. On the northern front, the Franks exploited Gothic paralysis to overturn the last vestiges of the strategic dominance created by Theoderic after 508. Between 531 and 534, they destroyed the independence of the Thuringian kingdom, formerly a staunch Gothic ally, and conquered the Burgundians in 532 and 533.[6]

Even more dangerous was the transformation fostered by these disputes in relations with Constantinople. From 527, the latter was ruled by an ambitious new Emperor, Justinian. Amalasuentha turned to Constantinople as a possible safe haven when fighting off the first challenge to her leadership, and, in return, provided logistic support for Justinian's general, Belisarius, against the Vandals in 533. Belisarius destroyed the Vandal kingdom between September 533 and March 534.[7] The continued uncertainty in the Italian kingdom, combined with the astounding success of Belisarius' expedition, encouraged Justinian to fish in troubled waters. Even before the fall of Amalasuentha, he made a series of formal complaints, although this was in part to disguise more clandestine contacts between himself and an increasingly

5 *Wars* 5.4.12ff, with *PLRE* 2, 65.

6 Wolfram, 1988, 335 with refs.

7 There is no better account of the expedition than Procopius' own: *Wars* 3–4.

threatened Gothic queen (Procopius *Wars* 5.3.12ff). After her fall, the diplomatic offensive continued, given added momentum by the claim that Amalasuentha had been Justinian's protégée. In the winter of 534/5, he was already trying to panic Theodahad into conceding sovereignty over Italy to the east (*Wars* 5.4.17ff). Justinian had not yet decided, however, to launch a full-scale attack.

Although Belisarius was despatched with a fleet to Sicily in 535, and another army to Gothic Dalmatia, Justinian's orders remained cautious. Belisarius was to survey the Gothic defences of the island, and withdraw if they seemed too formidable (*Wars* 5.5.6–7). In fact, Belisarius quickly took the island, and the Dalmatian expedition also prospered, so that Justinian renewed his diplomatic offensive with gusto in winter 535/6. Policy was still being improvised, however, and even Justinian's ambassadors were unsure whether the Emperor wanted to make limited territorial gains, or demand the Goths' total submission. Theodahad was on the point of surrender when news came, at Easter 536, of a successful Gothic counter-offensive in Dalmatia. Byzantine success in Sicily had now been matched by Gothic success in Dalmatia; both sides were ready for further trials of strength. The result was all-out war (*Wars* 5.6–7).

(ii) The struggle for Italy

The campaign for control of mainland Italy opened in earnest in summer 536. Belisarius landed in the south and besieged Naples, taking the city after a lengthy siege (it was in Byzantine hands by November 536). In the meantime, Theodahad, in Rome, did nothing; perhaps he still hoped for a negotiated solution. When the city fell, a powerful group among the leading Goths expressed their dissatisfaction by deposing and murdering the king (November/December 536: *Wars* 5.8.1–11, 9).

Thus perished the last male of Theoderic's line, and, in his place, the Goths elected Wittigis, who had recently shown himself a highly capable military commander (*Wars* 5.11.5). In a letter to all the Goths of Italy, Wittigis stressed that he belonged to Theoderic's line not by blood, but because his deeds were of similar stature (Cassiodorus, *Variae* 10.32). He did also marry Amalasuentha's daughter Matasuentha, but his own propaganda mentioned the marriage only in a letter to Justinian, and not in his communications to the Goths.[8]

[8] *Variae* 10.33: Wittigis claimed that the purpose of Justinian's war was fulfilled by the marriage and the death of Theodahad, both of which had avenged Amalasuentha.

No doubt the marriage was an attempt to counter the objections of Amal loyalists, but the ease with which the Amal family was ousted puts the dynastic propaganda of Theoderic's reign firmly into perspective. Most Goths clearly did not believe that Amal blood was a uniquely important qualification for rule (cf. p. 233). The Goths now had a regime as much committed to war as that of Justinian. In one sense, the events down to the fall of Naples had been something of a phoney war, and the real drama now unfolded in three acts. The first lasted from winter 536/7 to 540, when Wittigis surrendered both Ravenna and himself to Belisarius.

The defeat of Wittigis Wittigis spent winter 536/7 preparing for war. Leaving Rome in December, he went to Ravenna to gather and equip his forces. He also ceded to the Franks the Gallic territories which Theoderic had won in 508, and Tuluin extended in 523. This secured the Goths' northern border, and freed military forces which would otherwise have been needed for garrison duties (*Wars* 5.11.28–9). By February 537, Wittigis was ready, but Belisarius had already moved his relatively limited forces into Rome (9/10 December 536). The year 537 was thus spent in a fruitless Gothic siege of the former imperial capital. Its details are best encompassed by reading Procopius' gripping, first-hand account of the action. The bloodshed was briefly halted in December 537, when the arrival of Roman reinforcements prompted the Goths to make a three-month truce (*Wars* 5.14 to 6.6). The only other event of the year was another Gothic expedition to Dalmatia, which besieged, but failed to recapture, the city of Salona (*Wars* 5.16.8–18).

The stalemate around Rome was finally broken in winter 537/8, when Belisarius' cavalry raided Picenum (Figure 9.1). This was an area of dense Gothic settlement, and Belisarius' aim was to break the siege of Rome by threatening the wives and children of the men who had him penned in the city (*Wars* 6.7.28–34). The stratagem worked. By March 538, enough pressure had been applied for Wittigis to break up the siege. His army retreated north along the Via Flaminia, aiming to cut off and destroy the raiding force, which had established itself at Rimini (*Wars* 6.10). As he went, Wittigis established a series of strongpoints. The strategically placed city of Auximum was given a garrison of particular quality; other forces were left at Clusium, Urviventus, Tudera, Petra, Urbinus, Caesena and Montefertra (*Wars* 6.11.1–3; Figure 9.1). They were to keep Belisarius busy, while the Goths attacked Rimini.

But the Goths' retreat had restored Belisarius' freedom of

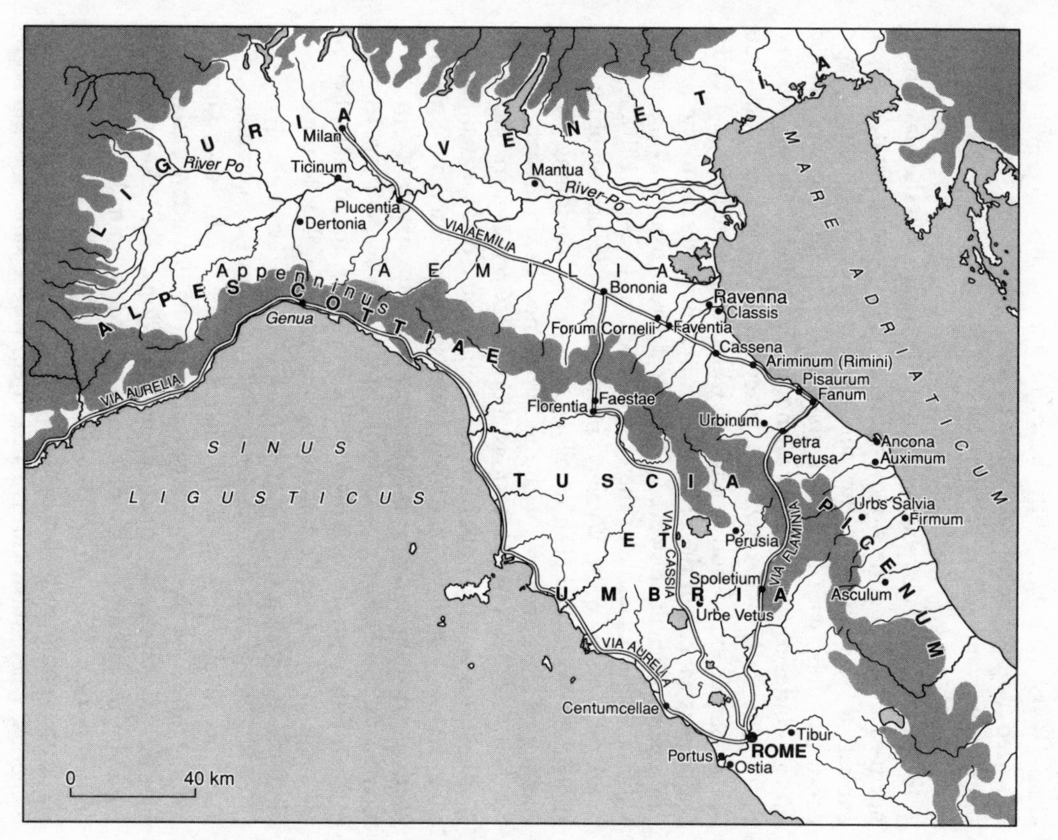

Figure 9.1 The first phase of the Gothic War (537–540)

movement. Rushing reinforcements to Rimini before Wittigis' main force could arrive there, he moved a second force by ship to Genoa. It proceeded north to take the surrender of Milan and other Ligurian cities (*Wars* 6.11–12). With the main part of his army, Belisarius followed Wittigis north-east into Picenum, where, on the receipt of more reinforcements, he began to work his way up the coast towards Ravenna (*Wars* 6.13, 16ff).

In 539, Belisarius largely retained the initiative. On the main front, north-east of Rome, he slowly tightened the noose around Wittigis' capital at Ravenna. As the summer progressed, Auximum was captured, along with Fiesole (*Wars* 6.23–7). These successes opened up two routes towards Ravenna, and, in December, Belisarius moved on the city itself (*Wars* 6.28.1ff). Elsewhere, Wittigis' nephew Urais led a counter-expedition to Liguria which recaptured the lost cities. Milan was sacked in the process. The Byzantine threat to the region remained sufficient, however, to prevent Urais from leaving the Po valley to defend Fiesole at the crucial moment (*Wars* 6.18ff).

By the end of 539, Wittigis' position was becoming untenable. Individual Goths and even whole groups were abandoning his cause, looking to come to terms with the Byzantines. Because of the threats to their families and possessions, both the Gothic garrisons of the Cottian Alps and the bulk of Urais' mobile force disappeared back to their homes (*Wars* 6.28.30–5). Increasingly isolated in Ravenna, Wittigis tried diplomacy instead, negotiating for assistance from the Lombards and Franks to the north, and, more desperately, from the Persian Empire to the east (*Wars* 6.22.9–20). He hoped that a Persian invasion of Syria would undermine Justinian's ability to pursue war simultaneously in Italy.

By the beginning of 540, Belisarius was firmly in command. But Ravenna itself, protected by marshes and walls, was virtually impregnable. Negotiations began, operating simultaneously on a number of levels. In open communications, the Goths offered formally to submit to Justinian, and to cede to him large tracts of Italian territory (*Wars* 6.29.1–3). Under this plan, Gothic rule would have been confined to lands north of the river Po – Liguria and the Venetias, where most Goths had settled. At the same time, in secret contacts, the Goths tried to seduce Belisarius away from his loyalty to Justinian, offering him *βασιλέα τῆς ἑσπερίας*: 'rule of the west'. Wittigis eventually opened the gates of Ravenna to Belisarius' forces in May 540, but the Goths had been tricked. As Procopius reports it, they surrendered thinking that Belisarius would declare himself western Emperor. Once Byzantine forces were inside the city, however, there was nothing that Wittigis could do. He and his chief supporters were detained, and the rest of the Gothic army sent home (*Wars* 6.29). With Belisarius' coup de théâtre, the war seemed over.

The successes of Totila The bulk of the Goths had been dispersed by military stratagem and diplomatic manoeuvre, however, not defeated in battle. Moreover, Belisarius had insufficient troops to occupy in force Gothic heartlands north of the Po. The only Roman unit in the area was a group of Heruli under Vitalius at Treviso. Hence, as the extent of Belisarius' trickery became clear, tactical opportunity and military manpower were both available for more energetic Gothic leaders to rekindle the fires of war. In the summer of 540, two in particular continued to resist: Urais in Pavia and Ildebadus at Verona. Neither conducted aggressive operations, but both refused to surrender (*Wars* 6.28.35; 29.39–41).

At this point, the Goths were still pressing Belisarius to accept the western imperium (*Wars* 6.30). Had he been able to move north of the Po in force, the war really could have been over. Troops, however, were not available, because war on the Persian front reopened in the summer of 540, and events went disastrously wrong for the eastern Empire. Antioch, second city of the Empire, was sacked, and Persian forces roamed free among the rich cities of Syria and Palestine. Justinian decided to recall Belisarius to deal with the Persians.[9] Belisarius thus left Ravenna in December 540, taking with him Wittigis and the other leading Goths, and all hope of seducing him away from Justinian had disappeared. Ildebadus rallied his supporters for war (*Wars* 7.1.25). Vitalius tried to nip the revolt in the bud, but was heavily defeated. The second phase of the Gothic war began in earnest; first, however, the Goths had to sort out their own power structures.

Initially, Urais deferred to Ildebadus. But power sharing was clearly not easy, and, when the two fell out (reportedly over their wives' competitive dressing), Ildebadus engineered Urais' death. This alienated a significant body of the Goths, who had Ildebadus killed in turn (*Wars* 6.30.4ff; 7.1.37–49). Both were dead by the end of 541. In the meantime, Eraric, leader of the Rugi within Ostrogothic ranks (p. 237), put himself forward. His main policy was to negotiate with Constantinople, reviving the idea of partitioning Italy. He too was murdered, however, at which point power passed to Ildebadus'

[9] Procopius describes Chosroes' attack, and the war which followed in Book II of the *Wars*. Bury, 1923, 89ff provides commentary.

nephew Totila (*Wars* 7.2). In the short term, Totila was committed to more martial options.

Totila's period of success, which lasted throughout the 540s, had two foundations. First, the war with Persia prevented Justinian from reinforcing his Italian armies. Secondly, Totila won some quick victories. Militarily, they allowed him to regain the tactical initiative; politically, they encouraged more of the Goths to throw in their lot with the revolt. Totila was also careful to treat prisoners leniently, so that many east Roman troops (often contingents of allied barbarians) eventually joined the Goths, especially when their pay failed to arrive. The relevant evidence is collected in App. 2, and suggests that certainly hundreds, and perhaps a few thousand Romans joined the Goths. Some Roman slaves also took their place in the Gothic army; Procopius gives us no idea of how many (*Wars* 7.16.15ff).

Faced with Totila and renewed revolt, 12,000 imperial troops moved north to besiege Verona, one of the centres of resistance, in winter 541/2. In spring, Totila went after them with 5,000 men, and won a resounding victory at Faenza, south of the Po, whence the Byzantines had retreated. Totila so distributed his forces that 300 of them charged the Romans' rear at the crucial moment. As Procopius reports it, Totila's support quickly rose to 20,000 after this success. He followed it up by besieging the Roman forces holding Florence, and won a second victory over a relief force (*Wars* 7.3–5). Between them, the two battles were sufficient to push the east Romans onto the defensive. Totila was able to spread his revolt south, taking Benevento, Cumae and eventually Naples in spring 543 (*Wars* 7.6–8).

In the next two campaigning seasons, Totila took a number of important centres, including the strategic fortress of Auximum. This cut off land communications between Rome and Ravenna (*Wars* 7.9–12), and prepared the ground for an escalation in his military ambitions. At the end of 545, Totila began his first siege of Rome. It was pressed throughout the following year, and the city finally surrendered on 17 December 546 (*Wars* 7.13–21). But Gothic manpower was being stretched to the utmost. In the same year, Totila handed over the province of Venetia to the Frankish king Theudebert, in order to free still more Goths from garrison duties (*Wars* 8.24). Totila also subdued in 546 a combined force of imperial troops and an irregular militia raised by a local landowner, Tullianus, which attempted to keep the province of Lucania free from Gothic interference (*Wars* 7.18, 22).

In the meantime, Justinian sent Belisarius back to Italy, in winter 544/5, but, without reinforcements, there was little he could do. He did reoccupy Rome in April 547, when Totila, short of manpower, decided not to hold it himself and failed to neutralize its defences. But Belisarius was unable to regain the initiative, and was eventually recalled to Constantinople in 548. Totila had in the meantime again upped the stakes, employing a two-fold strategy. On the one hand, he continued to bring under his control as much of Italy as possible. Rome was besieged a second time, for instance, from the summer of 549, until it fell to him again the following January (*Wars* 7.36). Gothic forces also captured a whole string of other fortresses, including Tarentum and Rimini (*Wars* 7.37). At the same time, Totila was endeavouring to spread the war. In 549, he created a fleet which was placed under the command of Indulf, a deserter from the Byzantine army. It was set loose on Byzantine possessions. The coast of Dalmatia was ravaged in 549, Sicily taken in 550 and Corfu and Epirus attacked in 551 (*Wars* 7.35, 37–9, 8.22).

Totila's underlying strategy seems clear. The Byzantine Empire possessed resources of wealth and manpower far in excess of his own. He had even been forced to cede part of Italy to the Franks to free Gothic manpower for his campaigns. Justinian's resources were also at this point being stretched by war on two fronts, but such a situation could not last indefinitely. In such circumstances, an outright Gothic victory was impossible and Totila could only hope to make a continued military option unattractively difficult for Justinian. Despite his vigorous pursuit of the war, Totila never lost sight of these realities. Occupying the strategic centres of Italy and spreading the effects of warfare via his fleet were both designed to make Justinian eschew conquest in favour of negotiation. Even at the height of his military success, therefore, Totila kept offering concessions. After his second capture of Rome, for instance, Totila sent his third embassy to Justinian, and, despite this Gothic success, its tone was highly conciliatory. In it, Totila offered to cede Dalmatia and Sicily to Constantinople, to pay an annual tribute, and to provide military contingents for the eastern Empire's campaigns (*Wars* 7.37.6–7; cf. 8.24.4). Without face-saving gains, Justinian would never be persuaded to end the war.

The destruction of the Goths Justinian, however, rejected all of Totila's approaches. From his point of view, one presumes, too much prestige had been invested in the conquest policy to abandon it. As the Persian war drew to a close – fizzling out in the later 540s, a formal peace treaty was agreed in 551 – the Emperor found the necessary forces to finish the job in Italy. His chosen strategy was a major land expedition through the Balkans into northern Italy: the

Plate 25 The Emperor Justinian (a close-up from the St Vitale mosaic in Ravenna)

route taken by Theoderic himself some 60 years before. Preparations began in 550, when the Emperor's cousin Germanus was appointed to command the expedition. Wittigis now dead, Germanus also married Matasuentha, Amalasuentha's daughter, in an attempt to confuse Gothic loyalties (*Wars* 7.39). Germanus, however, died in the year of his appointment, and it was not until early 552 that the expedition, under the command of the eunuch general Narses, was ready to move into Italy. The noose had already been tightening. In summer 551, an imperial force had utterly destroyed the Gothic fleet off Ancona (*Wars* 8.23).

In April 552, Narses advanced into Italy. Totila attempted to block the route to Ravenna (which remained in Byzantine hands), by flooding the land south of Verona. He also sent a force of his best men under Teias to harass Narses' army. Narses, however, moved methodically along the coast to Ravenna (*Wars* 8.26). A second Byzantine force also landed in Calabria in the south, where it defeated some Goths at Crotone. The scene was set for a showdown. Having replenished his stores at Ravenna, Narses advanced. He eventually met Totila in battle – at the end of June, or in early July – on a level plain in the northern Appenines called Busta Gallorum. Totila had gathered most of his available troops, and the central act of the encounter was a charge by the Gothic cavalry, the elite of his army. The charge was broken, and the Goths fled, leaving 6,000 dead on the battlefield. Totila himself was mortally wounded in the rout (*Wars* 8.28–32).

One last effort remained. Teias gathered as many Goths as he could at Pavia, and, realizing he needed help, made a further alliance with the Franks. Battle was renewed in October 532, in the south, at Mons Lactarius in Campania. Another fierce struggle ensued. Teias died, breathing defiance, and the remnants of the Goths negotiated an armistice (*Wars* 8.33–5). This was not quite yet the end. Early in 553, the Frankish assistance purchased by Teias, an army largely of Alamanni, arrived in Italy. After Teias' death, at least three Gothic leaders had continued the struggle. Indulf retreated to Pavia with 1,000 men (*Wars* 35.37), Aligern fought on at Cumae (*Wars* 8.34. 19–20) and Ragnaris was holding out in Conza della Campania (Agathias 2.13–14). The Frankish army advanced south through Liguria and Aemillia, and won some Gothic support. One of its leaders, Butilinus, was even offered the Gothic kingship. Narses, however, was ready. In 553, his troops subdued the whole of Tuscany, and, in December, brought Aligern to surrender. Butilinus' expedition itself was eventually defeated in 554, at the battle of Casilinum, as a result of which Ragnaris' followers surrendered in spring 555 (Agathias 2.1–14).

Between 558 and 560, imperial control was re-established in Liguria, Histria and most of Venetia. Only eastern Venetia was left unsubdued, and it was this region which witnessed the last flicker of Gothic revolt. In 561, a Gothic count called Widin rebelled in Brescia and called again for Frankish help. The manoeuvre failed.[10] Widin's defeat marked the final extinction of Gothic resistance to the Byzantine conquest of Italy.

[10] Paul the Deacon, *History of the Lombards* 2.2 with commentary of *PLRE* 3, 924.

(iii) Integratio interrupta: Goths and Romans in time of war

Much ink has been expended on the attitude of the Italo-Roman population to the war, more than one scholar having concluded that the locals essentially supported Justinian's policy. Thus Tullianus raised a military force to keep Totila out of Lucania, and, various individuals took either a pro-Byzantine stand, or calculated that the safest policy was to surrender to them: Datius in Milan, Marcius in Verona or the Pope and leading notables in Rome as early as December 536.[11] But different individuals reacted to events in a variety of ways, and attitudes changed as the war progressed.

Some Romans supported the Goths' cause initially, for instance, but not later. Not least among these was Cassiodorus. He continued as Wittigis' Praetorian Prefect, but had abandoned the Goths by the time of Wittigis' defeat (540). Others took a different view. Totila still had a Roman Praetorian Prefect, and, at one point, attempted to reconstitute a Senate of Goths and Italo-Romans. This suggests that Italo-Romans did not, even in the late 540s, feel entirely alienated from the Goths.[12] Indeed, a few committed individuals aside, most Italo-Romans were civilian by-standers, desperately trying to avoid damage and loss. Such a stance was deliberately encouraged by Byzantine policy. Belisarius made an example of Naples, because the city's population had helped its Gothic garrison resist his troops (*Wars* 5.9.8 ff).

The approach of the Goths was similar. Gothic kings were repeatedly disappointed not to get more positive support from Italo-Romans,[13] but, for the most part, this lack of active support did not lead to conflict. Only a positively pro-Byzantine approach on the part of Italo-Romans elicited a violent Gothic response. Thus Milan was deliberately sacked by the Goths after it had been surrendered to the Byzantines by some of its leading inhabitants (*Wars* 6. 12. 26 ff, 21. 38–9). The one apparent exception to this is Wittigis' massacre of some senatorial hostages during the siege of Rome in 537, but this was perhaps because the city had earlier been surrendered to Belisarius without a fight (*Wars* 5. 26. 1; cf. 5. 14). Faced with two military forces ready to punish active support for the other, it is hardly surprising that most Italo-Romans swung with the wind. Neutrality born of fear seems the most accurate characterization of the Italo-Roman response.

11 E.g. Thompson, 1982, ch. 5.
12 On elite Romans and the war, see now Schäfer, 1991, esp. 276ff.
13 E.g. *Wars* 5.18.40, 20.11–14; 6.6.15ff; cf. Thompson, 1982, 104–5.

One basic effect of 25 years of conflict, therefore, was to repolarize the Gothic and Roman elements of the Italian population. Byzantine policy positively discouraged the latter from assisting the former, and the bulk of the war was directed firmly at the Goths. This was true not only of the pitched battles, but also of the cavalry raid on Picenum which turned the tide of the first phase of the war. John, its commander, was ordered to attack only Gothic non-combatant personnel and their possessions (*Wars* 6. 7. 28 ff). As we have seen, Italo-Romans had been militarized to a degree, but mainly to provide city garrisons. There is no evidence of Italian counterparts to the Gallo-Roman senators who died fighting for the Visigoths at Vouillé (chapter 7).

In overall terms, the Byzantine campaigns progressively wore down the Goths' military capacities. By 'the Goths', I have in mind the fully enfranchised adult male element of Theoderic's following, which may have numbered something in the region of 5,000–10,000 individuals per generation (App. 1). The political attitudes of the rest of Theoderic's followers – even adult male ones – of lesser status were not of such central importance, since they were tied to, and probably dictated by, those of their superiors. Some of the events show up the importance of this group with great clarity. Gothic resistance to the first Roman move into Dalmatia collapsed, for instance, after heavy casualties to the Gothic elite of the region. Even though the Romans withdrew from Salona, the loss of their elite made the Goths refrain from taking possession of the city (*Wars* 5.7.3–10). When a Gothic relief force withdrew, the remnants of the original Gothic population simply surrendered (*Wars* 7.7. 26–37). Given previous losses, the latter presumably belonged to other than the elite caste. The sequence of events nicely illustrates, then, the degree to which military resistance depended upon the elite, those with most invested in being 'Gothic'. This can be demonstrated in other ways. Procopius has the Goths of the region of Pavia emphasize, in conversation with Urais, for instance, the importance of the number of elite casualties already suffered (*Wars* 6.30.7). Or again, threats to Gothic non-combatants altered the course of the war. Wittigis' siege of Rome was broken up by the cavalry raid on Picenum directed specifically at Gothic women and children. Likewise, Urais' relief force for Wittigis in Ravenna, again composed of many of the elite, melted away when it became known that its womenfolk and children were in Roman hands (*Wars* 6.10. 1ff; 28.29ff).

I have argued above that it was the attitudes of this elite group which underlay the creation of the Ostrogoths in the Balkans. It was their collective realization that they stood to do better, in dealings with Constantinople, as a united group which both put a break on dynastic competition, and led the Thracian Goths to join Theoderic the Amal after 483/4 (chapter 5). In many ways, the Byzantine conquest of Italy saw the processes witnessed in the Balkans go into reverse. Over 25 years, the war destroyed the ability and the willingness of this elite caste to maintain its cohesion by cooperative political action. The war lasted such a long time (535/6–61), of course, that more than one generation of the Gothic elite was involved in the fighting. When thinking of the war's effects, therefore, we should probably have in mind a figure of up to 15,000 crucial individuals.

The destruction of their group solidarity was achieved in a number of ways. For some, diplomatic pressure, backed by a display of military force, was sufficient. The attitude of Theodahad, as we have seen, was highly ambivalent. For most of his reign he was more ready to surrender his kingdom to the Byzantines, than to fight them for it. His son-in-law, Ebrimud, was like-minded. Quite similar too is the case of Pitzas. He lived in what was clearly the periphery of Gothic settlement in southern Samnium, and persuaded many of his neighbours, as far north as the river Biferno, to surrender to Belisarius (*Wars* 5.15.1–2). Procopius makes no reference to the social status of those involved, but they are likely enough to have belonged to the elite.

These instances aside, what is striking about Procopius' narrative, however, is the coherence and vigour of Gothic resistance. As the length of the war suggests, the Goths were not ready, on the whole, to subject themselves to Byzantine rule without the fiercest of struggles, and it took 25 years of warfare, operating on a number of levels, to destroy the coherence of this critical group. Not least important was death in battle. Procopius' narrative records a number of duels, for instance, but such conflict can hardly have caused significant losses.[14] Much more important were losses to the Gothic elite in the bigger engagements. In one of the battles outside Rome, 1,000 of 'those [Goths] who fight in the front rank' (i.e. the elite) were killed (*Wars* 5.18.14). Another substantial group of the elite died when Justinian's naval forces destroyed Totila's fleet. Much of the surviving elite had been allocated to it, and Procopius records the deflating effect that news of the fleet's destruction had on Gothic morale (*Wars* 8.23.29 ff; cf. 23.10; 24.3). Likewise, a further 6,000 Goths were killed at Busta Gallorum, and many more (although no figures are given) in Teias' last stand. We have no information on how many of the dead, in these last

14 E.g. *Wars* 6.1.23ff, 36; 8.28.11–16.

two battles, belonged to the elite, and the available information is obviously incomplete. There were enough hard-fought engagements in the 25 years of warfare, however, substantially to erode elite numbers.

To the disruptive effects of death in battle, the Byzantines added a policy of removing troublesome Goths from Italy and resettling them in the east. This was not, to begin with at least, imperial policy in all cases; it would have only stimulated greater resistance. After the surrender of Wittigis, Belisarius sent all but the king's closest henchmen back to their estates (*Wars* 6.29.35–8), and Narses did the same after Mons Lactarius.[15] Justinian's pragmatic sanction of 554, intended to restore order after the war, also stressed that land transactions which had taken place down to the reign of Theodahad remained legally valid. This would have included all the transactions under Theoderic by which the Goths had originally acquired their estates. None the less, in the course of the war, many Goths, again clearly including substantial numbers of the elite, were shipped out of Italy. Wittigis and his closest advisers were taken to Constantinople at the end of 540 (*Wars* 6.21.28). In 538/9, the Gothic garrisons of Petra, Clusium, Tudra and Auximum had not been allowed to return home. Many were transported away from the war zone to Naples and Sicily. Their final destination is not reported, but was, I suspect, the east (*Wars* 6.11.19ff; 13.2ff; 27.31ff.). This was certainly the case for much larger numbers of Goths in the 550s. It would seem, as one might expect, that, when revolts continued even after the deaths of Totila and Teias, Byzantine policy hardened. After Ragnaris' death, his 7,000 men were shipped to Constantinople (Agathias 2.14.7). The same treatment was accorded those who, in 561, supported the revolt of Widin in Brescia and Verona (Paul the Deacon *History of the Lombards* 2.2).

Twenty-five years of war, numerous casualties, and a significant number of deportations were thus required to break the resistance of the politically enfranchised caste of the Gothic population of Italy. Byzantine pressure had reduced elite numbers until the Ostrogoths had ceased to be viable as an independent socio-political unit. Different Goths realized this at different moments. Some, such as Theodahad, Ebrimud or Pitzas, were ready to throw in the towel as soon as Belisarius landed in southern Italy. Most, however, were made of sterner stuff. Even in the 550s, opinions differed. Aligern, for instance, decided that the enterprise of Butilinus – the Frank turned

[15] Agathias 1.1.1 to be preferred to Procopius *Wars* 8.35.33–6 who reports that the surviving Goths were to leave Italy.

Gothic king – was not something worth supporting. In Aligern's view, Butilinus' movement was not really Gothic at all, and one might as well surrender to the Byzantines (Agathias 1.20.1–11). Others were ready to continue fighting, even down to 561. Overall, the ability of the Goths to sustain the revolt even after the extinction of their royal dynasty, not to mention a second significant portion of their upper nobility with Wittigis in 540, confirms, it seems to me, the general picture of 'Gothicness' constructed above. While not shared in equally by all of Theoderic's followers, neither was it confined to a very small minority of the conquerors of Italy. On the contrary, a numerically significant cross-section of the immigrant group had a stake in this identity, and, in many cases, their collective allegiance to it could be overcome only by death or transportation. Some Goths certainly survived as landowners in Italy after 561.[16] They were no longer numerous enough, however, to assert an independent identity. The Ostrogoths had ceased to exist.

B. Redefining Gothic: The Visigoths in Spain

Where the Ostrogothic kingdom foundered in the mid-sixth century, overwhelmed by outside aggression, the Spanish kingdom of the Visigoths survived. It only did so, however, by overcoming external threats and internal political chaos. In surviving these difficulties, the kingdom was fundamentally transformed. By *c.* AD 700, the Visigoths of the fourth and fifth centuries were as much an institution of the past as the Ostrogoths, their identity pulled apart by other, less violent, means. In what follows, the names of the Law Codes are given in English in the text (*Visigothic Code*, *Code of Euric*), but cited in the footnotes by their Latin abbreviations: *LV (Leges Visigothorum)* and *CE* (*Codex Euricianus*) respectively.

(i) Sixth-century collapse

The middle years of the sixth century saw protracted political turmoil in the Visigothic kingdom.[17] It had a number of causes. Most

[16] The classic study is Schmidt, 1943, but some of his Gothic survivors were probably Lombards. The names at Schmidt, 1943, 9 should be checked against *PLRE* 3, drawing on Brown, 1984.

[17] There are many available narratives. In English, see especially, Thompson, 1969, chs 1–4; Collins, 1983, ch. 2. The most influential of the many narratives in Spanish: Orlandis, 1977; Garcia Moreno, 1989. Most instructive too is Claude, 1971.

important, perhaps, was the destruction of political continuity within the kingdom in the first decade of the century. In 511, the kingdom was hijacked, as we have seen, by Theoderic the Ostrogoth. When his united Gothic realm broke up in 526, its former Visigothic territories devolved to a son of Alaric II, Amalaric. For this, as we have seen, Theudis, Theoderic's right-hand man in Spain turned rebel, seems to have been chiefly responsible (chapter 8). Amalaric's succession was the result of new power structures, not old ones.

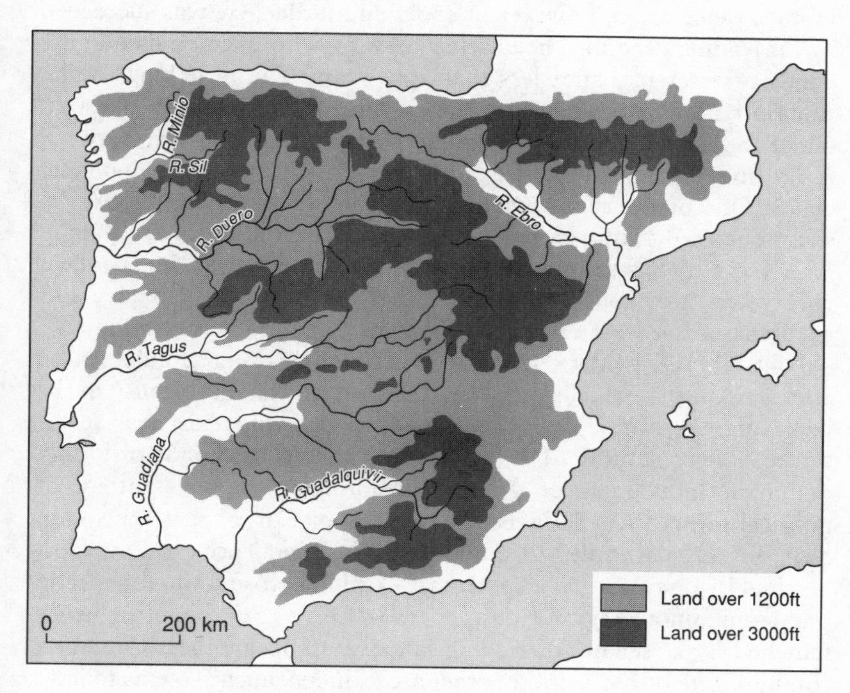

Figure 9.2 The physical geography of Spain

In addition, Frankish pressure continued to undermine the security of the kingdom. The new king Amalaric attempted to defuse this problem by marrying a Frankish princess, Chrotildis. As reported by Gregory of Tours, however, he then attempted to convert Chrotildis to Arianism from Catholicism, which gave one of her brothers, king Childebert, a pretext for invasion (Hist. 3.10). I doubt that this is the full story, but the effects of Frankish intervention are clear enough. The Visigothic army was defeated, Narbonne taken, and Amalaric fled south of the Pyrenees to

Barcelona, where he was murdered by some of his own men.[18] Theudis was implicated in the murder, and certainly its prime beneficiary. He became king after Amalaric's death in 531.

With Amalaric perished the last member of the old Visigothic ruling dynasty. While there had always been much political turmoil behind the façade of dynastic continuity, the sixth century saw ambitious Gothic nobles competing openly for the throne. Theudis' reign was lengthy (531–48), and even involved military success against the Franks. Once again, however, it ended in murder. He was succeeded by his leading general, Theudisclus (548–9), who likewise died at the hands of assassins, after less than two years. The next king, Agila, ruled for just two years more, before open revolt again broke out, under the leadership of Athanagild. The resulting civil war between Agila and Athanagild added a further dimension to the political chaos. One of the two – which is the subject of varying report[19] – summoned a Byzantine army, which duly arrived in southern Spain in 552. Once in Spain, however, it swiftly carved out an independent enclave in the south. Its extent has been much debated, but encompassed at least Cartagena, Malaga, Sagontia and Assidonia.[20]

Political crisis at the centre had other, perhaps more fundamental, effects upon the balance of power between centre and locality in the peninsula. As a new political order struggled into existence at the centre, power naturally fell (or was taken) into the hands of locally dominant individuals or groups, operating in a wide variety of political forms.[21] As early as 550, the city of Cordoba, in the south, beat off Agila's armies to establish its independence (Isidore *Hist. Goth.* 45). Elsewhere, a local dynast, Aspidius, rose to dominance in one mountainous region (John of Biclar *Chron.* 36), his prominence matched by a 'senate' of leading landowners in another: Cantabria (Braulio, *Life of Emil.* 26). In other areas, independence seems to have been asserted by political units descended from some of the Iberian tribes originally conquered by Rome.[22] The collapse of Roman power in the peninsula in the fifth century had had precisely the same effect, control falling, as we have seen, into the hands of a whole series of

[18] Further comment: Wood, 1994, 169ff.

[19] Isidore *Hist. Goth.* 47 states that Athanagild summoned the Byzantines; Jordanes, *Getica* 303 implies that it was Agila.

[20] See, with refs, Thompson, 1969, 320ff. (App.), and the article of R. M. Sanz Serrano in *Les Wisigoths*.

[21] E.g. Collins, 1983, 1–10.

[22] E.g. the mysterious Sappi (John of Biclar *Chron.* 27) and Suani (ibid. 39); cf. Claude, 1971, 55–9.

local independencies (chapter 7). It must be a moot point, therefore, whether barely a decade of undisturbed Visigothic rule (arguably only *c*.495–505) had been sufficient for the Goths properly to subdue them.

The power vacuum at the centre of the kingdom in the mid-sixth century was temporary, however, not permanent. There remained sufficient forces interested in reasserting centralized dominion to achieve this end, if only they could once be united. A beginning was perhaps made by Athanagild, who enjoyed unchallenged rule after the murder of his rival Agila in 554, down to 568. On his death, power passed to Liuva, who, within a year, associated his brother Leovigild with his rule, before dying in 571 or 572. In the reign of Leovigild (569–86), local autonomy throughout the peninsula was brought firmly to heel. In part, the renewed political stability which allowed Leovigild to suppress local autonomies, may have been an undocumented legacy from Athanagild. But it was also of his own creation. Successful military campaigns bring their originator enormous prestige, and endow him with plentiful gifts to pass on to grateful supporters. Leovigild may have been lucky enough to be in the right place at the right time, but military success was the hallmark of his reign.

John of Biclar provides a comprehensive, if annalistic, account of Leovigild's campaigns. The list is one of striking success. His first victories were against the Byzantines in 570 and 571 (the sacking of Malaga and capture of Medina Sidonia: *Chron.* 12, 17). The independence of Cordoba was curbed in 572 (*Chron.* 20), and subsequent campaigns followed annually down to 577. These probably worked methodically from north-west to north-east, along the line of the Pyrenees and into Galicia. They subdued, in turn, Sabaria and the Sabi, the so-called senate of Cantabria (whose leading lights were massacred), Aspidius' realm in the 'Agregensian mountains' and the territory of Orospeda (*Chron.* 27, 32, 36, 47). After all this martial success, John of Biclar reports (51), 'King Leovigild having everywhere destroyed the usurpers and the despoilers of Spain, returned home seeking rest with his own people and he built a town in Celtiberia, named Reccopolis after his son [Reccared].' A southern enclave remained in Byzantine hands, but most of the peninsula had been reunited. In the next decade, Leovigild further extended the kingdom by conquering the Suevic Kingdom of the north-east.

Suppressing local autonomies represents a major upheaval in itself, however, and it is hardly surprising that there remained a body of disaffected opinion within the kingdom. The military operations had also been accompanied by the elimination of political opponents: the execution or exile of many of the most powerful men of his kingdom (Isidore *Hist. Goth.* 51; Gregory of Tours, *Hist.* 4.3). When, therefore, Leovigild's eldest son, Hermenigild, fell out with his father in 579 (why is not recorded), supporters rallied to his cause. The rebellion began in Seville, where Leovigild had already established Hermenigild as sub-king, but swiftly spread. It also underlined the existence of a more fundamental division within the kingdom.

In *c.*500, Catholic churchmen and Arian kings alike were content to ignore their religious differences (above pp. 214, 225). Three generations later, this religious *modus vivendi* was beginning to break down. Why is unclear, but Christianity has always emphasized that there is only one path to Truth and Salvation. I suspect, therefore, that as the 'strangeness' of the intruding Goths disappeared (see below), it became increasingly impossible for either party to tolerate the existence of parallel and separate Churches. The first move may have been made by Leovigild. In 580, he called an Arian synod in Toledo, which significantly modified to the doctrinal teaching of the Gothic Chruch. The full and equal Divinity of the Son was acknowledged, but the Holy Spirit continued to be relegated to an inferior position. This was not a novel doctrinal position, and is traditionally called Macedonianism. Armed with this new doctrine, Leovigild attempted to unite religious observance within his kingdom. The synod also decided that it was not necessary to rebaptize Catholics who wished to change allegiance, removing a great ceremonial stumbling-block to conversion. Leovigild achieved some successes. At least one Catholic bishop, Vincent of Zaragoza, moved into his camp. It emerges clearly from the *Lives of the Fathers of Merida*, even though it is heavily biased against Leovigild, that strong-arm methods of persuasion were not the general rule.

What was Leovigild trying to achieve? Some have thought that he was trying to cement Arian Gothic domination of the peninsula. Given the wider context of his reign, however, this seems mistaken. Leovigild determinedly restored political unity to the kingdom, and attempted to establish it on stronger foundations. He recast the monarchy along new lines, to serve as a unifying focus for the whole population of the kingdom (see below). Even more strikingly, he overturned the law which had previously banned intermarriage between Roman and Goth. Against this backdrop, championing a compromise doctrinal settlement between the Arian and Catholic positions, and then attempting to build consensus around it, can surely only be read as a serious attempt to create religious unity within

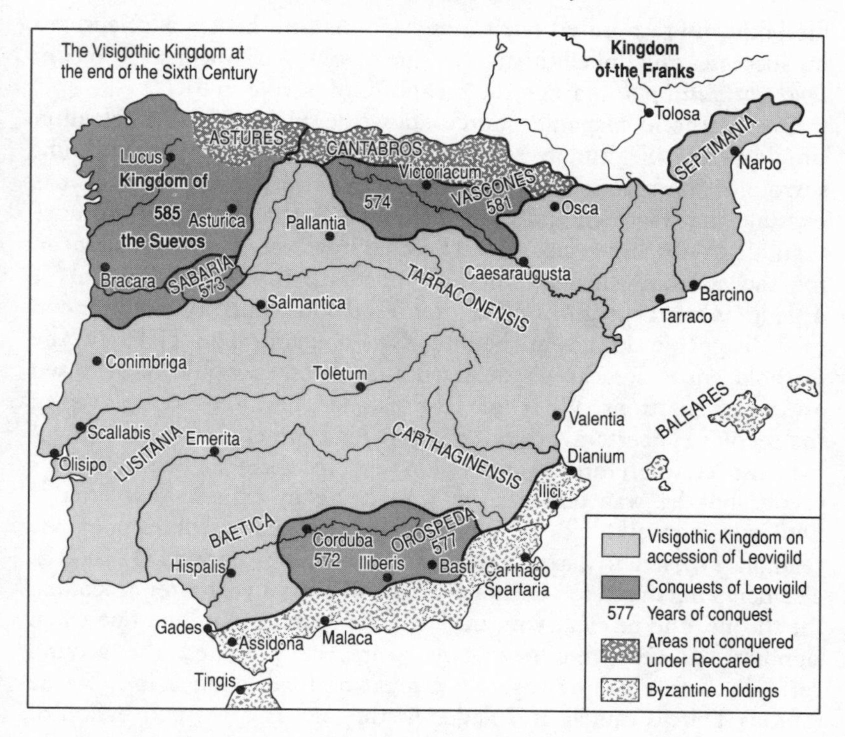

Figure 9.3 The campaigns of Leovigild

his kingdom. For the bulk of the population, the divide between Gothic and Catholic Christianity was perhaps not so great as Catholic churchmen liked to think.[23]

If religious unity was Leovigild's aim, this ambition overreached his power. Despite the conversions, the bulk of the Catholic population of the peninsula remained Catholic. The main effect of his policy was to generate a climate of religious tension, which his rebellious son seems to have exploited. At some point in his revolt, Hermenigild declared himself Catholic, taking the name John. It is unclear whether this was before or after the synod, but he did attempt to use his Catholic conversion as a weapon against his father. Perhaps in 580, Hermenigild issued a coin, inscribed *regi a Deo vita*, which emphasized the God-appointed nature of his rule. Leovigild replied in kind. As he

[23] Thompson, 1969, 78ff argued the case for Leovigild promoting Arian, Gothic domination. I echo what is otherwise the general consensus, refs as footnote 17 at p.276.

methodically recaptured territories from his son, his coins celebrated his successes and linked them to Divine favour. An issue inscribed *cum Deo optinuit Spali* marked the recapture of Seville in 584.

Our Catholic hispanic sources describe Hermenigild's rebellion simply as the illegitimate revolt of an erring son. Thus much doubt surrounds the precise role played by religion in the events, and it is possible that Hermenigild's conversion to Catholicism was no more than a last desperate measure. There is, however, an obvious reason for the sources' silence. They all postdate the Third Council of Toledo, when Leovigild's other, non-rebellious son, Reccared, united the Visigothic kingdom behind Catholicism. To celebrate the Catholicism of Reccared's defeated elder brother would have raised awkward questions. What role, for instance, had Reccared played in the revolt? He certainly didn't support his brother.

I suspect, therefore, that religion was an issue in Hermenigild's revolt, but he was defeated in 584, dying in exile a year later.[24] Leovigild himself died in 586, leaving the final resolution of the religious problem to his second son and successor, Reccared (586–601). The new king opted for Catholicism in 587, just a year after ascending the throne, and he clearly meant his move to have more than personal significance. Over the next two years, he prepared the ground carefully before calling together a great national council in 589: the famous Third Council of Toledo. At this meeting, the conversion of the Goths to Catholicism was proclaimed in a formal document. Eight named Arian bishops and their subordinates, five named lay Gothic *viri illustri* and all the leading men of the Goths (*omnes seniores Gothorum*) declared their conversion to Catholicism alongside that of their king. The Council drew a ceremonial line under the history of the Arian Church of the Visigoths, and, following Leovigild's lead, proclaimed rebaptism an anathema, thus smoothing the way for Arian converts.[25]

Conversion was accompanied, however, by no less than four separate revolts. In 587/8, a number of Gothic counts, including the future king Witteric, launched a conspiracy in Merida, together with Sunna, the Arian bishop of the city (*Lives of the Fathers of Merida* 5.10). In 588, an Arian bishop, Udilo, probably the bishop of Toledo, and a Visigothic Queen attempted a coup d'état (John of Biclar

[24] The evidence is set out conveniently in the contradictory arguments of Hillgarth, 1966, and Collins, 1980. I tend to follow the former.

[25] Conciliar acts: Vives, 1963, 107–45 (Gothic signatories at 122–3). For further commentary, see the works cited at footnote 17, at p. 276 together with Fontaine, 1967.

Chron. 90). Probably a year later, at Narbonne, two leading Gothic nobles, Granista and Vildigern, combined in revolt with the Gothic bishop of the city, Athalosus, and 'many Arians' (*Lives of the Fathers of Merida* 5.12). A final act of resistance in 589/90 involved a royal attendant, the *dux* Argimund, who was scalped and lost his right hand (John of Biclar, *Chron.* 94).[26] It has sometimes been said that the conversion of the Goths was achieved relatively painlessly, but four revolts in two years seems like rather a lot.

Without an ultimate willingness to constrain Arian hardliners, therefore, Reccared would never have achieved his religious aims. Like its political reformation under Leovigild, the Visigothic kingdom's new religious unity was a hard-won achievement. Overall, the paralysis which had crippled central power structures in the middle part of the century had been overcome. Unification was subsequently crowned by the conquest of the remaining Byzantine territories in the south. Under Sisebut (612–21), the Byzantines were reduced to a small enclave in the Algarve, and Suinthila (621–31) achieved their final expulsion in 624. There is no space here, and, indeed, it would hardly be appropriate in a book specifically about Goths, to undertake a full survey of the Visigothic kingdom which emerged from the momentous reigns of Leovigild and Reccared. It is very much to the point, however, to ask a more restricted question. What meaning, if any, was retained by the terms 'Goth' and 'Gothic' in the new Visigothic kingdom of the seventh century?

(ii) Goths in the seventh-century kingdom

In the seventh century, 'Goth' and its derivatives were still used in important contexts. The state was conceived of by its inhabitants as the kingdom or indeed nation (*gens*) of the Goths. Isidore of Seville, Julian of Toledo, occasional references in the *Visigothic Code*, all describe the kingdom in such terms.[27] Perhaps the most striking illustration of this important point, however, is to be found in the canons of the Fourth Council of Toledo (633). Amongst other things, these laid down that the population of the kingdom should take a sanctified oath to preserve the stability of the Gothic nation.[28] The Fifth and Sixth Councils of

[26] The chronology and circumstances of these revolts are far from straightforward. For further commentary, see Thompson, 1969, 103–4 and the relevant entries in Garcia Moreno, 1974.

[27] See, in more detail, Reydellet, 1981, 508–96; Teillet, 1984.

[28] 4.57. On the importance of oaths in the Visigothic kingdom, see Claude, 1976.

Toledo (636 and 638) further laid down that only a noble of the Gothic nation should be king (canons 3 and 17 respectively), the Eighth (653) that he should be chosen by the bishops and the great nobility (canon 10). Julian of Toledo's *History of King Wamba* describes the election of that king (672–80) in precisely such terms.[29] On a quite different level, various individuals continued to refer to themselves in the seventh century, or were known to others as 'Goths', particularly Bishop Renovatus of Merida in the 630s (*Lives of the Fathers of Merida* 5.14), and one Sinticius (d. 639), of whom it is recorded that he was a Goth on his father's side (Vives, 1969, n.86).

As these texts make clear, only Goths could participate fully in the political processes of the kingdom. In notional terms, at least, only Goths could aspire to the throne, and participate in royal elections. Asserting ethnic Gothic status may have had a financial point. A sixth-century law preserved in the seventh-century *Visigothic Code* records that any Goth who had subsequently taken from the Romans more than his allotted two-thirds share in the original land partition (chapter 7), was to return the extra 'so that the royal treasury shall sustain no loss'.[30] On the face of it, this implies that the Goths' original lands were granted tax free, and the law was still considered worth copying in the seventh century. It seems unlikely that all lands held by recognized Goths were tax free, however; at most, tax-free status probably applied to a particular set of lands, transferred to immigrants in the early years of the kingdom. For a variety of reasons, therefore, it was still clearly important to be a Goth in the seventh century. But what exactly was a seventh-century Goth?

The Goths of the fourth and fifth centuries consisted, as we have seen, of an elite caste of freemen and quasi- or would-be nobles, somewhere between one-fifth and one-half of the adult male population of the group as a whole.[31] Within this elite, some were more powerful than others, but important aspects of legal and political enfranchisement were shared widely among them. By the end of the seventh-century, this elite had been replaced by a dominant nobility with deeply entrenched rights.

Sixth-century legal texts preserved in the *Visigothic Code* show that

[29] V Tolet. *3 nec Gothicae gentis nobilitas* ...; VI Tolet. 17 *nisi genere Gothus*; VIII Tolet. 10. On the *Hist. Wamb.*, see Collins, 1977.

[30] *LV* 10.1.16: *ut nihil fisco debeat deperire*. The law is labelled *antiqua* signifying that it was taken from Leovigild's sixth-century lawbook.

[31] Although Garcia Moreno, 1994 contains much relevant information, it starts from the view that ethnicity in the Migration Period depended upon royal lineages. I consider this deeply mistaken.

this fundamental transformation was by then already underway. Many different laws make a distinction within the free class, allocating different rights and punishments to lesser and greater freemen. The latter are referred to variously, in strikingly comparative language, as *major* ('greater'), *honestior* ('more honourable') and *potentior* ('more powerful'). These are presumably synonyms. It is generally assumed that this distinction was based essentially on wealth. If so, richer freemen were bolstering their economic advantages with legal privilege. In the seventh century, the gap widened. A century earlier, all freemen had the same *wergild*, enjoying the same degree of financial protection under the law. By the time that King Erwig revised the *Visigothic Code* in 681, however, greater freemen were enjoying a higher and separate *wergild* (compare the original and revised versions of *LV* 8.4.16). The growing width of this divide is also reflected in other seventh-century legislation which forbade lesser freemen from bringing accusations against their betters (e.g. *LV* 6.1.2). The old social caste of freemen, guardians of 'Gothicness' in the Migration Period, had been destroyed. Full political and legal enfranchisement was now the preserve of a more restricted social group: an increasingly well-defined nobility.[32]

In this, the Visigothic kingdom parallels other successor states to the western Roman Empire. By the end of the seventh century, the 'Franks' of Neustria were a nexus of some half-dozen or so interrelated noble clans. Others of the so-called barbarian law codes, likewise, distinguish between lesser and greater freemen, and some even name clans with very particular privileges.[33] Some of the transformations underlying the emergence of this dominant nobility in Spain are well-evidenced in the sources, and have been much discussed. There is no need, therefore, to provide anything more than a broad outline of them here.[34]

[32] This has long been recognized. See most recently, Garcia Moreno, 1989, 247ff; Claude, 1971, 80ff. Some examples of rulings dividing the free class: *LV* 2.4.2; 8.3.6, 8.4.24; 9.3.3.

[33] Neustria: Gerberding, 1987, ch. 6. Divided free class: Burgundian *Book of Constitutions* 2.2; *Pactus Legis Alamannorum* (only in certain contexts) 2.1–11 with 14.6–11. Special families: *Lombard Laws*; Preface to *Edict of Rothari* (Lombard Laws); *Bavarian Laws* 3.1.

[34] Some bibliographical orientation: on estates and their survival, see Garcia Moreno, 1989, 225ff; Diaz Martinez, 1987, pt. 2, 1992–3. Money and trade: Barral I Altet, 1976; Keay, 1984a, 1984b; Reynolds, 1993. Social relations: Garcia Moreno, 1989, 237ff; Bonnassie, 1991, ch. 1; Claude, 1971, 84ff; Sanchez, 1989, 114ff.

Their economic context was, it seems, the survival and, indeed, the build up of large, self-sufficient landed estates (Latin *latifundia*). The old expectation was that most villas would have been destroyed in the troubles of the fifth century. More recently, pottery evidence for their survival has emerged in such widespread areas as the Guadalquivir valley, Lusitania, Rioja, Aragon and the Mediterranean coast. Monastic writers of the Visigothic kingdom also generally assume that religious foundations would be maintaining themselves from their large, self-sufficient, holdings. Of course, rich Hispano-Romans always had been landowners, but, in the Visigothic kingdom, landed wealth incorporated new powers and possibilities.

It seems to be generally assumed that the prevalence of large landed estates increased in the Visigothic period. This is probably, but not certainly, true. What is clear, is that their economic and social function underwent considerable transformation. Economically, estates became increasingly self-sufficient, as more sophisticated economic structures disappeared. Some coins were minted, but only gold ones (the *triens* = one-third of a standard Roman solidus). There was thus no small change in the economy, and such a switch to gold (paralleling developments everywhere in the former Roman west) is normally associated with a decline in exchange. Likewise, while import/export links with the wider Mediterranean did not disappear overnight, there was a progressive decline in such economic contacts, in so far, at least, as they can be measured in the types and quantities of non-indigenous pottery types reaching the peninsula. What evidence there is for local industry and craft specialization – at this point basically confined to pottery industries – also suggests simplification. Specialized wheel-made wares were replaced in many areas by hand-made ones, distributed only locally.

These economic trends had social implications which stemmed from the rise of these self-sufficient estates. At the top end, the landowning class translated its wealth into power by recruiting private armies. The most often cited case is that of Theudis. As we have seen, he married a Hispano-Roman senatorial lady in the early sixth-century, and, on the basis of her wealth, built up a personal army of 2,000 men (Procopius *Wars* 5.12.50–4). Some of the individuals involved in these military retinues were freemen. Visigothic legal texts define at least two different mechanisms for establishing dependence in such cases: the institutions of *buccellarii* and *saiones* (governed by somewhat different rules and expectations). Other dependants were unfree, either freedmen bound to perpetual service (*in obsequio*) of the lord who freed them and his heirs, or slaves, some of whom were also used for military service. Through these different institutions, elite individuals could build up private military forces. The new lords of the Visigothic kingdom also exercised considerable legal powers of a more general nature over their dependants. Increasingly, therefore, a single term came into use to cover both free and unfree dependants: *clientes*. In social terms, as well as economically, the great estates of the Visigothic kingdom were increasingly self-sufficient.

Most studies of these developments have related them to the history of the Visigothic state *per se*.[35] They certainly generated an overall decline in centralized state power, the ultimate destination of which is often taken to be the career of one Theodimer. At the time of the Muslim conquest, in the early eighth century, Theodimer agreed terms with the new masters of the peninsula. In return for an annual payment, he retained autonomous control of a region made up of seven towns of the south-east: Orihuela, Valencia, Alicante, Mulsa, Bigastro, Eyyo (Elche?) and Lorca.[36] Whether such complete regional autonomy reflects conditions prevailing under the later Visigothic monarchy, or was more the product of the Muslim conquest, seems to me a moot point. For our purposes, however, the main significance of these developments lies elsewhere. The Goths of the seventh century hispanic kingdom were no longer members of a caste of freemen. An elite class of landowners, they now exercised a widespread social dominance over the descendents of many of those, who, one hundred years earlier, would have been at least their notional equals.

In an important sense, the seventh-century definition of 'Goth' was thus narrower than its predecessors. In another, it was probably wider. The evidence is not complete, and the subject has occasioned much debate. Two particular types of evidence – the administrative organization of the seventh-century kingdom, and personal naming patterns – have been taken to suggest the newly dominant nobility of the period really was composed largely of ethnic Goths: the direct descendants of the immigrants of *c.*500. It seems more likely, however, that the 'Gothic' landowning class of the seventh century was composed as much, if not more, of individuals biologically of Roman descent.

Although not without disruption, much of the pattern of Roman administration, as we have seen, survived intact into the Visigothic kingdom (chapter 7). None of it was still functioning, however, in 654

[35] They have often been seen as generating a 'feudal' or 'protofeudal' state, since the pioneering work of Sanchez-Albornoz, 1947, 1974 (cf. Garcia Moreno, 1989, 333ff).

[36] Text: Simonet, 1903, 797ff.

when Reccesuinth issued his revised version of the *Visigothic Code*. In particular, the curial classes, who had run the cities in the Roman period, had been replaced by a system based on counts and a series of officials – some, like the *thiufadus* with Gothic names – with largely military responsibilities. E.A. Thompson argued that the replacement of Roman structures in local government with simpler, more martial, alternatives signified that Goths had taken over from Romans as the dominant force in local government.[37]

It is unlikely, however, that the administrative transformations had such an ethnically pointed significance. The changes affected the entire kingdom, for instance, but, as we have seen, Goths had not settled evenly across the peninsula. The Visigothic kingdom also demanded military service from its subjects without ethnic distinction. This is explicit in late seventh-century edicts of King Erwig,[38] but Romans had been performing military service in the Visigothic kingdom since the early sixth century. They fought and died at Vouillé, of course, and the later sixth-century *dux* Claudius, a Catholic and explicitly Roman supporter of Reccared, is described as an 'experienced soldier, well-versed in the arts of war'.[39] There is no reason to think Claudius exceptional in anything other than the degree of his distinction. This being so, the dominance in local government of military officers by no means signifies a Gothic take-over. The men holding these offices in the seventh century were just as likely militarized Romans.

Personal naming patterns among the seventh-century elite have to be reconstructed largely from lists of signatories to the great councils of church and state which occurred periodically at Toledo. The almost complete lack of seventh-century narrative sources from Spain is here a considerable handicap, especially for the lay aristocracy, of whom only a small proportion witnessed conciliar proceedings.[40] In the period 507–711, only 232 elite laymen are known, of whom some 72 have Roman names. It is hard, if not impossible, to draw any conclusion from such a small sample.

The sample of episcopal names is more complete, and shows an interesting pattern. The overall percentage of Roman-named bishops between 507 and 711 is 72 per cent, but, after *c.*650, declines to only

[37] See, e.g. *LV* 1.2.7; 1.5.2 with the arguments of Thompson, 1969, ch. 11.

[38] *LV* 9.2.8–9; cf. Sanchez, 1989.

[39] *Lives of the Fathers of Merida* 10.6–7: *in bellica studia eruditus, in causis bellicis nihilominus exercitatus.*

[40] Julian of Toledo *History of King Wamba* is the only exception.

48 per cent, and bishops with Germanic names are found throughout the peninsula. From this, it has been argued that Goths at least came to dominate the episcopate, since we have no explicit case of an Hispano-Roman taking a Gothic name. This conclusion is extremely insecure. The conciliar witness lists give only names, and no precise information on the ethnic background of signatories. Ethnic information tends to be given only in narrative sources, which are, of course, conspicuously lacking. There is no known case of a Roman taking a Gothic name, but Goths took Roman, especially Christian Roman names, and, in contemporary Frankish Gaul, Gallo-Romans of all kinds adopted Germanic, Frankish names.[41]

Given the small size of the sample and the lack of narrative information, it is a huge assumption from silence that only Goths were using Gothic names by *c.* AD 700. It is much more likely that the spread of Gothic names, certainly among the episcopate, and perhaps more generally among the elite, actually means that a general practice of using Gothic names was gaining wider currency. Neither shifting administrative patterns nor shifting naming patterns provide a strong indication that the Visigothic kingdom had come to be dominated by an elite of ethnic Goths. On the contrary, a wide variety of evidence suggests that what really emerged in the sixth and seventh centuries was an elite which called itself Gothic, but which was, in biological terms, a mixture of Goths and Hispano-Romans.

Down to the reign of Leovigild, intermarriage was formally banned, but, even in this period, one famous case is known: Theudis and his senatorial lady (p. 241).[42] After the removal of the ban, the lack of seventh-century narrative sources means that precise information is scanty. Even so, the inscription celebrating the Gothic descent of Sintiacus on his father's side, would imply that his maternal line was Hispano-Roman (p. 284). More generally, the law lifting the ban, envisaged intermarriage as an unexceptional event, already occurring on a substantial scale (*LV* 3.1). And 'Gothicness', it would seem, could be inherited from maternal as much as paternal lines. The late seventh-century King Erwig was the son of a renegade Byzantine, Artavasdus, and a Gothic mother, and yet succeeded to the throne.[43]

[41] Figures and ethnic analysis: Kampers, 1979, 160–1, 202ff, with refs (this study is an important prosopographical supplement to Garcia Moreno, 1974). Doubts: Claude, 1971, 112ff (with full listing of Goths with Roman names). Francia: e.g. Geary, 1985, 101–14 with refs.

[42] Thompson, 1969, 19 n.1 finds two other possible cases before Leovigild.

[43] Claude in *RgA* 7, 531ff.

Precise figures are unavailable, but Gothic and Roman elites probably intermarried freely between *c.*500 and *c.*700; if so, the seventh-century Visigothic elite was, in genetic terms, thoroughly mixed.

This genetic mixing was probably also matched by the full political integration of Hispano-Roman landowners into the public life of the kingdom. Although never quite as unstable as in the mid-sixth century, Visigothic politics from Leovigild onwards continued to exhibit a considerable capacity for violent upheaval. The seventh century saw the suppression of three minor kings (Liuva II (601–3), Reccared II (2 months of 621), and Tulga (639–42)), and numerous revolts. Some turned into successful seizures of the throne, others failed.[44] Leovigild himself dealt firmly with opponents, and his reputation was matched and surpassed by the mid-seventh-century king Chindaswinth (642–53). A Frankish chronicle reports that Chindaswinth put to death no less than 700 of his leading opponents (200 *primates Gotorum* and 500 *de mediogribus*: Fredegar 4.82). His son and successor, Reccesuinth, disassociated himself from his father's acts at the Eighth Council of Toledo in 653, and Bishop Eugenius of Toledo penned this charming epitaph:

> I Chindaswinth, ever the friend of evil deeds: committer of crimes Chindaswinth I, impious, obscene, ugly and wicked; not seeking the best, valuing the worst.

The upheavals of Chindaswinth's reign have sometimes been seen as marking the destruction of an old nobility based on inherited bloodlines and wealth, and its replacement by a new one more closely tied to royal office holding.[45] This, I suspect, is much too dramatic.

In such a context of extensive political conflict, allies among the landowning classes – all of whom had armed followings – are likely to have been valued, whatever their ethnic background. A case in point is again Claudius. In Reccared's reign, when conversion was being pushed through, we find him in Merida helping to put down a potential revolt by a group of Arians, composed, at least in part, of ethnic Goths. Among their number was Sunna, the Gothic Arian bishop of Merida, and a future Gothic King, Witteric (603–10) (p. 282). Thus at least

[44] Thanks to Julian of Toledo, we know much about the rebellion of the Septimanian *dux* Paulus, but other failed rebels, such as Indulf and Froila, are just names.

[45] For the details, see e.g. Thompson, 1969, 190ff; Collins, 1983, 108ff (esp. on Reccesuinth and Chindasuinth); Garcia Moreno, 1989, 161 ff. On the remodelling of the aristocracy, see e.g. Claude, 1971, 116–22.

one Gothic king found the support of an Hispano-Roman member of the elite quite invaluable against the machinations of some important Goths. Such a scenario probably repeated itself many times in the course of the sixth and seventh centuries. Violent political upheaval thus provided a further mechanism, beyond intermarriage, generating the integration of Roman and Goth.

The lifestyle and culture of this elite were also, in some senses, a mixture of Roman and non-Roman elements. Its general martial orientation represents a major break with the late Roman past, where elite young men had tended towards bureaucratic careers. One early medieval education manual, the *Institutionum Disciplinae* (usually thought to derive from the Visigothic kingdom), gives considerable space to the military training of elite youths, and refers in passing to the tales of the past which should also be passed on to them. The latter have occasioned much debate, and could have been as much Roman as Gothic in origin.[46] Military training, however, certainly affected the entire elite of the kingdom, and would have had great relevance for Hispano-Roman landowners required to lead military contingents in the service of their Gothic kings. In similar vein, a formula from the early seventh-century shows that it was by then standard for marriage arrangements to include a *morgengabe* consisting in part of weapons. The formula specifically characterizes the practice as 'Gothic'.[47]

Elite lifestyles owed quite as much, however, to Roman tradition. The marriage formula, for instance, was written in Latin verse and refers to the Goths as 'Getes' using a classicizing equation (cf. p. 13). A Latin Christianity, deriving from the Roman Empire, was also part and parcel of elite life. The *Institutionum Disciplinae* places as much emphasis on training in Christian Latin traditions as upon military exercises, for instance, and elite Christianity must be given due weight. An excellent illustration is king Sisebut. His reign saw much warfare, against both Byzantines and northern rebels. None the less, he had the time and interest to produce Latin hymns, and a lengthy verse epistle on eclipses, which shows him to have possessed a good knowledge of Lucretius and antique astronomical poetry. He also wrote much prose, including a saint's life and letters. His diplomatic letters, in particular, are striking for their Christian moralizing tone, and extensive Biblical echoes. As much recent work has rightly emphasized, sixth- and seventh-century kings and aristocrats, throughout the post-Roman

[46] On this text, see Riché, 1971.
[47] Form. Wis. 20 (ed. Gil, 1972, 90).

+PRECURSORDNIMARTIRBABTISTAIOHANNES
POSSIDECONSTRUCTAMINETERNOMUNERESEDE
QUAMDEUOTUSEGOREXRECCESUINTHUSAMATOR
NOMINISIPSETUIPROPRIODEIUREDICAUI
TERTIIPOSTDECMREGNICOMESINCLITUSANNO
SEXCENTUMDECIESERANONAGESIMANOBEM

Plates 26 and 27 The Visigothic Church of St Juan de Banos with Reccesuinth's building inscription

west, participated (no doubt to varying degrees) in a Christian Latin culture, which was a central influence on their lives.[48]

Many churches, likewise, were built by Visigothic nobles on their estates. Some of them even survive: St Juan de Banos, Quantanilla de la Vinas and San Fructuoso de Montelius (plate 27). Nor was it a clerical conspiracy, as used to be thought, to stress the religious role of kings in the seventh century. The Spanish episcopate represents no separate force in the kingdom, but was appointed from the kingdom's elite, and hence reflected its general cultural outlook.[49] Alongside its gifts of weapons to wives, the Visigothic elite took Christianity, and hence Latin too, very seriously.

The whole style of the Hispano-Visigothic monarchy, indeed, was deeply influenced by Roman example. Its court offices were in part descended directly from Roman ones, if in part non-Roman creations too. The offices of *comes spatariorum*, *comes patrimonii*, *comes cublicularium* and *comes notariorum* all have Roman ancestry others such as *comes armigri*, *comes stabuli*, and *comes scanciarum* arguably reflect old Gothic institutions. And, at least from the time of Leovigild onwards, royal ceremonial closely followed contemporary east Roman example. In the use of an elevated throne, in its vestments and in its symbols of authority, the Visigothic monarchy echoed Roman ceremonial forms. In addition, some of its practices were also Roman. Leovigild (at different moments) associated two of his sons with his rule in his own lifetime, an innovation for the Goths, but established practice for Romans. He also founded and named cities, another mode of behaviour with ancient precedents, one of which, Reccopolis, is under excavation. The site is Zorita de los Canes, some 30 miles east of Madrid. What has emerged (cf. figure 9.4) is a strongly Roman-style complex of buildings, where the palace, including an enormous pillared hall 135 long by 12 wide, is connected to the basilica.[50]

Material culture followed a similar pattern of development. Excavations of the *Reihengräber* cemeteries of the Meseta have shown that Gothic or Danubian dress customs were maintained by one group of their occupants down to the middle of the sixth century

[48] On Sisebut, see Fontaine, 1980; Collins, 1983, 67–9. His works are edited in Gil, 1972. See generally, e.g. Riché, 1976, chs 2, 4, 6, with, more recently McKitterick, 1991 (esp. papers by Collins and Wood).

[49] See in general, Collins, 1977, 1983; Linehan, 1993, ch. 2; Claude, 1971, 77ff, 108ff.

[50] See generally, Garcia Moreno, 1989, ch. 7; Claude, 1971, 59ff; King, 1972, chs 3–5. To Reccopolis, a good introduction is Ripoll, Lopez, 1994.

Plate 28 Leovigild's new town: Reccopolis

(chapter 7). From that period onwards, however, both dress styles and types of object and ornament buried with the dead came to reflect a particular variation on a common Christian, Mediterranean, Koine.[51] A similar picture emerges in a different way from Gothic Gaul: Septimania north of the Pyrenees. Up to *c.*500, this region was closely tied to the rest of Aquitaine. Local pottery and marble trades, for instance, distributed their goods throughout the region. In the sixth century, however, Septimania went its separate way. After *c.*500, inferior local marble was used for sarcophagi in place of better quality imports from what was now Frankish-held Aquitaine. Pottery

[51] See e.g. Bierbrauer, 1980, 1991; Ripoll Lopez, 1989, 1993–4; Kazanski, 1991, 101ff.

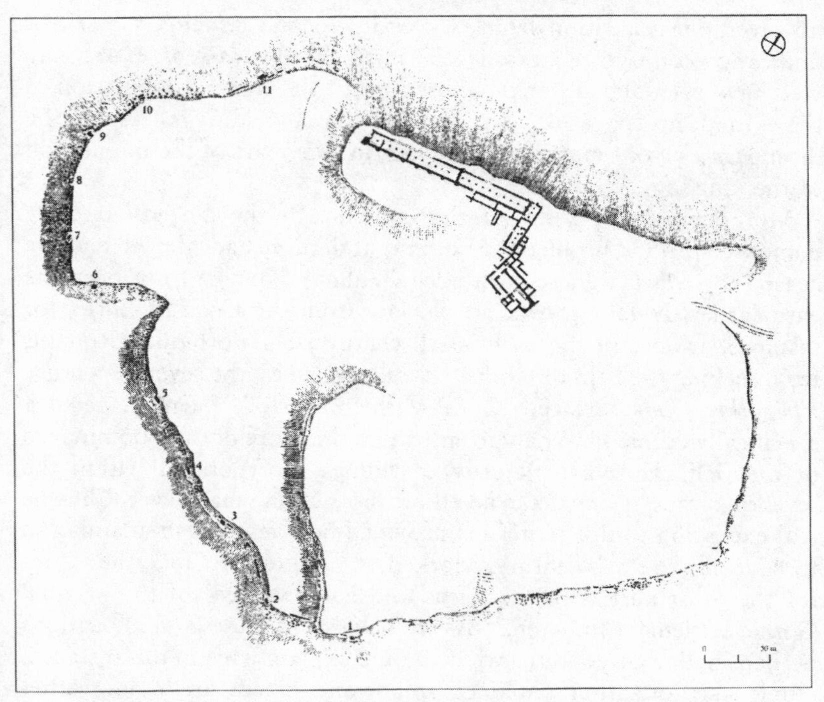

Figure 9.4 The palace and basilica at Reccopolis

distributions, likewise, came to reflect closely the new frontier between Frankish and Gothic Gaul. The archaeological remains of Septimania thus provide a striking illustration of how the new kingdom generated material cultural synthesis within its own borders.[52]

In legal terms too, old ethnic distinctions had disappeared within the kingdom by *c.* AD 700. Sometime in the middle of the seventh century, perhaps with the publication of Chindaswinth's code in 643/4, the *Breviary of Alaric* lost its validity. A pattern of two valid texts (the *Breviary* plus the *Code of Euric* and its successors), was replaced by one: the *Visigothic Code*. According to traditional interpretations, this transformation beautifully symbolized the new synthesis of Hispano-Roman and Goth. Separate personalized texts for Roman and Goth gave way to a unified body of law, as the kingdom's population itself united.[53] Even on my reading of the evidence,

[52] James, 1980, 1991.
[53] Date and (traditional) significance of the Code: e.g. King, 1980 (cf. King, 1972, ch. 1) drawing on a tradition going back to Zeumer, 1898–1901.

however, the transition from two codes to one remains a mark of unification, on two separate levels. First, the *Breviary of Alaric* may well have been aimed, for the most part, at the Roman population of the kingdom (p. 196), so that its passing did represent the disappearance of separate Roman law for one part of the population of the kingdom.

More important, some of the contents of the *Visigothic Code* demonstrate that problems of ethnic affiliation had almost entirely ceased to be a matter requiring legal rulings. This had not been the case earlier. In taking over an old law from the *Code of Euric*, for instance, which, in the early sixth century, had forbidden Romans from seeking the help of Goths to win legal cases, the seventh-century *Visigothic Code* replaced 'Goth' with 'powerful'.[54] Patronage of a specifically ethnic kind had given way to the more normal dominance of the rich. The vast majority of rulings incorporated within the seventh-century *Code* make no ethnic distinction whatsoever. The one real exception to this pattern is provided by a few laws remaining in force from the sixth century. Marked *antiqua* in the *Code*, they dealt for the most part with the terms and consequences of the original Gothic settlement in Spain.[55] As we have seen, these land allocations perhaps had tax-free status which would explain why, in this instance, ethnic categorization remained important. There are a few other instances of ethnic language in seventh-century laws, but in contexts so vague as to suggest it was employed merely for rhetorical flourish.[56] Otherwise, the *Visigothic Code* gives not the slightest hint that the seventh-century kingdom was composed of Goths and Romans with legally defined differences in rights and status. The really important thing was whether you were greater or lesser free, freedman or slave (e.g. LV 5.1.2).

Because of the 'shape', as it were, of the available source material, particularly the lack of detailed narrative sources, it cannot conclusively answer all our questions. And despite all the evidence for integration, it is not impossible that a disproportionate percentage of the 'Gothic' landowning elite of the seventh century were descended from Gothic immigrants from Aquitaine. An original ethnic difference could have transformed itself into a socio-economic one, for instance, through a determined land-grabbing exercise as the Goths entered Spain. To be able to assert this with any confidence,

54 Contrast *CE* 312 and *LV* 5.4.20; cf. Thompson, 1969, 124.
55 *LV* 10.1.8–9, 16; 10.2.1, 10.3.5.
56 *LV* 2.1.6; 3.1.6; 9.2.2.; 9.2.9.

however, we would need to know much more about individual family histories, and this information simply does not exist. Without the capacity to investigate the origins, land-holdings and marriages which produced the great men of the seventh century, we are forced back on evidence of a more general kind.

This, as we have seen, suggests a somewhat different picture. A Gothic rhetoric or ideology was maintained within the kingdom, reflected perhaps in naming patterns, as well as in self-definitions of the kingdom in formal contexts. Along with this went certain customs which were, or came to be thought of, as Gothic: *morgengabe* and the military training of elite youths. At the same time, the monarchical institutions and ideologies of the kingdom echoed late Roman and Byzantine norms, and elite culture was as much Latin and Christian as martial and Gothic. Intermarriage could occur freely after *c.*575, and chronically turbulent politics meant that kings and would-be kings were always in need of support. It thus seems most unlikely that a stable oligarchy of landowners of Gothic descent held tight control of the kingdom. Rather, the landowning class of the peninsula – a mixture of migrant Goths and indigenous Romans – had fought and married its way to unity and synthesis under a Gothic flag of convenience.

The sixth and seventh centuries thus saw the destruction of the Goths as they had existed in the fourth and fifth centuries. In Italy, this came about by outside force of arms, in Spain by the total transformation of the immigrant Goths. The Goths *par excellence* of the Migration Period were a particular and distinct caste within Gothic migrant groups, who shared important legal and political rights, and a determination to preserve their independence, especially in the face of Roman power. In Italy, the Byzantines had destroyed this caste by *c.*560. In Spain, all of its apparatus of ethnicity had disappeared by *c.*700. A separate Gothic language and religion had been dealt a death blow by the Third Council of Toledo in 587, but was anyway under pressure. Two Gothic Arian bishops signed their names there in Latinized forms, for instance, suggesting that Latin was already their main language, and Gothic Catholics are known from well before 587.[57] Above all, the equality and unity of the Gothic freeman caste had disappeared, most likely destroyed in the land-grabbing which

[57] Bishops Ubiligisclus (Willegisel) of Valencia and Froisclus (Frawigisel) of Tortosa: Schaferdiek, 1967, 161 n.97. The Catholic Goth Glismoda is attested as early as 455: Schaferdiek, 1967, 10ff.

marked the Goths' entry into Spain. The Gothic kingdom of *c.*700 no longer comprised an inner core of ethnically defined migrants. It was a unified state which defined itself as Gothic, not by reference to a Roman stratum within its own population, but against outsiders: the Franks of Gaul and the Romans of Constantinople.

10

Symbols, Mechanisms and Continuities

Gothic ethnicity incorporates a whole series of issues. How powerful an influence did Gothic identity exercise upon individuals within Gothic groups? To what degree was it shared by all the members of such groups? And what combinations of shared past experience and commonalities of current practice ('myth/symbol complex': p. 5) were used to comprehend and express a sense of difference? We are posing these questions, of course, of socio-political entities, who, between them, enjoyed a dramatic history lasting the best part of 700 years. There is every reason to suppose *a priori*, therefore, that Gothic identity and its modes of expression will not have gone unchanged. And although the Goths are in many ways the best documented Germanic group of the late Roman and Migration Periods, there are still many gaps in the evidence.

A. The 'Spread' of Gothic Identity

The foundation of my thinking on this subject is provided by Procopius of Caesarea in his *Gothic Wars*. This, it seems to me, shows the continued existence and active political involvement of a substantial social group within the immigrants who followed Theoderic to Italy. The elite of 'notables', who constituted a distinct and dominant caste within the population, should clearly be numbered in thousands, and perhaps comprised somewhere between one fifth and one half of the total male population. There are thus too many of them for us to translate 'notable' as 'noble', and Procopius' narrative picks out no other defined elite among the Goths. Comparing this evidence with other, more or less contemporary, indications, Procopius is probably documenting the survival and continued influence of a Gothic freeman class in the Italian kingdom (App. 1).

This leads me to stand apart, to some extent, from current scholarly thinking on the nature of social development and ethnic identity among the Goths between the fourth and the sixth centuries. Internal Gothic political activity centred on generating and maintaining consensus among this caste of freemen. One can see this in Procopius' narrative, and it also emerges from other well-informed sources, such as Ammianus (p. 57), who consistently show the constraints operating on Gothic leaders between the fourth and sixth centuries. I hesitate, therefore, to follow the chronology suggested by E.A. Thompson, in a series of studies, for the emergence of a dominant Gothic nobility. He considered this to have happened by the fourth century.[1] There clearly were substantial differences of wealth and social influence within the freemen class at all points between the fourth and sixth centuries. None the less, the critical break in its unity should, to my mind, be situated, in Visigothic Spain at least, between the sixth and seventh centuries, when the freeman class was subdivided in formal, legal, terms into higher and lower grades with different rights (chapter 9).

In similar vein, I would argue that the existence and range of activities of this group makes it most unlikely that Gothic identity, even in the sixth century, was the product of anything other than its self-perceptions. Again, this leads me to postulate a vision of Gothic identity which differs significantly, but not totally, from the influential definition generated by Wenskus, and followed by Wolfram, of the Gothic *Traditionskern*. For Wenskus, Gothic identity was carried essentially by a relatively few ('how many' is a question never really addressed) noble or royal clans, and the traditions surrounding them. Wenskus developed this view in necessary reaction to romantic nineteenth-century visions of free Germanic tribesmen opposing themselves to the oppressive imperialism of Rome.[2] The main evidence in favour of it, however, is provided by later dynastic propaganda. In particular, the propaganda of the Amal family

[1] Especially Thompson 1963, 1966.
[2] Wenskus, 1961; Wolfram, 1988.

preserved in Jordanes' *Getica* and Cassiodorus' *Variae* portrays the dynasty as a uniquely royal house which had ruled Goths for centuries. As we have seen, however, it is an odd mixture of Gothic and classicizing materials, and its correspondence to historical reality extremely limited.

The Amal family first rose to prominence in *c.*450, there is no good evidence that members of it had ever before ruled large numbers of Goths. Its last representative was also unceremoniously dumped upon failing to provide effective leadership in the war against Belisarius. The history of the Visigothic Balth dynasty is not dissimilar, so that such royal clans do not, it seems to me, provide pillars of sufficient strength upon which to rest Gothic identity. Just as political participation remained more communal than Thompson suggested, so, I would argue, did the generation of Gothic ethnic identity. Both were centred on the same group within Gothic society: the caste of freemen.

This is not, I must emphasize, a return to the nineteenth-century view of Germanic groups. In my view, the caste of freemen was itself a dominant and restricted social elite: a minority, but not a tiny one, within the total adult male population of groups calling themselves Gothic. Even before the arrival of the Huns, political enfranchisement in the fourth-century Gothic kingdoms was not shared in equally by the totality of the population. Former Roman prisoners clearly remained a distinct underclass, and the same may have been true of other groups, such as Dacians and Sarmatians, who had fallen under the sway of Gothic immigrants in the third century (chapter 3). Identifying the freemen group as the peculiar carriers of 'Gothicness' in the Migration-Period, defines an intermediate position between nineteenth-century visions, which seem too broad, and more modern ones, which seem too restrictive. This wider vision of ethnic participation still leaves plenty of room for envisaging an underclass, with more restricted rights, who actually composed the majority of the population of migrant groups. For the sixth century, as we have seen, Procopius provides some interesting indications of the lower level of political commitment which existed among them. When all the 'notables' of Dalmatia were killed in battle, the rest of its Gothic population simply surrendered (p. 273). The Visigothic (and other) legal evidence would suggest that there were at least two, ranked, subordinate social categories – slave and freed – beneath that of the freemen. These categories appear only in later (sixth – and seventh-century) sources, but probably give us insight into the general nature of social subordination among Germanic groups of the late Roman period.

I would also simply echo some of the revisionist points made by Wenskus and Wolfram. Membership of the elite caste was, on a number of levels, clearly not fixed. Although we lack explicit examples of this for the Goths, it is extremely likely that individuals of lower status, or groups of them, could acquire freedom, together with full social and political enfranchisement. The former Roman prisoners, or their descendants, among the fourth-century Gothic kingdoms seem to have been half way towards such an assimilation. Although still a distinguishable group, who, to judge by Ulfila, continued to use Latin and Greek, they also spoke Gothic, and those who fled south of the Danube with Ulfila in 347/8 did not fit back easily into mainstream Roman society (chapter 3).

It was also possible for individuals and groups to join Gothic units in other than the subordinate ranks of slave and freed. We hear of Alans and Huns among the Visigoths, for instance, and of semi-autonomous Rugi within the Ostrogoths. Similarly, in the course of Totila's campaigns, many units of the east Roman army chose to attach themselves to the Goths (App. 2). The question in all these cases is the degree of attachment involved. Did these groups became fully enfranchised Goths, or were they merely thought of as allies?

Certain individuals clearly made a total transition. Of the deserters, Procopius subsequently characterizes Indulf and Coccas as belonging to the caste of Gothic notables.[3] Likewise, the Rugi, even if they had refused to intermarry with the rest of the Goths, did put forward Eraric, at one point, as a candidate for the overall leadership of the Ostrogoths. Their political assimilation, at least, would seem pretty complete. But this is not true of all the non-Gothic groups we find among the Visigoths and Ostrogoths. If the Huns who followed Athaulf to Italy in 408 really had been operating with the Goths since autumn 377, as I suspect (pp. 175f), then they too are likely to have been fully integrated. On the other hand, Narses espoused a policy of deliberate generosity towards deserters from the east Roman army. Many of those who had joined Totila subsequently returned to their former allegiance. Likewise, some Alans moved in and out of Athaulf's following in Gaul in the early 410s (Paulinus *Euch.* 379–85).

A balance has to be maintained. Gothic royal dynasties were much more ephemeral than their propaganda liked to pretend. This, combined with the existence of a relatively large enfranchised class,

[3] App. 2; the same may also be true of Ragnaris, described by Agathias as a Bittigure Hun (2.13.3), but it is unclear whether he had only recently joined the Goths when he is first mentioned in the early 550s.

suggests that Gothic identity was associated with a substantial group among the population, not a very restricted minority. On the other hand, the freeman class was itself a minority, and not absolutely exclusive in membership. Individuals and groups from subordinate levels (freed and slave) could be promoted to freedom and full membership, and outsiders integrated. The conditions leading to such developments are unfortunately obscure, but the aims of the particular individuals, their length of involvement, loyalty, intermarriage and extent of any outside threat were probably among the crucial variables. It was the threat of extinction at the hands of the east Romans, for instance, which prompted Totila's generosity towards Roman deserters. But processes of integration, particularly full integration, did not always operate. Many of those who followed Theoderic to Italy remained in only subordinate social positions within the Ostrogoths.

B. *The Strength of Gothic Identity*

If the social extent of Gothic identity can be pinned down to the caste of freemen, the strength of its hold over individuals is harder to gauge. Of the Gothic entities of the first and second centuries in northern Poland, we know little. This was a world, as we have seen, of small units, endemic political realignment, and overlapping identities. Primary political affiliations existed alongside cult leagues, and, as we have seen, the peculiarities of the Wielbark culture suggest that its boundaries may reflect the extent of one such league. Even if Goths formed a single, discrete unit in this period, which is not certain, it seems unlikely that inherited Gothic identity was a major factor shaping the lives of individual members of the group.

By the fourth century, much had changed. To judge by the Tervingi, at least, a paradoxical pattern of development had occurred. In migrating to lands north of the Black Sea, the Goths had fragmented politically into a number of separate kingdoms, perhaps as many as a half dozen or more. At the same time, Gothic identity, although now the preserve of only a minority, had become more aggressively self-assertive. The Tervingi had a strong sense of their own territory, manifested in Athanaric's determination to make Valens recognize the boundaries of his kingdom. They likewise tried to assert a sense of religious solidarity around their own traditional cults, identifying Christianity as an alien intrusion from the Roman Empire. While in many senses a client state of the Empire, they resisted the more overt symbols of its domination, and, at times, even succeeded in asserting a less unequal relationship (chapter 3).

The Tervingi, of course, were gathered around a particular dynasty, and there is always a potential gap between the aims and views of leaders and led. Certainly, the led would seem to have been less hostile than their leaders to Christianity. None the less, fourth-century Gothic monarchs could not, as Athanaric's eventual fate shows, operate without support among their followers, so that a general willingness on the part of the latter to resist Roman domination seems manifest. Indeed, many recent studies of ethnicity have stressed the extent to which identity is actually forged in conflict.[4] The Goths, it would seem, provide another example of this phenomenon. Faced with the power of the Roman state, the new Gothic kingdoms of the Pontic littoral defined themselves more strongly and operated more aggressively, in comparison to their first- and second-century ancestors.

The subsequent period of Hunnic domination saw further transformations. Conflict became still more intense. Goths had to fight both Huns and the Roman state to preserve their autonomy. In the process, one Gothic political order was destroyed and a new one created. The Huns conquered or displaced the Gothic elites who had generated the fourth century kingdoms, and some of the latter reformed themselves to create two new supergroups: the Visigoths and Ostrogoths (Part 2). An already fairly powerful sense of Gothic identity was reinforced in these further conflicts. Other options, of course, were still available. At different moments in the fourth and fifth centuries, various Gothic individuals made their way in the world as Roman generals, and whole Gothic groups as bodies of allied Roman soldiery. Among the latter, the defeated supporters of Radagaisus drafted into the Roman army by Stilicho and the Gothic *foederati* of the eastern Empire, who revolted on Aspar's assassination in 471, stand out as particularly numerous examples. For most Goths, however, consonant with what we have observed of the fourth-century kingdoms, a desire for independence eventually won out over the financial and other blandishments of serving the Roman Empire. Most of the individuals known to have become officers of the imperial army were defeated candidates for the overall leaderships of the new Gothic supergroups (or their associates). These men had been driven from Gothic society by the possible consequences of feud (p. 143). Likewise, the two largest known bodies of allied Gothic troops in the

[4] E.g. Smith, 1981, 1986.

Roman army eventually chose to attach themselves to the new Gothic supergroups. Stilicho's allies joined Alaric because their families were attacked, clearly a negative response to Roman power. Aspar's allies attached themselves to Theoderic, partly to circumvent Zeno's policy of divide and rule, and partly because, operating with other Goths, they could achieve a better outcome for themselves. Once again, the importance of Roman power in the creation of a Gothic sense of identity could hardly be clearer.

The longer-term history of Visigothic Spain underlines still further its importance. In the absence of any Roman threat, Gothicness came to be redefined there in relation to landowning. As far as we can tell, this new definition broke up the unity of the freeman class of the Migration Period. The descendants of some Gothic freemen were demoted to second-class status, and those of some Roman landowners were included among the new elite. There is much evidence that substantial differences in wealth had existed from at least the fourth century. None the less, the free class would appear to have preserved its unity into the sixth century, not least as a vehicle to ensure the survival of its members' political independence in the face of the Roman state. Once the threat of Rome disappeared, economic logic replaced political logic, as it were, and the richer members of the freeman class – their wealth translated into land – made common cause with their local Gallo- or Hispano-Roman counterparts (chapter 9).

I would stress, however, that this was the longer term. Initial steps along the same path were also taken in Ostrogothic Italy. But when Belisarius' army arrived, 40 years after Theoderic's forces had conquered the peninsula, the Gothic freeman class remained identifiable and politically dominant. The war was carried on essentially by this group, and ended when its will to resist had been broken. Forty years is not quite two generations, so that this is perhaps not too surprising. The unity of Visigothic freemen is likely to have lasted at least that long.[5]

The new Gothicness of the seventh-century Visigothic kingdom was itself no weak force. By the last quarter of the sixth century, it had generated a material cultural unity throughout the kingdom, as Gothic modes of female burial dress were abandoned. In this case, the new unity echoed general Mediterranean norms, so that this is not

[5] In some senses, the differences between my views and those of Thompson, and Wenskus and Wolfram relate to the chronology of social processes, rather than to the processes themselves.

particularly impressive evidence of a new, clearly defined, 'Visigothicness'. In similar vein, Catholic Christianity and elements of Latin culture combined to create a new spirituality which united kings and nobles as much as churchmen. Again, this was a variation on a general post-Roman norm in the west, rather than something individual to the Iberian Visigoths. Perhaps above all, then, the kingdom generated a political unity within the peninsula. Again, this was not without caveats, since the central structures of the kingdom existed alongside locally dominant lords. None the less, the peninsula had never before operated as a unitary state, and it successfully generated a material cultural unity between its possessions in Septimania, north of the Pyrenees, and the rest of its holdings south of them. The achievement of sixth-century Visigothic kings in making local elites take notice of, and indeed direct their political lives around, the court at Toledo, should not be underestimated.

The narrative of Gothic political action between the third and seventh centuries suggests, then, that Gothicness operated as a powerful force in two different contexts. Individuals in the fourth and fifth centuries had to unite to survive, especially in the face of Roman power. Once that threat disappeared, old unities broke down in Spain, and new processes set in. Roman landowners desired to be numbered among the elite of the kingdom, and the body politic needed to include all, or most, of the locally powerful figures within it to create internal unity and guarantee frontier security. Between them, these forces generated a new 'Gothic' landowning elite, composed of the descendants not only of Gothic immigrants, but also (it seems) of many Hispano-Romans.

A picture of a significant, very pragmatic, Gothicness can thus be built up from the narrative of political events. Some inherited senses of identity, however, constrain the individual to act beyond the pragmatic. They are too powerful to be easily manipulable towards those ends which, by straightforward material calculation, would appear the most desirable. Once strong senses of identity exist, individuals can be forced to act in certain ways *because* they exist (chapter 1). Is there any evidence that Gothicness in this period ever went beyond the manipulable, a force of sufficient power to constrain individual choice away from the materially pragmatic?

This is an extremely difficult question. Even in modern case studies, with access to detailed first-hand accounts of personal experience, the conclusions of anthropologists differ radically over what significance to accord ethnic identity as a force shaping individual action. With the sources at our disposal, no conclusive argument for the Goths is possible. There is just about enough, and I would not want to press matters further, to suggest that, in certain instances, Gothicness may have been sufficiently powerful to have lain beyond individual pragmatic manipulation.

To start with, there is the general point that most of the main contributors to the new supergroups of the Migration Period – the Visigoths and Ostrogoths – would seem to have been Gothic (chapter 6). This point would not go undisputed by others, and Gothicness was certainly not exclusive. None the less, this pattern does suggest that, when forming voluntary relationships, groups deriving in some way from the fourth-century Gothic kingdoms were more likely to operate with one another than with others. We might also consider Gothic reactions to the other main attractive option open to them in the Migration Period: military service for the Roman state (being part of the Hunnic Empire was an involuntary and unattractive option). At different points, various Gothic groups served the Roman state as allied, semi-autonomous, groups within the Roman army: the Tervingi and Greuthungi after 382; some of the followers of Radagaisus after 405/6; the Thracian Gothic *foederati* in the middle of the fifth century. Conditions varied, and some of these groups served for longer than others. The Thracian Goths may have served Constantinople for two generations (p. 127). The vast majority of individuals within these categories eventually preferred a 'Gothic option', however, rather than to continue in Roman service. Why they did so is arguable. Some, particularly Radagaisus' ex-followers, were forced out by the massacres which followed Stilicho's fall from power. Likewise, the Thracian Goths may have felt that the rise of the Isaurians reduced the likely profitability of continued service. On the other hand, a straightforward assertion of Gothicness might also have been attractive, especially in the case of the Thracian Goths for whom the possibility now existed of uniting with the Pannonian Goths to create a much more powerful grouping.

Moreover, having taken possession of Italy, these Goths, on the whole, were ready to die to keep it. Theoderic erected, as we have seen, a façade of *Romanitas*, and some Goths were ready to surrender quickly and easily to Justinian's forces. Most, however, fought long and hard, and were not ready to accept the option, readily available in 540, of abandoning political sovereignty in return for keeping their Italian estates. They preferred to continue fighting, even though the Byzantines were willing to acknowledge most of the Goths' economic gains (chapter 9). This pattern of events makes it at least possible that group pride and solidarity operated among the Italian Goths of the freeman caste in ways that went beyond straightforward material calculation. The four, seemingly small-scale and hopeless, revolts against Reccared, occasioned by his conversion of the Visigothic kingdom to Catholicism (pp. 282f), might also fall into the same category.

A similar conclusion is suggested by one or two other, smaller-scale pieces of action. In 479, a Goth called Sidimund threw over a well-established career in the east Roman Empire, to cast in his lot with Theoderic the Amal, who, at that point, was in a far from secure position. Sidimund had investigated a Roman option, and even prospered by it – he had been granted estates in the region of Epidamnus – but eventually decided to assert his Gothicness (p. 161). One could balance Sidimund's choices with those of other Goths, who became Roman generals, and even, like Sarus or a certain Veteric (if he was a Goth), fought against their compatriots.[6] But many of the latter were, as we have seen, defeated candidates for the leadership of the Goths, who became Romans because it was no longer possible for them to remain Goths.

One final incident illustrates the difficulties involved in estimating the strength of Gothic ethnicity. Late in 400 or early 401, Gainas, a Roman general of Gothic origin realized that there was no further place for him in the political establishment of the eastern Empire. He decided, as a last resort, to seek his fortune north of the Danube. Before leaving Roman territory, his Gothic followers killed the general's remaining Roman supporters. This is a perplexing incident. Gainas himself would clearly have preferred to be Roman, but no longer could be. His followers were perhaps less committed to that line, since they could presumably have negotiated their way towards a rapprochement with Constantinople, and did not have to flee, especially, for instance, if they had handed over their leader. The Romans, it seems, were suspected of harbouring such designs, and that is why they were killed. In these particular (and very dire) circumstances, Romans threatened group solidarity, and Goths preferred to stick together.[7]

When sources are few and the questions complicated, historical argument tends to come to rest at the point where matters are beyond dispute. This can generate a tendency to disregard the different

[6] Respectively *PLRE* 2, 978–9, 1157.
[7] Zosimus 5.21.6: these 'barbarians' were perhaps the survivors of the Greuthungi led to the Danube by Odotheus in 386, and into revolt by Tribigild in 399: ch. 4.

possibilities that the evidence leaves open. The fact that you cannot *prove* that Gothic ethnicity constrained individual choice, at least among the elite freeman caste, is hardly surprising and essentially meaningless. Given the general lack of first-hand biographical information available, it could hardly be otherwise. The fact that some of the surviving information makes it *possible* that Gothic ethnicity might have been a real constraint is, in context, well worth pointing out. The lowest common denominator, the point at which no one disagrees, is the easiest point for an argument to come to rest, but can nevertheless be misleading. In the case of the Goths, I would argue that the sources provide many hints that 'Gothicness' was a more powerful force than the absolute minimum required to explain most of the sequences of events in which we know that Goths were involved.

C. *Symbols and Mechanisms*

Matters become even more difficult when it comes to the symbols by which Gothic ethnicity may have been expressed. What peculiarities, if any, of practice and custom made a Goth distinctive at any given time? Two points of reference must be kept in mind. First, there is no reason to suppose that the same symbols will have been used in every period where our sources report the existence of Goths. We do not have to find unchanging cultural constants to prove the existence of Goths as a historically continuous entity. Secondly – the reason why this is so – it is the reaction of individuals to such peculiarities, not the items themselves, that are important. Identity is an internal attitude of mind which may express itself through objects, norms or particular ways of doing things. These may be more or less consciously used as symbols, and, as circumstances change, unconscious symbols can evolve into conscious ones. But, in all cases, symbols are the *result* and not the *cause* of any sense of separate identity. Particularities can symbolize and express identity, but identity cannot be reduced to a process of listing differences between groups. In some contexts, differences can even disappear, but a sense of separateness remains (chapter 1).

For the earliest period where Goths are known to have existed, the southern shores of the Baltic Sea in the first and second centuries, we have nothing but archaeological evidence. The population of the Wielbark culture was distinctive in two kinds of ways: burial rituals and female dress (chapter 2). While certainly distinctive, these practices probably did not distinguish Goths *per se*, since Goths were only one element of the population within the area covered by the Wielbark culture. This is not to say, of course, that a more particular Gothicness was not expressed in some other way, which we cannot now read.

The archaeological evidence for the Migration Period and successor states throws up more possible symbols of Gothic ethnicity. The Černjachov culture maintained, if to a lesser degree, the Wielbark tendency to produce bi-ritual cemeteries. But burial practice may well have been changing generally towards inhumation, and the subject awaits detailed study. Weapons too, for the most part, were still not buried with Gothic dead, neither in southern Russia, nor in the successor states, in so far, at least, as Gothic burials have been identified in Spain and Italy. These practices may thus have been, or became, emblematic of Gothicness,[8] but there is too much still to be learned, especially about practices in fifth-century Aquitaine, to say anything very conclusive.

Other features of the archaeological remains may provide further clues. The distribution of combs in fourth-century Černjachov remains is very interesting. They do not seem to have been a feature of earlier archaeological cultures on the fringes of the Carpathians, but are frequently found in Černjachov burials.[9] Hair styles were sometimes emblematic among Germanic groups, the Suevic knot being a famous example (Tacitus *Germania* 38). This suggests, especially given the interesting evidence for Černjachov comb production (see below), that combs themselves might have been important symbols. The use of certain types of pendant also seems to have transferred itself from northern Poland to the shores of the Black Sea in the train of Wielbark expansion.

Female clothing styles, likewise, may have carried significance. As we have seen, a distinctive Wielbark habit of using two brooches is also found among Černjachov populations. This transferred itself more generally to Germanic groups subject to Hunnic domination in the so-called Danubian style of the fifth century. In the Hunnic Empire, therefore, two brooches were employed too generally to signify anything very specific. The evidence from Visigothic Spain, however, is another matter. From the last two decades of the fifth century, for the best part of another 100 years, a minority of the population in certain areas of the north of the peninsula chose to bury their female dead in the Germanic, Danubian style. Although it is not

[8] The line adopted in various studies by Bierbrauer, e.g. 1991.
[9] Heather and Matthews, 1991, 94.

absolutely certain, there is a good chance that this minority was composed of immigrant Goths and their descendants (chapter 7). If not specific compared to other fifth-century Germanic groups, this style of female dress certainly was specific compared to Hispano-Roman dress modes. The new element in the elite of the peninsula may well have chosen to assert their Gothic origin in clothing – if only for such ceremonial purposes as burial – because belonging to the immigrant group was the source of their claim to landed wealth and social prominence.

In Ostrogothic Italy, something of the same may also have been true, but the archaeological evidence for displayed difference is much less striking. In all, only 126 burials have been found with any kind of Gothic association, and there are no Italian *Reihengräber* cemeteries.[10] There may be a reason for this. A relative lack of ethnic assertion would be in tune with Theoderic's self-presentation of his rule as the Roman Empire continued, and one of the *Variae* expressly ordered Theoderic's officers to reclaim valuables buried with the dead (*Variae* 4.34). The order was justified on the grounds of utility, but this may not have Theoderic's real motivation. Dress remained important among the Italian Goths as an expression of status. The competitive dressing of the wives of Ildebadus and Urais, for instance, is said to have led their husbands into mutually destructive conflict (Procopius *Wars* 7.1.40). This being so, Theoderic's order was perhaps designed to undercut the competitive displays of some of his grander subordinates (cf. p. 239). Whether dress also functioned as a symbol of ethnicity in Italy is less clear.

At different moments, then, a case can be made for seeing a variety of customs or objects as markers of Gothic ethnicity. All apply only to specific contexts, and this is what we should expect. The idea that there should be one concrete item or custom performing this job throughout the time and space of Gothic history is a misunderstanding of how symbols work. It is an expectation based firmly on old conceptions of ethnicity as an unchanging constant. A good final illustration of this is provided by a recent study of eagle brooches (*fibulae*, found occasionally in Ostrogothic Italy, and more commonly in the probable Gothic remains of the Spanish kingdom). Made of gold and inlaid with semi-precious stones, they are one of the richest individual items buried with the dead, and surely must have been used to express elite status. They are the product of an adaptation of other ways of using the eagle to the brooch form which occurred in the fifth

10 Bierbrauer, 1975.

century. The eagle was a symbol of power among both Romans and Huns, but there is no sign that it had ever previously been an important symbol to Goths. Hence, the emergence of such brooches as a symbol of power among the Goths, it has been argued, may reflect the influence upon them of Huns and Romans.[11] This is perfectly likely, if in the end unproveable. Primarily, however, the argument underlines the point that, according to the influences exerted on a population group, its chosen symbols will indeed change.

The archaeological evidence raises one further issue of importance. If items such as brooches or combs were symbolic, how were they manufactured and distributed? Royal or communal control of important symbolic items would imply very different pictures of the dynamics of ethnicity. Could kings, for instance, influence ethnicity by picking and choosing who was to receive the crucial items? High status items, such as eagle *fibulae*, surely were made in a few workshops, probably under royal control. Annual military musters for the distribution of rewards seem to have been a regular feature of Gothic life, and provide an obvious context for their distribution.[12] Likewise, the finds at Bîrlad Valea-Seacă, of at least sixteen comb-makers' huts (p. 81), suggest that comb production was also centralized within Černjachov lands. Again, especially if combs were symbols, this production centre may also have been under royal control.

But it would be rash to conclude from these finds that ethnicity as a whole was under royal control, that Gothic kings could make anyone a Goth by giving them the key items. The example of the eagle brooches makes the point well. These were very probably royal gifts, and equally probably marked a claim to high status. They were worn, however, as a pair on each shoulder, in line with a norm of female dress style, which went back to the first century among Gothic and other Wielbark groups. By such gifts, kings could exercise enormous influence, especially over relative status within the group, but the form of the gift, a pair of fine brooches, was dictated by an ancient norm. Brooches are as much evidence for the importance of inherited communal norms, therefore, as they are for that of royal influence.

Between the fourth and seventh centuries, other possible symbols of Gothic ethnicity are suggested by the literary sources. The most obvious and much discussed of these is the so-called Arian form of

11 Greene, 1987.

12 Narses displayed 'bracelets, necklaces, and gold bracelets' as potential rewards to his troops before the battle of Busta Gallorum to encourage them to fight harder: *Wars* 8.31.8–9.

Christianity which was characteristic of Goths of both kinds in western Europe in AD 500. As we have seen, the leaders of the Tervingi seem to have espoused it as they crossed the Danube in 376, because it was, at that point, the brand of Christianity favoured by the Emperor Valens. It was also consonant with the teachings of Ulfila, missionary to the Goths in the 340s, and translator of the Bible into Gothic. Here again, the pattern is interesting. There was nothing specifically Gothic about Ulfila's teachings, the religious doctrine the Goths adopted from 376. Ulfila taught that the Son was 'like', rather than 'of one substance with', the Father. The latter definition, put forward at the Council of Nicaea in 325, eventually became the hallmark of Catholic orthodoxy. 'Likeness' was one of a number of old established positions, however, which had previously been acceptable, rather than some radical new heresy.[13] In 376, then, the Goths adopted an established form of Roman Christianity as part of their attempt to persuade a Roman Emperor to admit them into the Empire.

Soon after 376, however, the eastern half of the Empire joined the west in definitively adopting the Nicene definition of faith. Although the Goths had become Christians, it seems, to please a Roman Emperor, they did not follow suit. Instead, they held to Ulfila's teachings, which became, over time, increasingly a distinctive cultural feature of Goths (although Roman 'Arians' continued to exist well into the fifth century). In the sixth century, Italian papyri refer to the Goths' non-Nicene Christianity as *lex Gothorum* – the law of the Goths – and the Visigothic king Amalaric seems to have caused a diplomatic incident by demanding that his Catholic Frankish wife convert (pp. 245, 277). The Goths' brand of religion was in origin an entirely Roman phenomenon, and, by its nature, could never separate itself completely from the Roman culture in which it had been born. Ulfila's Gothic translation was made from a standard Greek Bible of the fourth century. Later on, it was reworked, probably in the fifth century, against the Latin Biblical texts with which Goths had now come into contact. The effects of this are particularly evident in the Epistles, which (rather than the Gospels) were the battleground of theological argument.[14] Likewise, the Goths did not separate themselves from the rest of Christian history. The same writing

[13] It was condemned by Nicenes primarily because it did not exclude more radical Arian positions: see Heather and Matthews, 1991, ch. 5 with refs.

[14] Friedrichsen, 1926 pt. A, 1939 pt. 4.

Plate 29 A sixth-century Italian bookmaster at work (the Codex Amiatinus *of c. AD 700, after an earlier Italian original)*

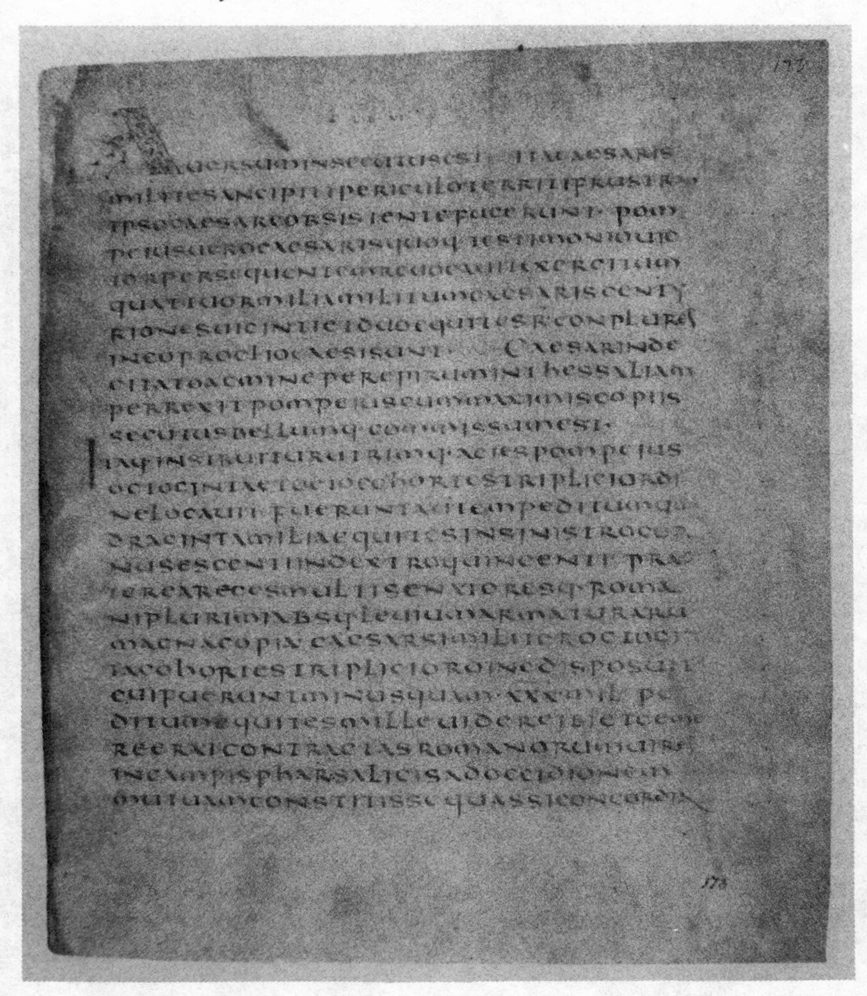

Plate 30 Viliaric's manuscript of the church historian Orosius

office, attached to the Theoderic's Arian cathedral of St Anastasius in Ravenna, which produced the great Gothic biblical masterpiece of the *Codex Argenteus*, also produced a beautiful Latin manuscript of Orosius' account of the unfolding of God's providence in history.[15] Ulfila's brand of Christianity operated as a distinctive mark of Gothicness, only in a context where Goths were living alongside Romans who generally held to Nicaea.

15 Tjäder, 1972.

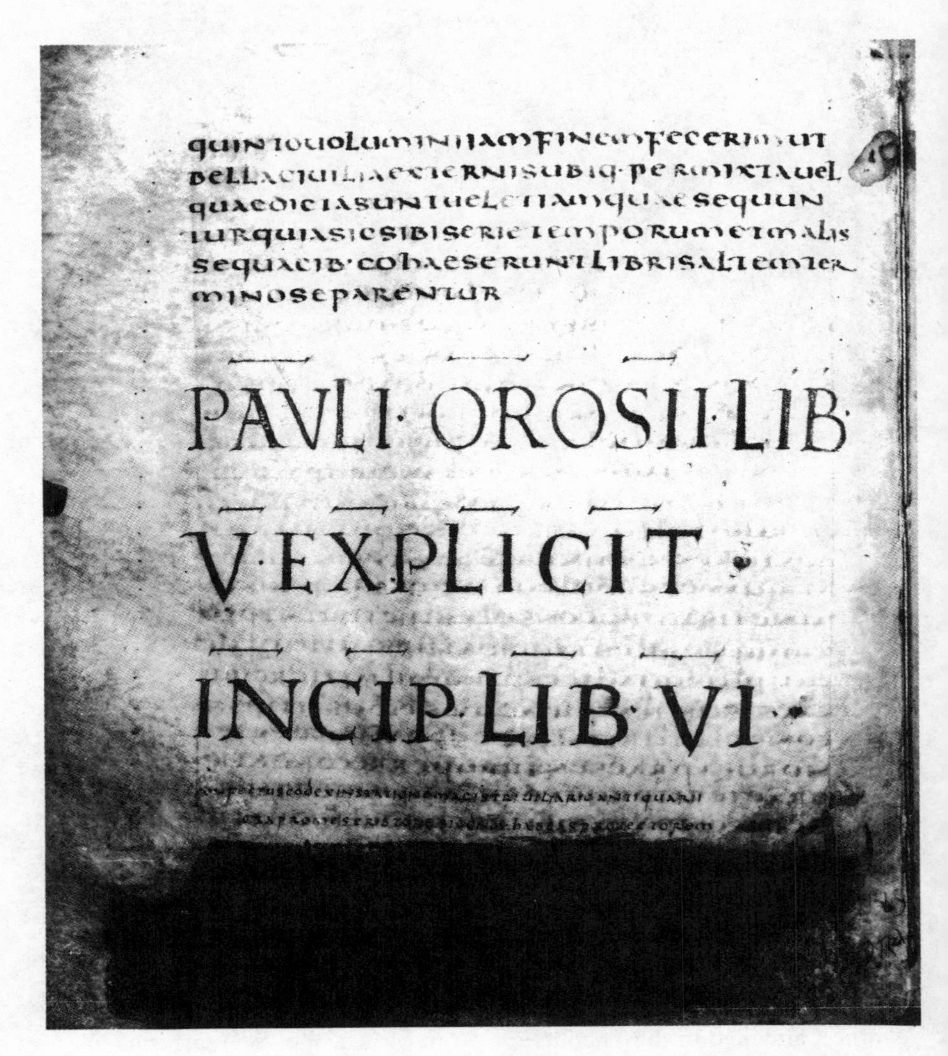
PAVLI· OROSII· LIB
V· EXPLICIT
INCIP· LIB· VI·

Plate 31 Viliaric's signature in Latin from the Orosius manuscript (compare plate 21)

This process of development nicely illustrates two things. First, the way in which ethnic symbols are specific to particular contexts. And, secondly, how an underlying sense of difference will find expression, even when profound cultural exchange – such as that necessary to improve one's text of the Bible and knowledge of

Christian history – was unavoidable. If the Goths had crossed the Danube slightly later, in the reign of Theodosius, and hence adopted Catholic Christianity, symbols of difference other than Arianism would have emerged to express the socio-political distinctiveness of, and conflict between, Roman and Goth.

The sources also suggest, appropriate to different contexts, other possible symbols. Religion, for instance, had been deliberately used as a symbol even before the Goths entered the Roman Empire. The non-Christian leaders of the Tervingi periodically persecuted Christians among them, and demanded public acts of conformity to the ways of traditional Gothic religion. They did this because Christianity was identified with the Roman state (chapter 3). The Goths' distinctive Christianity built on a history of using religion to express separation, and, once again, the importance of the Roman Empire as a negative stimulus to self-assertion is clear. Likewise, the Goths are likely to have had their own legal norms and peculiarities of dispute settlement. I do not believe in the concept of 'personality of law', and would argue against there having been separate legal texts for Roman and Goth in the successor states (chapter 7). Nevertheless, the legal systems of the Visigothic and Ostrogothic kingdoms both envisaged cases where a Gothic and a Roman judge would sit together to hear disputes between members of the two groups. We know very little about how dispute settlement may have worked among the Goths, but such arrangements do suggest, as one would anyway expect, that it was different from Roman legal practice. Otherwise, it is likely enough that ethnic difference found expression in other ways, which, in the absence of properly Gothic sources, we have no means of charting: moral norms, social values, clothing colours or even hairstyles (combs, as we have seen, were important, at least in the fourth century). There is much more that one would like to know, but it does seem to me that the archaeological evidence and literary sources provide enough evidence about symbols to show both that they existed, and that they worked as anthropological studies might lead one to predict. There was no unchanging mark of Gothicness, but, in different contexts, different customs, outward features or beliefs became emblematic. The constant was an underlying sense of difference, especially among the elite, freeman caste of Gothic groups.

This being so, I would like to reflect, finally, on some of the mechanisms by which knowledge of who was who might have been maintained among the elite freeman caste, particularly (but not entirely) in the successor states. On the move, when Gothic groups, for reasons of safety, operated in relatively compact masses, mutual recognition was not so much of a problem. Dispersal over the Italian or Iberian countryside was a much greater hindrance to group solidarity.

Public oath-swearing was a standard mechanism with a variety of functions. Athanaric swore a great oath not to set foot on Roman soil (AM 27.5.9), oaths had to been sworn by Gothic village authorities, after 369, that there were no Christians amongst them (*Passion of St. Saba* 3). Likewise, Gothic unity may have been buttressed in 376 by an oath not to be seduced by Roman blandishments (Eunapius fr. 59). The later hostility of a group of Goths to their Hunnic masters was also encapsulated in an oath (Priscus fr. 49), Theoderic wanted to extract oaths from Zeno and the senate of Constantinople that agreements would be honoured (Malchus fr. 18.2), and Visigothic rulers and subjects swore mutual oaths on the accession of new kings.[16] These different oaths were sworn variously by individuals and groups, sometimes buttressing group solidarity, otherwise placing obligations on particular individuals. They were all, however, public declarations in front of witnesses. They involved the gathering together and mutual recognition of a qualified social group to give and hear the oath. Used regularly, especially in relation to norms of political or religious behaviour (as in these examples), it is precisely the kind of mechanism which would have perpetuated solidarity among a dominant and mutually recognizable caste, such as the Gothic freemen of the Migration Period.

In the successor states, other mechanisms performed the same function. The whole process of allocating land, for instance, involved identifying a qualified group, and handing over to its members designated rewards. Mutual recognition and definition must have been part and parcel of this activity, therefore, especially if these lands were subsequently held tax free (p. 284). A similar function must have been performed by the distribution of annual donatives, at least in the Ostrogothic kingdom. As we have seen, this again involved the identification of a qualified group: those liable to military service in the field army, their names probably registered on lists. This group consisted largely of immigrants (and their descendants) of the right age for military service. An annual gathering of these men to receive rewards not only made them richer, but maintained group solidarity and recognition (chapter 8). Such mechanisms did not make it impossible for non-immigrants to have access to these privileges. Men such as Cyprian, who fought with Theoderic's army, may well have

[16] Claude, 1976.

gained the right thereby to share in donatives. But mechanisms such as these maintained a broad sense of group solidarity in a context where it might otherwise have lapsed.

Oath-swearings, land allocations, lists and gatherings for the distribution of donatives are all occasions organized by a central authority. Although material becomes thinner at this point, the sources also suggest that there were locally centred mechanisms perpetuating solidarity among Gothic freemen. Goths of both the fourth and sixth centuries also had their local authorities. As described by the *Passion of St. Saba*, village authorities mediated the effects of persecution within their own communities in the fourth, and, in the sixth, a mechanism existed for choosing a local leader, a *prior*, at least among the Goths of Reate and Nursia Cassiodorus, (*Variae* 8.26). This is very little to go on, but the Reate election was probably matched by similar events elsewhere, since local solidarities are evident among the Goths of Italy. Thus local politics also perpetuated mutual recognition among a qualified group: those allowed to influence the choice of *prior*.

I suspect also that local political enfranchisement was accompanied by the possession of particular legal rights, to hear evidence, give testimony and participate in judgements. As social mechanisms, they would all have tended to provide periodic occasions on which individual claims to a particular status would have been staked and recognized by peers. Such thoughts are based on analogy, rather than specifically Gothic evidence. They are all attributes of freemen in early medieval – so-called 'barbarian' – law codes from other kingdoms. While begging certain questions, I doubt that it is making too radical a leap to import these perspectives. The same codes also suggest that marriage taboos surrounded the equivalent free castes in other kingdoms. Individuals were allowed to marry only someone of equivalent standing on pain of total loss of status. Similarly, any change of status (from slave to freed, or free) was accompanied by a public ceremonial act witnessed by the local community.[17] The operation of these or similar mechanisms among the Goths would explain the kind of society we observe in Procopius' *Wars*. Without them, it is hard to explain why, 40 years after the conquest, Ostrogothic freemen still formed a discrete group which could be so

[17] The social significance of critical legal rights emerges clearly from Davies and Fouracre, 1986. Marriage and Manumission: e.g. *Lombard Laws* 221, 224–6; *Burgundian Code* 35, 40; *Alamannic Laws* (Lantfridana MSS) 16, 17; *Bavarian Laws* 8; *Salic Law* 13, 26.

clearly targeted by Belisarius. Of course, these institutions were themselves situational constructs, and, in new contexts, especially once Roman power had been removed, they gave way before new forces uniting Roman and Gothic landowners. In the right context, however, they functioned to preserve mutual recognition among a politically and socially enfranchised caste: the freemen.

In none of its manifestations was Gothicness a force akin to modern nationalism. But in at least two different forms, in two different periods, it was strong enough to shape individual action, and, through aggregations of individuals, European history. Between the later third and earlier sixth centuries, it was the product of, and itself influenced an elite of freemen, defined by certain political and legal rights held in common. In Spain, in the later sixth and seventh centuries, the unity of freemen was replaced by a community of landowners.

There is no reason why one of these manifestations should be considered more legitimately 'Gothic' than the other. Indeed, in broad terms, each stage of Gothicness did evolve out of its predecessor. Again, I would emphasize that I am arguing here for some broad, but by no means total, continuity. The fourth century Gothic kingdoms were created by substantial numbers of armed immigrants from northern Poland. This being so, their dominant caste of freemen is likely to have been composed in the first instance of the immigrants. Likewise, the successor states were created by large armed groups, dominated by the kind of freemen who had defined their superiority in the third and fourth centuries. Passages in the *Getica* would suggest, indeed, that the earlier Gothic historian Ablabius had found similar stories of the distant past being told among the Goths he knew, probably fifth-century Visigoths in Gaul, as Jordanes heard among sixth-century Goths in Constantinople.[18] The more dominant, at least, of the Gothic immigrants into western Europe, then turned themselves into landowners in the successor states as they extracted appropriate rewards from their leaders for past loyalty. Thus the overlap between immigrant freemen of the fourth to sixth centuries, and later Gothic landowners of the sixth to seventh centuries is likely to have been considerable. Indeed, without such an overlap, the determinedly Gothic rhetoric of the seventh-century Hispanic kingdom makes no sense. Another way of making the same point, is that preserved oral memories of the past are certainly myths – stories adapted to make particular points – rather than straightforward

[18] *Getica* 28–9; cf. Heather, 1991, 328.

history. At the same time, should they depart too far from historical reality, they have no force. Not, of course, that the overlaps and continuities between any of the manifestations of Gothicness were absolute.

It is likely enough, although we lack specific evidence, that some Roman prisoners and indigenous inhabitants of the north Pontic region eventually won Gothic freeman status. The descendants of many Hispano-Roman landowners – by intermarriage, political association and shared battles – also seem to have been numbered among the Goths of the seventh century. None the less, it has been one of the aims of this study to make the case for seeing migration, at least in relation to Goths, as a phenomenon of real importance in European history between the second and the sixth centuries. The migration of substantial numbers of 'Polish' Goths in the second and third centuries, and of substantial numbers of Gothic freemen from northern Danubian lands in the fourth and fifth centuries, provides, to my mind, a line of real continuity between the different manifestations of Gothicness. Depending on one's interests and points of view, of course, one might choose to emphasize either the continuities or the discontinuities. Any object can be described from the top downwards, or from the bottom upwards. Continuities and discontinuities are both essential to the full story, but, without the continuities, there would be no story at all.

Appendix 1

Procopius and the Gothic Elite

Procopius devoted the best part of four out of the eight books of history he wrote to the east Roman conquest of Italy, amounting to three whole volumes, or over 500 pages of Greek text in the Loeb edition. At no point does he provide a detailed, analytical account of Gothic social structure. His work contains, however, a huge amount of relevant information, and an extremely interesting and important picture of the social structure of the Goths of Italy emerges from the wide range of vignettes of which Procopius' work is composed.

Above all, Procopius' writings make it absolutely clear that a defined and recognizable elite existed among the Ostrogoths of Italy. To describe it he uses three Greek terms: *λόγιμος* ('worth mentioning' or 'remarkable'), *δόκιμος* ('esteemed' or 'notable'), and *ἄριστος* ('the best'). *A priori*, these look like synonyms employed to provide sylistic variation, rather than separate technical terms, and a closer look at Procopius' usage of them confirms that this is so.

On a very specific level, for instance, two of them are used to describe the same Gothic force of whom the garrison of the fortress of Auximus was composed at one point in the war (*δόκιμοι*: *Wars* 6.23.8; *ἄριστοι*: *Wars* 6.20.2). More generally, the three labels are attached to Goths engaged in the same range of activities.

1 All three terms are applied to significant individual Goths *λόγιμος*: *Wars* 5.4.13; *δόκιμος*: *Wars* 6.1.36; 6.20.14; 7.18.26; 8.26.4; *ἄριστος*: *Wars* 7.1.46).
2 Small numbers qualified by the terms are found taking part, alongside (or sometimes in opposition to) Gothic kings, in taking

important policy decisions (λόγιμος: *Wars* 5.13.26; 7.24.27; 8.35.33; δόκιμος: *Wars* 6.28.29; ἄριστος: *Wars* 6.8.9 (n.b. 7.1.46 again).

3 All three terms are sometimes applied to rather larger Gothic forces:
   (a) λόγιμος: *Wars* 8.23.10 (these Goths man 47 ships).
   (b) δόκιμος: *Wars* 3.8.12 (1,000 of them attend Theoderic's sister when she married Thrasamund, king of the Vandals); 6.23.8 (they comprise the garrison of Auximus); 8.26.21 (they comprise Teias' force sent to Verona).
   (c) ἄριστος: *Wars* 5.13.15 (they comprise the whole of Marcias' army sent to Dalmatia); 6.20.2 (garrison of Auximus; 6.28.29ff. (many (πολλοί) of them defend the Cottian Alps).[1]

The terms are used to designate an elite, they are not technical, and they are applied to groups engaged in the same range of activities. It is very hard not to see them, therefore, as synonyms.

In the course of his narrative, Procopius employs a number of other terms much more rarely, which may also be synonyms for the same group.

1 'Those who fight in the front rank' (ἄνδρες οἵ ἐν τοῖς πρώτοις ἐμάχοντο). One thousand of these men were killed in the fighting outside Rome (*Wars* 5.18.14).
2 Men 'of no mean station' (οὐκ ἀφανὴς). Applied to an individual wearing a helmet and corselet (*Wars* 5.23.9), and to another involved in a hostage exchange (6.7.13).

If these are further synonyms, these references raise the possibility that the Gothic elite was recognizable by a particular role in battle (although 'those who fight in the front rank' is an old classical term) and particular equipment.[2] These points cannot be pressed, but the existence of a Gothic elite is clear enough.

How should we describe this elite? At different places, Procopius applied all three of the central terms to very substantial military forces: to garrisons; the complements of 47 ships; entire military units

[1] It is unclear to me whether the incident at *Wars* 5.7.3, where a Gothic force in Dalmatia loses all its ἄριστοι, should be placed under 2 or 3.

[2] Cf. *Wars* 5.22.4 which seems to imply that there was something exceptional about the armour worn by an individual Goth hit by Belisarius' missile from the walls of Rome.

(the forces of Marcias and Teias) and to losses in the range of four figures. The terms encompass, then, at least several thousands of individual males within a total force of, at most, *c*.30,000 (p. 164). At the same time, not every adult male belonged to this social group. The terms are in themselves exclusive, implying the existence of other, lesser Gothic social groups. Procopius' narrative confirms the point. When the elite among the Goths of Dalmatia were killed, for instance, the rest of the Gothic population of the area surrendered to the invading east Romans (p. 273). One passage, indeed, gives some indication of the proportion of the elite to the rest of the Gothic population. The bodyguard sent with Theoderic's sister to Vandal Africa comprised 1,000 men from the elite, and a body of attendants (θεραπείας) amounting to a total of 5,000 fighting men (*Wars* 3.8.12). The lesser social group or groups, just as much as the elite, then, were considered fighting men, and the elite in this force, at least, amounted to about one-fifth of the total. It is impossible to be sure that the proportions of these social groups in Amalafrida's bodyguard reflected their proportions in the Ostrogoths as a whole. If anything, one might expect a rather grand force (with perhaps more attendants per member of the elite than usual) to have been sent out to impress the Vandals. I would suggest, therefore, that we must envisage an elite social caste among the Italian Goths of at least one-fifth of the total adult male population.

Who were these men? *A priori*, one might be tempted to think of them as a Gothic nobility, but their numbers seem far too large. Procopius does pick out a few individuals as even grander, using the superlative forms of the terms applied generally to the elite. Thus the three men who were Amalasuentha's chief opponents (of whom two were probably Tuluin and Osuin: p. 261) are called λογιμώτατος (*Wars* 5.2.21; cf. 3.11), and three of Totila's military commanders (one of whom was a renegade soldier from Belisarius' army) δοκιμωτάτος (*Wars* 8.23.1). It is very unclear that Procopius' usage is picking out any more than a pre-eminence acquired in the given individuals' own lifetimes, rather than an inherited social distinction which I take to be central to any concept of nobility. There is more than a little evidence that a Gothic nobility was beginning to differentiate itself from this caste of 'notables', but Procopius' evidence would not seem to be referring to this, still more elite, group (see further chapter 6).

On reflection, this social caste comprising perhaps at least one-fifth of the adult males of the group can only be equated, it seems to me, with the so-called 'free' class which one encounters in many of the sixth- and seventh-century so-called 'barbarian' law codes. To cite this evidence is a little problematic, since much of it, if only slightly, postdates Procopius, and we have no law code of this kind from the Ostrogothic kingdom. There is also the general problem that one can never be sure of the extent to which social norms laid out in law codes reflect reality. But evidence for a military elite attended by equally militarized servants is quite generally available for this period. Thus allied barbarians (*foederati*) in the western Roman army of the fifth century were expected to have slaves (*C.Th.* 7.13.16), and a Lombard contingent for Justinian's wars in Italy was composed of 2,500 'good fighting men' (ἄνδρας ἀγαθοὺς τὰ πολέμια) and 3,000 fighting servants (θεραπεία ... μαχίμων ἀνδρῶν: *Wars* 8.26.12). In this case, the proportions of higher and lower men were more like 50:50, and this, rather than 20:80, may have also been true of the Ostrogoths as a whole, as opposed to Amalafrida's guard of honour.

There is thus no reason to reject Procopius' evidence. Indeed, it is of great general significance, although there is no space to develop the point fully here. Many studies of the late nineteenth and early twentieth century – labelled, not inappropriately, by some the 'Romantic' period in the study of the Germanic peoples of the Roman and Migration Periods – laid enormous stress on the free class. It was seen as comprising, at least in the Migration Period, virtually all adult males, and taken, especially on the basis of material in the law codes, to have exercised an early form of democratic control over group action. In a necessary reaction to this, more recent scholarship has emphasized the extent to which Germanic groups, even in this early period, were hierarchic, and tended to look to more restricted social groups, nobilities, as the source of political initiative and decision-making.[3] Procopius' evidence, it seems to me, allows us to bridge the gap between the two perspectives. If we may generalize from his account, the free ('notable') class was still important in the sixth century, at least among the Ostrogoths. It did not comprise all or even most, however, of the adult male population. Rather, it was a restricted, oligarchic elite of somewhere between, perhaps, one-fifth and one-half of the Gothic population. The rights of full social, political and legal participation accorded this group in the law codes thus extended to only a minority, if a substantial one, of the population. Thus Procopius' *Wars*, the most detailed account of any

[3] Esp. the so-called 'new teaching' (*Neue Lehre*) on early Germanic history which has its roots in the classic study of Wenskus, 1961, cf. Garcia Moreno, 1994.

Gothic group – or, indeed, any Migration Period group in general – in action, leads us to a compromise position on the distribution of power in at least some Germanic societies of *c.*500. Not just the property of a restricted nobility, it was by no means distributed equally throughout the whole group. Power did continue to be shared in by a free class, but this class was itself an elite social caste.

Appendix 2

Non-Goths in the Army of Totila

In the course of the war against the Byzantines, Totila found himself very short of military manpower. One response was to cede part of Venetia to the Franks to release Gothic manpower from garrison duties in the area to take part in the war. More generally, Totila was careful to treat Roman prisoners with great kindness to encourage elements of the east Roman army to join his cause (cf. Procopius *Wars* 7.5.19). Three distinct levels of participation can be observed.

1 Certain individuals went over whole-heartedly to the Goths and became influential figures, particularly Indulf (e.g. *Wars* 8.23.1) and Coccas (*Wars* 8.31.11–16).
2 Certain groups became firmly attached to the Goths because they had killed their imperial commanders to revolt: *Wars* 8.33.9 ff.
3 Other groups joined on a more contingent basis, particularly because their pay failed to arrive (e.g. the threat reported at *Wars* 7.30.7–8). Some of them informed the imperial authorities that they would return to their former allegiance as soon as a major east Roman army appeared (*Wars* 7.39.22), and Narses was equipped with plenty of money to attract them back (*Wars* 8.26.6). Procopius makes the following references to Roman troops in Gothic ranks:
   (a) *Wars* 7.18.26: in the garrison of Bruttium (mixed with Goths).
   (b) *Wars* 7.23.3: in the garrison at Spoleto (mixed with Goths).
   (c) *Wars* 7.26.10: 70 Roman deserters go over to the Goths.
   (d) *Wars* 7.30.19ff: 220 out of the 300 of the garrison of

Rusciane join the Goths.

(e) *Wars* 7.35.22: 6,000 Lombards nearly join the Goths, but go home instead.

(f) *Wars* 7.36.19: 700 Roman troops join Totila.

(g) *Wars* 7.39.5: the garrison of Rhegium joins the Goths.

Bibliography

Primary Sources

Acta synhodorum habitarum Romae, ed. Th. Mommsen (*MGH AA* 12).

Agathias, *The Histories*, trans. J.D. Frendo (Berlin, 1975).

Alamannic Laws, trans. in Rivers, 1977.

Ambrose, *Expositio Evangelii secundum Lucam*, CSEL 32.

——*De Spiritu Sancto*, CSEL 79.

Ammianus Marcellinus, trans. J.C. Rolfe, Loeb, 3 vols (London, 1950–2).

Anonymous Valesianus, trans. Rolfe in vol. 3 of his Loeb Ammianus.

Aurelius Victor, *Caesares*, trans. H.W. Bird (Liverpool, 1994).

Auxentius (of Durostorum?), *Letter on Ulfila*, trans. in Heather and Matthews, 1991.

Bavarian Laws, trans. in Rivers, 1977.

Boethius, *Tractates, Consolation of Philosophy*, trans. H.F. Stewart et al., Loeb (London, 1973).

Braulio of Saragossa, *Works*, trans. Fathers of the Church, vol. 63.

Breviary of Alaric (= *Lex Romana Visigothorum*), ed. G. Haenel (Berlin, 1849).

Burgundian Code, trans. K.F. Drew (Pennsylvania, 1972).

Caesar, *Gallic War*.

Caesarius of Arles, *Life, Testament, Letters* trans. W. Klingshirn (Liverpool, 1994).

Cassiodorus, *Variae*, ed. A. Fridh (CCSL 96), summary trans. T. Hodgkin, *The Letters of Cassiodorus* (London, 1886); partial trans. S.J.B. Barnish, *Cassiodorus: Variae* (Liverpool, 1992).

Chronica Minora, vols 1 and 2, ed. Th. Mommsen, *MGH AA* 9 and 11.

Claudian, *Poems*, trans. M. Platnauer, Loeb, 2 vols (London, 1922).

Codex Euricianus, ed. K. Zeumer in *Leges Visigothorum*, *MGH*, *Leges* 1.

Codex Theodosianus, trans. C. Pharr (New York, 1952).
Collectio Avellana, ed. O. Guenther (CSEL 35).
Councils of Toledo, ed. Vives, 1963.
Dexippus, ed. *FHG* 4.
Dio, *Roman History*, trans. E. Cary, Loeb, vol. 9 (London, 1927).
Edict of Theoderic, ed. F. Bluhme *MGH, Leges*, 5.
Ennodius, *Works*, ed. W. Hartel (CSEL 6) (*Life of Epiphanius*, trans. Fathers of the Church, vol. 15).
Epiphanius, *Panarion*.
Eunapius, ed. and trans., Blockley 1983.
Formulae Wisigothorum, ed. Gil, 1972.
Fredegar, *Chronicle*, Bk. 4, ed. and trans. J.M. Wallace-Hadrill (London, 1960).
Gregory of Tours, *Histories*, trans. L. Thorpe, Penguin Classics (London, 1974).
Hydatius, *Chronicle*, ed. and trans. Burgess, 1993.
Isidore of Seville, *History of the Goths*, trans. Wolf, 1990.
John of Antioch, ed. *FHG* 4, 5; the fragments in vol. 4 are translated in Gordon, 1966.
John of Biclar, *Chronicle*, trans. Wolf, 1990.
John Malalas, *Chronicle*, trans. E. Jeffreys et al. (Melbourne, 1986).
Jordanes, *Getica, Romana*, ed. Th. Mommsen, *MGH AA* 5; Getica, trans. C.C. Mierow (New York, 1912).
Julian of Toledo, *History of King Wamba*, ed. W. Levison, reprinted Corpus Christianorum, vol. 115.
Laws of the Salian and Ripuarian Franks, trans. T.J. Rivers (New York, 1986) (= *Salic and Ripuarian* Laws).
Leges Visigothorum, ed. K. Zeumer, *MGH, Leges* 1.
Libanius, *Select Orations*, trans. A.F. Norman, Loeb, 2 vols (London, 1969, 1977).
Lives of the Fathers of Merida, ed. A. Maya Sanchez, Corpus Christianorum, Series Latina 116 (Turnholt, 1992).
Lombard Laws, trans. K. Fischer Drew (Pennsylvania, 1973).
Malchus of Philadelphia, ed. and trans. Blockley, 1983.
Maurice, *Strategicon*, trans. G.T. Dennis (Philadelphia, 1984).
Merobaudes, ed. and trans. F.M. Clover, *Transactions of the American Philological Society* 61 (1971).
Miracles of St. Demetrius, ed. with Fr. trans. P. Lemerle, 2 vols (Paris, 1979).
Olympiodorus, ed. and trans. Blockley, 1983.
Panegyrici Latini, ed. with fr. trans. E. Galletier, 3 vols (Paris, 1955).
Passion of St. Saba, trans. in Heather and Matthews, 1991.

Paul the Deacon, *History of the Lombards*, trans. W.D. Foulke (Pennsylvania, 1974); this includes translations of the *Origins of the Lombard People* and the *Codex Gothanum*.
Paulinus of Pella, *Eucharisticon*, ed. and trans. H.G. Evelyn White in vol. 2 of his Loeb Ausonius (London, 1921).
Paulus Orosius, *History Against the Pagans*, trans. Fathers of the Church, vol. 50.
Petrus Patricius, ed. *FHG* 4.
Philostorgius, *Ecclesiastical History* ed. J. Bidez (Leipzig, 1913).
Photius, *Bibliotheca*, ed. with Fr. trans. R. Henry (Paris, 1959–77).
Pliny, *Natural History*.
Possidius, *Life of Augustine*, trans. Fathers of the Church, vol. 15.
Priscus of Panium, ed. and trans. Blockley, 1983.
Procopius of Caesarea, *Works*, trans. H.B. Dewing, Loeb, 7 vols (London, 1914–40).
Ptolemy, *Geography*.
Ruricius of Limoges, *Epistulae*, ed. B. Krusch, *MGH AA* 8 (Berlin, 1887).
Rutilius Namatianus, *De Redito Suo*, ed. J. Vesserau and F. Prechac (Paris, 1933).
Salic Law, trans. K.F. Drew (Pennsylvania, 1991).
Salvian, *On the Government of God*, trans. E.M. Sanford (New York, 1966).
Scriptores Historia Augusta, trans. D. Magie, Loeb, 3 vols (London, 1922–32).
Sidonius Apollinaris, *Poems and Letters*, trans. W.B. Anderson, Loeb, 2 vols (London, 1935, 1965).
Socrates, *Ecclesiastical History*, trans. *Nicene and Post-Nicene Fathers*, vol. 3.
Sozomen, *Ecclesiastical History*, trans. *Nicene and Post-Nicene Fathers*, vol. 3.
Strabo, *Geography*.
George Syncellus, ed. B.G. Niebuhr, 2 vols (Bonn, 1829).
Synesius of Cyrene, *Works*, trans. A. Fitzgerald (London, 1930).
Tacitus, *Germania*, *Annals*, *Histories*, *Agricola*.
Themistius, *Orationes*, ed. G. Downey and A.F. Norman, 3 vols, Teubner (1965–74). Orations 8 and 10 trans. in Heather and Matthews, 1991; Orations 14–16 in Moncur and Heather, 1996.
Theophanes, *Chronicle*, ed. C. de Boor, 2 vols, Teubner (1883–5).
Zonaras, *Chronicon*, ed. L. Dindorf, 3 vols (Bonn, 1868–75).
Zosimus, *New History*, ed. with Fr. trans. F. Paschoud, 3 vols (Paris, 1971–89), Eng. trans. R.T. Ridley (Canberra, 1982).

Secondary Sources

Achelis, H. 1900, 'Der älteste deutsche Kalender', *Zeitschrift für die neutestamentliche Wissenschaft* i, 308–35.

Adams, W.Y. 1978, 'On Migration and Diffusion as Rival Paradigms', in Dake, 1978, 1–5.

Amory, P. 1993, 'The Meaning and Purpose of Ethnic Terminology in the Burgundian Laws', *Early Medieval Europe* 2.1, 1–28.

Anokhin, V.A. 1980, *The Coinage of Chersonesus*, BAR, IS 69 (Oxford).

Antony, D.W. 1990, 'Migration in Archaeology: The Baby and the Bathwater', *American Anthropologist* 92, 894–914.

Arrhenius, B. 1985, *Merovingian Garnet Jewellery. Emergence and Social Implications* (Stockholm).

Bacal, A. 1991, *Ethnicity in the Social Sciences. A View and a Review of the Literature on Ethnicity* (Coventry).

Barnish, S.J.B. 1983, 'The *Anonymous Valesianus II* as a Source For the Last Years of Theoderic', *Latomus* 42, 472–96.

——, 1986, 'Taxation, Land and Barbarian Settlement in the Western Empire', *PBSR* 54, 170–95.

——; 1988, 'Transformation and Survival in the Western Senatorial Aristocracy, *c.* AD 400–700', *PBSR* 65, 120–55.

——1990, 'Maximian, Cassiodorus, Boethius, Theodahad: Literature Philosophy and Politics in Ostrogothic Italy', *Nottingham Medieval Studies* 34, 16–31.

——1992, *Cassiodorus: Variae* (Liverpool, Translated Texts for Historians).

Barral I Altet, X. 1976, *La circulation des monnaies suèves et visigothiques* (Munich).

Barth, F. 1969, *Ethnic Groups and Boundaries. The Social Organisation of Cultural Difference* (Oslo).

Bentley, G.C. 1987, 'Ethnicity and Practice', *Comparative Studies in Society and History* 29, 24–55.

Bichir, Gh. 1976, *The Archaelogy and History of the Carpi*, BAR, IS 16 (Oxford).

Bierbrauer, V. 1975, *Die ostgotischen Grab- und Schatzfunde in Italien* (Spoleto).

——1980, 'Zur chronologischen, soziologischen und regionalen Gliederung des ostgermanischen Fundstoffs des 5. Jahrhunderts in Südosteuropa', in Wolfram and Daim (eds), 1980, 131–42.

——1986, 'Frühgeschichtliche Akkulturationprozesse in den Germanishcen Staaten am Mittelmeer (Westgoten, Ostgoten, Langobarden) aus der sicht des Archäologen', in *Atti di VI congresso internazionale di studi sull 'Alto Medioevo* (Spoleto), 89–105.

——1989, 'Ostgermanische Oberschichtsgräber der römischen Kaiserzeit und des frühen Mittelalters', in *Peregrinatio Gothica* 2, 40–106.

——1991, 'Die Goten vom 1.–7. Jahrhundert n.Chr.: Siedelgebiete und Wanderbewegungen aufgrund archäologischer Quellen', in *Peregrinatio Gothica* 3, 9–43.

Billy, P.-H. 1992, 'Souvenirs wisigothiques dans la toponymie de la Gaul meridionale', in Fontaine and Pellistrandi, 1992, 101–23.

Birley, A. 1966, *Marcus Aurelius* (London).

Blockley, R.C. 1983, *The Fragmentary Classicising Historians of the Later Roman Empire: Eunapius, Olympiodorus, Priscus and Malchus*, vol. 2 (Liverpool).

Blosiu, C. 1975, 'La nécropole de Letçani (dép. de Jassy) datant du IVe siècle de n.è.', *Arheologia Moldovei* 8, 203–80.

Böhme, H. W. 1975, 'Archäologische Zeugnisse zur Geschichte der Markomannenkriege (166–80 n. Chr.)', *Jahrbuch des römisch-germanischen Zentralmuseums Mainz* 22, 155–217.

Bona, I. 1991, *Das Hunnenreich* (Stuttgart).

Bonnassie, P. 1991, *From Slavery to Feudalism in South Western Europe*, trans. J. Birrell (Cambridge).

Braund, D.C. 1984, *Rome and the Friendly King: The Character of the Client Kingship* (London).

Brogiolo, G.P. and Castelletti, L. 1991, *Archeologia a Monte Barro* vol. 1 (Lecco).

Brooks, E.R. 1893, 'The Emperor Zenon and the Isaurians', *EHR* 8, 209–38.

Brown, T.S. 1984, *Gentlemen and Officers. Imperial Administration and Aristocratic Power in Byzantine Italy A.D. 554–800* (Rome).

Burgess, R.W. 1993, *The Chronicle of Hydatius and the Consularia Constantinopolitana: Two Contemporary Accounts of the final years of the Roman Empire* (Oxford).

Bury, J.B. 1923, *History of the Later Roman Empire* vol. 2 (London).

Cameron, A.D.E. 1970, *Claudian: Poetry and Politics at the Court of Honorius* (Oxford).

Cameron, A.D.E. et al. 1993, *Barbarians and Politics at the Court of Arcadius* (Berkeley).

Cataniciu, I.B. 1981, *Evolution of the System of Defence Works in Roman Dacia*, BAR, IS 116 (Oxford).

Cesa, M. 1994, *Imperio Tardantico e Barbari: La crisi militare da Adrianopoli al 418*, Biblioteca di Athenaeum 23 (Como).

Chadwick, H. 1981, *Boethius: The Consolations of Music, Logic, Theology, and Philosophy* (Oxford).
Childe, C.G. 1926, *The Aryans: A Study in Indo-European Origins* (London).
——1936, *Man Makes Himself* (London).
Chrysos, E.K. 1972, *Τὸ Βυζάντιον καὶ οἱ Γοτθοι* (Thessalonika).
Claude, D. 1971, *Adel, Kirche und Königtum im Westgotenreich* (Sigmaringen).
——1976, 'The Oath of the Allegiance and the Oath of the King in the Visigothic Kingdom', *Classical Folia*, 30, 3–26.
——1978, 'Universale und partikulare Zuge in der Politik Theoderichs', *Francia*, 6.
——1980, 'Die ostgotischen Königserhebungen', in Wolfram and Daim (eds), 1980, 149–86.
——1989, 'Zur Begrundung familiärer Beziehungen zwischen dem Kaiser und barbarischen Herrschern', in E.K. Chrysos and A. Schwarcz (eds), *Das Reich und die Barbaren* (Vienna), 25–56.
Clover, F.M. 1978, 'The Family and Early Career of Anicius Olybrius', *Historia*, xxvii, 169–96.
Collins, R. 1977, 'Julian of Toledo and the Royal Succession in Late Seventh-Century Spain', in P.H. Sawyer and I.N. Wood (eds), *Early Medieval Kingship* (Leeds), 30–49.
——1980, 'Merida and Toledo: 550–585', in James, 1980, 189–219.
——1983, *Early Medieval Spain: Unity in Diversity 400–1000* (London).
Courtois, C. 1955, *Les Vandales et l'Afrique* (Paris).
Cribb, R.J. 1991, *Nomads in Archaeology* (Cambridge).
Croke, B. 1977, 'Evidence for the Hun Invasion of Thrace in AD 422', *GRBS* 18, 347–67.
Dake, P.G. et al. (eds) 1978, *Diffusion and Migration: Their Roles in Cultural Development*, Archaeological Association of the University of Calgary (Calgary).
Davies, W. and Fouracre, P. 1986, *The Settlement of Disputes in Early Medieval Europe* (Cambridge).
Demougeot, E. 1969, *La formation de l'Europe et les invasions barbares: i. Des origines germaniques à l'avènement de Dioclétien* (Paris).
——1979, *La formation de l'Europe et les invasions barbares: ii. De l'avenèment de Dioclétien (284) à l'occupation germanique de l'Empire Romain d'occident (debut du VIe siècle)* (Paris).
Diaconu, Gh. 1977, 'L'ensemble archéologique de Pietroasele', *Dacia* n.s. 21, 199–220.

Diaz Martinez, P.C. 1987, *Formas economicas y sociales en el monacato Visigodo* (Salamanca).

——1992–3, 'Propiedad y exploitacion de la tierra in al Lusitania Tardoantigua', *Historia Antiqua* 10–11, 297–309.

——1994, 'La ocupacion Germanica de valle de Duero: Un Ensayo interpretativo', *Hispania Antiqua* 18, 457–76.

Drinkwater, J. and Elton, H. (eds) 1992, *Fifth-Century Gaul: A Crisis of Identity* (Cambridge).

Durliat, J. 1988, 'Le salaire de la paix sociale dans les royaumes barbares (Ve–VIe siècles)', in H. Wolfram and A. Schwarcz (eds) *Anerkennung und Integration: Zu den wirtschftlichen Grundlagen der Völkerwanderungszeit (400–600)*, Denskschriften der Österrichischen Akademie der Wissenschaften, Phil.-Hist. Kl. 193 (Vienna).

Dvornik, F. 1966, *Early Christian and Byzantine Political Philosophy: Origins and Background* (Washington D.C.).

Eggers, H.J. 1949/50, 'Lübsow, ein germanischer Fürstensitz der älteren Kaiserzeit', *Prähistorische Zeitschrift* 34/35, 155–231.

Ensslin, W. 1947, *Theoderich der Grosse* (Munich).

Fontaine, J. 1967, 'Conversion et Culture chez les Wisigoths d'Espagne', *Settimane di studi sull'Alto medioevo* 14, 87–147.

——1980, 'King Sisebut's *Vita Desiderii* and the Political Function of Visigothic Hagiography', in James, 1980, 93–129.

Fontaine, J. and Pellistrandi, C. (eds) 1992, *L'Europe heritière de l'Espagne wisigothique* (Madrid).

Friedrichsen, G.W.S. 1926, *The Gothic Version of the Gospels: A Study of its Style and Textual History* (Oxford).

——1939, *The Gothic Version of the Epistles: A Study of its Style and Textual History* (Oxford).

Frolova, N.A. 1983, *The Coinage of the Kingdom of Bosporos AD 242–341/2*, BAR, IS 166 (Oxford).

Gamillscheg, E. 1934, *Romania Germanica*, vol. 1 (Berlin-Leipzig).

Garcia Moreno, L.A. 1974, *Prosopografia del reino Visigodo de Toledo*, Acta Salmanticensia, Filosofia y letras 77 (Salamanca).

——1989, *Historia de Espana Visigoda* (Madrid).

——1994, 'Gothic Survivals in the Visigothic Kingdoms of Toulouse and Toledo', *Francia* 21/1, 1–15.

Geary, P. 1985, *Aristocracy in Provence. The Rhone Basin at the Dawn of the Carolingian Age* (Philadelphia).

Gebühr, M. 1974, 'Zur Definition älterkaiserzeitlicher Fürstengraber vom Lübsow-Typ', *Prähistorische Zeitschrift* 49, 82–128.

Gej, O.A. 1980, 'The Cherniakhovo Culture Sites of the North Pontic Area', *SA* 1980/2, 45–51.

Gellner, E. 1983, *Nations and Nationalism* (Oxford).
Gerberding, R.A. 1987, *The Rise of the Carolingians and the Liber Historiae Francorum* (Oxford).
Gil, J. 1972, *Miscellanea Wisigothica* (Seville).
Godłowski, K. 1970, *The Chronology of the Late Roman and Early Migration Periods in Central Europe*, Prace Archeologiczne 11.
——1986, 'Gegenseitige Beziehungen zwischen der Wielbark und der Przeworsk-Kultur. Veränderungen ihrer Verbreitung und das Problem der Gotenwanderung', in *Peregrinatio Gothica* 1, 125–52.
Goffart, W. 1980, *Barbarians and Romans AD 418–584: The Techniques of Accommodation* (Princeton).
——1988, *The Narrators of Barbarian History (AD 550–800): Jordanes, Gregory of Tours, Bede, and Paul the Deacon* (Princeton, N.J.).
Gordon, C.D. 1966, *The Age of Attila: Fifth-Century Byzantium and the Barbarians* (Ann Arbor).
Greene, K. 1987, 'Gothic Material Culture', in I. Hodder (ed.), *Archaeology as Long-Term History* (Cambridge), 117–42.
Grierson, P. 1985, 'The Date of Theoderic's Gold Medallion', *Hikuin* 11, 19–26.
Haarnagel, W. 1979, 'Das eisenzeitliche Dorf 'Feddersen Wierde', in H. Jankuhn and R. Wenskus (eds), *Geschichtswissenschaft und Archäologie* (Sigmaringen), 45–99.
Hachmann, R. 1970, *Die Goten und Skandinavien* (Berlin).
——1971, *The Germanic Peoples* (London).
Hagberg, U.E. (ed.) 1972, *Studia Gotica* (Stockholm).
Hall, J.B. 1988, 'Alaric's First Invasion of Italy', *Philologus* 132, 245–57.
Halsall, G. 1992, 'The Origins of the *Reihengräberzivilisation*: Forty Years On', in Drinkwater and Elton, 1992, 196–207.
Hannestad, K. 1960, 'Les forces militaires d'après la guerre gothique de Procope', *Classica et Mediaevalia*, 21, 136–83.
Harhoiu, R. 1977, *The Treasure from Pietroasa, Romania*, BAR, IS 24 (Oxford).
Harries, J. 1994, *Sidonius Apollinaris and the Fall of Rome* (Oxford).
Heather, P.J. 1986, 'The Crossing of the Danube and the Gothic Conversion', *GRBS* 27, 289–318.
——1987, 'The Two Thousandth Year of Gothic History and Theoderic's Intervention in Visigothic Spain', *XXXIV corso di cultura sull'arte ravennate e bizantina* (Ravenna), 171–8.
——1988, 'The Anti-Scythian Tirade of Synesius' *De Regno*', *Phoenix*, 42, 152–72.

——1989, 'Cassiodorus and the Rise of the Amals: Genealogy and the Goths under Hun Domination', *JRS* 79, 103–28.

——1991, *Goths and Romans 332–489* (Oxford).

——1993, 'The Historical Culture of Ostrogothic Italy', *Atti del XIII Congresso internazionale di studi sull'Alto Medioevo* (Spoleto), 317–53.

——1994a, 'Literacy and Power in the Migration Period', in Bowman, A.K. and Woolf, G. (eds), *Literacy and Power in the Ancient World* (Cambridge), 177–97.

——1994b, 'New Men for New Constantines. The Creation of an Imperial Elite in the Eastern Mediterranean', in P. Magdalino (ed.), *New Constantines: The Rhythmn of Imperial Renewal in Byzantium* (London), 11–33.

——1995a, 'The Huns and the End of the Roman Empire in Western Europe', *English Historical Review* 110, 4–41.

——1995b, 'Theoderic King of the Goths', *Early Medieval Europe* 4.2, 145–73.

——, 1996, 'Signs of Ethnic Identity: Disappearing and Reappearing Tribes', in W. Pohl (ed.), *Kingdoms of the Empire* (Brill) (forthcoming).

Heather, P.J. and Matthews, J.F. 1991, *The Goths in the Fourth Century* (Liverpool).

Hedeager, L. 1978, 'Processes Towards State Formation in Early Iron Age Denmark', in Kristiansen and Paludan-Muller (eds), 1978, 191–216.

——1987, 'Empire, Frontier and the Barbarian Hinterland. Rome and Northern Europe from AD 1–400', in K. Kristiansen et al. (eds), *Centre and Periphery in the Ancient World* (Cambridge), 125–40.

——1988, 'The Evolution of Germanic Society 1–400 AD', in R.F.J. Jones et al. (eds), *First Millennium Papers: Western Europe in the First Millennium* BAR, IS 401 (Oxford), 129–44.

——1992, *Iron Age Societies. From Tribe to State in Northern Europe 500 BC to AD 700*, trans. J. Hines (Oxford).

Hedeager L. and Kristiansen, K., 1981, 'Bendstrup – A Princely Grave from the Early Roman Iron Age: Its Social and Historical Context', *Kuml*, 150–62.

Hillgarth, J. 1966, 'Coins and Chronicles: Propaganda in Sixth Century Spain', *Historia* 16, 482–508.

Horedt, K. 1986, *Siebenburgen im Frühmittelater* (Bonn).

Hübener, W. 1970, 'Zur Chronologie der Westgotenzeitlichen Grabfunde in Spanien', *Madrider Mitteilungen* 11, 187–211.

——1973, 'Probleme der westgotenzeitlichen Nekropolen Spaniens aus mitteleuropäischer Sicht', *Mitteilungen der Berliner Gesellschaft für Anthropologie, Ethnologie und Urgeschichte* 2/3, 129–43.

Ilkjaer, J. 1995, 'Illerup Adal (Danemark). Un lieu de sacrifices du IIIe siècle de n.è. en Scandinavie meridionale', in Vallet and Kazanski, 1995, 101–12.

Ilkjaer, J. and Lonstrup, J. 1983, 'Der Moorfund im Tal der Illerup-Å bei Skanderborg im Ostjütland', *Germania* 61, 95–126.

Ioniţă, I. 1975, 'The Social-Economic Structure of Society During the Goths' Migration in the Carpatho-Danubean Area', in Constantinescu, M. et al. (eds), *Relations Between the Autochthonous Population and the Migratory Populations on the Territory of Romania* (Bucharest), 77–89.

James, E. 1980, 'Septimania and its Frontier: An Archaeological Approach', in James (ed.), 1980, 223–42.

——1980 (ed.), *Visigothic Spain: New Approaches* (Oxford).

——1988, *The Franks* (Oxford).

——1991, 'Les problèmes archéologiques du sud-ouest wisigothique et franc', in Perrin, 1991, 149–53.

Johnson, M.J. 1988, 'Towards a History of Theoderic's Building Programme', *DOP*, 42, 73–96.

Jones, A.H.M. 1962, 'The Constitutional Position of Odoacer and Theoderic', *JRS* 52, 126–30 = P. A. Brunt (ed.), *The Roman Economy (Oxford, 1974) 365–74].*

——1964, *The Later Roman Empire: A Social Economic and Administrative Survey* (Oxford).

Kampers, G. 1979, *Personengeschichtliche Studien zum Westgotenreich in Spanien* (Münster).

Kaster, R.A. 1988, *Guardians of the Language: The Grammarian and Society in Late Antiquity* (California).

Kazanski, M. 1991a, *Les Goths (Ier.-VIIe. après J.-C.)* (Paris).

——1991b, 'Contributions a l'étude des migrations des Goths à la fin du IVe siècle et au Ve siècle: le témoignage de l'archéologie', in Perrin (ed.), 1991, 11–25.

Kazanski, M. and Legoux, R. 1988, 'Contribution a l'étude des témoignages archéologiques des Goths en Europe orientale à l'epoque des Grandes Migrations: la chronologie de la culture de Černjahov récente', *Archéologie Médiévale* 18, 8–53.

Keay, S. 1984a, *Late Roman Amphorae in the Western Mediterranean. A Typology and Economic Study: The Catalan Evidence*, BAR, IS 196 (Oxford).

——1984b, 'Decline or Continuity? The Conventus Tarraconensis from the Fourth to the Seventh Centuries', in T. Blagg et al. (eds), *Papers in Iberian Archaeology*, BAR, 193 (Oxford), 552–69.

Kershaw, A.C. 1978, 'Diffusion and Migration Studies in Geography', in Dake, 1978, 6–13.

Khazanov, A.M. 1984, *Nomads and the Outside World*, trans. J. Crookenden (Cambridge).

King, C. 1992, 'Roman, Local and Barbarian Coinages in Fifth-Century Gaul', in Drinkwater and Elton (eds), 1992, 184–95.

King, P.D. 1972, *Law and Society in the Visigothic Kingdom* (Cambridge).

——1980, 'King Chindasvind and the First Territorial Law-Code of the Visigothic Kingdom', in James (ed.), 1980, 131–57.

Kivisto, P. 1989, *The Ethnic Enigma: The Saliance of Ethnicity for European Origin Groups* (Philadelphia).

Klingshirn, W.E. 1994, *Caesarius of Arles. The Making of a Christian Community in Late Antique Arles* (Cambridge).

Klose, J. 1934, *Roms Klientel-Randstaaten am Rhein und an der Donau: Beiträge zur ihrer Geschichte und rechtlichen Stellung im 1. und 2. Jhdt. n. Chr.* (Breslau).

Kmieciński, J. 1962, 'Problem of the So-called Gotho-Gepiden Culture in the Light of Recent Research', *Archaeologia Polona* 4, 270–85.

——1972, 'Die Bedeutung der Germanen östlich der Oder während der ersten Jahrhunderte nach Christi Geburt im Lichte der neueren Forschungen, in Hagberg (ed.), 1972, 72–80.

Kobylinski, Z. (ed.) 1991, *Ethnicity in Archaeology* (special theme), *Archaeologia Polona* 29.

Kokowski, A. 1995, *Schätze der Ostgoten* (Stuttgart).

Korkannen, I. 1975, *The Peoples of Hermenaric: Jordanes Getica 116*, Annales Academie Scientiarum Fennicae, Series B 187 (Helsinki).

Kossina, G. 1926, *Die Herkunft der Germanen: zur Methode der Siedlungsarchäologie*, 2nd edn (Wurzburg).

Kristiansen, K. and Paludan-Muller, C. (eds), 1978, *New Directions in Scandinavian Archaeology* (Copenhagen).

Liebeschuetz, J.H.W.G. 1990, *Barbarians and Bishops* (Oxford).

——1992, 'Alaric's Goths: Nation or Army?', in Drinkwater and Elton (eds), 1992, 75–83.

Linehan, P. 1993, *History and The Historians of Medieval Spain* (Oxford).

Macartney, C.A. 1934, 'The End of the Huns', *Byzantinisch-Neugreichische Jahrbucher*, 10, 106–14.

MacCormack, S. 1983, *Art and Ceremony in Late Antiquity* (Berkeley).

Maenchen-Helfen, O.J. 1973, *The World of the Huns* (Berkeley).

Magomedov, B. 1995, 'La stratification sociale de la population de la culture de Černjachov', in Vallet and Kazanski, 1995, 133–8.

Mango, C. 1990, *Le développement urbain de Constantinople (IVe-VIIe siècles)*, Travaux et Memoirès, monographies II (Paris).

Mathisen, R. 1979, 'Resistance and Reconciliation: Majorian and the Gallic Aristocracy After the Fall of Avitus', *Francia* 7, 597–627.

——1984, 'Emigrants, Exiles, and Survivors', *Phoenix* 38, 159–70.

Matthews, J.F. 1975, *Western Aristocracies and Imperial Court AD 364–425* (Oxford).

McKitterick, R. (ed.) 1991, *The Uses of Literacy in Early Medieval Europe* (Cambridge).

Mikat, P. 1984, *Dopplbesetzung oder Ehrentitulatur – Zur Stellung des westgotisch-arianischen Episkopites nach der Konversion von 587/9* (Opladen).

Minns, E.H. 1913, *Scythians and Greeks: A Survey of Ancient History and Archaeology of the North Coast of the Euxine From the Danube to the Caucasus* (Cambridge).

Molinero Perez, A. 1948, *La necropolis visigoda de Duraton* (Madrid).

——1971, *Aportaciones de las excavaciones y hallazgos casuales (1941–1959) al Museo de Segovia* (Madrid).

Momigliano, A. 1955, 'Cassiodorus and the Italian Culture of His Time', *Proceedings of the British Academy* 4, 207–45.

Moncur, D. and Heather, P. 1996, *Themistius: Select Orations*, Translated Texts for Historians (Liverpool) (forthcoming).

Moorhead, J. 1984, 'Theoderic, Zeno and Odovaker', *Byzantinische Zeitschrift*, 77, 261–6.

——1992, *Theoderic in Italy* (1992).

Myhre, B. 1978, 'Agrarian Development, Settlement History and Social Organization in Southwest Norway in the Iron Age', in Kristiansen and Paludan-Muller (eds), 1978, 224–35, 253–65.

Nelson, J. 1978, 'Queens as Jezebels: the Careers of Brunhild and Balthild in Merovingian History', in D. Baker (ed.), *Medieval Women* (Oxford), 31–77 (reprinted in J. Nelson, *Politics and Ritual in Early Medieval Europe* (London, 1986)).

O'Flynn, J.M. 1983, *Generalissimos of the Western Roman Empire* (Edmonton, Alb.).

Orlandis, J. 1977, *Historia de Espana: La Espana Visigotica* (Madrid).

Ørsnes, M. 1963, 'The Weapon Find in Ejsbøl Mose at Haderslev, *Acta Archaeologica* 34, 232–47.

—— 1968, *Der Moorfund von Ejsbøl bei Hadersleben. Deutungsprobleme der grossen nordgermanischen Waffenopferfunde*, Abhandlung der Akadmie der Wissenschaft in Gottingen (Gottingen).

Oxenstierna, E.C. 1945, *Die Urheimat der Goten* (Leipzig).

Palade, V. 1966, Atelierele pentru lucrat pieptini din os din secolul at IV-leas e.n. de la Bîrlad-Valea Seacă', *Arheologia Moldovei* 4, 261–77.

—— 1980, 'Éléments géto-daces dans le site Sîntana de Mureş, de Bîrlad-Valea Seacă, *Dacia, N.S. 24, 223–53.*

De Palol, P. and Ripoll Lopez, G. 1990, *Les Goths. Ostrogoths et Wisigoths en Occident, Ve-VIIIe siècle* (Paris).

Pearson, M.P., 1989, 'Beyond the Pale: Barbarian Social Dynamics in Western Europe', in J.C. Barrett et al. (eds), *Barbarians and Romans in North-west Europe from the Later Republic to Late Antiquity* BAR; IS 471 (Oxford), 198–226.

Peregrinatio Gothica 1, 1986, Archaeologia Baltica VII (Lodz).

Peregrinatio Gothica 2, 1989, Archaeologia Baltica VIII (Lodz).

Peregrinatio Gothica 3, 1992, Universitetets Oldsaksamlings Skrifter, NY rekke 14 (Oslo).

Perrin, P. (ed.), 1991, *Gallo-Romains, Wisigoths et Francs en Aquitaine, Septimanie et Espagne*, Actes des VIIe Journées internationales d'Archéologie merovingienne, Toulouse 1985 (Paris).

Pohl, W. 1980, 'Die Gepiden und die *Gentes* an der mittleren Donau nach dem Zerfall des Attilareiches', in Wolfram and Daim (eds), 1980, 239–305.

——1988, *Die Awaren* (Munich).

Prostko-Prostynski, J. 1994, *Utraeque res publicae: The Emperor Anastasius I's Gothic Policy* (491–518) (Poznan).

Randsborg, K. 1991, *The First Millennium in Europe and the Mediterranean* (Cambridge).

Rau, G. 1972, 'Körpergraber mit Glasbeigaben des 4. nachchristlichen Jahrhunderts im Oder-Wechsel-Raum', *Acta praehistorica et archaeologica* 3, 109–214.

Raev, B.A. 1986, *Roman Imports in the Lower Don Basin*, BAR, IS 278.

Renfrew, C. 1991, *Archaeology: Theories, Methods, and Practice* (London).

Reydellet, M. 1981, *La Royauté dans la littérature latine de Sidoine Apollinaire à Isidore de Séville* (Rome).

Riché, P. 1971, 'L'Education à l'époque Wisigothique: les Institutionum Disciplinae', *Annales Toledanos* 3, 171–80.

——1976, *Education and Culture in the Barbarian West*, trans. J.J. Contreni (South Carolina).

Ripoll Lopez, G. 1985, *La necropolis visigodo de El Carpio de Tajo (Toledo)* (Madrid).

——1989, 'Caracteristicas generales del poblamiento y la arqueologia funeraria visgoda de Hispania', *Espacio, Tiempo Y Forma, Revista de la Facultad de Geografia e Historia*, Serie 1. 2, 389–418.

——1993, 'La necropolis Visigoda de El Carpio de Tajo. Una nueva lectura a partir de la Topocronologia y los adornos personales', *Bulleti de la Reial Academia Catalana de Belles Arts de Sant Jordi* VII-VIII, 187–250.

——1994, 'Archeologia visigota in *Hispania*', in Arslan et al. 1994, 301–27.

Rivers, T.J. 1977, *Laws of the Alamans and Bavarians* (Pennsylvania).

Roosens, E.E. 1989, *Creating Ethnicity: The Process of Ethnogenesis* (California).

Rostovzeff, M.I. 1922, *Iranians and Greeks in South Russia* (Oxford).

Rouché, M. 1986, 'Les Wisigoths en Aquitaine. Peuple ou armée?', in *Peregrinatio Gothica* 1, 283–94.

Rousseau, P. 1992, 'Visigothic Migration and Settlement 376–418: Some Excluded Hypotheses', *Historia* 41, 345–61.

Sallares, R. 1991, *The Ecology of the Ancient Greek World* (London).

Sanchez, D. 1989, *El Ejercito en la Sociedad Visigoda* (Salamanca).

Sanchez-Albornoz, C. 1947, *El 'Stipendium' Hispano-Godo y los Origenes del Beneficio Prefeudal* (Buenos Aires).

——1974, *En Torno a los Origenes del Feudalismo*, vol. 1 (Buenos Aires).

Schäfer, C. 1991, *Der weströmische Senat als Träger antiker Kontinuität unter den Ostgotenkönigen (490–540 n. Chr.)* (St Katharinen).

Schaferdiek, K. 1967, *Die Kirche in den Riechen der Westgoten und Suewen bis zur Errichtung der westgotischen katholischen Staatskirche* (Berlin).

Schmidt, L. 1933, *Geschichte der deutschen Stämme bis zum Ausgang der Völkerwanderung. Die Ostgermanen*, 2nd edn (Munich).

——1943, *Die Letzten Ostogoten*, Abhandlung der Prussischen Akademie der Wissenschaften, Phil.-Hist. Kl. 10 (Berlin).

Scorpan, C. 1980, *Limes Scythiae*, BAR, IS 88 (Oxford).

Ščukin, M. 1989, *Romans and the Barbarians in Central and Eastern Europe 1st Century BC–1st Century AD*, BAR, IS 542 (Oxford).

Shennan, S.J. 1989, *Archaeological Approaches to Cultural Identity* (London).

——1991, 'Some Current Issues in the Archaeological Identification of Past Peoples', in Kobylinski, 1991, 29–38.

Simonet, F.J. 1903, *Historia de los Mozarabes de Espana* (Madrid).

Smith, A.D. 1981, 'War and Ethnicity: The Role of Warfare in the Formation, Self-images and Cohesion of Ethnic Communities', *Ethnic and Racial Studies* 4, 375–95.

——1986, *The Ethnic Origins of Nations* (Oxford).

Sorabji, R. 1983, *Time, Creation and the Continuum: Theories in Antiquity and the Early Middle Ages* (London).

Speidel, M.P. 1977, 'The Roman Army in Arabia', *ANRW* II.8.

Steuer, H., 1982, *Frühgeschichtliche Sozialstrukturen Mitteleuropa* (Göttingen).

Streitberg, W. 1920, *Gotisches Elementärbuch*, 5th and 6th edn (Heidelberg).

Svennung, J. 1967, *Jordanes und Scandia* (Stockholm).

——1972, 'Jordanes und die gotische Stammsage' in Hagberg (ed.), 1972, 20–56.

Syme, R. 1968, *Ammianus and the Historia Augusta* (Oxford).

——1971a, *Emperors and Biography: Studies in the Historia Augusta* (Oxford).

——1971b, *The Historia Augusta: A Call for Clarity* (Bonn).

Teillet, S. 1984, *Des Goths à la nation gothique: Les origines de l'idée de nation en Occident du V.e au VII.e siècle* (Paris).

Tejral, J. 1986, 'Fremde Einflüsse und kulturelle Veränderungen nordlich der mittleren Donau zu Beginn der Völkerwanderungszeit' in *Peregrinatio Gothica* 1.

——1988, 'Zur Chronologie und Deutung der südöstlichen Kulturelemente in der frühen Völkerwanderungszeit Mitteleuropas', *Anzeiger des Germanischen Nationalmuseums* 1987, 11–46.

Teodor, D.G. 1980, *The East Carpathian Area of Romania V–XI centuries AD*, BAR, IS 81 (Oxford).

Thompson, E.A. 1956, 'The Settlement of the Barbarians in Southern Gaul', *JRS* 46, 65–75.

——1963, 'The Visigoths from Fritigern to Euric', *Historia* 12, 105–26.

——1965, *The Early Germans* (Oxford).
——1966, *The Visigoths in the Time of Ulfila* (Oxford).
——1969, *The Goths in Spain* (Oxford).
——1982, *Romans and Barbarians. The Decline of the Western Empire* (Madison).
——1995, *The Huns* (Oxford).
Tjäder, J.-O. 1972, 'Der Codex argenteus in Uppsala und der Buchmeister Viliaric in Ravenna', in Hagberg (ed.), 1972, 144–64.
——1982, *Die nichliterarischen Lateinischen Papyri Italiens aus der Zeit 445–700*, vol. 2 (Stockholm).
Todd, M. 1975, *The Northern Barbarians 100 BC–AD 300* (London).
——1992, *The Early Germans* (Oxford).
Tomka, P. 1986, 'Die hunnische Fürstfund von Pannonhalma', *Acta Archaeologica Hungaricae* 36, 423–88.
Tudor, D. 1974, *Les Ponts Romains du bas Danube* (Bucharest).
Ucko, P.J. 1995, *Theory in Archaeology: A World Perspective* (London).
Vallet, F. and Kazanski, M. (eds) 1995, *La Noblesse romaine et les Chefs barbares* (Paris).
Van Es, W.A. 1967, *Wijster: A Native Village Beyond the Imperial Frontier 150–425 AD* (Groningen).
Vives, J. 1963, *Concilios Visigoticos e Hispano-Romanos* (Barcelona and Madrid).
——1969, *Inscripciones Cristianas de la Espana Romana y Visigoda*, 2nd edn (Barcelona).
Vulpe, R. 1957, *Le Vallum de la Moldavie inferieure et le 'Mur' d'Athanaric* (The Hague).
Wallace-Hadrill, J.M. 1961, 'Gothia and Romania', *Bulletin of the John Rylands Library, Manchester*, 44 = *The Long-Haired Kings and Other Studies in Frankish History* (London, 1962), 25–48.
Ward-Perkins, B. 1984, *From Classical Antiquity to the Middle Ages: Urban Public Building in Northern and Central Italy AD 300–850* (Oxford).
Wenskus, R. 1961, *Stammesbildung und Verfassung: Das Werden der frühmittelalterlichen Gentes* (Cologne).
Werner, J. 1956, *Beiträge zur Archeologie des Attila-Reiches*, Bayerische Akademie der Wissenschaften, Phil.-Hist. Kl., n.f. 38A.
Whitby, M. 1988, *The Emperor Maurice and His Historian: Theophylact Simocatta on Persian and Balkan Warfare* (Oxford).
Whittaker, C.R. 1994, *Frontiers of the Roman Empire* (Baltimore).
Wickham, C. 1984, 'The Other Transition: From the Ancient World to Feudalism', *Past and Present* 103, 3–36.

Les Wisigoths, Dossiers histoire et archéologie no. 108 (Paris, 1986).
Wolf, K.B. 1990, *Conquerors and Chroniclers of Early Medieval Spain* (Liverpool).
Wolfram, H. 1988, *History of the Goths* (Berkeley).
Wolfram, H. and Daim, F. 1980, (eds), *Die Völker an der mittleren und unteren Donau im fünften und sechsten Jahrhundert*, Denkschriften der Österriechischen Akademie der Wissenschaften, Phil.-Hist. Kl. 145 (Vienna).
Wolfram, H. and Pohl, W. 1990, (eds), *Typen der Ethnogenese unter besonderer Berücksichtigung der Bayern*, Denkschriften der Österreichischen Akademie der Wissenschaften, Phil.-Hist. Kl. 201 (Vienna).
Wood, I.N. 1985, 'Gregory of Tours and Clovis', *Revue Belge de Philolgie et d'Histoire* 63, 249–72.
——1990, 'Ethnicity and the Ethnogenesis of the Burgundians' in Wolfram and Pohl, 1990, 53–69.
——1994, *The Merovingian Kingdoms 450–751* (London).
Wormald, P. 1977, '*Lex Scripta* and *Verbum Regis*: Legislation and Germanic Kingship, from Euric to Cnut', in P.H. Sawyer and I.N. Wood (eds), *Early Medieval Kingship* (Leeds, 1977), 105–38.
Zeiss, H. 1948, *Die Grabfunde aus dem spanischen Westgotenreich* (Berlin-Leipzig).
Zeumer, F. 1898–1901, 'Geschichte der westgotischen Gesetzgebung', *Neues Archiv* 23, 419–516; 24, 39–122; 26, 91–149.

The Wielbark and Černjachov Cultures

A. General Studies of Gothic-Related Archaeological Materials

Arslan, E.A., et al. (eds), *I Goti*, Milan, 1994.
Bierbrauer, V., 'Die Goten vom 1.-7. Jahrhundert n.Chr.: Siedelgebiete und Wanderbewegungen aufgrund archäologischer Quellen', in *Peregrinatio Gothica* 3, 9–43.
Kazanski, M., *Les Goths (Ier.-VIIe. après J.-C.), Paris, 1991.*
Peregrinatio Gothica 1, Archaeologia Baltica VII, Lodz, 1986.
Peregrinatio Gothica 2, Archaeologia Baltica VIII, Lodz, 1989.
Peregrinatio Gothica 3, Universitetets Oldsaksamlings Skrifter, Ny rekke 14, Oslo, 1992.

B. Wielbark Culture

(i) General studies

Dabrowska, T., 'The Cultural Changes of Masovia and Polasie in the Period of the Roman Influence', *Wiadomosci Archeologiczne* 54.1 (1980), 45–58.

Godłowski, K., *The Chronology of the Late Roman and Early Migration Periods in Central Europe*, Prace Archeologiczne 11, 1970 (still labelled the 'East-Pomeranian Masovian culture').

——, 'Gegenseitige Beziehungen zwischen der Wielbark- und der Przeworsk-Kultur. Veränderungen ihrer Verbreitung und das Problem der Gotenwanderung', in *Peregrinatio Gothica* 1, 125–52.

Kmieciński, J., 'Problem of the So-called Gotho-Gepiden Culture in the Light of Recent Research', *Archaeologia Polona* 4, 1962, 270–85.

——, 'Die Bedeutung der Germanen östlich der Oder wahrend der ersten Jahrhunderte nach Christi Geburt in Lichte der neueren Forschungen', in U.E. Hagberg (ed.), *Studia Gotica*, Stockholm, 1972, 72–80.

——, 'Kulturverbindugen Skandinaviens und sudlicher Ostseekuste in der Spat-Latene und Romischen Kaiserzeit', in *Peregrinatio Gothica* 1, 39–60.

Kuharenko, J.V., 'Le Problème de la Civilisation "Gotho-Gépide" en Polesie et en Volhynia', *Acta Baltico-Slavica* 5 (1967), 19–40.

Machajewski, H., 'The Wielbark Culture in Relation to the Przeworsk Culture in Wielkopolska (Great Poland), *Fontes Archaeologici Posnanienses* 29 (1978), 49–64.

Ščukin, M., *Romans and the Barbarians in Central and Eastern Europe 1st Century BC–1st Century AD*, BAR, IS 542 (Oxford), 1989.

Wolagiewicz, R., 'Wielbark Culture Ploughed Area From the Early Roman Period at Gronowo, Pomerania', *Wiadomosci Archeologiczne* 42.2 (1977), 227–44.

——, 'Die Goten im Bereich der Wielbark–Kultur', in *Peregrinatio Gothica* 1, 63–98.

(ii) Publications of basic materials

Dabrowska, T., 'The Cemetery of the Przeworsk and Wielbark Cultures at the Kozarowka Site, Bialystok voivodship', *Wiadomosci Archeologiscżne* 43.1 (1978), 62–82.

Grabarczyk, T., et al., 'Période Romaine en Pomeranie', *Inventaria Archaeologica Pologne* 43, Warszawa-Lodz, 1979.

Kempisty, A. and Okulicz, J., Periode Romaine tardive et période des migrations des peuples en Mazovie, *Inventaria Archaeologica Pologne* 15, Lodz, 1965.

Kmiecinski, J., *Odry, cmantarzyski kurhanowe z okresu rzymskiego w powiecie chojnickem* (*Odry, a tumulus cemetery from the Roman period in the district of Chojnice*), Lodz, 1968.

Kmiecinski, J., et al., 'Cmentarzyski kurhanowe ze starszego odresu rzyymskiego w Wesiorach w pow. kartuskim' ('A tumulus cemetery from the old Roman period at Wesiory', *Prace i Materialy Muzeum Archeologicznego i Etnograficznego w Lodzi* 12 (1965), 37–119.

Kuharenko, J.V., *Mogil'nik Brest-Trichin* (*The Cemetery of Brest-Trichin*), Moscow, 1980.

Pietrzak, M. and Tuszyska, M., 'Période romaine tardive (Pruszsz Gdanski 7)', *Inventaria Archaeologica Pologne* 60, Warszawa-Lodz, 1988.

Schindler, R., *Die Besiedlungsgeschichte der Goten und Gepiden im Unteren Wiechselraum auf Grund der Tongefasse*, Leipzig, 1940.

C. *'Intermediate' Cultures*

Borodzej, T., et al., 'Période romaine tardive et début de la periode des migrations des peuples (groupe de Maslomeicz)', *Inventaria Archaeologica Pologne* 61, Warszawa-Lodz, 1989.

Kokowski, A., 'Periode romaine tardive. Civilisation de Černjahov', *Inventaria Archaeologica Pologne* 50, Warszawa-Lodz, 1986.

——, 'La genèse des éléments culturels sur le territoire de la Pologne sud-est et de l'Ukraine ouest dans la période des influences romaines', in *Peregrinatio Gothica* 1, 153–74.

——(ed.), *Schätze der Ostgoten* (Stuttgart, 1995).

D. *Černjachov Culture*

(*i*) *Studies of general relevance*

Constantinescu, M., et al. (eds), *Relations Between the Authochthonous Population and the Migratory Populations on the Territory of Romania*, Bucharest, 1975.

Diaconu, Gh., 'On the Socio-economic Relations Between Natives and Goths in Dacia', in Constantinescu et al. (eds), *Relations*, 67–75.

Häusler, A., 'Zu den sozialökonomischen Verhältnissen in der Černjachov-Kultur', *Zeitschrift für Archaologie* 13, 1979, 32–65.

Horedt, K., *Siebenburgen im Frühmittelalter*, Bonn, 1986.

Ioniță, I., 'Contributii cu privire la cultura Sîntana de Mureș-Černeahov pe teritoriul Republicii Socialiste România', *Arheologia Moldovei* 4, (1966), 189–259 (French summary 252–7).

——, 'Probleme der Sîntana de Mureș-Černjachov Kultur auf dem Gebiete Romaniens,' in U.E. Hagberg, ed., *Studia Gotica*, 1972, Stockholm, 95–104.

——, 'The Social-economic Structure of Society During the Goths' Migration in the Carpatho-Danubian Area', in Constantinescu, M. et al. (eds), *Relations*, 77–89.

Werner, J., 'Dančeny und Brangstrup', *Bonner Jahrbuch* 188 (1988), 241–86.

Wolfram H. and Daim F. (eds), *Die Völker an der mittleren und unteren Donau im fünften und sechsten Jahrhundert*, Össterreichische Akademie der Wissenschaften, Phil.–Hist. Kl., Denkschriften 145, Vienna, 1980.

(ii) Chronology and identification

Bierbrauer, V., 'Zur chronologischen, soziologischen und regionalen Gliederung des östgermanischen Fundstoffs des 5. Jahrhunderts in Südosteuropa' in Wolfram and Daim (eds) *Die Völker*, 131–142.

Diaconu, Gh., 'Archäologische Angaben über die Taifalen', *Dacia* n.s. 7, 1963, 301–15.

——, 'Einheimische und Wandervölker im 4. Jahrhundert u.Z. auf dem Getiete Rumäniens (Tîrgșor-Gherăseni-Variante)', *Dacia* n.s. 8, 1964, 195–210.

Gey, O.A., 'On the Date of the Chernyakhovo Culture in the Northern Black Sea Area', *SA* 1986.1, 77–87 (English summary 87).

Ioniță, I., 'Die Romer-Daker und die Wandervölker im Donaulandischen Karpatenraum im 4. Jahrhundert', in Wolfram and Daim (eds) *Die Völker*, 123–9.

——, 'Chronologie der Sîntana de Mureș-Černiachov-Kultur', in *Peregrinatio Gothica* 1, 295–351.

——, 'Die Fibeln mit umgeschlagenem Fuss in der Sîntana-de-Mureș-Černjachov Kultur', in *Peregrinatio Gothica* 3, 77–90.

Kropotkin, V.V., 'Denkmäler der Przeworsk Kultur in der Westukraine und ihre Beziehungen zur Lipica- und Černjachov-Kultur', *Ausklang der Latène-Zivilisaton und Anfänge der Germanischen Besiedlung im mittleren Donaugebiet*, Bratislava, 1976, 173–200.

Mitrea, B., and Preda, C., 'Quelques problèmes ayant trait aux nécropoles de type Sîntana-Tcherniakhov découvertes en Valachie', *Dacia* n.s. 8, 1964, 211–37.

Palade, V., 'Éléments Géto-Daces dans le site Sîntana de Mureş de Bîrlad-Valea Seacă', *Dacia* n.s. 24, 1980, 223–53.

Ščukin, M.B., 'Das Problem der Černjachov-Kultur in der sowjetischen archäologischen Literatur', *Zeitschrift für Archäologie* 9, 1975, 25–41.

(iii) *Publications of basic materials*

Blosiu, C., 'La nécropole de Letçani (dep. de Jassy) datant du IVe siècle de n.è.', *Arheologia Moldovei* 8, 1975, 203–80 (French summary 239–42).

Diaconu, Gh., *Tîrgşor* Necropola din secolele III–IV E.N., Bucharest, 1965.

——, 'Das Gräberfeld von Mogoşani (Kreis Dimboviţa)', *Dacia* n.s. 13, 1969, 367–402.

Diaconu, Gh. and Anghelescu, N., 'Despre Necropoloa din sec. IV e.n. de la Radu Negru (r. Călărasi)', *Studii si cercetari de istorie veche si arheologie* 14, 1963, 167–74.

Diaconu, Gh. et al., 'L'ensemble archeologique de Pietroasele', *Dacia* n.s. 21 (1977), 199–220.

Gey, O.A., 'The Cherniakhovo Culture Sites of the North Pontic Region', *SA* 1980.2, 45–51 (English summary 51).

Ioniţă, I., *Das Gräberfeld von Independenţa, Walachei: zur relativen Chronologie und zu den Bestattungs-, Beigaben-, und Trachtsitten eines Graberfeldes der Černjachov–Sîntana de Mureş–Kultur*, Saarbrucker Beiträge z. Altertumskunde 10, 1971.

——, 'La nécropole du IVe siècle de n.è. à Miorçani', *Inventaria Archaeologica Roumanie*, fasc. 8, 1979.

Magomedov, B.V., *Tchernjahovskaja kul'tura Severo-Zapadnogo Pritchernomor'ja* (*The Černjachov Culture in the Regions Northwest of the Black Sea*), Kiev, 1987.

Materialy i Issledovniya po Arkheologii SSSR vols 82, 89, 116, 139.

Mitrea, B. and Preda, C., *Necropole din secolul al IV lea E.N. in Muntenia*, Bucharest, 1966 (French summary 165–88).

Mogil'niki tchernjahovskoj kul'tury (*Cemeteries of the Černjachov Culture*) 2 vols, Moscow, 1979 and 1988.

Palade, V., 'Nécropole du IVe et commencement du Ve siècle de n.è. à Bîrlad-Valea Seacă', *Inventaria Archaeologica Roumanie*, fasc. 12, 1986.

Rafalovic, I.A., *Dančeny. Mogil'nik Cernjachovskoj Kul'tury III-IV vv. n.e.* (*Dančeny: A Cemetery of the Černjachov Culture of the 3rd–4th Centuries AD*), Kichinev, 1986.

Index